ADVANCE PRAISE FOR *THE QURAN: WITH OR AGAINST THE BIBLE?*

"This book is an important contribution to interfaith understanding. Written by a committed, believing Muslim scientist and scholar, it offers a helpful and honest comparison of the Qur'an with the Hebrew Bible and New Testament that is neither polemical, apologetic nor triumphalist. It acknowledges both similarities and differences in a spirit of improving understanding and respect for the dignity of believers of other faiths.

Dr. Ejaz Naqvi does not ignore differences between Bible and Qur'an, nor does he try to reconcile them. There are various ways to treat differences. Historically, religious thinkers have tended to assume that if there is a discrepancy between scriptures, one scripture must be right and the others are wrong. Based on this simplistic thinking, one religion must therefore hold the key to divine truth while the others are false religions and provide no benefit. Dr. Naqvi provides a deeper and much more spiritual and sophisticated analysis by demonstrating how differences need not be threatening but in fact enlightening. He shows that different versions of the same message appeal to different communities and stimulate discussion so that we can learn to know and respect one another better. From the grand perspective, all three scriptures convey the identical vital concern for ethics, compassion, and the need to respond to the divine will. This book will become a primary tool for interfaith understanding through scriptural reasoning and the comparative study of religious text."

Rabbi Reuven Firestone, Author and Professor of Medieval Judaism and Islam, Hebrew Union College. Co-Director, Center for Muslim-Jewish Engagement at University of Southern California, Los Angeles.

"At a time of perceived conflict between Muslims and Christians across the globe, Naqvi's book reminds us all of the shared mores and values - not to mention myths and stories - that bind the Quran and the Bible together as a single unbroken revelation. This is not just a candid and thought-provoking review of major topics in both the Bible and the Quran, but also a much-needed corrective to the negativity and conflict that have marred relations between the Abrahamic traditions. "

Reza Aslan, author of *No god but God* and *Beyond Fundamentalism.*

"Dr. Naqvi invites the reader on a journey through the world's two most widely read books, the Quran and the Bible. Along the way, a lot of nonsense about the Quran is straightened out, especially for Western Jews and Christians. From the same pages, Muslim readers can gain a better understanding of what their cousins in monotheism believe. These three streams of religious revelation communicate more than articles of faith. In their language, their rhythms, and their textures, they contain the notes that comprise the very melodies playing through the souls of a few billion people on our planet. Dr. Naqvi's pages help us appreciate the harmony and the differences we share."

Michael Wolfe, Author of *The Hadj, One Thousand Roads to Mecca,* and *Taking Back Islam.*

"Ejaz Naqvi's lovely book will not only cause many to look at the scriptures of other faiths with greater openness, but it will also cause more appreciation for one's own sacred texts. Who knew, despite some core differences, that we have so much in common? As Jesus said, ' those who have ears, let them hear!'"

Rev. Brian Stein-Webber, Executive Director, Interfaith Council of Contra Costa County, CA.

"Ejaz Naqvi seeks to bridge the yawning gap that zealots have created between Muslims and non-Muslims. *The Quran: With or Against the Bible?* is not meant to stir up controversy; it is intended to squash it. Naqvi's primary audience may be Christians and Jews, but he speaks to fellow Muslims, too, "a significant number" of whom have many "misconceptions about the Holy Quran," he argues. Misconceptions of Islam's holy book teachings, writes Naqvi, have proliferated because most people, even most Muslims, "have never read it," let alone read it in its entirety. "Second-hand" exposure to the Quran is not limited to Westerners who base their views on the comments of pundits and politicians, he believes, but it is common among Muslims who are fed only selected passages by preachers and rabble-rousers, whose education in the faith is often incomplete.

In a perfect world, explains the author, everyone would read the Quran in Arabic from cover to cover. The next best thing is for people to read it in their own language. Naqvi believes that if people did so they would grasp the goodness of this "guide"; they would see how much it has in common with the scriptures and traditions of the Judeo-Christian world.

Naqvi is an American medical doctor and a "born-again" Muslim, a unique combination that allows him to speak to a Western audience in ways someone born overseas in a culture of Islam might find difficult. All but the last chapter are organized like college lectures, complete with a summary of points to study and "to ponder."

Of the six sections into which these chapters are grouped, only the last one contains controversial material. That this is limited to one section is meant to show that the three "Abrahamaic books" (Old and New Testaments, Quran), as he puts it, have more in common than not. Naqvi acknowledges that the Bible is stronger as a history, whereas the Quran, which is far shorter, is more about the "moral of the story."

A portion of almost every page is given over to quotes, citations, or summaries of thoughts from one of the holy books. The similarities between the Bible and the Quran are made quite apparent in this way, whether it is the story of Mary or descriptions of the afterlife in Paradise.

What controversial material there is here is limited to two of the four chapters in part six—on Jihad and the role of women. Naqvi demonstrates that on the latter point the Old Testament and the Quran are strikingly similar. He also notes that while modern Western culture and its laws may not always "correspond" to the guidelines of the holy book, "the scriptures do not encourage people to 'take the law into their own hands' if there is a discrepancy between the divine law and the law of the land."

This book should be required reading for anyone seeking to find common ground, rather than division, through faith."

Mark McLaughlin, ForeWord Reviews
Clarion Review-Five Stars (out of five).

"A sober, probing exploration of the relationship among the three Abrahamic faiths—Islam, Judaism and Christianity.

Virginia Woolf once asked, "Ought not education to bring out and fortify the differences rather than the similarities?" Modern discussions of Islam tend to do just that, hastily pegging the youngest of the major monotheisms as different, foreign and far-off. In his accessible new contribution to the field of comparative religion, Naqvi tries to bridge the gaps that have too long separated Islam from Christianity and Judaism, arguing in essence that the three faiths are more alike than most people suspect. To do so, he engages in a "topic-by-topic review" that compares Muslim beliefs on a variety of themes—e.g., God, Scripture, science, ethics—to their Judeo-Christian counterparts. His review leads him to a number of basic insights that are nonetheless crucial reminders that what unites believers is often greater than what divides. Jews, Christians and Muslims all revere the patriarchs: Abraham, Isaac, Jacob and Joseph. Islam venerates Jesus, a man who is, for Muslims, a prophet and teacher of the highest regard. Naqvi also argues that Muslim ethics—outlined in the Five Pillars of Islam—are quite similar to Judeo-Christian moral teachings. But while the author gravitates toward likeness, he doesn't ignore differences; he honestly and objectively explains how the three religions sometimes diverge, and he ends each chapter with a set of provocative discussion questions that challenge readers to ponder these weighty topics. Naqvi does it all with an intelligence, grace and evenhandedness that make his project appealing for believers and nonbelievers alike.

A superb comparative look at Islam and its sister faiths, perfect for promoting a spiritual dialogue."

Kirkus Reviews-Kirkus Star for books of exceptional merit.

THE QURAN: WITH OR AGAINST THE BIBLE?

A Topic-by-Topic Review
for the Investigative Mind

Ejaz Naqvi, MD

iUniverse, Inc.
Bloomington

The Quran: With or Against the Bible?
A Topic-by-Topic Review for the Investigative Mind

iUniverse books may be ordered through booksellers or by contacting:

iUniverse
1663 Liberty Drive
Bloomington, IN 47403
www.iuniverse.com
1-800-Authors (1-800-288-4677)

Because of the dynamic nature of the Internet, any web addresses or links contained in this book may have changed since publication and may no longer be valid. The views expressed in this work are solely those of the author and do not necessarily reflect the views of the publisher, and the publisher hereby disclaims any responsibility for them.

Any people depicted in stock imagery provided by Thinkstock are models, and such images are being used for illustrative purposes only.

Certain stock imagery © Thinkstock.

ISBN: 978-1-4759-0774-2 (sc)
ISBN: 978-1-4759-0776-6 (e)
ISBN: 978-1-4759-0775-9 (dj)

Library of Congress Control Number: 2012906551

Printed in the United States of America

iUniverse rev. date: 1/18/2013

In the name of God, the Most Compassionate, the Most Merciful

I ask for forgiveness from the Lord of the worlds if I have unintentionally misrepresented the message contained within the Holy scriptures.

For my parents:

For guiding me.

For showing me that there is no substitute for honesty and hard work.

And for everything else ...

Acknowledgments

Farhana, Alina, Mohsin, and my extended family, for filling my heart with joy, love, and tenderness that provide fuel and purpose to my life.

And above all, God Almighty, for all His blessings that I cannot even begin to enumerate.

An objective and comparative review of the major themes presented in the Quran and the Bible to find the answers to questions you were too afraid to ask, with surprising findings.

"Science without religion is lame. Religion without science is blind."

Albert Einstein

"It is the perfection of God's works that they are all done with the greatest simplicity. He is the God of order and not of confusion."

Sir Isaac Newton

"God, the Supreme Being, is neither circumscribed by space, nor touched by time; he cannot be found in a particular direction, and his essence cannot change."

Avicenna (Abu Sina): A tenth-century Muslim polymath, and a foremost physician, philosopher, and theologian.

ABOUT THE AUTHOR

Ejaz Naqvi, MD is currently the president of a local Islamic center in San Francisco Bay Area and has been actively involved in many other local Islamic centers in various capacities. He serves on the executive board of the Interfaith Council of Contra Costa County, California and is actively engaged in interfaith work. Dr Naqvi is on the advisory board of Abrahamic Alliance International, an interfaith organization whose purpose is to unite Jews, Christians and Muslims for active peace building and the relief of extreme poverty through educational empowerment and compassionate community service. He also serves on the Board of Directors of Islamic Scholarship Fund, a non-profit organization that aims to promote engagement of American Muslim students in mainstream through educational scholarships and mentorship programs. Dr. Ejaz Naqvi is the host of a radio talk show titled "Frank Talk with Dr. Ejaz- The Forum for Civil dialogue on Religion, spirituality and Wellness" on Toginet Radio- an Internet radio station.

A practicing physician and a "born-again Muslim" after reading the Quranic translation for the first time in its entirety about two decades ago, he has since then pondered over the verses of the Quran and discovered that many of its teachings remain arcane. Eager and in search of finding the common grounds, his subsequent study of the Quran and the Bible has led him to finding significant similarities in the teachings of the Scriptures, which he shares in this book

TRANSLATIONS OF THE HOLY QURAN

The English translations of the verses from the Quran, unless otherwise indicated, are taken from Abdullah Yousuf Ali's *The Holy Quran: Text, Translation and Commentary*, USA edition, 2001, published by Tahrike Tarsile Qur'an, Inc., Elmhurst, New York. I have used the modern English, replacing certain words like "ye," or "Thou" with "you." The other two translations of significant proportions are taken from the following two sources and are specified in parentheses at the end of the quotations.

1. Shakir, M. H. *The Quran: Arabic Text and English Translation*, published by Tahrike Tarsile Qur'an, Inc., Elmhurst, New York (compilation by M. H. Shakir).

2. Malik, M. Farooq-i-Azam. *Al-Qur'an, Guidance for Mankind: The English Translation of the Meaning of Al Qur'an,* Institute of Islamic Knowledge, Houston, Texas. At times, I have substituted certain English words when using this translation (e.g., "Lord" or "Sustainer" for *"Rabb"* and "apostle" or "messenger" for *"Rasool"*).

On rare occasions, other translations are used and are clearly indicated in parenthesis at the end of the quotations.

TRANSLATIONS OF THE HOLY BIBLE

1. New Living Translation (NLT) Bible Translation, Tyndale House Publishers Inc., Carol Stream, Illinois. Unless otherwise indicated, all scripture quotations are taken from the Holy Bible, New Living Translation copyright © 1996, 2004, 2007 by Tyndale House Foundation. Used by permission of Tyndale House Publishers Inc., Carol Stream, IL 60188. All rights reserved.

2. New American Standard Bible (NASB), by the Lockman Foundation. scripture taken from the *New American Standard Bible ®*, copyright © 1960, 1962, 1963, 1968, 1971, 1972, 1973, 1975, 1977, 1995 by the Lockman Foundation. Used by permission.

When quoting the verses from the Quran and the Bible, I have bolded certain portions for emphasis. I have also often used brackets for alternative word choices and for the purpose of clarification.

CONTENTS

Author's Note

What I present in this book is the outcome of an investigative analysis of a set of topics from the Holy Quran, the Islamic Holy scripture, which I conducted over the last two decades. As an investigator, I put myself in the position of a critical analyst, rather than that of a religious scholar or expert, or a devoutly religious person.

The purpose of my investigation and critical analysis was to compare the teachings of the Holy Quran and the Holy Bible; in doing so, I investigated parallel teachings wherever I could. The aim of this work is to impress upon the reader the remarkable similarities in the paths of guidance that the two scriptures have bestowed upon their followers. I also acknowledge that, at times, significant differences exist. My focus, however, will be to highlight the teachings of the Holy Quran and focus on the similarities with those of the Holy Bible.

I have taken utmost care to be respectful to people of all faiths and especially toward the scriptures as well as the noble figures, including the prophets. I have often mentioned them by their common names only, though I have fully intended to follow in my mind the Islamic tradition of adding "Peace be upon him" (PBUH) when mentioning their names. I am aware that not all readers will agree with my discussions, my analytical techniques, or the results there from. Such disagreements are natural and even welcome as long as they are built on mutual respect and objectivity.

Ejaz Naqvi, MD

BEFORE WE START …

Religion seems to have once again taken a prominent role in our society, especially in politics. Most of us want to believe that our own religion is the right one. This in itself ought not to be an issue, unless we decide that for our religion to be "correct," other religions must be "wrong." Unfortunately "what's wrong" with other religions often takes the center stage rather than a mind-set of "what's right with our religion," leading to a neglect of practicing the "right" teachings of one's own religion. Though some scholars, like Rabbi Brad Hirschfield (*You Don't Have to be Wrong for Me to be Right*) and Dr. David Liepert (*Muslim, Christian, and Jew*) have been promoting this concept, we mostly tend to highlight our differences rather than our similarities. This is true for religion in general and the Holy scriptures in particular. In my book, the focal point is the Holy Quran, since it has recently come under the spotlight with widely divergent opinions. I will review a selection of the major themes in the Quran and compare them with corresponding passages from the Holy Bible. My conscious attempt to highlight the similarities of the teachings of the scriptures of the three Abrahamic faiths will hopefully serve to narrow the knowledge gap and bring people of different faiths closer together in their understanding of each other's scriptures.

No other book in the recent past has generated so much attention as the Holy Quran. The geo-political events in the last decade have provided the fuel to the fire. Up until just twenty-five years ago, very few in the Unites States knew much about Islam, Muslims, and the Holy Quran. They were known primarily through the Israeli-Palestinian conflict. The globalization of the economy and the advent of the Internet changed that to some extent. Then came the unfortunate events involving the New York World Trade Center towers, which impacted American lives, politics, and interfaith relations like never before. But even now Islam, Muslims, and their Holy scripture, the Quran, remain poorly understood. This seems to be mainly a result of a lack of knowledge and a lack of communication. A bottomless informational abyss exists between those with knowledge and those who are seeking it. Unfortunately, there has been some exploitation of the situation and spread of misinformation as well, which may be worse than having no information.

There is a clear need for better understanding among people of various faiths. The Quran, considered by Muslims to be the literal word of God, has come under severe scrutiny. Many wonder how a book that is considered Holy by 1.6 billion Muslims worldwide, and a source of internal peace and spiritual growth, could be considered the opposite by *some* non-Muslims. Though the latter may represent a small minority, a large majority of people living in the West still remain unaware of the teachings of the Quran. How could the same book be viewed with such divergent opinions and views? Is it blind faith versus pure bias? Is it a reflection of a lack of adequate information and education? Many questions still abound. Who wrote this book? Who is the "God" of the Quran? What's the Quranic view of the prophets, especially Moses and Jesus? What does the Quran teach about interfaith relations? Does the Quran promote peace and harmony between Muslims and the People of the Book or does it promote violence? How does the Quran compare to the Bible on important themes like worshipping God, the prophets, human rights, moral values, and fighting for justice and human dignity? Does the Quran render women as second-class citizens? This book is a humble effort to provide answers to these and many other questions.

Though many have read selected portions of the Quran, most people who carry negative opinions about the Quran have never read it in its entirety. Accordingly, my primary objective of writing this book is to provide an introduction to the key themes in the Quran. I will compare these themes with those in the Bible. *My primary intended audience, thus, are the non-Muslims, especially in the West and those unfamiliar with the Quran.* In doing so, this book will concentrate on the theological aspects and avoid any geo-political connotations.

A blunt truth, however, is that a significant number of Muslims around the world have some misconceptions about the Holy Quran. This results from the fact that the Quran was revealed in the Arabic language. Most Muslims have read the Quran, cover to cover, many times over, but in its original Arabic text. Only a tiny percentage of Muslims have actually read the entire Quran in *their native language,* and thus the scriptures remains arcane. They believe that reciting the Quran is a holy act in itself, which brings God's blessings to themselves, their house, and their place of worship. As good as these intentions are, they miss out on the very *reason* that the scriptures itself identifies as the divine purpose behind its bestowment: to serve as the guidance to mankind. Can people be guided if they do not understand the language of the guide? Their primary source of information remains second-hand knowledge acquired through periodic lessons, speeches, or sermons by local religious clerics. Nevertheless, the Quran invites people to not just read it but also make an effort to discern God's message. Then, there are those Muslims who did read the translations themselves, but *in bits and pieces*, which could lead to misinterpretation because of the risk of taking the messages out of context. *Accordingly, my secondary intended audience are the Muslims of the world who have yet to read the Quran in their native language from cover to cover.*

Though theologians may benefit from it, I would like to emphasize that this book is written in plain English, intended mainly for common people, who are intrigued by religion and have the desire and curiosity to learn about other scriptures. The topics picked are of common interest and are broad in nature. It is hoped that this book will serve as a stimulus to explore the scriptures further for a clearer and more thorough understanding of the scriptures, including the Quran.

At the risk of contradicting myself in a span of one paragraph, it must be pointed out that even though English (or any other translation) is a good way to understand the Quran, *the best way to study and understand the Quran is to study it in its original text in Arabic language*. This is because of the simple fact that the essence of even an ordinary book may be lost, or diluted, during a translation. According to the Muslim belief, the Quran is the literal word of God, and no translation can come close to the eloquence and the stunning beauty of its original text. Since studying the Quran in Arabic may not be practical for non-Arabic-speaking people, the next best way to understand is to study the translation in the language one understands best. Many people mistakenly believe that the Quran is not subject to interpretation by Muslims. The truth is that, though the original Arabic text has remained unchanged since it was revealed to Prophet Muhammad, the translations and interpretations have varied among Muslims. (Many Muslims also point out that one needs to study the teachings of Prophet Muhammad and the guidance of his noble family to appreciate and understand its truer meanings.) The Bible, too, faces similar challenges and is subject to human errors and interpretations during translations into English and other languages.

The only version of the Quran that is considered *the* Quran by Muslims is indeed the Quran in Arabic language. All the translations and commentaries are considered *just that;* they introduce a human element to the divine scripture. This book is not a translation or an exegesis of the Quran; it is divided into a number of sections, each further subdivided into chapters. Each section discusses one key theme in the Quran:

- God
- The Quran itself
- The Quran and science
- The Quran on other scriptures, prophets, and religions
- The Day of Judgment, hereafter, hell, and heaven
- Moral values, ethics, pillars of faith, and lessons for our daily lives

Under each section, these themes are analyzed and discussed in more detail under various chapters. Whereas it is of significant value to know the context of the revelations, various topics are reviewed mostly by quoting the verses from the Quran and the Bible. I will venture to let the Quranic verses and biblical passages convey their own message as much as possible, all the while limiting a commentary.

It is my hope that this book will serve as a catalyst for the reader to study and examine the Quran and the Bible in more detail, without prejudice and preconceptions.

Hopefully, such study will help bridge the gulf between people of various faiths.

Ejaz Naqvi, MD
January 2012

INTRODUCTION TO THE QURAN

Before discussing the key themes in the sections to follow, the Quran's divine source will be addressed as well as its authenticity, its compilation, and its organization. This will be compared to the composition and compilation of the Bible.

Muslims believe the Quran is the literal word of God, revealed to Prophet Muhammad, and that there is no doubt about its sacred nature or its content. Some of the verses are clear and explicit in nature; others are relatively implicit, with vague, multiple meanings. Muslims contend that the authenticity of the Quran can be appreciated by simply reading the Quran in its entirety. The Quran proclaims that the book itself is a miracle and that God promised to protect it from alteration and corruption. Later in this section, I will review the painstaking efforts by Prophet Muhammad himself, as well as his close companions right after his death, to compile the Quran in order to preserve its accuracy.

There are numerous passages in the Quran on "nature": references to human development, animal behavior, and astronomy, which are in conformity with the knowledge acquired mainly in the twentieth and twenty-first centuries. Muslims contend that these passages alone indicate the divine nature of a book that was revealed in the seventh century, though counterarguments have been put forth.

The challenges to the Quran existed even at the time of its revelation, and therefore there are many verses in the Quran addressing its own authenticity.

"This Book, there is no doubt in it, is a guide to those who guard (against evil)." 2:2 (Shakir)

"And if you are in doubt as to what We have revealed from time to time to Our servant, then produce a Surah [chapter] like thereunto; and call your witnesses or helpers (if there are any) besides Allah [God], if your (doubts) are true." 2:23

Those familiar with Arabic, both Muslims and non-Muslims, acknowledge the uniqueness of the poetic eloquence and believe that it is highly unlikely that mere mortals could have produced such a stunning work of magnificence and style. Invariably, though, much of the literal beauty gets diluted in the process of translations from the original Arabic text. Nonetheless, God cautions that the Quran is not a poetry book but a guide and a message to mankind:

"We have not taught him (Muhammad) poetry, nor does it behoove him. This is nothing but a reminder and a plain Qur'an." 36:69 (Malik)

There are just over six thousand verses and over seventy-nine thousand words in the Quran. However, there are only about two thousand unique words (or their derivatives) used in the entire Quran. Many see the use of so few unique words that deliver an eloquent yet very powerful message as yet another sign of the divine source of the Quran. Muslims contend that this message touches and tenderizes the heart if readers approach it with an open mind. Chapter 36, one of the more revered chapters in the Quran, named *"Ya'sin"* swears by the book itself:

"By the Quran, full of Wisdom, you [meaning Muhammad] are indeed one of the messengers, On a Straight Way. It is a Revelation sent down by (Him,) the Exalted in Might, Most Merciful." 36:2–5

And to the doubters, the Quran issues this challenge:

"This Quran is not such as can be produced by other than Allah; on the contrary it is a confirmation of (revelations) that went before it, and a fuller explanation of the Book—wherein there is no doubt— from the Lord of the worlds.

"Or do they say, 'He forged it'? Say: 'Bring then a Surah [chapter] like unto it, and call (to your aid) anyone you can besides Allah, if you speak the truth!'" 10:37–38

History

The Quran was revealed through Prophet Muhammad over a period of twenty-three years, though some Muslims believe that the entire Quran was revealed to him at once on the night of power (*Lailatul Qadr*), and under divine orders, he then revealed it to people in bits and pieces according to the circumstances. The first set of verses was revealed in the year 610 CE, when Prophet Muhammad was forty years old and was meditating near Mecca in a cave he often used to visit. It is reported that the Archangel Gabriel appeared in a human form and asked him to recite the following verses, that later became the first five verses of chapter 96 of the Quran (*Al-Alaq,* or "The Clot").

"Read in the name of your Lord Who created. He created man from a clot. Read and your Lord is Most Honorable, Who taught (to write) with the pen. Taught man what he knew not." 96:1–5 (Shakir)

In many ways, the Quran and Muhammad are inseparable. Prophet Muhammad is believed to have said nothing on his own except what was instructed by God to him through Archangel Gabriel. Quran asserts that the source of the revelations is the same as the prior scriptures revealed to the prophets that came before Prophet Muhammad, such as Prophets Abraham, Moses, David, and Jesus. Though highly revered, Prophet Muhammad is not considered the author, or the editor, of the Quran. Most

Muslims consider Prophet Muhammad to be illiterate (*ummi*), since he did not receive worldly education.

> *"And you [meaning Muhammad] were not (able) to recite a Book before this (Book came), nor are you (able) to transcribe it with your right hand: In that case, indeed, would the talkers of vanities have doubted."* 29:48

Composition of the Quran

The Quran has a total of 114 chapters, called *Surahs*, that vary in length from three to 286 verses, called *Ayahs*. The sequence of the chapters, however, does not reflect the chronological order of the verses as they were revealed to Prophet Muhammad, nor are the chapters arranged in a topical or thematic order. In addition to a number, each chapter has a name; for example, the first chapter is named *Surah Al-Fatiha*, or "The Opening."

To those unfamiliar with the Holy Quran and the readers of the Bible, it may seem disorganized as it seemingly moves from one topic to another frequently, often within the same chapter, and at times, even within a verse. The Quran is not a set of prescriptions or a detailed history of Arabs. This is in contrast to some of the very detailed accounts of Prophet Moses and the Israelites in the Torah. It encompasses a wide variety of subjects: from historical events like the creation of Adam, to warnings and glad tidings, as well as law giving. It does so in a seemingly haphazard manner, which Muslims feel is stunningly beautiful with unparalleled poetic eloquence. Unlike the book of Genesis (in the Old Testament), one won't find long accounts of creation in one chapter. For instance, Adam's creation is mentioned in chapter 2 (*Al-Baqr*, or "The Cow") in verses 30–39:

> *"Behold, your Lord said to the angels: 'I will create a vicegerent on earth.' They said: 'Will You place therein one who will make mischief therein and shed blood? While we do celebrate Your praises and glorify Your Holy (name)?' He said: 'I know what you*

know not.' And He taught Adam the names of all things; then He placed them before the angels, and said: 'Tell me the names of these if you are right.' They said: 'Glory to You, of knowledge We have none, save what You have taught us: In truth it is You Who are perfect in knowledge and wisdom.' He said: 'O Adam! Tell them their natures.' When he had told them, Allah said: 'Did I not tell you that I know the secrets of heaven and earth, and I know what you reveal and what you conceal?' And behold, We said to the angels: 'Bow down to Adam' and they bowed down. Not so Iblis [Satan]: he refused and was haughty (arrogant): He was of those who reject Faith. We said: 'O Adam! dwell you and your wife in the Garden; and eat of the bountiful things therein as (where and when) you will; but approach not this tree, or you run into harm and transgression.' Then did Satan make them slip from the (garden), and get them out of the state (of felicity) in which they had been. We said: 'Get you down, all (you people), with enmity between yourselves. On earth will be your dwelling-place and your means of livelihood—for a time.' Then learnt Adam from his Lord words of inspiration, and his Lord turned toward him; for He is Oft-Returning, Most Merciful. We said: 'Get you down all from here; and if, as is sure, there comes to you Guidance from me, whosoever follows My guidance, on them shall be no fear, nor shall they grieve. But those who reject Faith and belie Our Signs, they shall be companions of the Fire; they shall abide therein.'"

From this account, the verses then seamlessly move on to talk about the children of Israel. The Quran returns to the story of Adam's creation again in chapter 7, verses 19–25, as well as many other places.

However, this method of scattering is not necessarily unique to this scripture. For example, while describing the drunks in the

Samaria in the Northern Kingdom of Israel, the book of Isaiah refers to the Lord's instructions piece by piece:

> *"'Who does the LORD think we are?' they ask. 'Why does he speak to us like this? Are we little children, just recently weaned? He tells us everything over and over—one line at a time, one line at a time, a little here, and a little there!'"* Isaiah 28:9–10

The intention of this book is clearly not to reorganize the Quran in a topical format, as there is no one better to do so than the Lord Himself (if He had so willed), but to review various themes scattered at various places in the Quran. One has to believe that if a mere mortal can organize various subjects in a topical manner, then could not the Almighty, the All-Wise have done it Himself, through divine instructions to Prophet Muhammad when he was ordering the scribes to organize the Quran? This naturally leads one to wonder: so why didn't He? The answer, however, is not as simple, and frankly speaking, no one knows for sure. Before we delve in that arena, it should be pointed out that the Quran was not intended to be read like a novel or a history book, with a particular plot, with a beginning, middle, and end. By using these criteria, the Quran would indeed appear haphazard. The following is an attempt to relate plausible explanations. One reason might be that by dispersing various topics all over and repeating them often, one is bound to stumble upon more than just one particular topic and see the big picture. Otherwise one might just skip a chapter on a certain topic and might only study only the topic of interest. The scattered approach invites one to read the entire text. The scattering of themes perhaps makes it more resistant to willful alterations and deletions. Having the same topics dispersed all over does not make it impossible, but extremely difficult, to corrupt.

History without Specifics

The Quran narrates many stories, and many of them are found in the Bible as well. These include the stories of Adam, Noah, Abraham, Lot, David, Moses (and the pharaoh), Jesus Christ, the Virgin Mary, Zechariah, and others. The Quran mentions these stories without specific dates and oftentimes refers to people without their proper names. For example, in the story of Moses, the king is called *"Firawn"* (or Pharaoh), rather than by the specific pharaoh at the time of Moses. Similarly, in the story of Joseph, the son of Jacob, the woman who tried to seduce him is not named. The Quran's focus, when telling the stories of the past, is not on the specifics but rather the moral of the story.

Themes in the Quran

Many scholars have attempted to divide the Quranic teachings and the message into various sections based on the themes presented. For example, Amin A. Islahi (1904–1997), a South Asian Quranic scholar, divided the Quranic themes into seven sections: law (jurisprudence), Abrahamic religions, the struggle between truth and deceit, the proof of Muhammad as a messenger, the unity of God, the judgment, and warnings to nonbelievers. His exegesis, however, is relatively linear, based on the order of the chapters of the Quran, rather than dividing the Quran into various chapters based on the seven themes. This book attempts to cover various themes under different sections, by quoting verses from all over the Quran pertaining to a topic. This by no means is a complete list of the topics, the themes, or the verses in the Quran. More importantly, this is not an attempt to rearrange the order of the Quran, in accordance with the Muslim belief that no one has the authority to change the divine arrangement. This book should also not be considered an exegesis.

Compilation of the Quran

As the verses were revealed to Prophet Muhammad, he ordered his appointed scribes to store them in two forms: oral tradition (by memorization) and the written form. This was done with the clear intention of preserving the words from the Lord. Arabs had a strong tradition of memorizing stories and poetry. Most of his companions memorized large portions, and many memorized the whole Quran. This may seem strange to some in the West, but to this date, there are numerous Muslims who have memorized every single word of the Quran and can recite it from cover to cover. They are called *"Hafiz"* ("ones who memorize"). Muslims believe that this ability to memorize the entire Quran, in itself, is a miracle and yet another sign of the divine nature of the book.

To fully understand and appreciate how the Quran was organized and compiled into its current form, the methods behind how the other scriptures of the Abrahamic faith were organized and compiled should be examined.

Organization and Compilation of the Holy Bible

The following discussion regarding the compilation of the Holy Bible is undertaken with utmost sensitivity and respect for the scriptures from God, as well as the feelings of people of all faiths.

The Quran frequently makes references to the "People of the Book" and previous scriptures, especially *Torawt* (Torah), which was revealed to Prophet Moses; *Zabur* (Psalms), which were revealed to Prophet (King) David, and *Injil* (Gospel), which was revealed to Prophet Jesus Christ. These original scriptures are highly respected by Muslims, though they also believe that over a period of time, they have been modified and altered from their original content. There is a general consensus among many Muslim, Jewish, and Christian scholars that the original text of the Holy Bible is not available anywhere and what's currently available has been edited over the centuries, along with loss of many original verses, as explained below.

Composition of the Bible

The Bible is not one scripture but rather a set of scriptures. The word "Bible" means "the books" and is derived from a Greek phrase, *ton biblion*, meaning the "scroll" or the "book." *Byblos* was an ancient city, located in the current Lebanon, famous for supplying paper and paper products to the world, and became synonymous with the word "book."

The Christian Bible is divided into two parts. The first is called the Old Testament, containing the (minimum) thirty-nine books of Hebrew scripture, and the second portion is called the New

Testament, containing twenty-seven books. The first four books of the New Testament form the Canonical Gospels, which recount the life and teachings of Jesus Christ and are central to the Christian faith.

The Hebrew Bible (or Tanakh) consists of twenty-four books (corresponding to the thirty-nine books of the Old Testament in the Christian Bible) and has three main parts:

1. The Torah ("teaching" or "law") addresses the origins of the universe, Adam, Abraham and his descendants and the Israelite nation, its laws, and its covenant with the God of Israel. There are five books in the Torah.
2. The Nevi'im ("prophets"), containing the historic account of ancient Israel and Judah as well as the work of prophecy. There are eight books in this section.
3. The Ketuvim ("writings"), poetic and philosophical works such as the Psalms and the book of Job. There are eleven books in this section.

The first five books of the Hebrew Bible, making up the Torah, were revealed to Prophet Moses on Mount Sinai. These five books are **Genesis, Exodus, Leviticus, Numbers,** and **Deuteronomy.** The Christian Bible includes the books of the Hebrew Bible, but they are arranged in a different order: the Hebrew Bible ends with the people of Israel restored to Jerusalem and the temple, and the Christian arrangement ends with the book of the Prophet Malachi. It is to be noted that the arrangement and number of books vary among various schools of thoughts within Judaism, though the content remains the same.

The New Testament relates to the life and teachings of Prophet Jesus (**Gospels**), a life of the early church (Acts of the Apostles), and the letters from the apostles of Jesus (Paul and others). The Quran's mention of "Injil" revealed on Prophet Jesus Christ is what's known as the Gospel in the West. There are four Gospels: those written by **Matthew, Mark, Luke,** and **John.** These are not four entirely different scriptures but rather four versions of the same scripture on the life and teachings of Jesus Christ.

The word "Gospel" is derived from the Angelo-Saxon "god-spell," meaning "good news" or "good tidings." This word in turn is derived from the Greek word *"Evangelion"*, also meaning "good tidings."

The Gospel writers were among Jesus's twelve disciples (Matthew and John) or among close traveling companions of the apostle Paul (Mark and Luke). In Islam, John the Baptist is considered a prophet, mentioned in the Quran as *"Yahya."* These four Gospel writers took different approaches to the life of Jesus and, at times, differ when describing the same events or teachings. However, Matthew, Mark, and Luke share a number of similarities and are thus called "synoptic gospels," in Greek meaning "to view together."[1]

Compilation of the Bible

The term "canon" or canonization refers to the authoritative collection of sacred writings acknowledged by a particular religious community. The subject of canonization of the Holy Bible is complex, to say the least, with varying views, and the following is a very brief summary of what's accepted by the majority of scholars and historians.

"We do not possess any of the original writings of the biblical texts—Jewish or Christian."[2] The oldest *surviving* Christian Bibles are Greek manuscripts from the fourth century, and the oldest complete Jewish Bible is a Greek translation, also dating to the fourth century. The original texts were written on papyrus, which deteriorated over time. The oldest complete manuscripts of the Hebrew Bible (the Masoretic text) date from the Middle Ages. However, the discovery of the Dead Sea Scrolls reveal texts dating back to 70–150 BCE.

The Hebrew canon took place in stages. The first corpus to be canonized was the Torah, which is believed to have been canonized in 400 BCE. The canon of Nevi'im (Prophets) is less clear but is said to have occurred around 200 BCE; Ketuvim was put in place around 90 CE at the Rabbinical Council of Jamnia.

---

1 Jeffrey Geoghegan and Michael Homan, *The Bible for Dummies*, Wiley Publishing, Indianapolis, Indiana, 2003, p. 257.
2 Geoghegan and Homan, *The Bible for Dummies*, p. 15.

Following Moses, according to Jewish traditions, the teachings of the Torah were communicated in oral traditions and passed from one generation to another. The oral Torah is distinct from the written tradition. The oral Torah was not supposed to be written down. The intention was to maintain the sacred nature of the scriptures. Rabbi Arthur Kurzweil writes, "It was only after much debate and discussion that the great sages of the Jewish people decided to write down the oral teachings in a process that began a few thousand years ago. This compromise was based on the historical fact that the enemies of the Jewish people were killing so many of the children of Israel and the sacred traditions of the Jewish people were at a great risk of being lost."[3]

In 586 BCE, the Babylonians destroyed Jerusalem, including the Jewish temple and libraries containing the sacred texts. Many scrolls survived and were taken to Babylonia. In Babylon, these documents were edited and compiled. This process involved many people; the person credited with heading up the project was Ezra, a scribe and priest. Around 450 BCE, he brought these scrolls back to the rebuilt Jerusalem. During this time, additional works were penned and included in a relatively complete edition of the Jewish Bible.[4]

The Greek translation of the Hebrew Bible was done around 250–100 BCE. There were checks performed against the translations with Hebrew Bible as well as with oral traditions. "Yet, even with these various checks, most scholars found it a little unnerving that the oldest copies of the Hebrew Bible (called the Masoretic text, after the Jewish scribes responsible for its production) dated to around the tenth century CE, well over 1,500 years from the time many of the books of this library were written."[5]

The New Testament was originally written over a fifty- to seventy-five-year period. By traditions, these works were written by Prophet Jesus Christ's disciples and early church leaders. The first writings were likely started around 50–75 CE, and the

3 Arthur Kurzweil, *The Torah for Dummies*, Wiley Publishing, Indianapolis, Indiana, 2008, p. 14.
4 Geoghegan and Homan, *The Bible for Dummies*, p. 11.
5 Geoghegan and Homan, *The Bible for Dummies*, pp. 15–16.

other writings were nearly complete in various forms around 150 CE (but they were not in one single volume). Many scholars believe the initial texts were written before 70 CE, since they do not refer to the destruction of the second temple in Jerusalem by the Romans. Doubts were raised shortly thereafter about their authenticity, and in the second century CE, the canonization was ordered. The collection process was complete by the end of the second century CE, but it was not official until 367, when St. Athanasius, a bishop of Alexandria, used the word "canonization" in his Easter letter and determined the number of books in the New Testament to what it is currently: twenty-seven. The canon includes the letters of St. Paul, canonical Gospels, the Acts of the Apostles, and the book of Revelation. The first official canon was accepted in 393 CE in the synod of Hippo Regius in Africa (a synod is a council established by the church to determine a doctrine or other important affairs). The acts of this council are lost. In 397 CE, the synod of Carthage in Africa confirmed the New Testament canon to what's accepted today. A review of the process of canonization reveals many debates and disputes among church leaders as to which books and writings to include. Many books were eventually expunged (e.g., the book of 1 Clement and the Shepherd of Hermas). It is of note that Jesus spoke Aramaic, and God's revelations to him likely were in that language, yet there is no original Aramaic Gospel available.

From this brief discussion, one is tempted to ask the question: If the oldest surviving texts were not written for several centuries (Old Testament) and at least many decades to about 150 years (New Testament) after their revelations, how accurate are the current versions of the Holy Bible? Although great care has been taken to preserve oral traditions, as well as written texts over the years, there is ongoing debate among biblical scholars about the composition, compilation, translation, and the Bible's resultant accuracy. Churches of all dominions today almost universally accept the current New Testament's list of twenty-seven books. Many scholars insist that despite the challenges and some controversies early on, the current version of the

Bible, having gone through a process of canonization and being looked at by religious sages, is an accurate reflection of the original texts. "The material upon which the biblical books were written (usually Papyrus made from the tall water plant of the same name) deteriorated over time ... the books making up the Jewish and Christian Bibles had to be copied and recopied by hand to preserve them. Yet, the popular notion that this continued copying means that the books we now possess are hopelessly corrupted is inaccurate."[6]

We Now Return to the Compilation of the Quran

The history of the compilation of the Quran can be summarized in three phases:

1. During the lifetime of Prophet Muhammad (610–632 CE)
2. During the caliphate of the first caliph, Abu Bakr (632–634 CE)
3. During the caliphate of the third caliph, Uthman (644–656 CE)

1. During the Lifetime of Prophet Muhammad

The consensus among Muslims is that Prophet Muhammad himself, under divine instructions, organized the Quranic text in its current form and that the version we have currently available is the same as what was available at the time of Prophet Muhammad's death.

The Quran's compilation is made unique among all scriptures in that Prophet Muhammad appointed several scribes to write down the verses during his lifetime, and he directed its organization and placement of various chapters. The verses were written down on palm leaves, tablets of stone, leather, parchments, and other such material. The Quran points to the presence of a readable Quran on several occasions, which will be reviewed in more detail in chapter 8.

---

6 Geoghegan and Homan, *The Bible for Dummies*, p. 15.

"That this is indeed a Quran Most Honorable. In a Book well guarded, which none shall touch but those who are clean." 56:77–79

In his last sermon to a huge audience, when he was returning from the pilgrimage, about three months before he passed away, Prophet Muhammad addressed the audience of the Muslim pilgrims by stating:

"I leave amongst you two great things. The Book of God and my Ahlul-Bait (people of my household). Should you be attached to these two, never shall you get astray after me."[7]

Sahih Muslim is considered by most Muslims as one of the more authentic books of *Hadith* (the sayings of Muhammad). In the statement quoted above, the use of "the Book," and not "scripture" or "revelations," points to the presence of a written text at the time.

There are many passages in the Quran proclaiming its purity and divine source.

Other verses within the Quran itself also point to the writing down of the Quran at the time of revelation. For example:

"By no means (should it be so)! For it is indeed a Message of instruction: Therefore let whoso will, keep it in remembrance. (It is) in Books held (greatly) in honor. Exalted (in dignity), kept pure and holy, (Written) by the hands of scribes. Honorable and Pious and Just." 80:11–16

The Oral Quran: As the verses were revealed to Prophet Muhammad, in addition to dictating them to the appointed scribes, he would also reveal them to the appointed *Hafiz* (memorizers), who would repeat the verses back to him and memorize them. The following segment discusses how this oral tradition became an important part of the compilation of the Quran into a single volume.

The Quran was available in a textual form, and it was already named *Al-Quran*. Moreover, the following verse points to the Quran already separated into chapters, at the time of the revelations, during Prophet Muhammad's lifetime:

"Whenever there comes down a Surah, they look at each other, (saying), 'Does anyone see you? Then they turn aside'" 9:127

---

7 *Tafsi-e-Kabir,* and also *Sahih Muslim,* book 031, number 5920.

2. During the Caliphate of the First Caliph, Abu Bakr (632– 634 CE)

According to the most widely held view by Muslim scholars, within six months after the death of the Prophet Muhammad, about 700 *Hafiz* companions (who had memorized the whole Quran) were killed in the battle of Yamama. It was feared that the Quran's preservation would weaken. Abu Bakr then ordered a compilation from the collections of all scribes from the time of the Prophet Muhammad. This task was assigned to a well-known scribe, Zaid bin Thabit. The writings were checked against the memory of the other *Hafiz* companions and all writings from other reliable scribes; it was ensured that they had met strict criteria to be included in the one, authenticated text. The final product was passed on to Hafsah, the daughter of Umar and one of the widows of the Prophet Muhammad.[8]

After Prophet Muhammad's death in 632, several of his companions, including Ali Ibn Abi Talib, had already collected portions of the Quran as a whole book. Others included Abdullah Ibne Masood in Mecca and Obai Ibne Ka'b in Medina. Ali had handwritten a copy of the Quran, arranged not only in its current form (as dictated by Prophet Muhammad) but "because of his close relationship to Prophet Muhammad and long companionship, didn't only collect the dispersed scrolls of the Quran, but he rather could accompany it with a remarkable tafsir (commentary, or exegesis), mentioning the occasion of each verse's descension, and this was regarded as the first tafsir of Quran."[9] He also had the verses arranged in chronological order. According to some scholars, Ali was the first one to collect the Quran and wrote the first *tafsir*.

3. During the Caliphate of the Third Caliph, Uthman (644– 656 CE)

Later on, in the time of the Caliph Uthman, Islam spread fast, and many companions of Prophet Muhammad moved out of Arabia.

---

8   Sahih Bukhari 6:60:201, 6:61:509; Sohaib Sultan, *Koran for Dummies*, Wiley Publishing, Indianapolis, Indiana, 2004, pp. 27–29.
9   Maurice Bucaille, *The Bible, the Quran and Science*, Ansariyan Publications, 2007, p. 132.

Amongst the many countries and provinces that accepted Islam were Syria and Iraq, but their language was not Arabic. One of the Prophet Muhammad's companions, Huthaifah-ibn el-Yaman, during a visit to Syria and Iraq, learnt that people were reciting the Quran in different modes, dialects, or styles. This disturbed him very much, and upon his return, he requested Uthman to reproduce and distribute copies of the Quran that would help Muslims read or recite the Quran in a single consistent manner to avoid any conflict.

Uthman appointed twelve members, headed by Zaid bin Thabit (the same scribe used by Abu Bakr), to write the Quran in the mode of the tribe Quraish, the one used by the Prophet in his recitation. The intent was to preserve the Quran exactly as it was revealed and organized at the time of Prophet Muhammad. Uthman relied on two sources: the written text that had been previously ordered by Abu Bakr, and the various oral traditions of Muslims who memorized it during the lifetime of Prophet Muhammad. In Islamic history, there is no variation between these two sources, so the Uthmanic "rescension" is largely a codifying of a single version of a text. This version, the Uthmanic rescension, is the version of the Quran that has remained unchanged and is the one currently in use.

Of the completed official copies Uthman ordered, three were sent to Syria, Iraq, and Mecca, and one was kept in Medina. The original manuscript was returned to Hafsah. Uthman then ordered that all the other Quranic materials, whether written in fragmentary manuscripts or whole copies, be burnt. This was a precautionary measure taken to prevent any future conflict in the mode of recitation, thus preventing the Quran from fabrication or corruption.[10]

Some scholars suggest that the early Uthmanic texts of the Quran did not have the special markings that the current texts do. It is believed that early versions of the text did not contain diacritics, markers for short vowels, and dots that are used to distinguish similarly written Arabic letters.[11]

---

10 Sahih Bukhari, 6:61:510.
11 Youssef Mahmoud, *The Arabic Writing System and the Sociolinguistics of Orthographic Reform*, Ph.D. Dissertation, Georgetown University, 1979, p. 8.

Despite slight variations on the type of work and possible addition of diacritics for easier reading, it's unanimously agreed by all Muslims that the Quranic text and composition have been preserved, without any addition or deletions from the one that was revealed to Prophet Muhammad. The dialect present in today's texts is the same exact one since the days of Uthman, which is the same as organized by Prophet Muhammad.

Moreover, the entire Quran is the first person, literal word of God. This is in contrast to large portions of the Old Testament and the New Testament, which mostly consists of writings by apostles and the church leaders. "In Christianity and Judaism, the concept of the revelation as a book developed over a period of time. For Islam, the concept of revelation as a divine book is present from the very beginning."[12]

It is interesting to note that the word "Quran" itself has been noted in the Quran at least seventy times. The word "Gospel" is not found in current versions of the Bible. However, the Quran *does* name the prior scriptures as *Torawt* (Torah) and *Injil* (Gospel).

Recitation of the Quran

Muslims often claim, and some non-Muslim scholars concur, that the beauty of the Quran is best appreciated when it is recited (and understood) in its original Arabic language. It is a common custom in Muslim countries to recite the Quran in Arabic on various occasions. Not uncommonly, one hears the Quran being recited on audiotapes and CDs in beautiful melody, at mosques, as a ritual when someone dies, and at prayer gatherings. Malcolm Clark put it succinctly in his book, *Islam for Dummies*: "To read the Quran but never recite it in Arabic is like trying to appreciate a song by only reading the score."[13]

The Oldest Surviving Copy of the Quran

According to the Islamic traditions, the original Uthmanic texts are preserved in Topkapi Museum, in Istanbul, Turkey. A number

---

12 Malcolm Clark, *Islam for Dummies*, Wiley Publishing, Indianapolis, Indiana, 2003, p. 101.
13 Clark, *Islam for Dummies*, p. 103.

of ancient manuscripts of the Quran were discovered in Yemen in 1972. Carbon-14 dating traced these to the period between 645 and 690.[14] The calligraphic dating points to a date a little later, around 710–715.

The Secular View on Compilation

Most Western scholars basically accept the Uthmanic version of the compilation, but in addition, these scholars believe that other versions continued to circulate for centuries. They point out that texts from about 800 CE complain about the use of another version by Ibn Masud, indicating that after Uthman, at least one other version existed. Moreover, they point out that the earliest texts of any portion of the Quran that have been preserved date to the end of the seventh century. The Dome of the Rock in Jerusalem was inscribed in 691–692 with verses from the Quran. These manuscripts, it is said, have slightly different texts of some specific passages than in the Uthmanic texts and have a different way of writing some words. Muslims would contend that these slight variations are accounted for by various dialects and special markings that were added to make the reading easier for non-Arabic-speaking Muslims and don't alter the pronunciation, meaning, and message of the Quran. Malcolm Clark, in his book *Islam for Dummies,* writes, "Western scholars, such as Michael Cook, don't see it this way. What's striking isn't how many variants exist to the text of the Quran but how few exist, especially compared to the texts of the Jewish and Christian Bibles. What is surprising in this view isn't that the text wasn't fixed already in the times of Muhammad, but that it was fixed in written form as early as it was and transmitted as accurately as it was—again in contrast to the Bible."[15]

Points to Remember

- The Quran was revealed to Prophet Muhammad over a period of twenty-three years.

---

14 Carole Hillenbrand, *The New Cambridge Medieval History,* vol. 1, p. 330.
15 Clark, *Islam for Dummies,* p. 108.

- Muslims believe that Prophet Muhammad himself, during his lifetime, with divine guidance, ordered the placement of various chapters and verses and organized the Quran in its current form. Oral and written accounts existed in Prophet Muhammad's life, and the Quran as we see it today was available during the last few months of his life.
- Only the Quran in Arabic is considered *the* Quran. All other translations are considered interpretations, since it is impossible to precisely translate the Arabic version into any other language.
- Muslims believe that the Quran is the literal word of God. The current Quran is unaltered and uncorrupted from its original revelation to Prophet Muhammad.
- The scripts gathered in the days of the first caliph (Abu Bakr) and the third caliph (Uthman) were undertaken in an attempt to preserve the Quran in its original form, and Muslims believe the version available today is the same as the one at the end of Prophet Muhammad's life. Secular scholars generally agree with the traditional view but additionally believe that in addition to the Uthmanic script, there were other versions, available as late as 700 CE.
- The Torah existed in the oral form for five hundred to one thousand years, before attempts were made to capture it in textual form to preserve the divine message. The initial writings of the New Testament were not gathered until about fifty to seventy-five years after Christ and were not authenticated (in a process called canonization) until at least the end of the second century.
- The Quran refers to itself many times as "Al-Quran." The Torah (*Tawrat*) and the Gospel (*Injeel*) are mentioned by name in the Quran repeatedly.

Time to Ponder

- After the Torah and the Gospel were revealed, was another scripture (the Quran) needed, and if so, why? Similarly, after the Torah was revealed, why was another major scripture (the Gospel) needed?
- Why is the Quran not arranged in a topical or chronological order? Would it have made a difference if it were? Whereas mere mortals can write books in a well-organized, topical, or chronological order, why did God (or Muhammad, *if* one believes he wrote the book) choose not to arrange it that way?
- Why does the Quran repeatedly refer to the authenticity of the Quran (whereas the prior scriptures didn't)?

SECTION 1
GOD

CHAPTER 1
ALLAH = GOD

"Allah" is the Arabic word for "God." The word "Allah" is derived from two words: *Al* (the) and *Ilah* (deity), meaning "the deity" or simply, "God." Thus even though many people, including Muslims, may believe it is a proper name for God in Arabic, it literally means "the God," or "the sole God." The etymological origins of the word "Allah" are also found in other languages and appear in the Hebrew Bible (*Elohim*) and the Aramaic Bible (*Elaha*). Most English translations of the Bible have translated *Elohim* as God. Some in the West believe that Allah in the Quran is different than the "God" of the Bible. However, a close analysis of the Quran and the Bible and an examination of various cultural practices would argue against such a belief. According to *Columbia Encyclopedia*, Arabic speakers of all Abrahamic faiths, including Christians and Jews, use the word "Allah" to mean "God." These include Mizrahi Jews, Eastern Orthodox Christians, and Eastern Catholic Christians. Many others share this view.[16] Whereas many communities in the biblical and Quranic stories took on many deities as their god/s, the Quran and the Bible emphasize, over and over, that there is no god but God (the singular deity). Allah was also used in pre-Quranic Mecca by pagans as a deity, but one who had associates and was not considered the sole divine power. This polytheistic view was thoroughly rejected by Prophet Muhammad and the Quran. Muslims believe that the Quran is the final word from Allah, who is the Lord of the Worlds, the Creator of the universe, All-Knowledgeable, All-Powerful, All-Compassionate,

---

16   Bernard Lewis, P. M. Holt, Peter R. Holt, and Ann Katherine Swynford Lambton, *The Cambridge History of Islam*. Cambridge, UK, Cambridge University Press, 1977, p. 32.

and All-Merciful—the attributes shared by both the Quran and the Bible in reference to God.

Arabic translations of the Bible use *Allah* as the translation for the Hebrew Elohim. Thus "God," "Allah," and *"Elohim"* refer to the same deity.

"Elohim" is derived from *Eloah* (singular form), which is an expanded form of the Northwest Semitic noun *il*. It refers to the one God of Israel. The word *"elohim"* (with a lowercase *e*), on the other hand, is generally used in the Hebrew Bible to indicate plural pagan gods. *Elohim* is the first name for God used in the Torah: *"In the beginning, God (Elohim) created heavens and the earth."* Genesis 1:1. According to Jewish scholars, "Elohim" is the name given to God, the Creator, and generally implies power and justice. There is some argument that the similarities of the words "Allah," "Elah," and "Elohim" do not necessarily mean that these words refer to the same deity. The word *"Eloah"* is most often used in the book of Job (in debates between Job and his friends), and less so in Deuteronomy (32:15) and Psalms (50:22, 114:7, and 139:19).

Another divine name used in the Hebrew Bible is *"Yahweh,"* a proper name for the God of Israel. It is derived from a Hebrew word that's transcribed into Roman letters as *YHVH*. It is the most frequently used name of God in *Tanakh,* the Jewish Bible consisting of the Torah (teaching, or law), Nevi'im (Prophets), and Ketuvim (Writings). YHWH is considered to be an unutterable name of God of Israel and is often referred to as "tetragrammation" ("the four letters") since it's derived from four Hebrew letters: *Yod, Hey, Vav,* and *Hey.* The name YHVH implies God's mercy and the condescension of Almighty God. Bible describes Yahweh as the one true God who delivered Israel from Egypt and gave the Ten Commandments. Yahweh is also translated as Jehovah in English.

"I (am) Jehovah thy God, who hath brought thee out of the land of Egypt, out of a house of servants." Exodus 20:2 (translation from Darby; the King James, New Living Translation, and other modern translations have used "I am the LORD, your God" instead).

According to biblical accounts, God appeared to Moses and Abraham with different names, but it did not change the fact that He is the same God, regardless of what names He was called.

"And God said to Moses. "I am Yahweh—The Lord, I appeared to Abraham, Isaac, and Jacob as El-Shaddai, God Almighty, but I did not reveal my name Yahweh to them. And I reaffirmed my covenant with them." Exodus 6:2–3

(*El-Shaddai* is often used in the Torah and means "God, the Almighty.")

Allah, or God, is mentioned by various other attributes in the Quran, such as *Ar-Rehman* (The Most Compassionate), *Ar-Rahim* (The Most Merciful), *Al-Khaliq* (The Creator), and *Al-Nur* (The Light), among many other attributes. It is said that Allah has ninety-nine "names" in the Quran, although this actually refers to some of the qualities or attributes of God. Reading the attributes alone, one can conclude that the God in the Bible and the Quran have many of the same attributes.

Indeed *Allah* is the most often-repeated word used for God in the Quran. The following translators of the Quran have used the Arabic word *Allah* when translating the Quran into English, perhaps believing there is no corresponding word in English: Pickthall, Abdullah Yousuf Ali, Farooq-i-Azam Malik, Fakhry, Shakir, and Muhammad Ali.

Many other translators, especially in the modern times, have used the word "God" in translations for *Allah*. These include Asad, Yuksel, Pooya Yazdi, Al Ghazali, Emerick, Haleem, and Ali Unal.

The following verse is an example of the translations by the first group mentioned above:

"And your Allah is One Allah. There is no god but He, Most Gracious, Most Merciful." 2:163

If Allah is indeed a proper name, this translation does not seem very clear. However, if we take Allah as the Arabic word (and not a proper name) for God, here is how the same verse would be translated, with a much more clear message.

"And your God is One God. There is no god but He, Most Gracious, Most Merciful." 2:163

Therefore, when a verse is translated as "there is no god but Allah," it does not imply that "there is no God except the Arabic, or the Quranic, Allah." It simply means that "there is no god but God"—a more appropriate translation. (It is also the title of one of Reza Aslan's books, *No god but God*.)

Many passages in both the Quran and the Bible refer to the same historical events, like the creation of Adam, the floods in Noah's era, Abraham's sons Ishmael and Isaac, Moses and the Israelites, and so on. This would once again indicate that the Allah mentioned in the Quran and the God (or Yahweh) in the Bible is the same deity.

For these reasons, I am in agreement with the latter group of translators mentioned above, who have translated "Allah" to mean "God." And since Allah and God refer to the same deity, the words "Allah" and "God" in this book are used interchangeably.

Lord, Rabb, and Adonai

Another word used in the Quran for God is "*Rabb*," often translated as "Lord" or "Sustainer" in English, though some translators (e.g., Farooq-i-Azam Malik) have maintained that there is no English equivalent of the word. The word "*Adonai*" is used in the Hebrew Bible, usually side by side with Yahweh, and is often translated as "Lord" in English. Strictly speaking, "Adonai" is the plural of Adon, meaning lord and master, which became the replacement for YHWH, considered too holy to utter. Despite the linguistic origins, Adonai refers to a *singular* deity.

Is the God of the Quran the Same as the God of the Bible?

The doctrine of Trinity notwithstanding, the religious scholars of monotheistic faiths generally believe they worship the same God, the One who created the universe, the One who sent the prophets, the One who is eternal and will be the Master on the Day of Judgment.

Points to Remember

- Many Muslims and people of other faiths often think of "Allah" as a proper name of God. However, it is the Arabic word used *for* God, the singular deity. Many modern Quran translators have used "God" rather than retain "Allah" in their translations.
- "Elohim" is the Hebrew word for God. Yahweh is a personal, unutterable name of God, though it is often translated as "God" or "Lord" in English translations of the Holy Bible.
- Many non-Muslims, including Christians and Jews in the Arab world, use "Allah" to mean God. The Arabic versions of the Bible translate "Elohim" as "Allah."
- The God mentioned in the Bible and the Quran refers to the same deity, whether using the words "Allah," "Elohim," or "Yahweh."

Time to Ponder

- If the Torah, the Gospel, and the Quran refer to the same God, why do we not see the same name across all scriptures? Why was "Allah" not used in the Hebrew Bible, or "Elohim" not used in the Quran for God? Did God want us to remember Him in our own languages? If so, does it imply that how or what we call Him is not as important?
- Does the Quran insist that we know Him as Allah only? Does calling Him "God," instead, somehow imply one is lowering His status?
- Is the "God of Muslims" different than the "God of Jews" and the "God of Christians"? If one believes such a dogma, what's the theological evidence to support it?

CHAPTER 2
THE NATURE OF GOD

God's Existence

The question "Is there a God?" has probably existed in the minds of people since ancient times, and humans have gone back and forth in their argument. One of the fundamental beliefs among the monotheistic faiths, and for that matter most other religions, revolves around the existence of God, who created everything and to whom we shall all return. All scholars of monotheistic faiths agree that God's nature and His whereabouts are beyond finite human cognition. However, His signs are all around us. The Quran frequently invites man to ponder over the nature and the signs of His existence. The Quran further argues that the pondering should lead one to conclude that the universe and everything in it was created with an intelligent design by a supreme Creator, and that such creation was not fortuitous, for an accidental birth could not have resulted in such a complex yet orderly universe, in perfect harmony.

"Verily in the heavens and the earth, are Signs for those who believe. And in the creation of yourselves and the fact that animals are scattered (through the earth), are Signs for those of assured Faith. And in the alternation of Night and Day, and the fact that Allah sends down Sustenance from the sky, and revives therewith the earth after its death, and in the change of the winds, are Signs for those that are wise." 45:3–5

"Say: 'It is He Who has created you (and made you grow), and made for you the faculties of hearing, seeing, feeling, and understanding.'" 67:23

Similarly, Paul's invitation to study for signs of God in nature is apparent from this passage in the New Testament:

"For since the creation of the world His invisible attributes, His eternal power and divine nature, have been clearly seen, being understood through what has been made, so that they are without excuse." Romans 1:20[17]

The Quran's emphasis on pondering will be discussed in more detail in chapter 11.

The complex universe, from galaxies to biological cells, reveals intricate checks and balances that simply could not have evolved without supreme intelligence, leading to the only logical conclusion that the signs of God exist in "nature." Agnostics and atheists argue that natural phenomenon could be explained by "science." The question then is, who created the laws of science? Do scientific processes that explain the natural phenomena exclude the presence of, and the design by, God?

In his book *The Creator*, Brig. Aftab Ahmad Khan, a retired Pakistani army officer and an ardent student of Semitic religions, compares the concept of the existence of God to light and sound. He explains how light is real and has a source like the sun or electricity. Darkness, on the other hand, is simply the absence of light—a perception, not a reality. Similarly, sound is real; it has a measure, and silence is simply an absence of sound and a mere perception. Thus absence of God is a perception, and the existence of God is a reality with clear signs.[18]

In the following paragraphs, certain physiological phenomena are discussed that can trigger the curious minds to ponder whether these phenomena are accidental or a result of intelligent design. Human breast milk has a unique composition, with perfect balance in regards to the amounts of fluid, electrolytes, and other key nutrients—not more, not less than what a baby needs. Were it not for this perfect mix, the newborn would be in shortage or excess of either the fluids or the nutrients. Newborns have no teeth and can only swallow liquids, and no one taught

---

17 All biblical translations in this chapter are from the New American Standard Bible by the Lockman Foundation.

18 Brig. Aftab A. Khan, *The Creator*, p. 21.

them how to drink the only form of nutrition available: mother's milk. How did they learn to suckle mother's milk starting at birth? How does the process of evolution explain that? Were human babies at one time in the evolutionary process not able to suckle milk at birth? If so, the babies would have died, cutting off the human reproductive cycle. Moreover, human milk is low in iron, not enough to meet the needs of the newborn. However, the newborn liver has enough iron stores, acquired during pregnancy, to last about six months. That's about the amount of time before babies can begin to digest some form of solid food, rich in iron. Coincidence? Moreover, human milk is rich in antibodies (immunoglobulin A), especially in the first few days, to protect the newborn baby from infections during birth, when the baby passes through the birth canal—a place with a rich bacterial environment. Another coincidence?

How does the mother's birth canal learn to relax and open up when the baby is ready to be born? We know a head-down position is a very important factor in dilating the birth canal when the time is right. True, it can all be explained by physiological processes, but does a scientific explanation confirm evolution or intelligent design? Who put all this in motion? Another physiological phenomenon to ponder: during fetal life, lungs are formed but are not expanded, as the fetus does not breathe. If he or she did, he or she would have drowned in the fluid in which he or she lives (which serves as a shock absorber). So how does he or she get his or her oxygen and get rid of the dangerous carbon dioxide? There exists a unique system of dual blood supply from the mother through the umbilical arteries and veins, bypassing the need to exchange these gases through breathing. Is there evidence to show that at some point, the above mentioned phenomena did not exist, and humans somehow "learned" or evolved to fix these problem that otherwise existed? If humans existed at one time without these "corrective" or evolutionary mechanisms, it would have made reproduction impossible.

The oxygen cycle is another example of symbiosis—a process whereby two organisms exist in a mutually beneficial state. By far the largest reservoir of oxygen on earth is found in the silicate and oxide minerals in the crust and mantle of the earth (99.5 percent). Less than 0.4 percent is released in the atmosphere we breathe. The main source of the atmospheric oxygen is photosynthesis, a process by which plants on earth and the oceans produce oxygen that's critical to sustain human life. Is that a coincidence or the result of an intelligent design?

The subject of signs of God and the Quran and science will be discussed in more detail in section 3.

God Is One

The existence of God and the Oneness of God are inseparable concepts, representing the most fundamental teaching of the scriptures. "There is no god, but God" is the first half of Muslim's testimony (*Shahada)* to Islam. Anyone who associates other gods with Allah is considered a *mushrik*, a polytheist, or a pagan. It is considered a major sin. In the Quran, the Oneness of God, or *Wehdat,* is repeatedly emphasized. Some of the very basic teachings from the Quran about God are that there is no god but God, that there is only *one* God, that He has no partners, and that there is no one else worthy of worship.

The Quran further teaches that God is Omnipresent and Omnipotent. He is our Guardian, Helper, *the* Most Kind, *the* Most Merciful, *the* Most Loving, *the* Judge, *the* Most High, All-Knowing, *the* Hearer of all, *the* Seer of all, *the* Most Generous, All-Wise, *the* Majestic, *the* First, *the* Last, *the* Light, *the* Guide, and *the* Almighty. Scholars point out that these and other attributes of God are themselves a testimony to His Oneness. The complex doctrine of Trinity notwithstanding, the Bible and the Quran are congruent on many of these key beliefs.

"Your God is one God; there is no one worthy of worship except Him, the Compassionate, the Merciful." 2:163

"And God has said: 'Do not take to worshipping two (or more) deities.' He is the One and Only God: hence, 'of Me, of Me alone stand in awe!'" 16:51 (Asad)

"Do not associate another deity with Allah, lest you sit back, condemned, forsaken. Your Lord has decreed to you that: You shall worship none but Him." 17:22–23 (Shakir)

"That surely your God is One, the Lord of the heavens and of the earth and all that lies between them, and the Lord of the east (every point and place at the rising of the sun)." 37:4–5

"Say: He is Allah the One and Only; Allah is the Self-Sufficient (independent of all, while all are dependent on Him); He begets not, nor is He begotten; And there is none comparable to Him." 112:1–4 (Malik)

The Oneness of God in the Bible

The Ten Commandments of the Torah start with the declaration of the Oneness of God and a prohibition of polytheism, once again highlighting the emphasis put on this fundamental belief:

"I am the LORD your God, who brought you out of the land of Egypt, out of the house of slavery. You shall have no other gods before Me. You shall not make for yourself an idol, or any likeness of what is in heaven above or on the earth beneath or in the water under the earth. You shall not worship them or serve them." Exodus 20:2–5

"I am the LORD your God who brought you out of the land of Egypt, out of the house of slavery. You shall have no other gods before Me." Deuteronomy 5:6–7

"Hear, O Israel: The LORD is our God, the LORD is one." Deuteronomy 6:4

Jews recite a prayer known as *"Shema"* twice a day, and its words come from the Torah. It starts by the above-mentioned verse. In Hebrew the word *"Ekhad"* ("one") is used to describe God's Oneness. This word is strikingly close to the Arabic word *"Ehad,"* used in the Quran in relations to God, meaning one.

"Thus says the LORD, the King of Israel, and his Redeemer, the LORD of hosts: 'I am the first and I am the Last. And there is no God besides Me.'" Isaiah 44:6

In Islam, there are three key duties of man to God:

1. Submitting to God, submitting to His will.
2. Seeking His pleasure. Engaging in activities with the intention to please God.
3. Remembering Him (*"Dhikr"*). Remembering Him all the time so one doesn't move away from Him and thereby risk succumbing to the temptations and desires.

The concept of submission is at the core of Islamic beliefs. The word "Islam" means "submission" (to the will of God), and "Muslim" literally means "submitter." Islam is a way of life, rather than a religion consisting of a set of beliefs and rituals. According to this doctrine, one belongs to God and everything one does is for the purpose of pleasing, serving, and getting near to God, so much so that at the height of this state, God's will becomes your will.

"Nay, whoever submits His whole self to Allah and is a doer of good, He will get his reward with his Lord; on such shall be no fear, nor shall they grieve." 2:112

"We shall surely test your steadfastness with fear and famine, with loss of property, life, and produce. Give good news to those who endure with patience; who, when afflicted with calamity, say: 'We belong to Allah and to Him we shall return.'" 2:155–156 (Malik)

"Serve Allah, and join not any partners with Him." 4:36

"When Isa [Jesus] found out that they had no faith, he asked: 'Who will help me in the cause of Allah?' The Disciples replied: 'We will help you in the cause of Allah. We believe in Allah. Be our witness that we are Muslims.'" 3:52 (Malik)

Farooq-i-Azam and Yousuf Ali have translated the Arabic word *"Muslimoon"* at the end of the verse as "Muslims." Other translators have used the word "submitters", the literal meaning of the word "Muslim," instead of *Muslim* or *Muslimoon* (plural). For example, Asad translates the same verse as follows:

"And when Jesus became aware of their refusal to acknowledge the truth, he asked: 'Who will be my helpers in God's cause?' The white-garbed ones replied: 'We shall be (thy) helpers (in the cause) of God! We believe in God: and bear thou witness that we have surrendered (submitted) ourselves unto Him!'"

Remember God Often

The Quran not only commands followers to submit to His will but emphasizes that God must be remembered often, and His remembrance must be part of our daily lives.

"For sure, in the creation of the heavens and the earth and the alternation of the night and the day there are signs for men of

understanding. Those who remember Allah while standing, sitting, and lying on their sides, and meditate on the creation of the heavens and the earth, then cry out: 'Our Rabb [Lord]! You have not created this in vain. Glory to You.'" 3:190–191 (Malik)

Another verse is often cited about the remembrance of God:

"Therefore, remember Me, and, I will remember you, be grateful to Me and never deny Me." 2:152 (Malik)

The Arabic word for remembrance of God is *"Dhikr."* This can be in the form of repeating His name, keeping His name in the heart and mind, remembering His commands (doing good deeds and avoiding bad ones), as well as elevating and glorifying His name. Many consider this verse a bargain and sign of God's mercy. This verse seeks to elevate the spirituality and love for God by remembering Him and urges us to be grateful to Him in good times and bad times. In his commentary of the verse, Pooya Yazdi writes:

"To be grateful (*Shukr* in Arabic) is the key to the fulfillment and application of remembrance which neutralizes desires and generates joy of inner contentment—deep and peaceful. The opposite of this condition is *Kufr*—the falling over hurdles on the road of disobedience."

Submission to God in the Torah

The concept of submission is not unique to Muslims. It is similar to the concept of *d'veykut,* meaning "clinging" in Jewish tradition. *D'veykut* means one is clinging to God with such faith and devotion that his will and God's will merge into one will. The following is a passage from the Torah (Moses is addressing his people):

"Now, Israel, what does the LORD your God require from you, but to fear the LORD your God, to walk in all His ways and love Him, and to serve the LORD your God with all your heart and with all your soul and to keep the LORD'S commandments and His statutes which I am commanding you today for your good." Deuteronomy 10:12–13

And in the oldest prayer in Judaism, *Shema*:

"Hear, O Israel! The LORD is our God, the LORD is one! You shall love the LORD your God with all your heart and with all your

soul and with all your might. These words, which I am commanding you today, shall be on your heart. You shall teach them diligently to your sons and shall talk of them when you sit in your house and when you walk by the way and when you lie down and when you rise up. You shall bind them as a sign on your hand and they shall be as frontals on your forehead. You shall write them on the doorposts of your house and on your gates." Deuteronomy 6:4–9

The similarity of Quran verses 3:190–191, quoted above, and Deuteronomy 6:4–9 is striking: Both command the followers to remember God in all phases: sitting, standing, and lying. In addition to submitting to Him, the constant remembrance throughout the day is meant to encourage one to do good deeds and eschew bad deeds as ordained by God.

Submission in the New Testament

Friendship with the world is discouraged, as friendship with the world makes one an enemy of God; therefore, one must submit to Him and seek nearness to Him. Even though the passage quoted below is being addressed to adulterers, it can be easily applied to everyone, adulterers or not.

"Submit therefore to God. Resist the devil and he will flee from you. Draw near to God and He will draw near to you." James 4:7–8

God Is Light *(Nur)*

The Quran, the Old Testament, and the New Testament have all embraced the concept of the light *(Nur* in Arabic*)* of God. God is characterized as light, and all the light in the universe is a reflection of His light. A detailed discussion of God as light is beyond the scope of this book. This light is the source of guidance, and without this light, everything will be in total darkness, or ignorance. The divine light is knowledge, from which all forms of knowledge flow. The following verse in the Quran points to this luminous Glory of God in a verse that Muslims and many non Muslim Islamic scholars quote often to praise its immense poetic and literal beauty. This is from a chapter that itself is named *"An-Nur,"* or *"*The Light*"*:

"God is the light of the heavens and the earth. The example of His light is like a niche wherein is a lamp: the lamp is in a crystal, and the crystal shining as if a pearl-like radiant star, lit from the oil of a blessed olive tree that is neither of the east nor of the west. The oil almost gives light of itself though no fire touches it. Light upon light. God guides to His light whom He wills. God strikes parables for people. God has full knowledge of all things." 24:35 (Unal)

In his commentary to this verse, Yazdi writes, "The physical light is but a reflection of the true light in the realm of reality, and that true light is Allah. The performance of light is to manifest. It is Allah who manifests the universe. The divine light, according to the parable, is placed high above everything, all that which has been created, the whole universe. The lamp is the core of the real illumination. Due to the limitations of human experience, man cannot see the real light but perceive only the lighted objects." He further goes on to state that the light is a parable and to visualize God or His nature is humanly impossible. "The existence of the supreme being has been compared to light in order to make human intellect understand a great attribute of Allah. Otherwise He is the inconceivable absolute who has created the light. Light is His manifestation. It is not His being."

In his book *Torah for Dummies*, Arthur Kurzweil writes:

"The first spoken words by God as recorded in Torah are 'Let there be light.' (Genesis 1:3)" He goes on to write, "But when God says 'Let there be light', at the beginning of the Torah, this light exists before God's creation of the sun, moon, stars, and planets. God's divine light emanates from its divine source. According to the great sages of the Jewish tradition, everything in the world ultimately is formed by the primal light at the beginning of the creation story."[19]

When promising future glory for Jerusalem, the book of Isaiah foretells that the brightness from God's light will shine upon Jerusalem:

---

19 Kurzweil, *The Torah for Dummies*, p. 22.

"No longer will you have the sun for light by day, Nor for brightness will the moon give you light; But you will have the LORD for an everlasting light." Isaiah 60:19

Similar characterization is apparent in the book of Revelation, when God gives Jesus the vision of events to come. John also shares that vision. John then reports all that he saw during his trip to heaven:

"And the city has no need of the sun or of the moon to shine on it, for the glory of God has illumined it." Revelation 21:23

Points to Remember

- The Oneness of God is fundamental to the Quranic teachings and forms the cornerstone of the Islamic faith. Worshipping anyone other than God is the biggest sin. The Oneness of God is an essential part of the Ten Commandments in the Old Testament as well.
- Trinitarian Christians claim Oneness of God too, except that according to this doctrine, God appeared in three persons: the Father, the Son, and the Holy Spirit. This view is not shared by some Christian churches, as well as by Muslims, Jews, and other nonmonotheistic religions.
- "Islam" means submission. However, the concept of submission to the will of God is shared by all three monotheistic religions.
- There is consensus among the three faiths that it is beyond the cognitive capacity of humans to imagine God. "God's light" is a shared though complex concept. All the light in the universe is reflection of His light and He is the source of guidance. Without this light, one remains in the darkness (of ignorance).

Time to Ponder

- Does remembering God at all times mean one needs to "wear" one's religion on one's sleeve? If not, how can one remember God without appearing to do so?
- Can one align one's will with God's will without submitting to Him?

CHAPTER 3
GOD IS KIND AND LOVING

A not uncommon misgiving that abounds is that the "God of the Quran" and the "God of the Torah" is always angry, full of vengeance, and that the scriptures has used fear to subjugate followers. In this chapter, I will review the validity of this claim and compare relevant attributes of God mentioned in the Quran and the Bible.

This misconception is not unique to non-Muslims. Some Muslim priests, unwittingly, focus on God's vengeance and the Day of Judgment, and instead of describing how God will reward people for good deeds, they focus more on how He will punish them for bad deeds; they remind followers to always be on the right path, or else! Muslims often talk about the "ninety-nine names of Allah" with great reverence. They seem to forget, though, that by far the most often-repeated attributes of God in the Quran are *"Ar Rahman"* (the Most Compassionate) and *"Ar Raheem"* (the Most Merciful).

All chapters (Surahs) in the Quran, except chapter 9 (*Surah Tawba,* or "The Repentance"), start with the verse, *"Bismillah Ar Rahman Ar Raheem,"* meaning "In the name of God, the Most Compassionate, the Most Merciful." Various scholars have translated the word *Ar Rahman* into "the Most Kind," "the Most Compassionate," "the Most Gracious," or "the Most Beneficent." Moreover, the attributes *Ar Rahman* and *Ar Raheem* also appear *in the body* of many other chapters, including chapter 1, *Al-Fatiha* ("The Opening"). This small Surah will be discussed in chapter 5, but it is worth pointing out here that the verses proclaim God as the Lord (Sustainer) of all the worlds and that He is the Most Kind and the Most Merciful—period. Not just for Muslims, not just for people of faith or for only humans, but for the entire universe (and everything in it). Muslims are encouraged to recite the verse "In the name of God, the Most Compassionate, the Most Merciful," whenever they begin a task—when leaving home for work, on starting a journey, or during take-off when flying. The message is not just that Muslims are to remember God in their everyday life but to serve as a reminder that God wants them to remember Him as *the Most Kind* and *the Most Merciful*. God could have chosen many of His other attributes, for example, "In the name of God, the Almighty," or "In the name of God, the All-Knowing," or "In the name of God, the Creator," and so on. None of His attributes related to His Might and Justice are the chosen attributes for this oft-repeated verse. Here are some other names (attributes) often mentioned in the Quran that reflect God's kindness:

- *Al-Wadud:* The Loving One
- *Al-Ghaffar:* The Forgiving
- *Al-Ghafur:* The Forgiver and the Hider of Faults
- *Al-Karim*: The Most Generous
- *Al Wali*: The Protecting Friend
- *Al-Afu*: The Forgiver
- *Ar-Rau'f*: The Clement (Lenient)/Kind
- *As-Salam:* The Source of Peace
- *Al-Mujib:* The Responder to Prayers

It is indeed true that the Quran and the Bible repeatedly warn the people who do evil, often in graphic details; however, these verses in the Quran are often followed (or preceded) by verses alluding to the reward for good deeds and His mercy and forgiveness.

The following verses serve as a very small sample alluding to the love, kindness, and mercy of God:

"And He is the Oft-Forgiving, Full of Loving-Kindness." 85:14

"And there is the type of man who gives his life to earn the pleasure of Allah. And Allah is full of kindness to (His) devotees." 2:207

"Our Lord! You are indeed full of Kindness, Most Merciful." 59:10

"What is the matter with you, that you place not your hope for kindness and long-suffering in Allah?" 71:13 (Noah asking his people to seek forgiveness from God and warning them of the great flood.)

"But ask forgiveness of your Lord, and turn unto Him (in repentance): For my Lord is indeed full of mercy and loving-kindness." 11:90

The concept of accountability is pervasive in the Islamic doctrine. The Quran indicates that everyone is responsible for their actions—good and bad—and will have to answer to God on the Day of Judgment. However, most Muslims also believe that individuals will enter heaven on account of God's mercy, and not merely on their good deeds—a belief often shared by Christians and Jews.

The Kind and Loving God in the Bible

The Old Testament too has been a target of same type of criticism: "The God of the Old Testament is harsh and full of vengeance, and the God of New Testament is loving and kind." Once again, reading the scriptures, it becomes clear that the God of these scriptures indeed has the same attributes, for He is the same God. These few quotes cannot do justice to the immense subject of God's love and do not substitute a complete review of the texts:

"Nevertheless in Your great Mercy, You did not utterly consume them nor forsake them; For You are God, Gracious and Merciful." Nehemiah 9:31

"How precious is Your loving Kindness, O God! Therefore the children of men put their trust under the shadow of Your wings." Psalm 36:7

"I will mention the loving kindnesses of the LORD And the praises of the LORD, According to all that the LORD has bestowed on us, And the great goodness toward the house of Israel, Which He has bestowed on them according to His Mercies, according to the multitude of His loving kindnesses." Isaiah 63:7

"And we have known and believed the love that God has for us. God is love, and he who abides in love abides in God, and God in him." 1 John 4:16

"Don't tear your clothing in your grief, but tear your hearts instead. Return to the LORD your God, for He is Merciful and Compassionate, slow to get angry and filled with unfailing love. He is eager to relent and not punish." Joel 2:13

Should We "Fear" God?

Perhaps one of the reasons to believe that God should be "feared" is the word *"Taqwa,"* which is often translated as "to fear God." The person who practices *Taqwa* is known as *"Muttaqi,"* often translated as "God fearing." However, many others have more appropriately translated it as "God-conscious," "pious," "righteous," or "in awe of God." A similar parable is perhaps found in Hebrew. "The Hebrew word 'Yir'at HaShem' (year-ahtah-shehm) is sometimes translated as 'fear of God' but is better understood as 'in awe of God.'"[20] In fact in Jewish traditions, hell is despised since that means one will be not in the company of God, as the ultimate goal is to seek nearness to God.

In some ways, "fearing God" is similar to a loving parent-child relationship, whereby children do not want to do anything against the wishes of their parents, not because they are afraid of the parents, but out of love and respect for them. This is indeed the essence of the teachings of the scriptures. As we get to know God, we will then get close to Him, worship Him out of love, and be in awe of Him, not because of fear of Him or a fear of going to hell. For the ones "in awe of God," fear of hell is replaced by fear of disobeying Him, a fear of making Him unhappy.

Points to Remember

- The most frequent attributes of God mentioned in the Quran are *"Ar-Raheem"* and *"Ar-Rehman,"* meaning "the Most Kind" and "the Most Merciful."
- The Old Testament often refers to God's wrath (against wrongdoers for abominable acts) but also declares His mercy for the righteous. The Gospel repeatedly proclaims God's mercy and forgiveness. The teachings of Jesus

---

20 Kurzweil, *The Torah for Dummies*, p. 30.

Christ center on God's love, kindness, and forgiveness.

Time to Ponder

- If one believes that God is going to judge people based on their deeds alone, how is His mercy and kindness going to play out?
- Conversely, how is His clemency and kindness going to help if people continue to disobey His laws, without repentance, or if they reject His signs? If He forgives everyone out of His mercy, who will be the subjects of His judgment?

CHAPTER 4
GOD, THE CREATOR

Both the Quran and the Bible have put tremendous emphasis on God as the Creator of the universe—a belief central to the monotheistic faiths. God is the Creator of everything living and non-living; some can be seen and perceived by our special senses, others cannot. According to the Quran and the Bible, He existed before anything existed or was created. Moreover, He is eternal, whereas everyone else and everything else is mortal. Thus, He is the First (*Al-Awwal*) and the Last (*Al-Akhir*). The Quran asserts that God created the heavens and the earth and everything in between in perfect balance, proportion, and harmony. Every creation has a design and a plan, and each creation has a fixed term of existence. Though very intriguing and tempting, a detailed discussion on the merits of the creation and intelligent design versus theories of evolution is beyond the scope of this book. However, the subject of creation will be revisited in more detail under section 3, "The Quran and Science." This chapter will review some of the verses in the Quran and the Bible on the subject of creation and its various aspects.

God, the Creator of Everything

"Allah is Creator of all things, and He is the Guardian and Disposer of all affairs." 39:62

"Glory to Allah, Who created in pairs all things that the earth produces, as well as their own (human) kind and (other) things of which they have no knowledge." 36:36

"All praise is due to Allah, Who created the heavens and the earth and made the darkness and the light; yet those who disbelieve set up equals with their Lord." 6:1 (Shakir)

Where Does God "Live"?

Where is God's throne? In what part of the universe is heaven located? To be perfectly honest, no one knows the real answers.

People of the Abrahamic faiths believe God existed before the universe was created, therefore He must have been *outside* of the universe we know of. So is there a universe outside of the universe we know? God is also omnipresent. The Quran addresses that by stating that God is nearer to us than our jugular vein [*"And certainly We created man, and We know what his mind suggests to him, and We are nearer to him than his life-vein."* 50:16 (Shakir)], and He is with us all the time [*"He is with you wherever you are; and Allah sees what you do."* 57:4 (Shakir)]. The metaphoric reference "so close yet so far away" seems applicable in this regard (or more appropriately, "so far away yet so near"). It must be pointed out that trying to define where God lives as if He is a "person" is a fallacy, since all religious scholars concur that His nature is beyond the human imagination.

God creates with ease; the "Be verses". As complex and, at times, incomprehensible as the universe around us seems, the Quran states that not only has God created everything but also that the creation of the universe was very easy for Him:

"Rather, to Him belongs all that is in the heavens and in the earth; all are obedient to Him. He is the Creator of the heavens and the earth! When He decrees a thing, He needs only to say, 'Be,' and there it becomes." 2:116–117 (Malik)

"Verily, when He intends a thing, His Command is, 'Be,' and it is!" 36:82

"She said: My Lord! when shall there be a son (born) to me, and man has not touched me? He said: Even so, Allah creates what He pleases; when He has decreed a matter, He only says to it, 'Be,' and it is." 3:47 (This verse is about the Virgin Mary when the Angel Gabriel gave her the news that she will have a son, named Jesus Christ.)

However easy it is for God to create, it does not imply that the process of creation does not follow certain rules. According to the Quran, the process of creation is set in motion by the divine orders, and every living and nonliving creation then follows His commands to behave in a certain fashion (laws of science). Nothing in "nature" is without logic; the laws of physics, chemistry, and biology are set forth by divine orders. In other words, creation does not negate the laws of science but merely indicates that these laws were not spontaneous but were rather established by the Creator Himself.

God Created the Earth for Mankind's Benefit

According to the Quran, God is especially merciful to mankind, and everything on the earth was created for the benefit of man. He has made all that is between the heavens and the earth for man's service and made them subservient. This includes animals as well as "what's in the earth."

"How can you deny Allah? Did He not give you life when you were lifeless; and will He not cause you to die and again bring you to life; and will you not ultimately return to Him? It is He Who has created for you all that there is in the earth." 2:28–29 (Malik)

"Do you not see that Allah has made subservient to you whatsoever is in the earth and the ships running in the sea by His command? And He withholds heaven from falling on the earth except with His permission; most surely Allah is Compassionate, Merciful to men." 22:65 (Shakir)

"Do you not see that Allah has made what is in the heavens and what is in the earth subservient to you, and made complete to you His favors outwardly and inwardly?" 31:20 (Shakir)

God Made Humans Superior to Many Other Creations

"And surely We have honored the children of Adam, and We carry them in the land and the sea, and We have given them of the good things, and We have made them to excel by an appropriate excellence over most of those whom We have created." 17:70 (Shakir)

God, the Creator, in the Bible

In contrast to the Quran, the Old Testament gives a detailed account of the creation in one long sequence in chapters 1 and 2 of Genesis. The very first verse of the first chapter of the first book of the Bible speaks about the creation of heavens and the earth, underlining that the belief in God, as the Creator of the universe, is of utmost importance.

"In the beginning God created the heavens and the earth." Genesis 1:1[21]

And it goes on to describe the creation in more detail, explaining that God created celestial bodies, animals, and plants on successive days, interpreted by many Bible scholars as stages, though some argue that the sequence mentioned in Genesis is not consistent with current scientific knowledge regarding the creation of the solar system, as they point out that the sun ("the light") was formed before the planet earth. The passages start with the creation of earth first, which may be why the early Christian churches believed in a geocentric view of our solar system until Copernicus's and Galileo's description of the heliocentric solar system.

"The earth was formless and void, and darkness was over the surface of the deep, and the Spirit of God was moving over the surface of the waters. Then God said, 'Let there be light'; and there was light. God saw that the light was good; and God separated the light from the darkness." Genesis 1:2–4

In the next day, or stage, the oceans on earth and then the vegetation were produced. The next phase of creation was described:

"Then God said, 'Let there be lights in the expanse of the heavens to separate the day from the night, and let them be for signs and for seasons and for days and years; and let them be for lights in the expanse of the heavens to give light on the earth'; and it was so. God made the two great lights, the greater light to govern the day, and the lesser light to govern the night; He made the stars also. God placed them in the expanse of the heavens to give light on the earth, and to govern the day and the night, and to separate the light from the darkness; and God saw that it was good." Genesis 1:14–18

Man's creation is mentioned later in the same chapter:

"God created man in His own image, in the image of God He created him; male and female He created them." Genesis 1:27

What's in and on earth is made for the benefit of man. Plants were created for the benefit of mankind: This is pointed out in

---

21 All biblical translations in this chapter are from the New American Standard Bible by the Lockman Foundation, except as noted.

Genesis 1:29. Compare this with some of the verses from the Quran, quoted in the preceding segment.

"Then God said, 'Behold, I have given you every plant yielding seed that is on the surface of all the earth, and every tree which has fruit yielding seed; it shall be food for you.'" Genesis 1:29

All Creations Praise and Prostrate to God

According to the Bible and the Quran, humans are not the only creation praising and worshipping God. All creations, living or nonliving, worship and praise God but in their own unique ways.

The Biblical Account (the Biblical Version of the "Be Verse")

"Praise Him, all the angels. Praise Him, all the armies of the heavens! Praise Him, sun and moon! Praise Him, all you twinkling stars! Praise Him, skies above! Praise Him, vapors above the clouds! Let created thing give praise to the Lord, for He issued his command and they came into being." Psalm 148:2–5 (NLT)

The Quran's View

"To Allah prostrate all the creatures of the heavens and the earth, including the angels; and they are not arrogant." 16:49 (Malik)

"Whatever is in the heavens and the earth do prostrate before Allah Alone willingly or unwillingly, and so do their shadows in the mornings and evenings." 13:15 (Malik)

This prostration is not necessarily physical, like humans do. The prostration is described as submitting to, or obeying, the laws God has set forth. A related concept mentioned many times in the Quran is that all creatures glorify God but in their own unique ways:

"The seven heavens, the earth and all beings therein declare His glory. There is not a single thing but glorifies Him with His praise, but you do not understand their hymns of His glory. The fact is that He is very Forbearing, Forgiving." 17:44 (Malik)

"Do you not see that everything in the heavens and the earth glorify Allah, including the birds in flight? He knows the prayer of each one and its glorification, and Allah is Cognizant of what they do." 24:41 (Shakir)

The Purpose of Human Life

Why are we here? Why were we created? These questions are often triggered by pondering minds—at least the minds of those who believe in creation. The answer from the evolution perspective is rather simple: we fortuitously evolved into human form; therefore, there cannot be a defined purpose of our existence.

The Quran and the Bible are very clear as to where we came from and where are we going—we came from God and to Him we shall return. A detailed discussion of the purpose of life is beyond the scope of this book, but it would be prudent to mention that the Quran spells out three purposes of human creation in various places:

To worship God: *"I created the Jinn and humankind only that they might worship Me."* 51:56 (Pickthall)

(The *Jinns* or genies are often mentioned as creations of God in the Quran as one of the three sentient creations of God: angels, Jinns, and humans. The Jinns are made from smokeless fire. Both the Jinns and the humans have free will, whereas angels do not.)

However, in the next verse, the Quran goes on to clarify that God is free of all *need,* implying that to worship Him is in the human's own interest.

"I do not desire from them any sustenance and I do not desire that they should feed Me." 51:57 (Shakir)

To act as His viceroy or vicegerent: *"Behold, your Lord said to the angels: 'I will create a vicegerent on earth.'"* 2:30

This role makes humans responsible to represent God and His attributes, including compassion, mercy, and justice.

To test and try: Mankind is given the knowledge, the intellect, and all other necessary faculties to know God and the power to self-control, and yet have the free will to choose the right way or the wrong way. Only after giving them the knowledge, the guidance, and the faculties to make the right choices, will He judge mankind.

"He Who created Death and Life, that He may try which of you is best in deed: and He is the Exalted in Might, Oft-Forgiving." 67:2 (Shakir)

"Verily We created Man from a drop of mingled sperm, in order to try him: So We gave him (the gifts), of Hearing and Sight. Surely

We have shown him the way: he may be thankful or unthankful."
76:2–3

The Bible on the Purpose of Life

Though not mentioned explicitly in the Bible as the reasons for the creation of mankind, the concepts of worship, submission, and trial are fundamentally no different in Jewish and Christian traditions. The subject of submission to God was also discussed in chapter 2. In his book, *Torah for Dummies*, Rabbi Arthur Kurzweil writes, "Based on the Torah, Judaism takes the fundamental position that as with Abraham, life for each human is a series of tests of trials given by God for their benefit. All trials, from smallest frustration to the greatest tragedy, are really for the best even though you can't always see them that way. A basic tenant of Jewish faith is the principle that God knows what He is both doing and allowing and that the tests you face are for the benefit of your soul."[22] The Bible does not directly talk about man being God's viceroy. However, the book Genesis declares that man's creation was in God's image:

"Then God said, 'Let Us make man in Our image, according to Our likeness; and let them rule over the fish of the sea and over the birds of the sky and over the cattle and over all the earth, and over every creeping thing that creeps on the earth.' God created man in His own image, in the image of God He created him; male and female He created them." Genesis 1:26–27

However, one should not stretch the likeness to God and "created in His image" too far, to mean that men are "like God," as is explained elsewhere in the Bible:

"Remember the former things long past, For I am God, and there is no other; I am God, and there is no one like Me." Isaiah 46:9

"That there is no one like Me in all the earth." Exodus 9:14

Points to Remember

- According to the Quran and the Bible, God is the Creator of everything. He existed before anything existed. He will exist after everything ceases to exist (the *Awwal*

---

22 Kurzweil, *Torah for Dummies*, p. 75.

and the *Akhir*—or the First and the Last, the Eternal). The creation is an ongoing process, according to the Quran. God created everything with a designed plan, reflecting His tremendous wisdom.

- According to the Quran, the purpose of the creation of humans is to act as God's viceroy and to worship Him. Additionally, God created humans to be tested and tried. The Bible does not explicitly state the purpose of creation but makes references to the same purposes mentioned in the Quran.

- Both the Quran and the Bible make mention of humans as not the only creatures who worship and praise God. Other creations do too, but in their own unique way, and they follow the laws of God.

Time to Ponder

- Did we evolve or were we created? The scriptures unanimously and very clearly state that Adam was created and humans are descendants of Adam. Are the creation doctrine and evolution theories mutually exclusive? Is evolution part of God's intelligent design in creation?

CHAPTER 5
PRAISE THE LORD

A central theme according to the teachings of the Quran and the Bible is that all praise belongs to God, the Lord of the heavens and the earth. Submission to God, glorifying and praising Him, goes hand in hand. One cannot submit to God without glorifying Him. Conversely, one cannot glorify the Lord without fully submitting to Him. He alone is deserving of all the praise and the worship. As mentioned at the end of the last chapter, *all* creations of God praise and glorify Him, in one form or another.

The very first chapter of the Quran, named *Al-Fatiha*, or "The Opening," is considered by the Muslims to be the heart and soul of the Quran. It has been called "the Mother of the Book," its essence and its foundation. It is recited in all five daily, mandatory prayers, in all seventeen times a day.

"In the name of Allah, the Compassionate, the Merciful.

"All praise is for Allah, the Lord of all Worlds.

"The Compassionate, the Merciful.

"Master of the Day of Judgment.

"You Alone we worship and You alone we call on for help.

"Guide us to The Right Way.

"The Way of those whom You have favored (or bestowed grace); not of those who have earned Your wrath, or of those who have lost The Way." 1:1–7

Many commentators have written chapter after chapter on the exegesis of this Surah. Some key elements of the Surah are pointed out here by examining the sequence of verses alone, in a rather simplistic manner. The sequence is perhaps an indication how the Lord wants to be remembered. *In the name of God, the Compassionate, the Merciful"* is followed by the declaration *"All praise is for God, the Lord of all Worlds."* He is the Lord of the worlds (plural) because God created everything and thus existed before everything. The word "Lord" does not truly translate the essence of the Arabic word *"Rabb"* used here, which signifies the sustainer, someone who is the supreme caretaker. The verse calls for the *Rabb* to be the sustainer for all the worlds and not just the *Rabb* of the Muslims or the people of faith. He oversees and takes responsibility to take care of everything and everyone in all the worlds, and He provides sustenance and bounties for everyone (and everything), regardless of their faith in Him (or lack of it). This is followed by what may explain the prior verse further: *"The Compassionate, the Merciful,"* indicating He is the sustainer for all regardless of their beliefs *because* He is their Creator and the Most Compassionate and the Most Merciful. He then reminds us that He will be the *Master of the Day of Judgment.* Everything will perish, and just as He existed before anything was created, He will exist after everything vanishes. His Compassion and Mercy are mentioned *before* the Day of Judgment. This is then followed by a fundamental commandment: *You alone we worship and You alone we call on for help.* The Quran is very clear on its displeasure and prohibition of seeking help from or worshipping idols, other deities, or people besides God. This is a key concept of monotheism. Also note that worshippers address God in this verse by "You" and not in third person like "God" or "Lord," putting worshippers in direct, one-on-one communication with God after affirming their faith in Him. A prayer then follows: *Guide us to the Right Way.* This puts in perspective the asking Him for help in the previous verse. Seeking His help is not for worldly matters (a beautiful house, a beautiful spouse, job, money, etc.) but to be guided to the right path, as ordained by and leading to Him. It then goes on to further describe what the right path is: *"The Way of those whom You have favored (or bestowed grace); not of those who have earned Your wrath, or of those who have lost The Way."*

It is believed by many Muslim scholars that the opening chapter, *Surah Al-Fatiha,* is the prayer of the worshipper and the rest of the entire Quran is an answer to that prayer. Right after the end of this short Surah, which ends in a prayer ("*guide* us to the right way"), chapter 2 (*Surah Al-Baqarah* or "The Cow") opens with this declaration:

"*Alif Lam Mim (mystical Quranic letters). This is the scriptures whereof there is no doubt, a guidance unto those who ward off (evil)."* 2:1–2 (Pickthall) Also translated by Yahiya Emerick as follows: "*Alif Lam Mim. This is the Book, in which there is no doubt. It is a guide to those who are mindful (of their duty to God)."*

Many other verses in the Quran refer to God being the only one worthy of all praise:

"*Those who believe, and work righteousness, their Lord will guide them because of their faith: beneath them will flow rivers in gardens of bliss. (This will be) their cry therein: 'Glory to You, O Allah.' And 'Peace' will be their greeting therein! And the close of their cry (prayer) will be:* **Praise be to Allah, the Lord of the worlds!**"* 10:9–10 (The bolded verse is the same verse as *Surah Al-Fatiha's* verse 2).

The Quran makes numerous references to the prayers of many prophets praising the Lord.

Abraham Praising God

"*All praise is due to God, who has bestowed upon me, in my old age, Ishmael and Isaac! Behold, my Sustainer hears indeed all prayer."* 14:39 (Asad)

"*And say: 'All praise is due to God, who begets no offspring, and has no partner in His dominion, and has no weakness, and therefore no need of any aid and (thus) extol His limitless greatness.'"* 17:111 (Asad)

Noah Praising God

"*Then when you have embarked on the ark with your companions, say: 'Praise be to Allah Who has delivered us from the nation of wrongdoers.'"* 23:28 (Malik)

Moses Praising God

"*And Moses said: 'If you show ingratitude, you and all on earth together, yet is Allah free of all wants, worthy of all praise.'"* 14:8

David and Solomon Praising God

"We gave (in the past) knowledge to David and Solomon: And they both said: 'Praise be to Allah, Who has favored us above many of his servants who believe!'" 27:15

Praise the Lord in the Bible

"You alone we worship" in the Bible:

"He alone is your God, the Only one who is worthy of your praise, the One who has done these mighty miracles that you have seen with your own eyes." Deuteronomy 10:21

Praising the Lord is a central theme emphasized frequently in various books of the Bible. All the prophets have been given the commands to praise Him and taught how to praise Him. Subservience to God, praising and glorifying Him, forms the essence of the biblical teachings about God:

"'Praise the Lord,' Jethro said, 'for he has rescued you from the Egyptians and from Pharaoh.'" Exodus 18:10

"When you have eaten your fill, be sure to praise the Lord your God for the good land he has given you." Deuteronomy 8:10

"David replied to Abigail, 'Praise the Lord, the God of Israel, who has sent you to meet me today!'" 1 Samuel 25:3

The Lord's Prayer

Considered a basic prayer among Christians, the Lord's Prayer is memorized by heart by many; it was taught by Prophet Jesus Christ to his disciples. It is derived from the two passages from the New Testament: Matthew 6:9–13 and Luke 11:2–4. Compare it side by side with *Surah Al-Fatiha,* quoted at the beginning of this chapter, to appreciate resemblance of the two prayers considered central to Christianity and Islam:

"Our Father in Heaven,
"Hallowed be your name.
"Your Kingdom come,
"Your will be done,
"on earth as in heaven.

"Give us today our daily bread.
"Forgive us our sins,
"as we forgive those who sin against us.
"Lead us not into temptation,
"but deliver us from evil.
"For the kingdom, the power, and the glory are yours.
"Now and forever. Amen."

Points to Remember

- Praising the Lord is an essential part of prayer for people of the monotheistic faiths. Most prayers start with "praise the Lord." All prophets used the same phrase to honor God. Praising the Lord and worshipping Him go hand in hand.
- The opening chapter in the Quran, called *Surah Al-Fatiha*, or "The Opening," is in the form of a prayer. Some view the rest of the Quran as the guidance or the answer to that prayer of the worshipers. It bears resemblance to the Lord's Prayer.

Time to Ponder

- Can we worship God without praising Him?
- Can we praise holy figures without worshipping them? Where do we draw the line between praising the prophets, apostles, and other holy figures, and worshipping them? What differentiates the two acts?

CHAPTER 6
ATTRIBUTES OF GOD

"Ninety-Nine Names of God"

Muslims often refer to the "ninety-nine names of Allah" mentioned in the Quran. Table 1 lists these names, which are essentially His attributes; they shed light into His nature. However, it must be emphasized, again, that God is limitless and thus limiting His attributes to a certain number is assigning bounds for Him. A more appropriate way to put this in perspective might be to state, "There are ninety-nine names or attributes mentioned in the Quran," rather than, "God has ninety-nine names." These attributes relate to His nature, His Power, His Oneness, His Will, His Kindness, His being the ultimate Judge, and so on. God has no comparable. He is infinite, and the attributes mentioned in the Quran, and the Bible, are to help us humans understand Him with our finite ability.

"The most beautiful names belong to Allah; so call on Him by them." 7:180

"Say: 'Call upon Allah, or call upon the Most Gracious: by whatever name you call upon Him (it is well): To Him belong the Most Beautiful Names.'" 17:110

According to the teachings of the scriptures, God is not limited by time or space (or by anything, for that matter). He is self-sufficient and He has no partners and no equals. He has no form or figure. He has no needs. The various names can be grouped into categories referring to His various attributes. The following is a small sample from the Quran:

All-Knowing: Some of the names expressing this attribute are *Al-Khabir* (The Aware), *Al-Hakim* (All Wise), *Ar-Raqib* (The Watcher), *Al-Hadi* (The Guide), and *Al-Alim* (All-Knowing).

Most Merciful, Most Kind: *Ar-Rehman* (The Most Kind), *Ar-Raheem* (The Most Merciful), *Al-Wadud* (The Loving One), *Al-Ghaffar* (The Forgiving), *Al-Ghafur* (The Forgiver and The Hider of Faults), and *Al-Karim* (The Most Generous).

Almighty: He is Almighty, all-powerful, and to Him belongs everything in the universe, and everyone and everything is subservient to His will. Attributes related to His might and supreme nature include *Al-Malik* (The King), *Al-Qa'dir* (The Powerful), *Al-Azeem* (The Grand), *Al-Qawi* (The Strong and The Powerful), *Al-Aziz* (The Mighty), *Al-Kabeer* (The Most Great), *Al-Jalil* (The Mighty), and *Al-Muta'ali* (The Supreme One).

"It is He Who begins (the process of) creation; then repeats it; and for Him it is most easy. To Him belongs the loftiest similitude (we can think of) in the heavens and the earth: for He is Exalted in Might, full of wisdom." 30:27 (Malik)

And many of the attributes are mentioned in the following, oft-quoted set of verses:

"Allah is He, besides Whom there is no god, the Knower of the unseen and the seen. He is the Compassionate, the Merciful. Allah is He, besides Whom there is no god, the King, the Holy, the Giver of peace, the Granter of security, the Guardian, the Almighty, the Irresistible, the Supreme: Glory be to Allah! He is far above the 'shirk' they commit (by associating other gods with Him). He is Allah, the Creator, the Evolver, the Fashioner. His are the most beautiful names. All that is in the heavens and the earth declares His glory, and He is the All Mighty, the All Wise." 59:22–24 (Malik)

God: The Guardian and Helper

"Do you not know that to Allah belongs the dominion of the heavens and the earth, and that besides Allah, you have no protector ['Wa'li'] or helper ['Naseer']!" 2:107 (Malik)

The literal meaning of *Wa'li* is variously translated as "protecting friend" (Pickthall, Mir Ali), "protector" (Malik, Asad, Mir Ali, Fakhry, Emerick, and Yousuf Ali), "Guardian" (Ali Unal), and "Supporter" (Yuksel). *Naseer* is translated as "helper" (most translators) or "victor" (Yuksel). These two words are often used together to highlight that the believers should not make anyone else their guardian and helper.

"Surely Allah is the kingdom of the heavens and the earth; He brings to life and causes to die; and there is not for you besides Allah any Guardian or Helper." 9:116 (Shakir)

"Surely your Lord is Allah Who created the heavens and the earth in six periods, and He is firm in power, regulating the affair, there is no intercessor except after His permission; this is Allah, your Lord, therefore serve Him." 10:3

"And Allah best knows your enemies; and Allah suffices as a Guardian, and Allah suffices as a Helper." 4:45 (Shakir)

"Verily, my protector [Guardian] is God, who has bestowed this divine writ [scripture] from on high: for it is He who protects the righteous." 7:196 (Asad)

"So establish regular Prayer, give regular Charity, and hold fast to Allah. He is your Protector ['Maula']—the Best to protect and the Best to help." 22:78

(The word for "protector" used in Arabic in this verse is *"Maula."* Mir Ali translates *Maula* as "Master.")

Verse 5:55–56, however, ask the believers to take God as well as His apostle and those who believe as their guardians:

"Your real protecting friends are God, His Apostle, and the fellow believers—the ones who establish contact Salah [prayers], pay Zakah [charity] while they bow down. Whoever makes God, His Apostle, and the fellow believers his protecting friends, must know that God's party will surely be victorious." 5:55–56 (Mir Ali)

These two verses may appear to contradict the earlier verses. But the Muslim scholars reason that the apostle (Muhammad) and the believers were so close to God that their will became God's will (or God's will was their will), and thus the apostle and the fellow believers became an extension, or a vehicle, for God's protection. In the commentary of verse 5:55, *"pay Zakah (charity) while they bow down,"* Pooya Yazdi comments that this refers to Ali, Muhammad's son-in-law, when he gave his ring to a beggar when he was bowing down during a prayer.

The "ninety-nine names" only give a glimpse of God's attributes. The following verse puts it all in perspective:

*"(He is) the Creator of the heavens and the earth: He has made for you pairs from among yourselves, and pairs among cattle: by this means does He multiply you: **there is nothing whatever like unto Him** and He is the One that hears and sees (all things)."* 42:11

Simply put, God is way above our imagination, without similitude, a concept universally accepted by all people of faith.

Many of his attributes are eloquently expressed in the following verse (known by Muslims as *Ayatul Kursi*, or "the verse of the throne"):

"Allah! There is no god but Him: the Living, the Eternal. He neither slumbers nor sleeps. To Him belongs all that is in the heavens and the earth. Who can intercede with Him without His permission? He knows what is before them and what is behind them. They cannot gain access to any thing out of His knowledge except what He pleases. His throne is more vast than the heavens and the earth, and guarding of these both does not fatigue Him. He is the Exalted, the Supreme." 2:255 (Malik)

The following set is another example of glorification of God by referring to some of His attributes:

"Allah is He, besides Whom there is no god, the Knower of the unseen and the seen. He is the Compassionate, the Merciful. Allah is He, besides Whom there is no god, the King, the Holy, the Giver of peace, the Granter of security, the Guardian, the Almighty, the Irresistible, the Supreme: Glory be to Allah! He is far above the 'shirk' they commit (by associating other gods with Him). He is Allah, the Creator, the Evolver, the Fashioner. His are the most beautiful names. All that is in the heavens and the earth declares His Glory, and He is the All Mighty, the All Wise." 59:22–24 (Malik)

Table 1
Ninety-Nine Names (Attributes) of God Mentioned in the Quran

| *Ar-Rahman* | 1 | The All-Compassionate |

Ar-Rahim	2	The All-Merciful
Al-Malik	3	The Absolute Ruler
Al-Quddus	4	The Pure One
As-Salam	5	The Source of Peace
Al-Mu'min	6	The Inspirer of Faith
Al-Muhaymin	7	The Guardian
Al-'Aziz	8	The Victorious
Al-Jabbar	9	The Compeller
Al-Mutakabbir	10	The Greatest
Al-Khaliq	11	The Creator
Al-Bari'	12	The Maker of Order
Al-Musawwir	13	The Shaper of Beauty
Al-Ghaffar	14	The Forgiving
Al-Qahhar	15	The Subduer
Al-Wahhab	16	The Giver of All
Ar-Razzaq	17	The Sustainer
Al-Fattah	18	The Opener
Al-'Alim	19	The Knower of All
Al-Qabid	20	The Constrictor
Al-Basit	21	The Reliever
Al-Khafid	22	The Abaser
Ar-Rafi'	23	The Exalter
Al-Mu'izz	24	The Bestower of Honors
Al-Mudhill	25	The Humiliator
As-Sami	26	The Hearer of All
Al-Basir	27	The Seer of All
Al-Hakam	28	The Judge
Al-'Adl	29	The Just
Al-Latif	30	The Subtle One
Al-Khabir	31	The All-Aware
Al-Halim	32	The Forebearing
Al-'Azim	33	The Magnificent

Al-Ghafur	34	The Forgiver and Hider of Faults
Ash-Shakur	35	The Rewarder of Thankfulness
Al-'Ali	36	The Highest
Al-Kabir	37	The Greatest
Al-Hafiz	38	The Preserver
Al-Muqit	39	The Nourisher
Al-Hasib	40	The Accounter
Al-Jalil	41	The Mighty
Al-Karim	42	The Generous
Ar-Raqib	43	The Watchful One
Al-Mujib	44	The Responder to Prayer
Al-Wasi'	45	The All-Comprehending
Al-Hakim	46	The Perfectly Wise
Al-Wadud	47	The Loving One
Al-Majíd	48	The Majestic One
Al-Ba'ith	49	The Resurrector
Ash-Shahid	50	The Witness
Al-h Haqq	51	The Truth
Al-Wakil	52	The Trustee
Al-Qawi	53	The Possessor of All Strength
Al-Matin	54	The Forceful One
Al-Wáli	55	The Governor
Al-Hamid	56	The Praised One
Al-Muhsi	57	The Appraiser
Al-Mubdi	58	The Originator
Al-Mu'id	59	The Restorer
Al-Muhyi	60	The Giver of Life
Al-Mumit	61	The Taker of Life
Al-Hayy	62	The Ever Living One
Al-Qayyum	63	The Self-Existing One
Al-Wajid	64	The Finder
Al-Májid	65	The Glorious

Al-Wahid	66	The Only One
Al-Ahad	67	The One
As-Samad	68	The Satisfier of All Needs
Al-Qadir	69	The All Powerful
Al-Muqtadir	70	The Creator of All Power
Al-Muqaddim	71	The Expediter
Al-Mu'akhkhir	72	The Delayer
Al-Awwal	73	The First
Al-Akhir	74	The Last
Az-Zahir	75	The Manifest One
Al-Batin	76	The Hidden One
Al-Wali	77	The Protecting Friend
Al-Muta'ali	78	The Supreme One
Al-Barr	79	The Doer of Good
At-Tawwib	80	The Guide to Repentance
Al-Muntaqim	81	The Avenger
Al-Afu	82	The Forgiver
Ar-Ra'uf	83	The Clement
Malik al-Mulk	84	The Owner of All
Dhul-Jalali Wal-Ikram	85	The Lord of Majesty and Bounty
Al-Muqsit	86	The Equitable One
Al-Jami	87	The Gatherer
Al-Ghani	88	The Rich One
Al-Mughni	89	The Enricher
Al-Mani'	90	The Preventer of Harm
Ad-Darr	91	The Creator of the Harmful
An-Nafi	92	The Creator of Good
An-Nur	93	The Light
Al-Hadi	94	The Guide
Al-Badi	95	The Originator
Al-Baqi	96	The Everlasting One

Al-Warith	97	The Inheritor of All
Ar-Rashid	98	The Righteous Teacher
As-Sabur	99	The Patient One

Attributes of God in the Bible

God, the Creator

As mentioned earlier, the book of Genesis opens with verses on the creation of heavens and earth by God. Some of these verses have been mentioned in chapter 4 already but are worth repeating here:

"In the beginning God created the heavens and the earth." Genesis 1:1

"So God created man in His own image; in the image of God He created him; male and female He created them." Genesis 1:27

"You are worthy, O Lord, to receive glory and honor and power; for You created all things, And by Your will they exist and were created." Revelation 4:11

God's Oneness

The Jewish daily prayer, *Shema*, starts with the declaration:

"Hear, O Israel: The LORD our God, the LORD is One." Deuteronomy 6:4

God Is Gracious and Merciful

"But in your great mercy, you did not destroy them completely or abandon them forever. What a Gracious and Merciful God you are!" Nehemiah 9:31 (mentioned as *"Ar-Rehman"* and *"Ar-Raheem"* in the Quran repeatedly; see chapter 3).

"For the LORD your God is a Merciful God; he will not abandon or destroy you or forget the covenant with your ancestors, which he confirmed to them by oath." Deuteronomy 4:31

"Consider therefore the kindness and sternness of God: sternness to those who fell, but kindness to you, provided that you continue in his kindness. Otherwise, you also will be cut off." Romans 11:22

God Is Almighty

"The Lord, the Mighty One, is God! The Lord, the Mighty One, is God! He knows the truth, and may Israel know it, too!" Joshua 22:22

"Look, God is all-powerful. Who is a teacher like him?" Job 36:32

"'I am the Alpha and the Omega—the beginning and the end,' says the Lord God. 'I am the one who is, who always was, and who is still to come—the Almighty One.'" Revelation 1:8

God Is *the* Judge

"God is an honest judge. He is angry with the wicked every day." Psalm 7:11

"God alone, who gave the law, is the Judge. He alone has the power to save or to destroy. So what right do you have to judge your neighbor?" James 4:12

God Is Forgiving

"But the Lord our God is merciful and forgiving, even though we have rebelled against him." Daniel 9:9

"'The LORD is slow to anger, abounding in love and forgiving sin and rebellion. Yet he does not leave the guilty unpunished." Numbers 14:18

"O Lord our God, you answered them. You were a forgiving God to them, but you punished them when they went wrong." Psalm 99:8

God Is the First *(Al-Awwal)* and the Last *(Al-Akhir)*

"This is what the LORD says, Israel's King and Redeemer, the LORD Almighty: I am the first and I am the last; apart from me there is no God." Isaiah 44:6

And as quoted above: *"'I am the Alpha and the Omega, the beginning and the end,' says the Lord God. 'I am the one who is, who always was, and who is still to come—the Almighty One.'"* Revelation 1:8

Points to Remember

- The Quran refers to the "names" (*Asma'as*) of God, which are essentially His attributes. However, it must be emphasized that He is limitless, cannot be comprehended by humans' finite cognition, and cannot be bound by numbers. All of the attributes have one thing in common: they emphasize His Oneness.
- Similar attributes of God are mentioned in the Bible as well, though not all of them.
- The most frequently mentioned attributes in the Quran are *"Ar-Rehman"* and *"Ar-Raheem,"* meaning "The Most Kind" and "The Most Merciful."

Time to Ponder

- The descriptions of various attributes of God in the Quran and the Bible are very similar. Are the "God of the Quran" and the "God of the Bible" different Gods? If so, what's the basis for such a belief?

SECTION 2
THE QURAN
ON THE QURAN

CHAPTER 7
THE QURAN: GOD'S REVELATION

Healing and a Guide to Mankind

The readers of the Quran can quickly discover a feature unique to the scriptures: the Quran refers to itself in various forms. This section will focus on the Quran's self-references and proclamation as a complete guide to mankind and other matters such as the purpose of the revelations.

Islamic Tradition: Treating the book with utmost respect: Muslims are required to treat the Quran with utmost respect. One has to be physically and spiritually clean to touch it, to be free of "ill or sinful thoughts," when reciting or reading the Quran. The book must be kept in a clean place, often wrapped in a cloth or in a box. It is highly recommended, though not required, to do the *wadoo,* or ablution, a way to spiritually clean and purify oneself with water. There ought to be no background music or other means of distraction, like the sound of the radio or television, when reciting or studying the Quran.

The Quran Mentions Itself Often

The word "Quran" means *reading* or *recitation* and is derived from the word *"Qura,"* meaning to read or rehearse. The Quran refers to itself frequently in various forms such as *the Quran, the Revelations,* or simply *"Al-Kitab"* (The Book). *The Quran* generally refers to the scripture and the revelations, an inclusive term for the oral and textual forms, whereas the word *Al-Kitab* generally refers to the textual form.

The Quran

The word *"Al-Quran"* itself is mentioned seventy times in the Quran.

Quran: Healing for Mankind

The Quran boldly proclaims itself as healing and the recipe for mankind. This healing is the spiritual remedy from all the diseases of the heart and mind. To seek peace in the heart and mind and to attain complete spiritual health, the Quran instructs the readers to seek the remedy within the teachings of the Quran.

"O mankind! There has come to you a direction from your Lord and a healing for what (diseases are) in your hearts—and for those who believe, a guidance and a Mercy." 10:57

The word used in this verse for the cure or healing is *"Shifa,"* which is typically used to imply health, recovery, or healing. Note that the verse is addressed to mankind as it relates to the healing aspect and not only to Muslims or people of the faith. The disease is the lack of faith and the remedy is in the principles as taught by God in the Quran. The "direction" is in reference to the Quran itself.

Also note that the verse starts by pronouncing the Quran as healing for *mankind* but ends with the statement that the guidance and mercy in it are for *those who believe.* The Quran describes ways for the heart's purification through remembrance of God, submitting to the will of God, and following the path prescribed by Him. The Quran instructs readers to elevate the spiritual heart to a level that is in awe, as well as in love of God, and is in a state of gratitude and submission so much so that God's will becomes their will. In other words, this state of submission and containment softens the hearts and minds to allow God's light to enter one's soul and changes one's perception of the purpose of existence and living to be in complete alignment with the principles of living, as defined and prescribed by God. Those who believe and choose to follow the instructions, naturally, are the ones likely to benefit from it the most. This is similar to a remedy for an illness prescribed by a doctor. The remedy can cure the illness if one has faith in the doctor's ability and follows the instructions carefully, but if the instructions are not followed or the remedy is misused, it will not likely lead to healing from the ailment.

The Quran Revealed for Mankind, Not Only for "Muslims"

There are numerous passages in the Quran addressed to mankind, clearly indicating that the revelations are for the purpose of mankind, rather than a specific group of people. The word used in Arabic for mankind is *"An-Naas."* It has been variously translated as "mankind" (Pickthall, Asad, Yousuf Ali, Malik), "humankind" (Unal), "men" (Shakir, Asad), and "people" (Yuksel, Mir Ali-Pooya, Fakhry, Emerick).

"We have explained in detail in this Quran, for the benefit of mankind, every kind of similitude: but man is, in most things, contentious." 18:54

The following six short verses constitute an entire chapter, the last one in the Quran, in fact, named *Al-Naas* ("Mankind"). The Quran calls Allah as the Lord and the King (Master) for all mankind, not just the believers or Muslims. He is the Sustainer and the Caretaker for all mankind whether they are Muslims, Christians, Jews, Hindus, people of other faiths, or atheists. All mankind is told to seek refuge in Him:

"Say: I seek refuge with the Lord and Cherisher of mankind, The King [or Ruler] of mankind, The God of mankind, From the mischief of the Whisperer (of Evil), who withdraws (after his whisper)—(The same) who whispers into the hearts of mankind—Among Jinns and among men." 114:1–6

This address to mankind is generally related to the broad issues like the purpose of the revelation, God's Oneness, and belief in One God.

"This is a message unto all mankind. Hence, let them be warned thereby, and let them know that He is the One and Only God; and let those who are endowed with insight take this to heart!" 14:52 (Asad)

"This (revelation) is a means of insight for mankind, and a guidance and grace unto people who are endowed with inner certainty." 45:20 (Asad)

"Alif Lam Mim. God—There is no god but Him; the Living, the Eternal. He has revealed to you this Book (the Quran) with the Truth, confirming the scriptures, which preceded it, as He revealed the Tawrat [Torah] and Injeel [Gospel], before this, as guidance for mankind and also revealed this Al-Furqa'n (criterion for judgment between right and wrong). Surely those who reject God's revelations will be sternly punished; God is Mighty, capable of retribution." 3:1–4 (Malik)

"He makes His revelations clear to mankind so that they may take heed." 2:221 (Malik)

"O Mankind! Eat of what is lawful and clean on the earth and do not follow the footsteps of Shaitan [Satan]; surely he is your open enemy. He [Satan] enjoins you to commit evil and indecency and to say certain things against God about which you have no knowledge." 2:168–169 (Malik)

"It is the month of Ramadan in which the Quran was revealed, a guidance for mankind with clear teachings showing the Right Way and a criterion [Al-Furqa'n] of truth and falsehood." 2:185(Malik)

The Word "Quran" within the Quran on Other Occasions

"When the Quran is read, listen to it with attention, and hold your peace: that you may receive Mercy." 7:204

"It is We Who have sent down the Quran to you by stages." 76:23

"And when Our clear communications are recited to them, those who hope not for Our meeting say: 'Bring a Quran other than this or change it.' Say (O Muhammad): It does not beseem me that I should change it of myself; I follow naught but what is revealed to me." 10:15 (Shakir)

The above verses indicate the following:

1. The oral tradition, or recitation of the revelations, was practiced even in the days of Prophet Muhammad. (7:204)
2. The Quran was known as "the Quran" from the time of the initial revelations. (10:15 and others)
3. Prophet Muhammad had no power to change it, since the Quran is the literal word of God and God alone. (10:15)

"This Quran is not such as can be produced by other than Allah. On the contrary it is a confirmation of (revelations) that went before it, and a fuller explanation of the Book—wherein there is no doubt— from the Lord of the worlds." 10:37

"These are the verses of the Book that make things clear. We have revealed this Quran in the Arabic language so that you (Arabs) may understand. We relate to you the best of stories through this Quran by Our revelation to you (O Muhammad), though before this you were one of those who did not know." 12:1–3 (Malik)

"VERILY, this Quran shows the way to all that is most upright, and gives the believers who do good deeds the glad tiding that theirs will be a great reward." 17:9 (Shakir)

"Nay, this is a Glorious Quran, inscribed in a tablet preserved." 85:21–22

"Now whenever you happen to recite this Quran, seek refuge with God from Satan, the accursed." 16:98 (Shakir)

As mentioned in the introduction, the Quran was revealed in bits and pieces over twenty-three years, rather than all at once. In addition to verse 76:23 quoted above, the following verse also refers to that:

"(It is) a Quran which We have divided (into parts from time to time), in order that you might recite it to men at intervals: We have revealed it by stages." 17:106

The Quran speaks itself as the *"Al-Furqa'n,"* or the criterion, between truth and falsehood, and right and wrong. In other words, the teachings of the Quran shall serve as the criteria for contentious matters. In addition to verse 2:185 quoted above and some others, the following is another occasion:

"Blessed is the One Who has revealed Al-Furqa'n to His servant [meaning Muhammad], that he may be a Warner to the worlds." 25:1 (Shakir)

The Quran in Arabic

The Quran contains many references not only to the revelation in the Arabic language but to the rationale as well:

"We have sent it down as an Arabic Quran, in order that you may learn wisdom." 12:2

"(It is) a Quran in Arabic, without any crookedness (therein): in order that they may guard against Evil." 39:28

"Thus have we sent down this Quran in Arabic and clearly proclaimed in it some of the warnings so that they may take heed or that it may serve as a reminder to them. High and exalted be Allah, the True King! Do not hasten to recite the Quran before its revelation is completely conveyed to you, and then say: 'O Rabb [Lord]! Increase my knowledge.'" 20:113–114 (Malik)

"Surely this Quran is a revelation from the Rabb [Lord] of the Worlds. The trustworthy Spirit (Angel Gabriel) brought it down upon your heart so that you may become one of those who are appointed by Allah to warn the people in a plain Arabic language. This fact was foretold in the scriptures of the former people." 26:192–196 (Malik)

The phrase "former people" is in references to the People of the Book (Jews and Christians).

"This (Quran) is revealed by the Compassionate, the Merciful. A Book whose verses are well explained, A Quran in the Arabic language for people who understand. A giver of good news and admonition: yet most of the people turn their backs and do not listen." 41:2–4 (Malik)

"We have made it a Quran in Arabic, that you may be able to understand (and learn wisdom)." 43:3

"And before this, was the Book of Moses as a guide and a mercy: And this Book confirms (it) in the Arabic tongue; to admonish the unjust, and as Glad Tidings to those who do right." 46:12

"Verily, We have made this (Quran) easy, in your tongue, in order that they may give heed." 44:58

The verses quoted above are rather self-explanatory but it's worth pointing out that the Quran declares that the verses are well explained (41:2–4), they are easy to understand (44:58), and it was revealed to the people who spoke Arabic in their language, just like the Torah was revealed in Hebrew and the Gospel in Aramaic.

The question that can be asked concerning the Quran's Arabic language is: If it was meant for mankind, why was it only revealed in the Arabic language? There may not be a simple answer but the same is true for all other scriptures that were revealed in the native language of the prophet and the community it was revealed upon—the idea being for the "primary" audience to learn it and then spread it to others in their own languages with the invitation to eventually learn it in the scriptures's original language.

The Quran: Easy to Understand

"And We have indeed made the Quran easy to understand and remember: then is there any that will receive admonition?" 54:17

The same exact verse is repeated three more times in the same chapter: 54:22, 54:32, and 54:40.

These verses, among others, affirm the claim that the Quran is easy to understand, despite popular belief to the contrary among non-Muslims (as well as many Muslims). The following verse refers to the two simple purposes of the scriptures that the verse spells out clearly:

"Praise be to God Who has revealed the Book to His servant and did not make it complicated. It is straightforward so that He may warn about the terrible punishment for the unbelievers from Him and give good news to the believers who do good deeds that they shall have a goodly reward." 18:1–2 (Malik)

Some Verses Are Clear while Others Are Allegorical:
Clear verses form the foundation of the book:

The following verse addresses an important issue that has created many emotional debates about the clarity of the verses. It explains that some verses in the Quran are very clear, and others are more vague or allegorical. The translation used here is by Yousuf Ali and alternative translations are also noted in parenthesis, as noted by various scholars:

"He it is Who has sent down to you the Book: In it are verses basic or fundamental [also translated as decisive by Pooya Yazdi and Shakir, definite by Yuksel, and clear by Pickthall]; they are the foundation of the Book: others are allegorical [translated as ambiguous by Yazdi and multiple-meaning by Yuksel]. But those in whose hearts is perversity follow the part thereof that is allegorical, seeking discord, and searching for its hidden meanings, but no one knows its hidden meanings except Allah and those who are firmly

grounded in knowledge; they say: 'We believe in the Book; the whole of it is from our Lord': and none will grasp the Message except men of understanding." 3:7

In his commentary of this verse, Pooya Yazdi explains, "Most of the verses of the Quran are clear and decisive. There is no ambiguity in them. They are known as the *muhkamat* (basic, fundamental, decisive). They relate to the fundamentals of the faith, such as the Oneness of Allah, the directions pertaining to the practice of the faith, and the laws governing the day-to-day life of the faithful. They can neither be changed nor modified. Any man of average intelligence can understand and follow them." [23]

Then to explain the allegorical verses, he adds, "The *mutashabihat* (allegorical) are the verses which have been composed in subtle and profound diction and style. They carry implications other than the literal meanings, and therefore, are capable of giving different significations." He goes on to state that the phrase "those who are firmly grounded in knowledge" refers to Prophet Muhammad and his noble family, and thus one should use their teachings and examples for a more complete understanding of the Book. However, not understanding these ambiguous verses does not change the foundation of the Book, which, according to this verse, is made up of clear and decisive verses.

Allegorical verses notwithstanding, yet another verse proclaiming the simplicity of the Quran is quoted below:

"And We have revealed the Book to you explaining clearly everything, and a guidance and mercy and good news for those who submit." 16:89 (Shakir)

The above-mentioned verse contradicts the notion brought forth by some scholars, Muslims and non-Muslims alike, that the Quran is complex and complicated, emphasizing that the important and basic beliefs and the fundamental laws are made clear and easy to understand; though the Quran acknowledges the allegorical nature

---

23   Yazdi, Ayatullah Agha Pooya and S. V. Mir Ahmad Ali. *The Holy Qur'an— The Final Testament*, Tahrike Tarsile Qur'an, Elmhurst, New York: 2002. Quotes noted here are taken from the version on www.quran.al-islam.org, which varies slightly from the print version.

of some of the verses, *the foundation* of the Quranic teachings remains the verses that are made very clear.

Al-Kitab (the Book)

"This Book, there is no doubt in it, is a guide to those who guard (against evil)." 2:2 (Shakir)

"And this is a Book which We have sent down, bringing blessings, and confirming (the revelations) which came before it: that you may warn the mother of cities (Mecca) and all around her. Those who believe in the Hereafter believe in this (Book), and they are constant in guarding their prayers." 6:92

"A Book which We have revealed unto you, in order that you might lead mankind out of the depths of darkness into light—by the leave of their Lord—to the Way of (Him) the Exalted in power, worthy of all praise!" 14:1

A Book of Wisdom

Claiming repeatedly that it's a book of wisdom, the Quran invites deep thinking and reflection on God's signs that are abundant all around us. It challenges our intellect with the implication that if we contemplate the verses and study the nature, we will be led to the same conclusions as the teachings of the Quran. This wisdom is not necessarily reflected in one's genius as a mathematician or physicist, for example, but sets its own criteria. It provides guidance as it relates to the two paths: the straight path consisting of knowledge of God, surrendering to His will, commands, and laws, and the other, that's the opposite of the straight path. The destinations are also clearly spelled out for either path. The wisdom is then defined, not in terms of an IQ number, but whether one takes heed to the guidance and teachings provided therein. The Quran does not separate religion from science (or "nature"), nor science from religion.

"Alif Lam Ra (mystic Quranic letters). These are the Ayats [Ayahs or verses] of the Book of Wisdom." 10:1

"Alif Lam Mim (mystic Quranic letters). These are verses of the Book of wisdom, a guide and a mercy for the doers of goodness. Those who keep up prayers, pay the poor-rate [Zakah or charity] and

are certain of hereafter. These are on a guidance from their Lord, and these are they who are successful." 31:1–5 (Shakir)

"Yā Se'en. I swear by the Quran, which is full of Wisdom. That you [meaning Muhammad] are indeed one of the messengers. On a Straight way (path). A revelation by the Almighty, the Merciful." 36:1–5 (Shakir)

"By the Book that makes things clear, We have made it a Quran in Arabic, that you may be able to understand (and learn wisdom). And verily, it is in the Mother of the Book, in Our Presence, high (in dignity), full of wisdom." 43:2–4

Mother of the Book

The Mother of the Book, according to the explanation by Yahya Emerick, is the source of all the revelations by God. These include the Torah, the Gospel, the Quran, and all other scriptures. All of them have their foundation of wisdom rooted in the mystical source, and the source of knowledge is God.

According to Ali Unal's interpretation, the "Mother of the Book" refers to the preserved tablet *("Loh-e-Mehfooz")*, mentioned often in the Quran. The Quran originally existed in this mystical Mother Book, which exists with God. The Quran (the one on the preserved tablet) is high, exalted, and unfathomable to the human mind; however, God revealed it to Prophet Muhammad as a book in Arabic language so that people might be able to read and understand it.

Points to Remember

- The Quran makes frequent references to itself as "the Book," "Al-Quran," and "the revelations," indicating that this scripture was available in the textual form in the lifetime of Prophet Muhammad, and it was known as *the Quran* from the very beginning.
- Contrary to the popular belief by many Muslims and scholars of other faiths, the Quran is made easy to understand (and serves as guidance to mankind). However, some verses are allegorical and are specifically referred to as such. However, the foundation, or the

basis, of the book are the "clear" verses that relate to the fundamentals of the faith.

Time to Ponder

- What is God's purpose of leaving some verses allegorical intentionally?

CHAPTER 8
WHY WAS THE QURAN REVEALED?

What was the purpose of the revelation of the Quran? What if the Quran was never revealed? Would the faith in One God and our lives on earth be any different without it?

One may start by asking the basic question: why was *any* scripture needed? Why did God send the prophets? The basic purpose, theologians agree, was to provide an awareness of God and His laws. Of course God could have just inspired everyone to His way. But then if everyone was so inspired (and followed the right path), what then is the purpose of our creation? With this kind of inspiration and the resultant "righteous behavior," everyone would be leading the right path in this world. Were angels not enough, one might argue, as God's creation, to submit and worship to God constantly? The scriptures are in agreement that He chose the prophets to communicate His message to humans and gave humans the free will to accept the message or reject it. The essential purpose of the scriptures was to capture the message to serve as a guide for generations to come after the initial revelations.

The next question is why did God send down the Quran when humankind already had received multiple scriptures: the Torah, the Psalms, and the Gospel, among others. Why did the world need another prophet (Muhammad) after Moses and Jesus Christ? Muslim scholars contend that the Quran is the "Last Testament" and that it was required because people had deviated from the path shown by earlier scriptures, which had been modified, and even corrupted, and were no longer in their original form, thus necessitating another scripture that would stand the test of time. They further contend that faiths not intended by God had crept into societies, and a correction needed to be made to counter the misconceptions and practices of those faiths.

"Most surely there is a party amongst those who distort the Book with their tongue that you may consider it to be (a part) of the Book, and they say, It is from God, while it is not from God, and they tell a lie against God whilst they know." 3:78

"We certainly gave Moses the Book aforetime: but disputes arose therein." 41:45

"From those, too, who call themselves Christians, We did take a covenant, but they forgot a good part of the message that was sent them." 5:14

The Quran speaks about the religion of God, Islam, as basically one religion and one basic message and that God didn't intend to confuse mankind by sending various prophets with different messages. All prophets were "Muslims" (or submitters to the will of God) and brought the same basic religion to mankind, but those with scriptures were sent with a set of laws to conform to the needs of the communities it was revealed to. The topic of God's religion as one religion will be revisited in more detail in chapter 19.

One may also ask the same question about the other scriptures. After all, the Torah and the Gospel were not the first set of divine revelations. Before the Torah, there were revelations to other prophets (e.g., Adam and Abraham), though there does not seem to be any current recordings of these scriptures available. Why was the Torah necessary after the revelations were sent to Abraham? Why was the Gospel necessary after the Torah was revealed to Moses?

Muslims believe the Quran reaffirms many teachings of the prior scriptures while rejecting others that it says had been modified from their original, as well as establishing some laws not found in the prior scriptures. These are not necessarily a "new" set of laws but rather new aspects of the same old divine law.

In fact the message in the Quran is the same fundamental message as was in the preceding scriptures:

"Nothing is said to you [meaning Muhammad] that was not said to the messengers before you: that your Lord has at his Command (all) forgiveness as well as a most Grievous Penalty." 41:43

One may summarize the purpose of the Quran's revelations as following:

- Guidance, mercy, and healing
- Glad tidings and warnings

Guidance, Mercy, and Healing

This was discussed earlier in chapter 7. It's worth mentioning a few other verses to highlight the Quran's claim as a source of guidance and mercy:

"There is, in their stories, instruction for men of understanding. It is not a tale invented, but a confirmation of what went before it, a detailed exposition of all things, and a guide and a mercy to people who believe." 12:111

"This Book, there is no doubt in it, is a guide to those who guard (against evil)." 2:2

"When the Quran is read, listen to it with attention, and hold your peace: that you may receive Mercy." 7:204

In the following verse, the Quran lays some basic conditions to obtain its benefit. The precondition for getting the benefit is to have an open mind:

"Verily in this is a Message for any that has a heart and understanding or who gives ear and earnestly witnesses (the truth)." 50:37

Glad Tidings and Warnings

The basic underlying purpose of the prophets and the scriptures has been to inform mankind about God and to give good news about the consequences of good behavior, as well as warn about the consequences of bad behavior.

The Quranic references to the consequences of deeds imply accountability. This is analogous to informed consent before one goes through a surgical procedure. The physician typically goes over the pros and cons with patients, informing them of the intended (positive) outcomes as well as the potential adverse outcomes. He or she would also inform patients of the potential problems if they choose not to undergo the procedure. In much the same way, the Quran informs people about the two paths with their respective destinations. It then leaves the choice up to their free will.

The use of *glad tidings*, or *good tidings*, is somewhat unique in that the phrase often appears in the translation of the Quran and the Bible, and one hardly finds the usage in any other setting. The English word "tidings" has been in use since the eighteenth century; it means "news" or "information." Thus, "glad tidings" simply means "good news." Though "glad tidings" is often used in the scriptures, it is hard to find the opposite phrase, "bad tidings" (or "bad news") in the scriptures. Instead, the word "warning" is often used. The glad tidings are given in close proximity to the warning, and vice versa. In fact, in the Quran, the two phrases are frequently used together, in the same verse, or in consecutive verses. The words often used for the prophets in this context are *"Basheer"* (meaning "the bearer of glad tidings") and *"Nazeer"* (meaning "the warner"). The Quran repeatedly refers to Muhammad as the bearer of glad tidings and a warner. The following are some examples:

"That you should worship none but Allah (Say): 'Verily I am (sent) unto you from Him to warn and to bring glad tidings.'" 11:2

"We sent down the (Quran) in Truth, and in Truth has it descended: and We sent you but to give Glad Tidings and to warn." 17:105

"Verily We have sent thee in truth, as a bearer of glad tidings, and as a warner: and there never was a people, without a warner having lived among them (in the past)." 35:24

Other Apostles Were Also Sent as Bearers of Glad Tidings and as Warners

"Mankind was one single nation, and God sent Messengers with glad tidings and warnings; and with them He sent the Book in truth, to judge between people in matters wherein they differed." 2:213

"(We sent) messengers as the givers of good news and as warners, so that people should not have a plea against Allah after the (coming of) messengers; and Allah is Mighty, Wise." 4:165

"And We send (Our) message-bearers only as heralds of glad tidings and as warners: hence, all who believe and live righteously, no fear need they have, and neither shall they grieve." 6:48 (Asad)

Glad (Good) Tidings in the Bible

"The Spirit of the Lord GOD is upon Me, Because the LORD has anointed Me To preach good tidings to the poor; He has sent Me to heal the brokenhearted, To proclaim liberty to the captives, And the opening of the prison to those who are bound." Isaiah 61:1 (New King James Version).

This is a passage from the book of Isaiah, son of Amoz, considered by most biblical and Islamic scholars as a Hebrew prophet of Judah, who also prophesied about the birth of Jesus Christ and, according to Islamic scholars like Ibne Kathir and Kisa'I, foretold the prophecy of Muhammad. "Glad or good tidings" is used by various translations such as Darby, the King James Version, and the New King James Version, whereas others such as the New American Bible Standard and the New Living Translation have used "good news."

The Bible: The Warnings to Wrongdoers

The Bible sends clear warning to those who disobey the Lord and to the wrongdoers. The book of Jeremiah starts off by reminding the people of Israel and Judah about God's favors and also in the beginning how eager they were to please Lord (Jeremiah 2:1–2). In chapters 4, 5, and 6, Jeremiah goes on to warn the people of Israel and Judah of the oncoming disaster from the north. The whole sequence is one stern warning after another in rather graphic detail:

"Listen to this warning, Jerusalem, or I will turn from you in disgust. Listen, or I will turn you into a heap of ruins, a land where no one lives. This is what the LORD of Heaven's Armies says: 'Even the few who remain in Israel will be picked over again, as when a harvester checks each vine a second time to pick the grapes that were missed.'" Jeremiah 6:8–9

A few other verses that warn people in the Bible are quoted below:

"Now it came to pass at the end of seven days that the word of the LORD came to me, saying, 'Son of man, I have made you a

watchman for the house of Israel; therefore hear a word from My mouth, and give them warning from Me: When I say to the wicked, "You shall surely die," and you give him no warning, nor speak to warn the wicked from his wicked way, to save his life, that same wicked man shall die in his iniquity; but his blood I will require at your hand."' Ezekiel 3:16–18

And the LORD God of their fathers sent warnings to them by His messengers, rising up early and sending them, because He had compassion on His people and on His dwelling place. But they mocked the messengers of God, despised His words, and scoffed at His prophets, until the wrath of the LORD arose against His people, till there was no remedy." 2 Chronicles 36:14–16

The main distinction between "warnings" in the Quran and the Bible seems to be that the Quran warns wrongdoers and tyrants mainly about what's to come in the hereafter, whereas most of the warnings in the Bible refer to their fate in this world.

Points to Remember

- The basic message of the prophets was to convey the same message from God: to worship and seek His pleasure by following the laws established by Him.
- The scriptures serve as a source of divine laws, and the consequences of obeying and disobeying God are clearly outlined. The Quran speaks about people being bestowed with faculties to understand the message but leaves it up to them whatever path they choose at their free will.
- The Quran proclaims itself as guidance to mankind. Those who take heed will be the beneficiaries of the (spiritual) healing power of the scripture.

Time to Ponder

- If the scriptures did not give mankind clear warnings about the consequences of its actions, would it be fair for them to receive an adverse verdict on the Day of Judgment?

CHAPTER 9
RECITATION, TRANSLATION, AND INTERPRETATION OF THE QURAN

In ways similar to the Torah, the oral tradition of the Quran is considered as important as, if not more important than, the written text. It is worth repeating here that the most prudent way to understand the Quran is to study it in its original Arabic language. The next best way is to study a translation (realizing that translations don't always convey the true meaning and spirit conveyed by the original language of the scriptures).

Recitation (*Tilawat*)

The recitation of the Arabic Quran is a great tradition among the Muslims and is considered a source of blessings and a noble deed in itself. *Tilawat* is the word used to mean the recitation of the Quran. Many reciters (known as *"Qaris"*) develop their own unique style, and their melodious recitations have been sold on cassettes and CDs around the world. (Apologies to the young readers for using some obsolete words here like "cassettes.") These recitations are said to often leave deep impressions on even unfamiliar ears.

Tilawat comes from the root word *"Tala"* and has a wider meaning that includes to recite, rehearse, read, and meditate.

"When the Quran is recited, listen to it with complete silence so that you may be shown mercy." 7:204 (Malik). This is also translated by Yousuf Ali as *"When the Quran is read, listen to it with attention, and hold your peace: that you may receive Mercy."* In this verse,

listeners are instructed about the basic mannerism of listening to the Quran. Many Muslims do indeed stop talking when they hear the recitation:

"When you recite the Quran, seek Allah's protection from the accursed Shaitan [Satan], surely he has no authority over those who believe and put their trust in their Lord." 16:98–99 (Shakir)

Translation and Interpretation of the Quran

The following verse was quoted in the last chapter but is relevant to this discussion again:

"He it is Who has revealed the Book to you; some of its verses are decisive [unambiguous or 'muhkamat'], they are the basis [foundation] of the Book, and others are allegorical [ambiguous or 'mutashabihat']; then as for those in whose hearts there is perversity they follow the part of it which is allegorical, seeking to mislead and seeking to give it (their own) interpretation. But none knows its interpretation except God, and those who are firmly rooted in knowledge say: we believe in it, it is all from our Lord; and none do mind except those having understanding." 3:7 (Shakir)

Muslim (and many non-Muslim) scholars believe that the Quranic Arabic is archaic, reflecting seventh-century Arabic, not the modern-day Arabic. Moreover, when a text is translated into another language, there is always some inherent difficulty. Like the other scriptures, the Quran uses idioms frequently. For example, the idiom in English "carrying a chip on the shoulder" indicates someone getting angry at the slightest provocation or having a short fuse (which in itself is another idiom); it should not be literally translated into another language. The Quran is filled with colloquial terms—words that may have a different meaning during prior times. Furthermore, the Quran uses homonyms—words with multiple meanings. For example, the word *"Ayahs"* means a "sign," the "verse," or the "miracle." The translations often have subtle changes and variations from the original, at times influenced by culture, sectarian biases, and other ideologies, and they are thus often called interpretations, rather than translations. (Examples of such work include *The Meaning of the Glorious Koran* by Pickthall,

The Koran Interpreted by Arthur Arberry, and *An Interpretation of the Quran* by Majid Fakhry.)

The first person to translate part of the Quran was Salman Farsi, a noble companion of Prophet Muhammad from Persia, who translated *Surah Al-Fatiha* (the opening chapter) into Persian during the seventh century. The **first translation of the Quran** is believed to have been done in 884 in Sind (part of India at the time, now a part of Pakistan), by the orders of Abdullah bin Umar bin Abdul Aziz on the request of the Hindu Raja Mehruk. Robertus Ketenensis produced the **first Latin translation of the Quran** in 1143; it was titled Lex Mahumet pseudoprophete ("The law of Muhammad, the pseudo-prophet"). As the title suggests, it was negatively biased against the Quran. Many of the later European translations of the Quran were taken from Ketenensis's work.

The first translations into English were not undertaken by Muslims but by Christians who sought to debunk Islam and aid in the conversion of Muslims to Christianity. *The Al-coran of Mohamet* (1649) by Alexander Ross was the first English translation of the Quran. This translation was not from Arabic but rather based on Andre Du Ryer's French rendition, containing many distortions and misinterpretations. In 1734, George Sale produced the first English translation of the Quran from Arabic, *The Al Koran of Mohammed*. George Sale's translation was to remain the most widely available English translation over the next two hundred years, and it is still in print today, with release of a recent 2009 edition. According to a news brief from the Library of Congress dated January 3, 2007, Keith Ellison, the first Muslim US congressman, took the oath of office on Thomas Jefferson's personal copy of George Sale's 1734 translation of the Quran. Since George Sale, many English translations have been made available, each with its own set of strengths, weaknesses, biases, and varying level of scholarly research. The first Muslim to translate the Quran into English is said to be Dr. Mirza Fazl in 1910 in India; he arranged an English translation and the Arabic text side by side.

Exegesis (*Tafsir*)

A *tafsir* is an Arabic word for "exegesis," which means "explanation or commentary" and refers to the science of Quranic interpretation. It includes:

- Clarification of the meanings of verses
- Explanation of the underlying thoughts in metaphors
- Reconciling verses that seem contradictory
- Clarification of verses whose intents are not understood
- Explanation of the context of the verses

The *tafsir* cannot be based just on someone's own opinion, according to a saying (Hadith) of Prophet Muhammad. Though the Quran repeatedly asks readers to contemplate and ponder, an exegesis can only be written by someone with deep knowledge of the Quran, Hadith, as well as other reliable narrations. According to the Shia Muslim school of thought, the best *tafsir* is given by the family of the Prophet and the imams from his progeny, since they are believed to be the appointed successors of the Prophet Muhammad by divine instructions. It is also believed that Ali, Muhammad's son-in-law, was the first one to compile the Quran, and he wrote the first *tafsir*. However, no single volume of Quranic exegesis by Prophet Muhammad, his family, or the Imams is currently available.

Points to Remember

- The Quran was revealed in Arabic. Only the Arabic Quran is considered "the Holy Quran".
- The first translation was attempted by Salman Farsi, a companion of Prophet Muhammad. The first full translation was done in Sind (currently part of Pakistan) in 884. The first Latin translation was undertaken in the twelfth century, and the first English translation was in the eighteenth century. As with any other translations, there is an inherent loss of the true spirit and meaning during translations of the scriptures.

- A *tafsir* means an interpretation or exegesis with analysis of the deeper meaning and the context of the verses revealed.

Time to Ponder

- The Quran proclaims it is easy to understand, or at least the verses that form its foundation are. Does one need a Quranic scholar to properly understand the message and receive guidance? When should "the common person" seek the help of a religious scholar? The same questions apply to the Bible.

Section 3
The Quran
and Science

CHAPTER 10
THE UNIVERSE AND ASTRONOMY

Though very intriguing and tempting, a detailed discussion on the merits of the creation and intelligent design versus Darwin's theory of evolution is beyond the scope of this book.

The Quran repeatedly asks readers and followers to reflect and ponder. It has references to the creation of the universe, humans, the animal and plant kingdoms, as well as human embryology; this information was unknown or poorly understood at the time of the revelation some fourteen centuries ago. Many of the concepts outlined in the Quran have been discovered in the last two hundred years. Muslim scholars, therefore, point out that these scientific discoveries alone are proof of the divine nature of the Quran. Some non-Muslim scholars counter by stating that the translations are at times "stretched" to fit current scientific knowledge. Many Muslims also object to these references, believing that the Quran does not need to be "authenticated" by science and it should be the other way round. Still others contend the references are too vague. Similar debate exists for biblical references to science and nature. There are some similarities between the accounts of these scientific matters in the Quran and the Bible, as well as some stark differences. These objections and skepticism notwithstanding, these topics will be reviewed one at a time.

Ponder, Reflect, and Contemplate

Contrary to the popular belief, many scientists are and have been deeply affected by religion in their pursuit of the truth in science. Many have cited religion as the basis for their interest in science, and conversely the study of science has made them reflect deeper. For example, according to the famous physicist and Nobel Prize winner, Albert Einstein (1879–1955), "Science without religion is lame. Religion without science is blind."

Sir Isaac Newton (1643–1727), a famous English physicist, mathematician, astronomer, and theologian, was inspired by his religious faith and was an ardent Bible reader; he sought to understand its deeper meaning, especially as it relates to science. He said, "It is the perfection of God's works that they are all done with the greatest simplicity. He is the God of order and not of confusion." He also said, "God created everything by number, weight, and measure."

Numerous Muslim scholars and scientists during the Islamic golden age (seventh to thirteenth century), like Jabir Ibne Hayyan (721–815, considered the father of chemistry), Abu Sina (Avicenna; 980–1037, regarded as the most famous and influential Islamic polymath), and Ibne Al-Haytham (965–1040, considered father of optics and a pioneer of scientific methods), credited the Quran as the source of their inspiration to understand and explore nature, and many of them were deeply influenced by religion and their faith in God.

The Quran repeatedly draws the attention to "nature" and invites the reader to contemplate and think deeply.

"Do you not see that Allah is He, Whom obeys whoever is in the heavens and whoever is in the earth, and the sun and the moon and the stars, and the mountains and the trees, and the animals and many of the people." 22:18

The verse challenges the reader to ponder and reflect: *"Do you not see?"* It is a key concept in the Quran, not just for the matters related to astronomy but in all issues related to nature or otherwise.

"Most surely in the creation of the heavens and the earth and the alternation of the night and the day there are signs for men who understand. Those who remember Allah standing and sitting and lying on their sides and reflect on the creation of the heavens and the earth: Our Lord! You have not created this in vain." 3:190–191 (Shakir)

"(It is) a Book We have revealed to you abounding in good that they may ponder over its verses, and that those endowed with understanding may be mindful." 38:29 (Shakir)

In the following five verses (6:95–99), the Quran emphasizes and reminds everyone that it is God who makes things happen in "nature" and informs the believers that in nature there are His signs for people of knowledge and for those who ponder and reflect (Shakir):

"Surely Allah causes the grain and the stone to germinate; He brings forth the living from the dead and He is the bringer forth of the dead from the living; that is Allah! How are you then turned away?

"And He it is Who has made the stars for you that you might follow the right way thereby in the darkness of the land and the sea; truly We have made plain the communications for a people who know.

"And He it is Who has brought you into being from a single soul, then there is (for you) a resting-place and a depository; indeed We have made plain the communications for a people who understand.

"And He it is Who sends down water from the cloud, then We bring forth with it buds of all (plants), then We bring forth from it green (foliage) from which We produce grain piled up (in the ear); and of the palm-tree, of the sheaths of it, come forth clusters (of dates) within reach, and gardens of grapes and olives and pomegranates, alike and unlike; behold the fruit of it when it yields the fruit and the ripening of it; most surely there are signs in this for a people who believe."

In yet another series of verses, the Quran spells out some of His signs and invites the readers to reflect upon creation, human relationship, diversity, and the sleep cycle [*Surah Rum* or "Rome," 30:21–23 (Shakir)]:

"And one of His signs is that He created mates for you from yourselves that you may find rest in them, and He put between you love and compassion; most surely there are signs in this for a people who reflect.

"And one of His signs is the creation of the heavens and the earth and the diversity of your tongues and colors; most surely there are signs in this for the learned.

"And one of His signs is your sleeping and your seeking of His grace by night and (by) day; most surely there are signs in this for a people who would hear."

The following verses refer to the creation of the universe for an appointed term:

"Do they not see how Allah originates creation then repeats its process? Surely it is easy for Allah." 29:19 (Malik)

"Do they not reflect within themselves: Allah did not create the heavens and the earth and what is between them two but with truth, and (for) an appointed term?" 30:8 (Shakir)

Creation of the Universe

The Quran, unlike the Bible (in the book of Genesis), does not provide a continuous, stage-by-stage description of how the universe was created. This is in keeping with Quranic style. The verses are scattered throughout the scriptures. Taken together, these verses provide a powerful account of the creation of the universe that Muslim scholars believe is in line with currently accepted astrophysics laws and understanding.

The Big Bang Theory

The prevailing theory of the origin of the universe is commonly referred as the Big Bang theory. The theory is the most comprehensive and accurate explanation supported by scientific evidence and observation. According to this theory, the universe was one extremely hot and condensed mass, that very quickly cooled and expanded in a matter of seconds. This mass had incredibly high temperature, energy, and pressure. This tiny mass expanded extremely rapidly. Many varying models exist but according to a commonly held model, approximately 10^{-37} seconds into the expansion, a thermodynamic transition took place, causing cosmic inflation during which the universe grew exponentially. After the initial violent and massive explosion, some 13.75 billion years ago, there was a gradual expansion of this mass into galaxies, stars, and planets, including our own solar system.

Furthermore, modern astrophysicists agree that the universe is expanding. In fact, the model of the Big Bang was based on the observation that the distance between galaxies is increasing, indicating that the universe is in a constant state of expansion. If it is expanding with time, then working backwards, it must have been very small at one point in time.

The person credited with the theory is Monsignor Lemai'tre, a priest from Catholic University of Louvain, Belgium. His work was published in the early 1930s. The term "Big Bang" was first coined in 1949 by Fred Hoyle, a British astronomer and mathematician.

The Big Bang/Aquatic Origins of Life in the Quran

"And Allah has created from water every living creature: so of them is that which walks upon its belly, and of them is that which walks upon two feet, and of them is that which walks upon four; Allah creates what He pleases; surely Allah has power over all things."
24:45(Shakir)

The following verse, 21:30, is one of the most quoted verses by Muslim scholars in relation to the creation of the universe:

"Do not the Unbelievers see that the heavens and the earth were joined together (as one unit of creation), before we clove them asunder? We made from water every living thing. Will they not then believe?" (Yousuf Ali)

"Have not those who disbelieve known that the heavens and the earth were of one piece, then We parted them, and We made every living thing of water? Will they not then believe?" (Pickthall)

"Don't those who suppress (their awareness of the truth) see that heavens and earth were once fused together in a single piece, and then We split them apart? That we made every living thing from water? So won't they believe?" (Emerick)

This verse points to two key astrophysical and biological theories currently accepted by scientists: the Big Bang theory and the origin of life from water.

1. The splitting of the heavens and the earth: The word used in Arabic (*Fataq*) in this verse refers to a process of separation, breaking or splitting of something whose elements were initially fused together. Moreover, the word used for the skies ("heavens") is in plural, often used in the Quran in reference to all the zones of space in the universe.

2. The origin of life from water: The verse states, *"We made from water every living thing."* Scholars have used this to mean that every living object (protoplasm) is predominantly made of water. Other scholars have interpreted this in reference to the *origin* of life on earth from an oceanic source. There is no uniformly accepted model in terms of scientific theories about the origin of life on earth, but the "deep sea vent theory" is one of them, and many scientists believe that life on earth started on the oceanic floor. No matter how the second part of 21:30 is interpreted, either one seems to have scientific basis for it, according to current thinking.

The Universe as Smoke (Nebula)

It is widely believed that at one point in time, the whole universe was nothing but a cloud of smoke, consisting of highly opaque and hot gases, and the galaxies took shape much later. New stars and galaxies are still being formed from this smoke. Some of the amazing pictures sent by the Hubble telescope of stars being formed out of a cloud of smoke and dust (nebula) give us a visual clue to the origins of the universe.

"Moreover He comprehended in His design the sky, and it had been (as) smoke: He said to it and to the earth: 'Come you together, willingly or unwillingly.'" 41:11

The Universe Is Expanding

Another widely accepted model of the universe affirms that the universe is ever expanding. The terms "space" and "universe" are sometimes used interchangeably. However, space refers to a mathematical concept, whereas the universe is all the matter and energy that exists. Does space have an edge? Where does space start and stop? What space is the universe expanding into? These are very interesting questions, and scientists have varying theories. For example, the Finite theory supposes that space does not have an edge but rather space wraps around itself. So if we could theoretically travel through the universe, we will end up where we started. Verse 51:47 is often quoted to support the claim that the Quran hinted at the expanding universe:

"And it is We who have built the universe with (Our creative) power; and, verily, it is We who are steadily expanding it." (Asad) Also translated as *"We built the sky above with Our (special) ability and We are expanding it."* (Emerick) or *"We constructed the universe with Might and We are expanding it."* (Yuksel)

It should be pointed out that the above three translators are from recent times. A sample of older translations is noted below:

"We have built the heaven with might, and We it is who make the vast extent (thereof)." (Pickthall) Or *"With power and skill did We construct the Firmament: for it is We Who create the vastness of space."* (Yousuf Ali).

It can be argued that the modern translators "twisted" the translation to fit into the currently held scientific facts. However, it can be equally strongly argued that the earlier translators simply could not comprehend what later on became scientific facts, and they translated the verse according to the knowledge as it existed then. It is not necessarily giving new meaning to the words per se, but rather putting the correct meaning to a concept that evolved and became obvious with time as humans acquired more knowledge.

The Quran on the Collapse of the Universe Like a Scroll

It is widely believed that the earth and our solar system, like the other stars and galaxies, have a finite life and will eventually vanish. It is no longer a matter of if but when. The Quran (and the Bible) have many references to the end of time. The Quran and the Bible not only foretell the end of times for our planet and the sun, they discuss doomsday for the "heavens"—generally referring to the entire universe. Some of these verses will be reviewed in more detail again in section 5 ("The Quran and Eschatology").

"When the sun (with its spacious light) is folded up; When the stars fall, losing their luster; When the mountains vanish (like a mirage). 81:1–3

"The Day that We roll up the heavens like a scroll rolled up for books (completed), even as We produced the first creation, so shall

We produce a new one: a promise We have undertaken: truly shall We fulfill it." 21:104

The Bible on the Collapse of the Universe Like a Scroll

In a verse that has striking resemblance to the Quranic verse quoted above, the Bible foretells the end of times:

"*All the stars in the sky will rot. The heavens will be rolled up like a scroll. The stars will fall like leaves from a grapevine, like green figs from a fig tree.*" Isaiah 34:3–5

The Creation of the Universe and the Earth in Stages

"*And certainly We created the heavens and the earth and what is between them in six periods and there touched Us not any fatigue.*" 50:38 (Shakir). Or "*We created the heavens and the earth and all between them in Six Days, nor did any sense of weariness touch Us.*" (Yousuf Ali)

Another verse refers to the same stages:

"*Surely your Lord is Allah, Who created the heavens and the earth in six periods of time, and He is firm in power.*" 7:54 (Shakir).

The word for "days" used in Arabic is "*Ayyam,*" a plural for "*Yaum.*" In general, the word *Yaum* is translated as "a day." However, the plural *Ayyam* is also meant for "periods of time" and is used in the Quran to indicate periods of time as well, and therefore is meant to indicate stages rather than a time period between two successive sunrises or sunsets. It is of note that the book Genesis of the Old Testament starts with the creation and refers to the six days of the creation of the heavens and the earth. Biblical scholars have similarly argued that these "days" refer to periods or stages, rather than earthly days.

Time Is Relative

Einstein did not come up with his theory of relativity until 1905. It generalizes Galileo's theory of relativity, that all uniform motion is relative, and that there is no absolute and well-defined state of rest, contradicting the classical notion that the duration of the time interval between two events is equal for all observers. The Quran introduces the concept of a measure of a time, different from the earthly measures:

"He rules (all) affairs from the heavens to the earth: in the end will (all affairs) go up to Him, on a Day, the space whereof will be (as) a thousand years of your reckoning." 32:5

"The angels and the spirit ascend unto him in a Day the measure whereof is (as) fifty thousand years." 70:4

"Yet they ask you to hasten on the Punishment! But Allah will not fail in His Promise. Verily a Day in the sight of your Lord is like a thousand years of your reckoning." 22:47

The above three verses alone point to a concept, which fourteen hundred years ago was entirely obscure. That is, the definition of a day was basically the time interval between two successive sunrises or sunsets. It wasn't until much later, and in recent times, that we began to realize that a day on earth is not the same as a day elsewhere in the universe and that time is relative in space. In another sequence of verses, the Quran refers to the stages of the creation of the universe and the earth:

"Ask them: 'Do you really deny the One Who created the earth in two periods and do you set up rivals in worship with Him while He is the Lord of the worlds?' He set upon it mountains towering high above its surface, He bestowed blessings upon it and in four periods provided it with sustenance according to the needs of all those who live in and ask for it. Moreover, He turned toward the sky, which was but smoke, He said to it and to the earth: 'Come forward (into being) both of you, willingly or unwillingly,' and they submitted: 'We shall come willingly.' So, from this creation, He formed the seven heavens in two periods and to each heaven He ordained its laws. He adorned the lowest heaven with brilliant lamps (luminaries or stars) and made it secure. Such is the design of the All-Mighty, the All-Knowing." 41:9–12 (Malik)

In the above verses, Yousuf Ali and Pickthall translate the Arabic word for "the periods" as "days." One might wonder what was the measure of a day *before* the earth was created? It could *not* have been the days as measured by the rotation of the (then-nonexistent) earth upon its axis. However, the Quran clearly speaks of measurements of days other than the earthly days as noted above. Another point of contention can be the age of the earth, believed by scientists to be about 4.5 billion years, whereas the age of the universe is believed to be about 13.75 billion years. According to the verse noted above (*"He turned toward the sky, which was but smoke, He said to it and to the earth …"*), the earth and the smoky universe were ordered to come into being at the same time—an apparent contradiction to the currently held scientific view. The verse goes on to say, *"So, from this creation,"* which can be taken to indicate that the matters that eventually formed the earth and the heavens existed at the time of the divine orders, *"He said to it and to the earth: 'Come forward both of you (into being).'"* Who or what was God addressing as "earth" if earth had not fully been formed at the time?

The Quran and the Solar System

The Quran mentions the heavens and the earth (*"Samawaat"* and *"Ard"*) together frequently. Typically the word "heavens" or "skies" (plural) is mentioned before the earth (Verses 7:54, 10:3, 11:7, 91:5, 32:4, and many others), though the word "earth" is mentioned before "heaven" in verse 20:4. The Quran does not describe the creation in a step-by-step fashion, and the mention of heavens before earth (or vice versa) may not be a reference to the sequence of events.

Earth Is Round

Though the concept of a spherical earth was developed in ancient Greece around the seventh century BCE, starting with Pythagoras, the spherical shape of the earth remained speculative until the sixteenth century; many people believed in a flat earth model. Many ancient cultures had a varying opinion of earth being flat versus being round. The Indians and Greek believed in its spherical shape, while the roundness of the earth in China was not well known until the seventeenth century. Sir Francis Drake sailed around the earth in 1597 CE to show that the earth is spherical and not flat, a common view at the time. Though not an entirely unique concept at the time, the Quran does refer to the spherical shape of the earth:

"O company of Jinn and men, if you have power to penetrate (all) regions of the heavens and the earth; then penetrate (them)! You will never penetrate them save with (Our) sanction." 55:33 (Shakir)

The Arabic word used for "regions" in this verse is *"aqtar."* It is a plural of the word *"Qutr"* or "diameter" and is frequently used in Arabic geometry texts. Thus Yuksel has translated the verse as follows: *"O Tribes of Jinn and humans, if you can penetrate the diameters of heavens and earth ..."*

A diameter is obviously a measure for a spherical object. This verse points out that the earth is spherical, in an indirect way—not an uncommon approach by the Quran, leaving the reader to do the pondering. Moreover, there are several verses pointing out that the day and night merge into each other gradually:

"See you not that Allah merges Night into Day and he merges Day into Night; that He has subjected the sun, and the moon (to His law), each running its course for a term appointed; and that Allah is well-acquainted with all that you do?" 31:29

Though one might take the meaning at its face value (days gradually turning into night), the merging of day and night gradually indicate a rotating round earth and thus can only mean that the earth is not flat, otherwise the night and day will not "merge" but change suddenly.

Earth Is Like an Egg

Critics sometimes point out a "discrepancy" in the Quran by mentioning verse 79:30 to indicate the earth is egg-shaped. Verse 79:30 is translated by many as follows (the whole sequence is quoted for a better understanding of the context; 79:30 is bolded):

*"O mankind, is your creation harder than the heaven that He built? He raised its canopy and fashioned it to perfection. He gave darkness to the night and brightness to the day. **After that He spread out the earth**. Then from it He brought forth its water and its pasture, set its mountains. And made them beneficial for you and your cattle."* 79:27–33 (Malik)

*"The land after that, He made it **like an egg**."* 79:30 (Yuksel)

Some skeptics have used this to show contradictions to the scientific knowledge regarding the shape of the earth being like an egg (ovoid). The phrases that I bolded above, "spread out" and " like an egg," are translated from the Arabic word *"dahaha."* Yuksel, in his commentary, points out that the word is derived from the root word *"dahy,"* meaning further expansion of the earth, as well as an egg. Many Muslim scholars have interpreted it to indicate this was an allegorical description. However, it may indeed have been used to mean an egg-like earth, but not in reference to its shape.

Geologists have described the core of the earth in reference to an egg. The following is an excerpt from the web pages of University of Washington: "The inside of the earth is layered, something like an egg. Both have a thin, brittle shell. The crust of the earth is broken into pieces, like the cracked shell of a hardboiled egg. The mantle of the earth is like the egg white, and the core of the earth lies in the center, like the egg yolk."[24]

Earth's Protective Atmosphere and Ozone Layer

Earth's atmosphere protects the planet from harmful radiation. The stratosphere is the atmosphere that begins about ten miles above the earth surface and extends up to about thirty miles. The ozone layer in the stratosphere protects the earth from many harmful effects of the sun's ultraviolet radiation. We also know that many small meteorites crash into small pieces as they travel through the stratosphere, rather than hitting the earth. The ozone layer was not described until late 1800s and early 1900s. In addition to the protective atmosphere, a layer created by earth's magnetic field, called the Van Allen belt, serves to protect the planet from solar flares that can play havoc if they reach the earth.

"We made the sky a protective ceiling. Yet they are turning away from Our signs." 21:32 (Yuksel)

The "protective ceiling" is also translated as "sheltering canopy" (Emerick), "guarded canopy" (Shakir), and "canopy well guarded" (Yousuf Ali).

---

24   http://www.washington.edu/burkemuseum/earthquakes/bigone/science.html.

Once again, though the Quranic reference to the ozone layer and other protective layers is indirect, it clearly speaks about a ceiling that serves to protect the planet earth. If one argues about the verses being too vague and stretched to fit into modern concepts, then what alternative conclusions can be drawn from this and other indirect verses?

Sun Is the Light and the Moon Is Illuminated (Reflected Light)

Verse 10:5 talks about the nature of the brightness of the sun and the moon:

"He is the One Who made the sun an illuminator, and the moon a light, and He measured its phases so that you would know the number of the years and the calculations." (Yuksel)

Emerick in his commentary of the verse points out that the Arabic word used for the bright glowing of the sun is in the plural, indicating the many separate colors contained in sunlight. Moreover, the moonlight is referred to as the generic *"noor,"* which means any light shining upon something.

"Blessed is He Who made the constellations in the heavens and made therein a lamp [meaning sun that gives light] and a shining moon." 25:61

The sun is often referred to in the Quran as *"siraaj,"* which means a "torch," or as *"wahhaaj,"* which means "a blazing lamp." The moon is often referred to as *"munawwar,"* meaning "illuminated." Though Anaxagoras in ancient Greece may have described the moon reflecting sun's light as early as the fifth century BCE, it didn't become common knowledge until much later.

The Celestial Bodies Moving in Orbits

For many centuries, the concept of a geocentric universe was prevalent among European scientists, whereby the earth stood still in the center and everything else, including the sun, moved around the earth. In 1543 CE, Nicolaus Copernicus published his theory of a heliocentric system, whereby the earth moved around a stationary sun. The Quran described that the sun and other celestial bodies move in orbits:

"It is He Who created the Night and the Day, and the sun and the moon: all (the celestial bodies) swim along, each in its rounded course." 21:33 (Yousuf Ali), or *"And He it is Who created the night and the day and the sun and the moon; all (orbs) travel along swiftly in their celestial spheres."* (Shakir)

In another verse, the concept of the sun and the moon moving in their respective orbits is once again mentioned as follows:

"Neither is it allowable to the sun that it should overtake the moon, nor can the night outstrip the day; and all float on in a sphere." 36:40 (Shakir), or as translated by Pickthall: *"It is not for the sun to overtake the moon, nor doth the night outstrip the day. They float each in an orbit."*

The verse indicates that the celestial bodies not only move in an orbit but also implies that each has its own distinct orbit, as they cannot "overtake" each other.

Sun and the Moon Floating for an Appointed Term; the Sun Will Extinguish

It is widely believed by modern scientists that the chemical process in the sun that creates energy and light will eventually cease, and the sun will extinguish and turn into a white dwarf. The knowledge of the finality and the mortality of the sun was acquired within the past century.

In the following verse, not only does the Quran indicate the orbits for the sun and the moon, but also that they all are moving around for a definite, appointed term:

"He created the heavens and the earth in true (proportions): He makes the Night overlap the Day, and the Day overlap the Night: He has subjected the sun and the moon (to His law): Each one follows a course for a time appointed. Is not He the Exalted in Power—He Who forgives again and again." 39:5

In the verse 39:5 mentioned above, the verb used for overlap is *"yukaviru."* Yuksel translated that into "rolls over," thus the translation for the above verse, according to him, is *"He created the heavens and the earth in truth, He rolls the Night over the Day, and He rolls the Day over the Night."* This he believes was the indication that the earth also is rotating along its axis, making the night roll over the day and the day over the night.

"And the sun runs his course for a period determined for Him: that is the decree of (Him), the Exalted in Might, the All-Knowing." 36:38

"Allah is He Who raised the heavens without any pillars that you can see; is firmly established on the throne (of authority); He has subjected the sun and the moon (to his Law)! Each one runs (its course) for a term appointed. He does regulate all affairs, explaining the signs in detail, that you may believe with certainty in the meeting with your Lord." 13:2

The Bible and Astronomy

The book of Genesis starts with the creation, and the entire first chapter describes the various stages in which the universe was created, followed by the creation of man in chapter 2. Much like the Quran, there is a debate among scientists and biblical theologians about the accuracy of the biblical accounts of creation and astronomy, ranging from the age of the universe to the sequence of creation. Many theologians claim that there is no contradiction between modern knowledge and the biblical accounts.

The entire first chapter of Genesis is presented here, verse by verse:[25]

"In the beginning God created the heavens and the earth. The earth was formless and void, and darkness was over the surface of the deep, and the Spirit of God was moving over the surface of the waters. Then God said, 'Let there be light'; and there was light. God saw that the light was good; and God separated the light from the darkness. God called the light day, and the darkness He called night. And there was evening and there was morning, one day.

"Then God said, 'Let there be an expanse in the midst of the waters, and let it separate the waters from the waters.' God made the expanse, and separated the waters, which were below the expanse from the waters which were above the expanse; and it was so. God

---

25 All biblical translations in this chapter are from the New American Standard Bible by the Lockman Foundation.

called the expanse heaven. And there was evening and there was morning, a second day.

"Then God said, 'Let the waters below the heavens be gathered into one place, and let the dry land appear'; and it was so. God called the dry land earth, and the gathering of the waters He called seas; and God saw that it was good. Then God said, 'Let the earth sprout vegetation, plants yielding seed, and fruit trees on the earth bearing fruit after their kind with seed in them'; and it was so. The earth brought forth vegetation, plants yielding seed after their kind, and trees bearing fruit with seed in them, after their kind; and God saw that it was good. There was evening and there was morning, a third day.

"Then God said, "Let there be lights in the expanse of the heavens to separate the day from the night, and let them be for signs and for seasons and for days and years; and let them be for lights in the expanse of the heavens to give light on the earth'; and it was so. God made the two great lights, the greater light to govern the day, and the lesser light to govern the night; He made the stars also. God placed them in the expanse of the heavens to give light on the earth, and to govern the day and the night, and to separate the light from the darkness; and God saw that it was good. There was evening and there was morning, a fourth day.

"Then God said, 'Let the waters teem with swarms of living creatures, and let birds fly above the earth in the open expanse of the heavens.' God created the great sea monsters and every living creature that moves, with which the waters swarmed after their kind, and every winged bird after its kind; and God saw that it was good. God blessed them, saying, 'Be fruitful and multiply, and fill the waters in the seas, and let birds multiply on the earth.' There was evening and there was morning, a fifth day.

"Then God said, 'Let the earth bring forth living creatures after their kind: cattle and creeping things and beasts of the earth after their kind'; and it was so. God made the beasts of the earth after their kind, and the cattle after their kind, and everything that creeps on the ground after its kind; and God saw that it was good.

"Then God said, 'Let Us make man in Our image, according to Our likeness; and let them rule over the fish of the sea and over the birds of the sky and over the cattle and over all the earth, and over *every creeping thing that creeps on the earth.' God created man in His own image, in the image of God He created him; male and female He created them. God blessed them; and God said to them, 'Be fruitful and multiply, and fill the earth, and subdue it; and rule over the fish of the sea and over the birds of the sky and over every living thing that moves on the earth.' Then God said, 'Behold, I have given you every plant yielding seed that is on the surface of all the earth, and every tree which has fruit yielding seed; it shall be food for you; and to every beast of the earth and to every bird of the sky and to every thing that moves on the earth which has life, I have given every green plant for food'; and it was so. God saw all that He had made, and behold, it was very good. And there was evening and there was morning, the sixth day."* Genesis 1:1–31

Though some critics have pointed out the conflicts with the current knowledge, some passages that are consistent with modern knowledge are reviewed here.

A Formless Earth

"The earth was formless and void." Genesis 1:2

The following verses point out that the earth was filled with water (oceans) first and the land appeared later, a currently established scientific fact:

"Then God said, "Let the waters below the heavens be gathered into one place, and let the dry land appear"; and it was so. God called the dry land earth, and the gathering of the waters He called seas." Genesis 1:9–10

The references to the heavenly bodies are not limited to the book of Genesis. For example, the Bible speaks of the uniqueness of each star in the following verse:

"There is one glory of the sun, and another glory of the moon, and another glory of the stars; for star differs from star in glory." 1 Corinthians 15:41

Moon Is Luminous

"God made the two great lights, the greater light to govern the day, and the lesser light to govern the night; He made the stars also." Genesis 1:16

Though not as direct as the Quranic references to the moon's reflective brightness, this verse is cited by many as a reference that the moon is reflective of sunlight.

The Universe Is Expanding

The following verses, among others, have been put forth to support the claim that the Bible gave indication about an expanding universe (or *stretching* of the universe):

"It is He who sits above the circle of the earth, And its inhabitants are like grasshoppers, Who stretches out the heavens like a curtain And spreads them out like a tent to dwell in." Isaiah 40:22

"Thus says the LORD, your Redeemer, and the one who formed you from the womb. 'I, the LORD, am the maker of all things, Stretching out the heavens by Myself And spreading out the earth all alone.'" Isaiah 44:24

"It is He who made the earth by His power, Who established the world by His wisdom; And by His understanding He has stretched out the heavens." Jeremiah 10:12

Arguments Against the Biblical Accounts

As in the case of the Quran, critics have pointed out apparent contradictions in the Bible as well. The following is an incomplete account of some of this criticism by many scientists and some biblical scholars. It should be pointed out that this criticism is not necessarily directed toward the Holy scriptures but the authenticity of translations and narrations and the loss or alteration of original passages.

Earth is flat: In the following verse, they point out that the "four corners" of the earth indicate a flat earth, though it can be counterargued that this is used metaphorically to mean from all over the earth:

"And He will lift up a standard for the nations And assemble the banished ones of Israel, And will gather the dispersed of Judah From the four corners of the earth." Isaiah 11:12

Earth formed before the sun: The critics point to an apparent contradiction to the current knowledge about the evolution of our solar system. Genesis describes how God formed the earth on the first through the third day of creation, as well as its oceans and the herbs on the earth. Then on the fourth day (verses 14–19), He made the greater and lesser lights in the heavens (indicating the sun and the moon) as well as other stars.

Points to Remember

- The Quran refers to the creation of the universe and its expansion and many other physical concepts related to the sun, the moon, and the earth. Many of these astronomical phenomena were largely unknown, or not well known, some fourteen hundred years ago. The Quran refers to these in more direct terms (solar orbit, the sun's eventual demise, the moon's illumination), as well as in indirect fashion (the ozone layer, the Big Bang theory).
- The Bible gives a detailed account of creation of heaven and the earth in the book of Genesis in the first chapter, though there are other indirect references elsewhere. Not all critics and scholars agree on the accuracy of Quranic as well as biblical references.

Time to Ponder

- The Quran specifically invites the readers to ponder over God's signs. What's the purpose behind the indirect references in the scriptures rather than more direct ones? Would that have convinced skeptics to believe in Him? Could the direct references have confounded the ancient people?
- Should the discovery of laws or explanations for natural phenomena lead to a conclusion that there must not be a God?

CHAPTER 11
THE EARTH, AND PLANT AND ANIMAL KINGDOMS

The Quran has repeated references to the creation of the earth and many creations on the earth, both living and nonliving. These include many topics that can be classified under geology, geography, and oceanography, among others. There are many passages on mountains, the winds, the clouds and the rains, the sky, the oceans, as well as the living organisms of the animal and plant kingdoms. These references are mostly in relation to pondering God's signs in nature. Some of the verses have already been quoted previously in this book.

"Most surely in the creation of the heavens and the earth and the alternation of the night and the day, and the ships that run in the sea with that which profits men, and the water that Allah sends down from the cloud, then gives life with it to the earth after its death and spreads in it all (kinds of) animals, and the changing of the winds and the clouds made subservient between heaven and earth, there are signs for a people who understand." 2:164 (Shakir)

"And He it is Who spread the earth and made in it firm mountains and rivers, and of all fruits He has made in it two kinds; He makes the night cover the day; most surely there are signs in this for a people who reflect." 13:3 (Shakir)

Mountains Firmly Fixed

Mountains are formed as tectonic plates collide. One plate slides under the other, lifting it above the surface (thus forming a mountain). The other plate dips inward. Mountains have roots that are embedded deep into the earth's mantle, said to be many times the elevation above the surface. For example, Himalayas were formed some ninety million years ago by the movement of the Asian plate into the Indian plate, forcing the smaller Indian plate deep into the earth's mantle—a process called subduction. The Indian plate forming the basis of the Himalayas sank as deep as 155 miles below the surface. The tallest peak above the sea level is just over 5.5 miles (29,029 feet).[26] It is also described that these inward subductions serve as pegs to stabilize the earth.

Professor Frank Press, a geophysicist, former science advisor to President Jimmy Carter from 1976 to 1980, and president of National Academy of Sciences in Washington, DC, from 1981 to 1993, has written many books on the planet earth. In his book titled *Earth*, Press writes that mountains have underlying roots, embedded deep in the earth's mantle.[27]

The function and structure of mountains underneath the earth's surface was not well known until the last one hundred years or so. However, the Quran mentioned this fact some fourteen hundred years ago:

"Have We not made the earth as a wide expanse. And the mountains as pegs?" 78:6–7

"He created the heavens without any pillars that you can see; He set on the earth mountains standing firm, lest it should shake with you; and He scattered through it beasts of all kinds. We send down rain from the sky, and produce on the earth every kind of noble creature, in pairs." 31:10

The second part of this verse will be discussed later in this chapter.

There is evidence now that the tectonic plates under mountains move constantly. The movement of the earth's crust that they are located on causes this motion of mountains. The earth's crust "floats" over the mantle layer, which is denser. In the early twentieth century, Alfred Wegener, a German scientist, proposed that the continents of the earth had been attached together when it first

---

26 Anju Pandey, *A Study of the Himalayas*, National Oceanography Center, http://www.livescience.com/6595-depth-himalayan-mountain-roots-revealed.html.

27 Frank Press and Raymond Siever, *Earth*, p. 435.

formed, but then they drifted in different directions and thus separated as they moved away from each other. Wegener stated that the continents were joined together about 500 million years ago, and this large mass, called Pangaea, was located in the South Pole. Approximately 180 million years ago, Pangaea divided into two parts, which drifted in different directions. There are six major tectonic plates under the earth's surface that constantly move and carry with them the continents, the mountains, and ocean floors. The constant movement of the continents is referred to as the continental drift. The Quran refers to the moving of the mountains in the following verse (the drifting of the mountains is likened to the drifting or movement of clouds):

"And you see the mountains, you think they are solid, while they are passing by like the clouds, the making of God Who perfected everything. He is ever-aware of what you do." 27:88 (Yuksel)

While some of the earlier translators have interpreted this verse to mean that the mountains will fly away on the Day of Judgment, the more modern translators, like Yuksel, dispute that and feel the verse was in relation to the moveability of the mountains along with the tectonic plates. They point out that the end of the world will be chaotic, and this verse does not give that impression, and in fact the second part of the verse ("the making of God who perfected everything") clearly refers to creation and perfection rather than destruction and chaos on the final day.

Clouds, Winds, and Rain

Meteorologists describe many different types of clouds. One kind of rain cloud is cumulonimbus. Clouds go through the following stages to produce rain, hail, and lightning (these observations weren't made until this century):

- Cumulonimbus clouds begin to form when wind pushes some small pieces of clouds, called cumulus clouds, to an area where these clouds converge.
- More of these smaller clouds join together to form larger clouds.

- As they grow, there is an upward draft, which is the greatest near the center of the clouds thus formed. This results in stacking up of the clouds as the upward movement reaches the cooler regions of the atmosphere, where water drops begin to formulate, as well as hail, which grow heavier, so much so that the updrafts are unable to hold them. They begin to then fall as rain and hail.

The Quran talks about the clouds, the rain, and the lightning in many passages:

"Do you not see that God drives along the clouds, then gathers them together, then piles them up, so that you see the rain coming forth from their midst? And He sends down of the clouds that are (like) mountains wherein is hail, afflicting therewith whom He pleases and turning it away from whom He pleases; the flash of His lightning almost takes away the sight." 24:43 (Shakir)

"He it is Who shows you the lightning causing fear and hope and (Who) brings up the heavy cloud." 13:12 (Shakir)

The role of the winds in cloud formation is once again mentioned in the following verse:

"It is Allah Who sends the Winds, and they raise the Clouds: then does He spread them in the sky as He wills, and break them into fragments, until you see rain-drops issue from the midst thereof: then when He has made them reach such of His servants as He wills behold, they do rejoice!" 30:48

Moreover, cumulonimbus clouds can get very heavy and can carry up to 300,000 tons of water in them. This fact about the heavy weight of these clouds is mentioned in the following verse (the verse also refers to the mercy of God that the rains bring about in giving life to dead land, by making it more fertile):

"It is He Who sends the winds like heralds of glad tidings, going before His mercy: when they have carried the heavy-laden clouds, We drive them to a land that is dead, make rain to descend thereon." 7:57

The heavy clouds are also mentioned in verse 13:12, quoted earlier in this section, and translated as "heavy clouds" even by older translations such as by Pickthall.

The Oceans and the Seas

The Quran speaks of dividing barriers between seas. Oceanographers have pointed out that each sea has its own salinity, temperature, and density, which are maintained when the two seas meet. The Mediterranean Sea is warm, less dense, and more saline compared to the Atlantic Ocean. When the Mediterranean Sea enters the Atlantic over the Gibraltar sill, it moves several hundred kilometers into the Atlantic at a depth of about one thousand meters, with its own dense, saline characteristics.

"He has made the two seas to flow freely (so that) they meet together: Between them is a Barrier which they do not transgress." 55:19–20

"It is He Who has let free the two bodies of flowing water: One palatable and sweet, and the other salt and bitter; yet has He made a barrier between them, a partition that is forbidden to be passed." 25:53

The Water Cycle

The US Geological Survey (USGS) has identified sixteen components of the water cycle. In its very basic form, the water cycle describes how the water content on the planet earth remains constant and moves from one part to another and, eventually, back to where it started—in the oceans. It describes the rainwater gathering as underground springs, which then flow back into the oceans.

In the seventh century BCE, Thales of Miletus believed that surface spray of the oceans was picked up by the wind and carried inland to fall as rain. In 1580, Bernard Palissy was the first man to describe the present day concept of the water cycle. He described how water evaporates from the oceans and cools to form clouds. The clouds move inland where they rise, condense, and fall as rain. This water gathers as lakes and streams and flows back to the ocean in a continuous cycle.[28]

"He sends down water from the skies, and the channels flow, each according to its measure." 13:17

---

28   Bucaille, *The Bible, the Quran, and Science*, 2nd edition, pp. 173–174.

"And We send the fecundating winds, then cause the rain to descend from the sky, therewith providing you with water (in abundance), though ye are not the guardians of its stores." 15:22

These verses refer to what happens after rain and snow fall from the skies:

"Do you not see that Allah sends down rain from the sky, and leads it through springs in the earth? Then He causes to grow, therewith, produce of various colors: then it withers; you will see it grow yellow; then He makes it dry up and crumble away. Truly, in this, is a Message of remembrance to men of understanding." 39:21 (Shakir)

"And We send down water from the sky according to (due) measure, and We cause it to soak in the soil; and We certainly are able to drain it off (with ease)." 23:18

"Say: 'See you? If your stream be some morning lost (in the underground earth), who then can supply you with clear-flowing water?'" 67:30

"And We produce therein orchard with date-palms and vines, and We cause springs to gush forth therein." 36:34

Lastly, in this set of three verses, God is reminding us who really is behind the water cycle to function (56:68–70):

"Have you considered the water which you drink?

"Is it you that send it down from the clouds, or are We the senders?

"If We pleased, We would have made it salty; why do you not then give thanks?" (Shakir)

Animal Kingdom/Zoology

The Quran makes numerous references to the animal kingdom, animal behavior, and what we can learn from them.

Animal Societies

The modern-day animal ecology studies reveal how animals live in distinct societies. Birds flying together have been observed since ancient times. However, much of the knowledge of animal behavior was not known until more recent times. For example, ants are now known to have an extremely intelligent order of living including hierarchy, military planning, labor division, and advanced communications. The Quran refers to the animal societies in the following verse. In addition to the reference to the distinct animal societies, God also talks about something that is not given much thought: animals will be gathered at the end, just like the humans will be.

"There is not an animal (that lives) on the earth, nor a being that flies on its wings, but (forms part of) communities like you. Nothing have we omitted from the Book, and they (all) shall be gathered to their Lord in the end." 6:38

Honeybees

Honeybee colonies are some of the most fascinating studies in nature. Each colony has just one queen bee, a few hundred males, and up to eighty thousand worker bees. Each one of them has a distinct role. The queen bee's major functions are to lay eggs and secrete substances that maintain the unity of the colony as well as the integrity of the hives. The males' only function is to fertilize the queen, and that's pretty much it! (Tough job, but somebody has to do it.) Worker bees' functions include practically everything else, from gathering food and feeding the queen and the males, to building honeycombs, producing honey, cleaning up, and regulating the temperature of the hive. The worker bees are females but their ovaries do not mature, and thus are rendered infertile. In 1973, Karl von Frisch received the Nobel Prize in 1973 for his research on the behavior and communication of the bees. In what's called a "bee dance," the workers bees communicate to the other bees the exact distance and direction of the flowers to find the nectar.

*"And your Lord taught the Bee **to build** its cells (or hives) in hills, on trees, and in (men's) habitations: Then to eat of all the produce (of the earth), and **find with skill the spacious paths of its Lord**: there issues from within their bodies a drink of varying colors, wherein is healing for men: verily in this is a Sign for those who give thought."* 16:68–69

Chapter 16 of the Quran is named *"An-Nahl,"* meaning "The Bee." What's amazing isn't just that the Lord is ordering the bees to make colonies (common men knew that from simple observation in ancient times). The verb I bolded in the first line above ("to build") is the verb used *for females* in Arabic. That fact about the female worker bees' functions in a colony was not known until recent times. Many Muslim scholars believe the bolded phrase above refers to the bee dance.

Honey

Verses 16:68–69, mentioned above, not only refer to the female honeybee, they also make mention of honey's healing properties. Honey has been collected and used from ancient times in various capacities—as a source of nutrition, as well as embalming mummies, to its application on the wounds. Its various properties include antibacterial effects, wound healing, help with digestion, use in skin creams and lotions, calming effects, as well as antioxidant properties. It is commonly used for seasonal allergies from honeybee hives produced locally. It is also used for sore throats and coughs.

There is much interest in doing randomized, controlled trials, though only few exist today. Some have shown efficacy (e.g., in preventing catheter-associated infections in hemodialysis patients), others have not (e.g., honey-impregnated dressings for venous insufficiency ulcers). *Unfiltered*, pasteurized honey has been used to treat seasonal allergies, though one small study using *filtered* honey failed to show benefit in oculonasal allergies. Honey has been used since ancient times, but its antibacterial, antiseptic, and antioxidant effects have been more recently come to light. Though Western medical experts feel more research is needed to show the effectiveness of honey, many folk medicine practitioners are already convinced of its uses to heal various ailments.

A recent study titled, "Honey for wound healing, ulcers, and burns; data supporting its use in clinical practice," concluded, "The data presented here demonstrate that honey from different geographical areas have considerable therapeutic effects on chronic wounds, ulcers, and burns. The results encourage the use of honey in clinical practice as a natural and safe wound healer."[29]

---

29 N. Al-Waili, K. Salom, A. Al-Ghamdi, *Scientific World Journal*, April 5, 2011, 11:766–87.

It should be pointed out that honey's mention as a healing agent is not unique to the Quran. It is also mentioned in the Bible (*"My son, eat honey, for it is good, Yes, the honey from the comb is sweet to your taste." Proverbs 24:13*) and other scriptures. Ayurveda, an ancient Indian modality, has also used honey for various ailments for over four thousand years.

Cattle Made for the Benefit of Man

"And cattle He has created for you (men): from them you derive warmth, and numerous benefits, and of their (meat) you eat. And you have a sense of pride and beauty in them as you drive them home in the evening, and as you lead them forth to pasture in the morning. And they carry your heavy loads to lands that you could not (otherwise) reach except with souls distressed: for your Lord is indeed Most Kind, Most Merciful, And (He has created) horses, mules, and donkeys, for you to ride and use for show; and He has created (other) things of which you have no knowledge." 16:5–8

This verse is not intended to introduce us to the signs of God as much as a reminder to give thanks. In other verses, the Quran reminds readers that it's God who made them subservient to us.

In addition to the verses noted above, the Quran speaks about the flimsiness of spider webs (29:41) and mentions how ants talk to and communicate with each other (27:17–18). It wasn't until recently that we learned about the sophisticated life style, organization, and communication skills of ants. In fact, there are chapters named after them (chapter 27, *An-Naml,* or "The Ant," and chapter 29, *Al Ankaboot,* or "The Spider").

Plant Kingdom/Botany

Reproduction in the Plant Kingdom

Christian Konrad Sprengel, a German botanist, is credited with discovering plant sexuality; in 1793, he initially described pollination. There are two methods of plant reproduction. One asexual, the other is sexual. Sexual reproduction in the plant kingdom is carried out by the coupling of the male and female parts of the same (or another) plant. The Quran talks about the sexual reproduction of plant kingdom:

"He Who has made for you the earth like a carpet spread out; has enabled you to go about therein by roads (and channels); and has sent down water from the sky. With it have We produced diverse pairs of plants each separate from the others." 20:53

"You see the earth barren and lifeless, but when We pour down rain on it, it is stirred (to life), it swells, and it puts forth every kind of beautiful growth (in pairs)." 22:5. This is the last part of a verse that describes human reproduction.

It should be noted that the Arabic word used in these verses for "pairs" is *"Zauj,"* which is used variously for a couple, married couples, mates, or spouses. Thus Pickthall translates a similar verse as follows:

"And He it is Who spread out the earth and placed therein firm hills and flowing streams, and of all fruits He placed therein two spouses (male and female)." 13:3

The Fig and the Olive

The fig and the olive are mentioned in the Quran with reverence and are considered sacred trees (and fruits) in Islam. In fact, there is a chapter named *At-Tin* ("The Fig"). Figs and olives have been touted as foods with great nutritional value as well as possessing disease-preventing properties. Figs have high fiber content and are a good source of omega-3 and omega-6 fatty acids, which are shown to reduce cholesterol and prevent coronary artery disease. They also contain phytosterol, which helps eliminate cholesterol from the body. Figs also are good sources of iron, calcium, and iron.

The common fig tree and the fruit are also frequently cited in the Bible, and Genesis 3:7 describes Adam and Eve covering themselves with fig leaves. The fig fruit is also included in the list of food found in the Promised Land.

The benefits of olive and olive oil are also well documented. It is an excellent source of omega-6 fatty acids, an antioxidant, and is beneficial for cholesterol and healthy cardiovascular system, as well as for prevention of cancer. It is rich in Vitamins A, D, and K and thus helpful for bone and teeth growth. Olives are now being looked at for use as a renewable, green energy source, using waste produced from the olive plants as an energy source that produces 2.5 times the energy generated by burning the same amount of wood.

Olive trees and fruit are mentioned with respect in all religions and are mentioned in secular ancient history as well. The olive tree and olives are mentioned over thirty times in the Bible. It is one of the first plants mentioned in the Bible, and one of the most significant. For example, it was an olive leaf that a dove brought back to Noah to demonstrate that the flood was over.

The olive tree and olive oil are mentioned seven times in the Quran, and the olive is praised as a precious fruit. Chapter 95 starts with Lord's swearing, "By the fig ...," highlighting the importance of the fig and the olive:

"(I swear) By the fig and the olive." 95:1

"It is He who sends down rain from the sky: from it you drink, and out of it (grows) the vegetation on which you feed your cattle. With it He produces for you corn, olives, date-palms, grapes, and every kind of fruit: verily in this is a sign for those who give thought." 16:10–11

"Let man reflect on the food he eats. How We pour down rainwater in abundance and cleave the soil asunder. How We bring forth grain, grapes and nutritious vegetation; olives and dates, lush gardens, fruits and fodder, as a means of sustenance for you and your cattle." 80:24–32 (Malik)

These verses don't describe the virtues of the olive, the figs, and other fruits but instead invite the reader to reflect and ponder.

Creation of the Unknown

The Quran, in addition to referring to the creation of the known, refers to unknown creatures. Some Muslims believe that in these verses, the Quran is referring to microbes, which were unknown at the time of the revelation (however, microbes are likely only some of the creations unknown to man presently):

"And (He has created) horses, mules, and donkeys, for you to ride and use for show; and He has created (other) things of which you have no knowledge." 16:8

"Glory to Allah, Who created in pairs all things that the earth produces, as well as their own (human) kind and (other) things of which they have no knowledge." 36:36

The Bible on Earth, the Animals, and Plants

In general, the relationship between religion and science, and especially Christianity and science, has been hotly debated for centuries. Some scholars like Thomas Berry argue that the two are connected, whereas many others, including National Academy of Sciences (NAS), take the view that they are independent of each other, and some argue that they are at odds. NAS published a statement in 1984, and again in 1999, which stated, "Science is a particular way of knowing about the world. In science, explanations are limited to those based on observations and experiments that can be substantiated by other scientists. Explanations that cannot be based on empirical evidence are not a part of science."[30] It goes on to state that creationism should not be taught in school since it does not meet the criteria for scientific facts and evidence.

The Bible is not a science book; it merely gives pointers. The same can be said about the Quran, and though NAS did not specifically address the Quranic accounts of creation, its conclusions can be equally applied to the Quran. As mentioned earlier, Einstein, Newton, and scientists from the Islamic golden age used religion as their inspiration for scientific exploration and believed that science and religion cannot be separated.

Earth without pillars: *"God stretches the northern sky over empty space and hangs the earth on nothing."* Job 26:7

The Bible and the dinosaurs: The Bible has many references to animals, including, as some claim, the dinosaur:

"Take a look at Behemoth which I made, just as I made you. It eats grass like an ox. See its powerful loins and the muscles of its

---

30 *Science and Creationism: A View from National Academy of Sciences,* National Academy Press, 2nd edition. p. 2.

belly. Its tail is as strong as a cedar. The sinews of its thighs are knit tightly together. Its bones are tubes of bronze. Its limbs are bars of iron. It is a prime example of God's handiwork, and only its Creator can threaten it. The mountains offer it their best food, where all the wild animals play. It lies under the lotus plants, hidden by the reeds in the marsh. The lotus plants give it shade among the willows beside the stream. It is not disturbed by the raging river, not concerned when the swelling Jordan rushes around it. No one can catch it off guard or put a ring in its nose and lead it away." Job 40:15–24

This animal has been translated as elephant or another big animal, but the complete description does not fit any existing animal and most closely fits the Brachiosaurus, a dinosaur that ate plants and other vegetation and had long arms and a very long neck, which would have required enormous muscles to keep it above the ground.

Winds and the rain: Though not as elaborate as the repeated accounts in the Quran, the Bible points out that it is God who brings about the rain and orders the winds:

"God alone understands the way to wisdom; He knows where it can be found, for He looks throughout the whole earth and sees everything under the heavens. **He decided how hard the winds should blow and how much rain should fall.** *He made the laws for the rain and laid out a path for the lightning."* Job 28:23–26

The bolded portion above is translated in the King James Version as *"To make the weight for the winds; and he weigheth the waters by measure"*; the biblical commentators point out that the winds or air does have weight, and this was referred to in this verse before that became common knowledge. Also compare this to the Quranic verse on the rain falling in due measure: *"And He Who sends down water from the cloud according to a measure, then We raise to life thereby a dead country."* 43:11

The reference to the water cycle: *"All the rivers run into the sea, Yet the sea is not full. To the place from which the rivers come, There they return again."* Ecclesiastes 1:7

"For as the rain comes down, and the snow from heaven, And do not return there, But water the earth, And make it bring forth

and but that it may give seed to the sower. And bread to the eater."
Isaiah 55:10

Points to Remember

- The Quran and the Bible have numerous passages in reference to the planet earth and its inhabitants in the animal and plant kingdoms, as well as nonliving objects. The Quran speaks more specifically about some scientific phenomenon (unknown at the time) like the bee and other animal colonies and mountains being anchored like pegs. Both make reference to the water cycle, the winds, and the rain.
- The Quran, as well as the Bible, typically makes indirect references to natural phenomenon (though direct references exist). The Quran specifically asks readers to ponder over the signs for a more complete understanding.

Time to Ponder

- What's the alternate explanation for the passages in the Quran quoted in this chapter on mountains, winds, clouds, and various animals and their behavior, if one takes the critical view that these have been "stretched to fit" into the current scientific understanding? The same question applies to the biblical references.

CHAPTER 12
HUMANS AND HUMAN EMBRYOLOGY

In this chapter, the focus is mainly on human reproduction, though other aspects of human physiology will be presented as well. Though humans are directly involved in reproduction, God reminds everyone, in the form of a question to mankind, that the real Creator is Him.

"It is We Who have created you: why will you not witness the Truth? Do you then see? The (human Seed) that you throw out (emit)—Is it you who create it, or are We the Creator?" 56:57–59

In other words, human reproductive cells (sperm and ovum) join to start human development, but parents have little, if any, control over what happens next—modern technology for diagnosis and some interventions notwithstanding. The Quran and the Bible emphasize that the sequence of events is set in motion by divine orders and design.

Man Created from a Drop Emitted from Between Spine and Ribs

"Now let man but think [consider]. From what he is created! He is created from a drop emitted—Proceeding from between the back bone and the ribs." 86:5–7

In embryonic stages, the reproductive organs of the male and female (the testicles and the ovaries) begin their development near the kidney between the spinal column and rib cage. Later they descend to the pelvis (ovaries) or reach the scrotal sacs (testicles) before birth. Even in the adult after the descent of the reproductive organ, these organs receive their blood supply from the abdominal aorta, which runs near the spine. The lymphatic drainage and the venous blood go back to the same area.

Though rather indirect, many Muslims use this verse to show its relevance to the origin of the testicles during embryonic life. Critics have ruled this to be a stretch. If so, once again, one would be really challenged to come up with an alternative explanation for this verse.

In order to truly appreciate the references to human reproduction in the Quran, a basic knowledge of human embryology is needed. It must be emphasized at the outset that much of the knowledge of human reproduction started in the 1900s in very rudimentary form and was not known fully until later in the twentieth century.

- **Fertilization**: The male sperm meets the female egg (ovum), usually in the fallopian tubes of the female. The semen consists of fluid portion and sperm. A typical ejaculate consists of only few milliliters of fluid and contains about 250 million sperms, though only one is needed to fertilize the egg. (The total count, however, is an important factor determining fertility.) The sperms are produced in the testes. The fluid is produced in many areas along the way from the testes to the urinary tract: within the seminal vesicle (a gland adjacent to the prostate), the prostate, and the glands in the lining of the urinary bladder. Once fertilized by one sperm, the fertilized egg moves toward the body of the uterus.
- **Implantation:** On days five through seven, the fertilized egg attaches itself to the wall of the uterus. Implantation connections between the mother and the embryo will begin to form, including the umbilical cord.
- **Development of the embryo (embrogenesis):** The developing human is known as an embryo in the first eight weeks. After this period, the term used is "fetus." In weeks four through five, the brain and spinal cord take shape, along with the heart and circulatory system. The limb buds also appear, and organs start to develop. In weeks six through eight, muscles and nerves

are developed enough that movements start, though random and in twitches. Eyes begin to develop, and hair has started to form, along with facial features.

- **Fetal development** (weeks nine through forty): During this time, the organs and other vital structures like the brain and heart continue to grow and mature. Early on, the head makes up half the size of the fetus. The proportions start to take form toward the later part of pregnancy.

The following are examples of the verses that many Muslims use to show the Quran's references to various stages of human development:

Semen Formation

"Verily We created Man from a drop of mingled fluids." 76:2 (Emerick). Yousuf Ali translated this verse as *"Verily We created Man from a drop of mingled sperm."*

As mentioned above, the semen fluid is derived from various sources as the sperms pass up from the testes to the urinary tract before it's ejected. In prior commentaries, the mingled fluids were thought to be a reference to the fluids from the male and female during fertilization. However, modern commentators, including French physician Maurice Bucaille and the Supreme Council of Islamic Affairs in Cairo, say that the mingled fluids refer to the various sources of spermatic fluid.[31] In fact, Bucaille has dedicated a whole chapter on human reproduction in his book, *The Bible, the Quran, and Science.*

Fertilization and Implantation

Recall that only a small quantity of semen is required for successful fertilization:

*"Was he not a drop of sperm emitted (in lowly form)? Then did he become a **leech-like clot**; then did (Allah) make and fashion*

---

31 Bucaille, *The Bible, the Quran, and Science*, p. 202.

(him) in due proportion. And of him He made two sexes, male and female." 75:37–39

These verses summarize various processes:

1. Starting with a semen drop—obviously common knowledge by average men in the sixth century CE.

2. Which then develops into a leech-like mass in the process of implantation. The Arabic word used for the bolded word is *"Alaqa,"* derived from *"Al-Alaq,"* which has three meanings. One is "clot," the other is "leech," and the last one is "something that clings on." Earlier translators have used the word "clot," whereas more recent translators have used the word "leech" or "something that clings." Based on the process summarized earlier, all three translations seem appropriate. First, the early embryo does cling to the uterine wall. Second, the word "leech" seems to describe it well. The leech clings to something and sucks blood. The embryo does the same: it clings to the uterine wall and derives blood from the uterine wall. The clot is also a reasonable description in a broad sense, as the clotted blood does cling to the body parts, though it's not as accurate a description as the other two.

3. The last part of the verse goes on to describe the further development of the implanted embryo. Some critics might argue that the sequence is not consistent with development (e.g., we now know that gender is determined at fertilization and not after it has been proportioned). The counterargument is that the external reproductive organs are not identified until late first trimester or around the second trimester (when ultrasound can be used to detect the gender of the developing fetus).

"It is He Who has created you from dust then from a sperm-drop, then from a leech-like clot ['something which clings']." 40:67

"O mankind! if you have a doubt about the Resurrection, (consider) that We created you out of dust, then out of sperm, then out of a leech-like clot, then out of a morsel of flesh, partly formed

and partly unformed, in order that We may manifest (our power) to you; and We cause whom We will to rest in the wombs for an appointed term, then do We bring you out as babies, then (foster you) that you may reach your age of full strength; and some of you are called to die, and some are sent back to the feeblest old age, so that they know nothing after having known." 22:5

The above verse essentially talks about the entire life cycle, starting from the very beginning of creation (from Adam, if one believes in the creation theory), to fetal development, to old age and death. It also refers to senile dementia at the end.

Development of the Implanted Embryo

Multiple verses in the Quran refer to the development from something tiny and small and describe the development of bones, muscles, hearing, and sight, among other things. A few of them are quoted here:

"Indeed We have created man from an essence of clay, then placed him as a drop of semen in a firm resting place, then changed the semen into a leechlike mass, then leechlike mass into a fetus lump, then fetus lump into bones, then clothed the bones with flesh, and then We brought him forth as quite a different creature from the embryo—so blessed is Allah, the best of all Creators. Then after living for a while you shall all die, then most surely you shall be raised to life again on the Day of Resurrection." 23:12–16 (Shakir)

Once again, this verse refers to many stages from Adam's creation to describe the implantation and fetal development. Note that the bones are said to be formed first, then the muscles.

"He creates you in the wombs of your mothers—a creation after a creation—in triple darkness." 39:6 (Shakir)

"Triple darkness" is also translated as "three veils of darkness." (Yousuf Ali)

The above verse is believed to refer to the three walls the fetus is wrapped in: namely the maternal abdominal wall, the uterus, and the embryonic membranes. Others claim these three veils refer to three layers—endoderm, mesoderm, and ectoderm—that form the basis for all human structures. Critics have, once again, called this a stretch but without an alternate explanation for the triple darkness or veils reference.

Males Determine Baby's Gender

Until recently, it was a common belief, especially in Eastern cultures, that the mother determines the baby's gender. In fact, in some cultures, having a female baby is still considered "the mother's fault", especially when the father and the in-laws were hoping for a male baby, considered more prestigious in many cultures. Selective, gender-based abortion is still believed to occur in parts of India. It's common knowledge now that the sperm in the semen contains either X or Y chromosomes. The female egg has two X chromosomes. The offspring gets half of the chromosomes from the father and half from the mother. The resultant offspring thus is either a female (if the X chromosome from the father joins the X maternal chromosome, resulting in an XX baby) or a male (if the Y chromosome from the father joins the X maternal chromosome, resulting in an XY baby).

"That it is He who created in pairs—both male and female. From a drop of ejaculated semen." 53:45–46 (Malik)

Mother's Milk

This topic is obviously not related to human embryology but is nonetheless relevant to the subject in this chapter. In the twentieth century, artificial milk became fashionable. It was touted as good as, and sometimes better than, mother's milk. It was artificially "fortified" and thus was "new and improved" milk for newborn babies and infants. It soon became evident that mother's milk is far superior. Mother's milk not only provides necessary nutrients, it is digested more easily, helps babies fight infections better by virtue of its high immunoglobulin (antibodies) content, and also helps establish and maintain useful colon bacteria (probiotics). The other benefits include lowered risk of sudden infant death syndrome; increased intelligence; decreased likelihood of contracting middle ear infections, colds, and flu; decreased risk of asthma and eczema; and decreased dental problems. Moreover, breastfeeding also provides health benefits for the mother.

On January 15, 2011, the World Health Organization (WHO) published the following statement on breastfeeding: "WHO recommends mothers worldwide to exclusively breastfeed infants for the child's first six months to achieve optimal growth, development, and health. Thereafter, they should be given nutritious complementary foods and continue breastfeeding up to the age of two years or beyond."[32]

The Quran's advice on breastfeeding: *"The mothers shall give such [meaning suckling] to their offspring for two whole years."* 2:233

Even though this verse is in the context of a divorce and addresses the responsibilities for an infant, the recommendations are strikingly similar to our current knowledge and the WHO recommendations. Though it is likely that nursing for up to two years was relatively common knowledge in that era, its inclusion in the Quran highlights its importance and is unique to the scriptures.

The Bible and Human Development[33]

The Bible is very quiet on the subject of human embryology or development in stages. It is hard to find biblical verses on some of the specific topics mentioned above despite searching for them. The few passages that do refer to human development are of a very broad nature:

"For You formed my inward parts; You wove me in my mother's womb." Psalm 139:13

"God created man in His own image, in the image of God He created him; male and female He created them." Genesis 1:27

"Before I formed you in the womb I knew you, And before you were born I consecrated you; I have appointed you a prophet to the nations." Jeremiah 1:5 (This verse is in reference to Jeremiah)

---

32 http://www.who.int/nutrition/topics/exclusive_breastfeeding/en/.
33 All biblical translations in this chapter are from the New American Standard Bible by the Lockman Foundation.

Points to Remember

- Though far from being an embryology textbook, the Quran makes references to human development in various stages that are consistent with current knowledge. The Quran makes numerous references to developmental stages and gender determination.
- Some critics have not been impressed and claim the verses are too vague and that translators have stretched them to fit into modern scientific knowledge.

Time to Ponder

- Newborns cannot chew or digest solid food and can only ingest and digest liquids; they also have very little control on voluntary movements. However, they know how to suckle for milk at birth without any prior training. How does the evolution theory explain that?
- What starts the birthing process? How are the newborns being pushed out from the wombs? Is that a learned or evolved behavior? If so, is there some evidence that babies simply died, millions of years ago, before being born because the humans, or prehuman forms, simply did not know how to initiate this process? If they did not, how did the subsequent generations follow?

SECTION 4
THE QURAN ON
PROPHETS, SCRIPTURES,
AND PEOPLE OF THE BOOK

CHAPTER 13
THE PROPHETS

According to the Quran, Adam was the first prophet and Muhammad was the last prophet. The Quran recognizes (and commands believers to respect) all the prophets that came before Muhammad—from Adam, to Noah, to Abraham, to Moses, and Jesus, among others. The Quran mentions twenty-five prophets by name, twenty-one of whom also appear in the Bible. Although the total number of all the prophets sent down by God is not mentioned in the Quran, the Muslims believe, through Hadith, that God sent down 124,000 prophets in all.

"Of some messengers We have already told you the story; of others We have not; And to Moses Allah spoke direct." 4:164

"We did aforetime send messengers before you [meaning Muhammad]: of them there are some whose story We have related to you, and some whose story We have not related to you. It was not (possible) for any messenger to bring a sign except by the leave of Allah." 40:78

There are various words for prophets, which are often used interchangeably, but they have different connotations.

***Nabi* or Prophet**: In both Arabic and Hebrew, the word "*Nabi*" means a prophet (pronounced in Hebrew as "nâbîy," or *navi*). A prophet is chosen by God and receives divine inspirations from Him about theological and other teachings and then relays it to his nation. The noun *Nabi*, in its various forms, occurs seventy-five times in the Quran. The second subdivision of the Hebrew Bible, Tanakh (which stands for "Torah, Nevi'im, Ketuvim"), is devoted to the Hebrew prophets. *Navi* is derived from the term *niv safatayim*, meaning fruit of the lips, indicating the emphasis on speaking (on God's behalf).

Rasool (also spelled *Rasul*) is often translated as "apostle" by some Quran translators; it literally means "messenger." A *Rasool* is a prophet who brings a set of divine law or jurisprudence (*Sharia*) and is also given a scripture (e.g., the Torah, the Psalms, the Gospel, or the Quran). The word *Rasool* occurs more than three hundred times in the Quran. The term "apostle" in Christianity, however, is not used for prophets but rather for the original disciples of Jesus Christ sent out to various lands to convey his teachings. Abraham, Moses, David, Jesus Christ, and Mohammad are all considered God's messengers.

It is therefore important to understand that according to Islamic traditions, all apostles/messengers (*Rasools*) were prophets but not all prophets were apostles/messengers.

All monotheistic faiths concur that only God can choose the prophets. According to the Quran, the basic message and teachings as well as the warnings of *all* the prophets were the same: That there is only One God, and He is the only one worthy of worship. Moreover, most Islamic traditions hold the view that all prophets were *"Masum,"* meaning innocent, pure, and without sins. Still others believe the prophets had some flaws and may have committed minor mistakes but nonetheless lived without committing *major* sins.

Prophets in the Christian Bible: In Christianity, the prophets are inspired by God through the Holy Spirit to deliver specific messages. They delivered the truth about God and also warned their people of God's wrath for disobedience. Prophets are recognized to be human and fallible; they may make wrong decisions, have incorrect personal beliefs or opinions, or sin from time to time. Their hearing of God's revelation does not remove all their humanity or perfect them, nor did they always want to deliver the messages they had received. Though various prophets are mentioned in many books of the Bible (Judges, Samuel, Job, Psalms, etc.), the Christian Bible has a set of books on prophets, termed Major Prophets (Isaiah, Jeremiah, Lamentations of Jeremiah, Ezekiel, and Daniel) and Minor Prophets (twelve of them, from Hosea to Malachi). The terms "major" and "minor" are based on the length of the books, not the importance of the prophet. They are all part of the Old Testament portion of the Christian Bible.

Prophets in the Hebrew Bible: The Hebrew Bible ends before the Gospel of Matthew of the New Testament, as arranged in the Christian Bible. Like the Christian Bible, the prophets are mentioned in many places in the Old Testament, though there are books dedicated to the prophets and their stories. The Books of Prophets include "The Former Prophets" (Joshua, Judges, Samuel, and Kings), the "Latter Prophets" (Isaiah, Jeremiah, and Ezekiel), and "The Twelve" (which are the same as the Christian Minor Prophets).

There are fifty-five prophets of Israel named in the Hebrew Bible, or Tanakh (not recognizing Jesus and Muhammad as prophets). Nevi'im (Prophets) is a major section of the Hebrew Bible and deals with the stories of prophets; it falls between the Torah (Law) and the Ketuvim (Writings). However, many other books of the Hebrew Bible narrate stories of other prophets (Abraham, Isaac, Jacob, and Moses in the Torah, for example; the book of Daniel is considered part of the Ketuvim). A Jewish tradition suggests that there were twice as many prophets as the number of Israelites who left Egypt, which would make 1.2 million prophets, far more than the traditional Islamic belief. The Talmud is a central text of mainstream Judaism, from a record of rabbinic discussions pertaining to Jewish law, ethics, and customs. It recognizes the existence of forty-eight male prophets, who gave permanent messages to mankind. According to the Talmud, there were also seven women prophets, whose message bears relevance for all generations: Sarah (wife of Abraham), Miriam (sister of Moses and Aaron), Deborah (wife of Lapidoth), Hannah (mother of the Prophet Samuel), Abigail (a wife of King David), Huldah (from the time of Jeremiah), and Esther (a queen of Persia, raised by her cousin, Mordecai).

The Belief in Prophets

In addition to belief in One God, the Quran demands belief in all prophets. The Quran recognizes all "Hebrew" prophets, as well as prophets who came before and after, and of course Prophet Muhammad, who the Quran often refers to as the "seal of the prophets," meaning the last of the prophets.

"Say: We believe in God, and in that which has been bestowed from on high upon us, and that which has been bestowed upon Abraham and Ishmael and Isaac and Jacob and, their descendants, and that which has been vouchsafed (given) to Moses and Jesus; and that which has been vouchsafed to all the (other) prophets by their Sustainer: we make no distinction between any of them. And it is unto Him that we surrender [submit] ourselves." 2:136 (Asad)

Pooya Yazdi writes in his commentary of this verse, "The religion of Islam is universal, for all people, in every age. Therefore, it is necessary for every follower of Islam to believe in all the prophets and messengers of Allah and in what was revealed to them. No other religion besides Islam demands from its followers to believe equally in the sinless purity of the conduct and character of other prophets of Allah, and in the truthfulness of other sacred scriptures as the revealed words of Allah."

Named prophets in the Quran: The following is a list of the twenty-five prophets named in the Quran. The Quranic names are used here, with the English names in parenthesis. The names that do not appear in the Bible are mentioned by their Quranic names only:

- Adam (Adam)
- Idris (Enoch)
- Nuh (Noah)
- Houd
- Saalih
- Ibrahim (Abraham)
- Isma'il (Ishmael)
- Ishaq (Issac)
- Lut (Lot)
- Yaqub, or Israel (Jacob)
- Yousuf (Joseph)
- Shu'aib
- Ayub (Job)
- Musa (Moses)
- Haroon (Aaron)
- Dhul-Kifl (Ezekiel)

- Dawood (David)
- Sulaiman (Solomon)
- Ilyas (Elijah or Elyas)
- Al-Yasa (Elisha)
- Younus (Jonah)
- Zakariyya (Zachariah)
- Yahya (John the Baptist)
- Isa (Jesus)
- Muhammad

The following verses alone mention seventeen prophets by name, and Prophet Muhammad is addressed without naming him at the end.

"That was the reasoning about Us, which We gave to Abraham (to use) against his people: We raise whom We will, degree after degree: for your Lord is full of wisdom and knowledge. We gave him Isaac and Jacob: all (three) guided: and before him, We guided Noah, and among his [meaning Abraham's] progeny, David, Solomon, Job, Joseph, Moses, and Aaron: thus do We reward those who do good: And Zechariah and John, and Jesus and Elias: all in the ranks of the righteous: And Ishmael and Elisha, and Jonas, and Lot: and to all We gave favor above the nations: (To them) and to their fathers, and progeny and brethren: We chose them, and we guided them to a straight way. This is the guidance of Allah: He gives that guidance to whom He pleases, of His worshippers. If they were to join other gods with Him, all that they did would be vain for them. These were the men to whom We gave the Book, and authority, and prophethood: if these (their descendants) reject them, Behold! We shall entrust their charge to a new people who reject them not. Those were the (prophets) who received Allah's guidance: Copy [follow] the guidance they received; Say [addressing Muhammad]: No reward for this do I ask of you. This is no less than a message for the nations." 6:83–90

The exalted prophets (*"Ulul Azm Ambia"*): Even though Muslims are asked to respect and recognize all prophets, some are given preferences over the others. There are five messengers, traditionally considered *"Ulul Azm,"* or exalted prophets. They are Prophets Noah, Abraham, Moses, Jesus, and Muhammad.

"Allah did choose Adam and Noah, the family of Abraham, and the family of Imran above all people." 3:33

Imran is considered the father of Mary and *"Al-e Imran,"* or the "family of Imran," include Mary and Jesus. In another family tree, and commentary by Pooya, Imran is shown as the father of Moses and Aaron.

"And it is your Lord that knows best all beings that are in the heavens and on earth: We did bestow on some prophets more (and other) gifts than on others: and We gave to David (the gift of) the Psalms." 17:55

"These are the Signs [rvelations] of Allah: we rehearse them to you [meaning Muhammad] in truth: verily you are one of the messengers. Those (some) messengers We endowed with gifts, some above others: To one of them Allah spoke; others He raised to degrees (of honor); to Jesus, the son of Mary We gave clear (Signs), and strengthened him with the holy spirit." 2:252–253

Though David is not mentioned by Muslim scholars as one of the *"Ulul Azm,"* or exalted prophets, his name is mentioned among the "preferred prophet" in verse 17:55 quoted above.

The Purpose of Sending the Prophets

As mentioned in chapter 8 under "Glad Tidings and Warnings," the purpose of sending all prophets according to the Quran was the same: to teach their people that there is One God, and no one else is worthy of worship. The prophets served two basic purposes. They were warners and bearers of glad tidings.

"Not a messenger did We send before you without this inspiration sent by Us to him: that there is no god but I; therefore worship and serve Me." 21:25

"(We sent) messengers who gave good news as well as warning, that mankind, after (the coming) of the messengers, should have no plea against Allah: For Allah is Exalted in Power, Wise." 4:165

God chose the prophets from within the same communities, who spoke their own language. The purpose was to make it easy on the people to understand the clear message.

"We sent not a messenger except (to teach) in the language of his (own) people, in order to make (things) clear to them." 14:4

Every community received a messenger: The Quran also mentions that the messengers were sent to guide every nation or community.

"To every people (was sent) a messenger: when their messenger comes (before them), the matter will be judged between them with justice, and they will not be wronged." 10:47

"Verily We have sent you in truth, as a bearer of glad tidings, and as a warner: and there never was a people, without a warner having lived among them (in the past)." 35:24

"For We assuredly sent amongst every People a messenger, (with the Command), "Serve Allah, and eschew [shun] evil."" 16:36 (Pickthall translated the bolded word as "false gods.")

God took covenant from all prophets: The Old Testament (as well as the Quran) refers to the well-chronicled covenant from Prophet Abraham and Israelites. Additionally, the Quran makes several references to the covenants from all prophets to carry out their mission of proclaiming the truth and passing out the message from God to their people.

"And remember We took from the prophets their covenant: As (We did) from you [referring to Muhammad]: from Noah, Abraham, Moses, and Jesus the son of Mary: We took from them a solemn covenant." 33:7

Obeying messengers is obeying God: Because the messengers simply were passing on the commandments from God, obeying them is tantamount to obeying God.

"He who obeys the Messenger [meaning Muhammad], obeys Allah." 4:80

"Obey Allah, and obey the Messenger, and beware (of evil)." 5:92

Some of the messengers and the prophets will be discussed in more detail in the chapters that follow.

Points to Remember

- The Quran instructs followers to recognize and respect all prophets. Among the prophets, in Islam, there are five exalted ones (*Ulul Azam*): Prophets Noah, Abraham, Moses, Jesus Christ, and Muhammad.

- The Quran mentions twenty-five prophets by name. The Hebrew Bible names fifty-five prophets.
- The basic purpose of all the prophets, from Adam to Muhammad, was the same: to give the singular message about One God and to worship Him only, to warn people of the consequences for nonbelief and bad deeds, and to give glad tidings to those who believe and do good deeds.

Time to Ponder

- Why did God have to send 124,000 prophets (according to Muslim belief), or over a million prophets (according to Jewish traditions)? What if He had stopped after sending a few? Conversely, why did He stop sending prophets after Muhammad (according to Muslims), Jesus (according to Christians), and Malachi (believed to be the last of the Hebrew prophets)?
- Did the prophets give different messages (or "religions") to their communities? If one believes that, then how can one reconcile varying religions coming from the same God?

CHAPTER 14
ADAM AND NOAH

"Allah did choose Adam and Noah, the family of Abraham, and the family of 'Imran above all people." 3:33

Adam was the first man God created, according to the Quran and the Bible. He was also the first prophet. The basic story of creation of Prophet Adam is fairly similar in the Quran and the Bible, though there are some differences, as outlined later in this chapter. The story of Adam is mentioned in four different chapters of the Quran. The Quran speaks of the creation of Adam from clay and that God then inspired the body of Adam with "holy spirit" to give him life. He then created Eve. Both lived in heaven and were forbidden to eat from "that tree." God gathered all the angels and the *Jinns*, including Satan (*Shaitan* or *Iblees*, as he is called with this specific name in the Quran), and then God asked everyone to prostrate to Adam. Jinns are known by Muslims to be one of the creations of God, believed to be created from "the fire of scorching wind, or intensely hot fire." (15:27) Jinns, like humans, have free will but are invisible to humans. The assembly of the angels and the Jinns obeyed God's order except Satan, as he became arrogant and cited his superiority for being made from fire, rather than from clay. The early part of chapter 2 of the Quran refers to the creation of Adam, and his eventual expulsion from paradise, which is mentioned in a fairly long set of verses (2:30–39), quoted earlier in the introduction of this book.

In another verse, God addresses mankind as "children of Adam" and warns them of the seductive powers of Satan.

"O you Children of Adam! Let not Satan seduce you, in the same manner as He got your parents out of the Garden, stripping them of

their raiment, to expose their shame: for he and his tribe watch you from a position where you cannot see them." 7:27

Though not mentioned in the Quran, Muslims believe that Adam and Eve were sent down to the earth, at a place currently known as Mecca, Saudi Arabia: Adam on the mountain *Safa*, and Eve arrived on mountain *Marwa*. These are two most famous hills in Mecca, near Kaaba, the holiest Islamic shrine. Adam and Eve are said to have wept for forty years in repentance for their disobedience, until their repentance was accepted by God, at which time God sent them the Black Stone, which is considered by Muslims to be a piece of rock from heaven. It is a part of one of the corners of Kaaba. It is believed that at this time, God taught Adam the initial rituals of Hajj around Kaaba, which is covered in more detail in chapter 23, "Pillars of Islam."

Variations in Quranic and Biblical Accounts[34]

Most of the story of Adam and Eve, from the creation from clay, to the temptation and deceit of Satan, to their expulsion from heaven and Satan being cursed eternally, are similar in both the Bible and the Quran. There are, however, some differences in the two accounts, and though the focus of this book is to highlight the similarities, it would be counterintuitive to completely ignore the differences; a few of them are listed below.

- In the Bible, Eve was created from Adam's ribs.

  "The LORD God fashioned into a woman the rib which He had taken from the man, and brought her to the man. The man said, 'This is now bone of my bones, And flesh of my flesh; She shall be called Woman, because she was taken out of Man.'" Genesis 2:22–23

  Some biblical scholars feel this was metaphoric and meant Eve was created side by side with Adam.

  The Quran does not specifically contradict the biblical account of Eve's creation from Adam's ribs but refers to the

---

34 All biblical translations in this chapter are from the New American Standard Bible by the Lockman Foundation.

creation of "its mate of the same" in verse 4:1. *"O people! Be careful of (your duty to) your Lord, Who created you from a single being and created its mate of the same (kind) and spread from these two, many men and women."* (Shakir)

- The Bible states Adam's age. He lived for nine hundred and thirty years (Genesis 5:5). The Quran makes no mention of Adam's lifespan on earth.

- The Quran states Satan deceived both Adam and Eve and seems to put the blame equally on both of them for disobeying. The Bible states that the serpent (who was Satan in the form of a serpent) tempted Eve into eating the forbidden fruit, and she in turn asked Adam to eat it. *"But from the fruit of the tree which is in the middle of the garden, God has said, 'You shall not eat from it or touch it, or you will die.' The serpent said to the woman, 'You surely will not die! For God knows that in the day you eat from it your eyes will be opened, and you will be like God, knowing good and evil.' When the woman saw that the tree was good for food, and that it was a delight to the eyes, and that the tree was desirable to make one wise, she took from its fruit and ate; and she gave also to her husband with her, and he ate.'"* (Genesis 3:3–6) This made God angry at the serpent, Eve, and Adam. The serpent for deceiving Eve, Eve for getting deceived and disobeying God, and Adam for listening to Eve and disobeying God. *"Then the LORD God said to the woman, 'What is this you have done?' And the woman said, 'The serpent deceived me, and I ate.' The LORD God said to the serpent, 'Because you have done this, Cursed are you more than all cattle, And more than every beast of the field; On your belly you will go, And dust you will eat All the days of your life; And I will put enmity Between you and the woman, And between your seed and her seed; He shall bruise you on the head, And you shall bruise him on the heel.' To the woman He said, 'I will greatly multiply your pain in childbirth, In pain you will bring forth children; Yet your desire will be for your husband, And he will rule over you.' Then to Adam He said, 'Because you have listened to the voice of your wife, and have eaten from the tree about which I commanded you, saying, 'You shall not eat from it'; Cursed is the ground because of you; In toil you will eat of it All the days of your life.'"* Genesis 3:13–17

- As noted above, in the Quran, God informed the angels and the Jinns that he is creating a vicegerent on earth and asked the angels and the Jinns to prostrate to Adam. Satan refused. The Bible makes no such references.

The Lessons in Adam's Story

Many Quranic and biblical scholars have drawn their take-home message from Adam's story as told in the Quran and the Bible, which can be summarized as follows:

The man is a viceroy of God on earth. God created Adam and Eve, told them to live in the beautiful gardens in heaven, where they were spiritually pure and innocent, until they sinned and disobeyed God as they succumbed to the temptations by Satan. The humans, too, are pure, when they are born. They can stay pure or succumb to the temptations. Just like Adam and Eve had to face the consequences of their actions, so will the rest of mankind. Satan was one of God's most ardent worshippers until he refused to prostrate to Adam out of his arrogance, and he became a subject of God's wrath and anger. The Quran and the Bible repeatedly instruct man to avoid arrogance and teach humility.

Noah (Nuh, Noach)

The Quran does not specify the lineage of Prophet Noah, like the Old Testament does. As mentioned earlier, Noah is considered one of the exalted prophets in the Quran, who received inspirations from God and preached to his people, who remained sinful and extreme in transgression and remained unrepentant, which eventually led God to punish them with the famous deluge.

The Quran mentions Noah and his story many times, and chapter 71 is named after him (*Nuh*, or "Noah"). Chapter 71 contains twenty-eight verses and is entirely dedicated to the story of Noah, a rarity in the Quran. The chapter refers to the sinful nature of the people of Noah and names the idols they used to worship (*Wadd, Suwa, Yaghut, Yaüq,* and *Nasr*). According to the commentary by Pooya Yazdi, these five false gods represented the following:

Name	Shape	Quality represented
Wadd	Manly	Powers
Suwa	Woman(ly)	Beauty
Yaghut	Lion (or Bull)	Brute strength
Yaüq	Horse	Swiftness
Nasr	Eagle (or Falcon)	Insight

Noah's story is not limited to chapter 71; it is spread throughout the Quran. The story is well summarized in the following five verses of chapter 7, *Al-A'raaf* ("The Heights").

"We sent Noah to his people. He said: 'O my people! Worship Allah! you have no other god but Him. I fear for you the punishment of a dreadful day!' The leaders of his people said: 'Ah! we see you evidently wandering (in mind).' He said: 'O my people! No wandering is there in my (mind): on the contrary I am a messenger from the Lord and Cherisher of the worlds! I but fulfill toward you the duties of my Lord's mission: Sincere is my advice to you, and I know from Allah something that you know not. Do you wonder that there has come to you a message from your Lord, through a man of your own people, to warn you, so that you may fear Allah and haply receive His Mercy?' But they rejected him, and We delivered him, and those with him, in the Ark: but We overwhelmed in the flood those who rejected Our signs. They were indeed a blind people!'" 7:59–64

Noah builds the ark: *"And it was revealed to Noah: 'None of your people will believe now, other than those who have already believed. So do not grieve at their evil deeds. Build an ark under Our supervision in accordance with Our revelation, and beware not to plead with Me on behalf of those who are wrongdoers: for they are all to be drowned in the flood.' So he started to build the ark; and whenever the chiefs of his people passed by him they laughed at him. He said: 'Laugh at us now if you will, soon the time is going to* come when we too will laugh at you as you are laughing at us. Soon you will come to know who will be seized by a humiliating scourge, and who is afflicted with everlasting punishment.' Finally when Our Command came and the water from Al-Tannūr (the fountains of the earth) gushed forth! We said to Noah: 'Take into the Ark a pair from every species, your family—except those against whom the Word has already gone forth—and the believers and those who believed with him were only a few.' Thus he said: 'Embark in it, in the name of Allah in whose hands is its sailing and its stopping; surely my Lord is Forgiving, Merciful.'" 11:36–41 (Malik)

And on one of the rare occasions, the Quran does give specific information about a prophet's time or age, and according to this verse, Noah lived for nine hundred and fifty years:

"We sent Noah to his people and he lived among them a thousand years less fifty." 29:14

Variations in the Quranic and Biblical Accounts

While the story of Noah by and large is similar in both the Quran and the Bible, there are some differences. Both talk about Noah being a righteous person and a messenger of God. ("These are the records of the generations of Noah. Noah was a righteous man, blameless in his time; Noah walked with God." Genesis 6:9) Both talk about his people ridiculing him when he was building the ark, God's ordering Noah to include all animals in pairs (one male and one female from each species), and the deluge.

- The Bible names three sons of Noah. The Quran does not.

- The Quran mentions the son of Noah who did not take heed and was among those left behind and died in the floods. The Bible states the three sons and their wives accompanied him on the boat.

  "As the ark floated with them on board over the mountainous waves and Noah called out to his son, who stood apart: 'O my son! Embark with us and be not with the unbelievers! He replied: 'I will take refuge on some mountain, which will *save me from the flood.' Noah said: 'None shall be secure today from the judgment of God, except the one on whom He has mercy!' And thereupon a wave came between them and he (Noah's son) became among one of those who drowned."* 11:42–43

"But I will establish My covenant with you; and you shall enter the ark—you and your sons and your wife, and your sons' wives with you." Genesis 6:18

- The Quran states Noah's wife was also among the ones left behind, and was not among the righteous: *"For those who are bent on denying the truth God has propounded a parable in (the stories of) Noah's wife and Lot's wife: they were wedded to two of Our righteous servants, and each one betrayed her husband; and neither of the two (husbands) will be of any avail to these two women when they are told (on Judgment Day), 'Enter the fire with all those (other sinners) who enter it!'"* 66:10 (Malik)

- According to the Quran, the ark came to rest on Mount Judi. The Bible states it came to rest on Mount Ararat. The Al-joudi (Judaea) is a mount in the biblical range of Ararat. The Quran cites a particular mount in the Ararat Range, and the Bible mentions the Ararat Range. Judaea is still present in the Ararat Range in Turkey, so perhaps they are both talking about the same area. Moreover, the Bible gave a specific time the ark was afloat for (the duration of the flood), as noted here:

"Then the word went forth: 'O earth! Swallow up thy water, and O sky! Withhold (your rain)!' and the water abated, and the matter was ended. The Ark rested on Mount Judi, and the word went forth: 'Away with those who do wrong!'" 11:44

"In the seventh month, on the seventeenth day of the month, the ark rested upon the mountains of Ararat." Genesis 8:4 (Some translations have put this number at "exactly one hundred

and fifty days" or five months: New Living Translation and New Century Version.)

- The Bible gives very detailed instructions about the ark, as well as about the duration and timings of the great flood. The Quran does not mention the dimensions.

"This is how you shall make it: the length of the ark three hundred cubits, its breadth fifty cubits, and its height thirty cubits. You shall make a window for the ark, and finish it to a cubit from the top; and set the door of the ark in the side of it; you shall make it with lower, second, and third decks." Genesis 6:15–16

One cubit is 1.5 feet, and many translations have used the measurements in feet. This would come out to be about one and half the length of a US football field and about five stories tall.

- Noah getting drunk: According to the Bible, Noah started to drink and lay naked. The Quran (as well as the Bible) considers drunkenness a sin and regards the prophets, especially an exalted prophet like Noah, as sinless: *"Then Noah began farming and planted a vineyard. He drank of the wine and became drunk, and uncovered himself inside his tent. Ham, the father of Canaan, saw the nakedness of his father, and told his two brothers outside. But Shem and Japheth took a garment and laid it upon both their shoulders and walked backward and covered the nakedness of their father; and their faces were turned away, so that they did not see their father's nakedness."* Genesis 9:20–23

Despite these differences, the moral of Noah's story is essentially the same in both Genesis (Old Testament—the Torah) and the Quran. They both outline Noah's righteous character and prophetic teachings. Only those who were on the ark survived, including animal species. The rest of the people drowned and were killed for their transgressions. Noah carried on humankind upon his return to dry land. Noah is thus referred to in Islamic traditions as *"Adam-e-Saani,"* or "Second Adam," as he was literally the father of mankind that survived the great flood.

Points to Remember

- The basic story of Adam and Eve is similar in the Quran and the Bible. Adam was the first human created. Eve was the first woman created. They were tempted by Satan and were expelled from paradise for disobeying God, though God accepted their repentance.
- The basic story of Noah is also fairly similar in the Quran and the Bible, who was a righteous person and one of the exalted and sinless prophets in the Quran. The Bible also calls him righteous and "blameless," but subsequently also talks about his drunkenness.

Time to Ponder

- Satan (*Iblees*) was a believer (in God, paradise, angels, etc.) and was one of the most devout worshippers of God until he disobeyed God's orders after creation of Adam. As a result, he was expelled from paradise and cursed forever. Why did he disobey, and what lessons can one draw from the story?

CHAPTER 15
ABRAHAM: THE FATHER OF MONOTHEISTIC RELIGIONS

This chapter pertains to the stories of the patriarchs of the monotheistic religions: Abraham, Isaac, and Jacob, as well as Ishmael and Joseph, as told in the Quran and the Bible. The story of Abraham is reviewed first.

Abraham (Avraham or Avaram in Hebrew), or *Ibrahim*, as he is known in the Quran, is highly revered and an exalted prophet according to the Quran and is the second most-mentioned prophet (sixty-nine times) after Moses. There is a chapter named *Ibrahim* after him (chapter 14). Prophet Abraham is considered the father of the monotheistic religions: Judaism, Christianity, and Islam. However, both the Quranic and biblical commentators point out that he was not the "pioneer" of the concept of monotheism, which had preceded Abraham. The Quran does not relate Abraham's genealogy, but according to the biblical accounts, he was the tenth generation from Noah. The Quran talks about God's covenant with Abraham with a promise to exalt his descendants. Abraham and his first son, Ishmael (*Ismail*), built Ka'aba, the cubical structure in Mecca, considered the holiest shrine in Islam. The Quran also narrates the sacrifice of his son as a test, which Abraham passed with flying colors, and God promised him an exalted status, as well as exalted his descendants. The sacrifice alone was of course not the only reason for his exalted status.

"Abraham was indeed a model, devoutly obedient to Allah, (and) true in Faith, and he joined not gods with Allah: He showed his gratitude for the favors of Allah, who chose him, and guided him

to a Straight Way. And We gave him Good in this world, and he will be, in the Hereafter, in the ranks of the Righteous." 16:120–122

God honors Abraham by calling him His friend: God gives Abraham one of the highest honors a human can have, by calling him a friend, hence his nickname in Arabic, *"Khaleelal Allah,"* meaning "the friend of God."

"Who can be better in religion than one who submits his whole self to Allah, does good, and follows the way of Abraham—the true in Faith? For Allah did take Abraham for a friend." 4:125

Brief Life History

Most biblical commentators agree that Abraham was born in a city called Ur, in the present country of Iraq. Abraham's first wife Sarah had borne him no children. She had a handmaid whose name was Hagar (*Hajirah*). In their old age, having no hope for children from herself, she gave her permission to Abraham to take Hagar as a wife, in order to have children and maintain his progeny. From this marriage, they had a son named Ishmael, who became a source of friction between Hagar and Sarah. The peace and harmony of the family was disturbed. Sarah asked Abraham to send them away. Abraham sought God's help and was directed to send away Hagar and Ishmael to a place currently known as Mecca. They stopped at a place where Ka'aba now stands. Islamic traditions hold that Archangel Gabriel informed Abraham that it was a land full of God's blessings and bounties, and there used to be a house (known as *baytul mamur)* in that place, which was held sacred and venerated by mankind in ancient times, and that it was God's will that Abraham and Ishmael should rebuild the ruined house again, which they eventually did. As Abraham was leaving them on his way back to his native land, he said a prayer:

"O our Lord! I have made some of my offspring to dwell in a valley without cultivation, by Your Sacred House; in order, O our Lord, that they may establish regular Prayer: so fill the hearts of some among men with love toward them, and feed them with fruits: so that they may give thanks." 14:37

Soon Hagar and the very young Ishmael ran out of water and lay on the desert sand, crying in thirst while Hagar ran back and forth between the mountains of *Safa* and *Marwa*. When she was at *Safa*, she saw water in the direction of *Marwa*—a mirage. Upon reaching *Marwa*, she looked back and once again saw the same in the direction of *Safa*. She ran back and forth seven times in search of water. God showed mercy on them, and a spring of fresh and sweet water gushed forth from the earth under the feet of Ishmael, from a well that came to be known as *Zamzam*. The word is derived from the word *Zome*, meaning "stop", named after Hagar's telling the gushing water to stop when she saw water that kept gushing forth and wouldn't stop. This well is still present in the Grand Mosque of Ka'aba and is considered holy water by Muslims around the world. Moreover, the pilgrims performing Muslim Hajj are required to walk between *Safa* and *Marwa* seven times to honor the memory of Hagar and Ishmael.

Though a common belief among Muslims, the Zamzam well is not mentioned, or even referred to, in the Quran. Interestingly, though, it is recorded in the Old Testament, in the book of Genesis chapter 21. This will be reviewed in more detail later in this chapter, under "Ishmael in the Bible."

The flow of water increased day by day, and the surrounding land became fertile. People began to come and settle there. Soon it became a flourishing town. When Abraham returned, he found the wasteland in the desert a busy trade center.

Abraham's attempted sacrifice of his son, Ishmael (and passing the test): Though the name Ishmael is not mentioned in the verse, Muslims commonly believe the son Abraham attempted to sacrifice was Ishmael, and not Isaac as mentioned in Genesis. They point out the verse after the sacrifice, where God gives him the good news about another righteous son, Isaac.

"(Abraham) said: 'I am going to take refuge with my Lord, He will surely guide me. O Lord! Grant me a righteous son.' So We gave him the good news of a gentle son. When he reached the age to work with him, (Abraham) said to him: 'O my son! I have seen a vision that I should offer you as a sacrifice, now tell me what is your view.' He replied: 'O my father! Do as you are commanded: you will find me, if Allah so wills, of the patient.'

And when they both submitted to Allah and (Abraham) laid down his son prostrate upon his forehead for sacrifice; We called out to him: 'O Abraham stop! You have fulfilled your vision.' Thus do We reward the righteous. That was indeed a manifest test. We ransomed his son for a great sacrifice and We left his good name among the later generations. Salutation (and peace) to Abraham. Thus We reward the righteous. Surely he was one of Our believing devotees. We gave him the good news of Isaac —a prophet—one of the righteous." 37:99–112

Abraham and Ishmael build Ka'aba with a prayer: Upon his return to Mecca, and when Ishmael grew older, the father and the son built Ka'aba at the ancient site, where many Muslim scholars believe Adam built the original house of worship.

"And remember Abraham and Ishmael raised the foundations of the House (With this prayer): Our Lord! Accept (this service) from us: For You are the All-Hearing, the All-knowing." 2:127

In another set of verses, the Quran mentions Abraham's prayers:

"Remember Abraham said: 'O my Lord! make this city one of peace and security: and preserve me and my sons from worshipping idols.

"'O my Lord! they have indeed led astray many among mankind; He then who follows my (ways) is of me, and he that disobeys me, but You are indeed Oft-forgiving, Most Merciful.

"'O our Lord! I have made some of my offspring to dwell in a valley without cultivation, by Your Sacred House; in order, O our Lord, that they may establish regular Prayer: so fill the hearts of some among men with love toward them, and feed them with fruits: so that they may give thanks.

"'O our Lord! truly You do know what we conceal and what we reveal: for nothing whatever is hidden from Allah, whether on earth or in heaven. Praise be to Allah, Who hath granted unto me in old age Ishmael and Isaac: for truly my Lord is He, the Hearer of Prayer!

"'O my Lord! make me one who establishes regular Prayer, and also (raise such) among my offspring O our Lord! and accept You my Prayer.'

"'O our Lord! cover (us) with Your forgiveness—me, my parents, and (all) Believers, on the Day that the Reckoning will be established!'" 14:35–41

Abraham Not a Jew or a Christian

The Quran addresses the dispute among people whether Abraham was a "Jew," a "Christian," or a "Muslim."

"People of the Book! Why dispute you about Abraham, when the Law [Torah] and the Gospel were not revealed till after him?" 3:65

It further goes on to say:

Ibrahim was not a Jew nor a Christian but he was (an) upright (man), a Muslim [submitter], and he was not one of the polytheists. Most surely the nearest of people to Ibrahim are those who followed him and this Prophet [Muhammad] and those who believe. And Allah is the guardian of the believers." 3:67–68 (Shakir)

God Shows Abraham a Miracle from Dead Birds

The Quran narrates a story when Abraham asked God to show how He will bring life to the dead:

"When Abraham said: 'Show me, Lord, how You will raise the dead,' He replied: 'Have you no faith?' He said 'Yes, but just to reassure my heart.' Allah said, 'Take four birds, draw them to you, and cut their bodies to pieces. Scatter them over the mountaintops, then call them back. They will come swiftly to you. Know that Allah is Mighty, Wise.'" 2:260

A similar story is told in Genesis, except there are multiple animals, rather than four birds; and it is not in reference to God's giving life to the dead. It ends somewhat abruptly as Abraham falls asleep.

"And Abram [Abraham's birth name] believed the LORD, and the LORD counted him as righteous because of his faith. Then the LORD told him, 'I am the LORD who brought you out of Ur of the Chaldeans to give you this land as your possession.' But Abram replied, 'O Sovereign LORD, how can I be sure that I will actually possess it?' The LORD told him, 'Bring me a three-year-old heifer, a three-year-old female goat, a three-year-old ram, a turtledove, and a young pigeon.' So Abram presented all these to him and killed

them. Then he cut each animal down the middle and laid the halves side by side; he did not, however, cut the birds in half. Some vultures swooped down to eat the carcasses, but Abram chased them away. As the sun was going down, Abram fell into a deep sleep, and a terrifying darkness came down over him." Genesis 15:6–12[35]

Abraham in the Bible

As in the Quran, the Bible holds Abraham in high esteem. He has an exalted status among the followers of the Old Testament, as well as the New Testament. He is considered the father of the Jewish and Christian faiths. According to Genesis, his birth name was Abram (*Av Aram*), meaning "father of Aram," or "exalted father," which was changed by God to Abraham (*Avraham*), meaning "father of many (nations)," as God promised him that he would be the father of many nations (Genesis 17:5). At the same time, God also changed the name of his first wife, *Sarai* (meaning "my princess") to *Sarah* (meaning "princess to all nations of the world").

God's first call to Abram, as he is known then, is mentioned in Genesis chapter 12. God called on Abram to leave for the Promised Land. This journey took Abram from Ur to Haran (near the Turkey-Syria border today), to Schechem (West Bank of Israel today), to Bethel (West Bank), to Egypt, and eventually to Hebron (West Bank of Israel today).

"Now the LORD said to Abram, 'Go forth from your country, And from your relatives And from your father's house, To the land which I will show you; And I will make you a great nation, And I will bless you, And make your name great; And so you shall be a blessing; And I will bless those who bless you, And the one who curses you I will curse. And in you all the families of the earth will be blessed.'" Genesis 12:1–3

Ishmael's Birth: Sarah and Hagar Don't Get Along

God once again talks to Abraham in Genesis 15 and promises great descendants. Abraham replies that he does not even have a son and

---

35 All biblical translations in this chapter are from the New American Standard Bible by the Lockman Foundation.

worries that his servant will be the heir, whereupon God gives him the good news of a son as well as having as many descendants as stars in the sky:

"Then behold, the word of the LORD came to him, saying, 'This man will not be your heir; but one who will come forth from your own body, he shall be your heir.' And He took him outside and said, 'Now look toward the heavens, and count the stars, if you are able to count them.' And He said to him, 'So shall your descendants be.' Then he believed in the LORD; and He reckoned it to him as righteousness." Genesis 15:4−6

Chapter 16 of Genesis goes on to tell the story of Ishmael's birth. Sarah had attained old age; she was in her sixties and was barren, so she gave permission for Abraham to take her Egyptian maid as his wife:

"After Abram had lived ten years in the land of Canaan, Abram's wife Sarai took Hagar the Egyptian, her maid, and gave her to her husband Abram as his wife." Genesis 16:3

The chapter describes how the relationship between the two wives sours. Chapter 17 of Genesis deals with God's covenant again and explains that in return, Abraham and his progeny must be circumcised. (Genesis 17:5)

Isaac Is Born, Informed by the Angels on the Way to Sodom and Gomorrah

In the meantime, angels visit Abraham on the way to the twin cities of Sodom and Gomorrah. They tell Abraham that they are on the way to where Lot (a prophet and a nephew of Abraham) lives and that God is going to bring about destruction of the twin towns. This happens despite Abraham's plea to spare them. This story is also told in the Quran. The angels also gave the glad tidings of the birth of Isaac:

"He [meaning one of the angels] said, 'I will surely return to you at this time next year; and behold, Sarah your wife will have a son.' And Sarah was listening at the tent door, which was behind him. Now Abraham and Sarah were old, advanced in age; Sarah was past childbearing. Sarah laughed to herself, saying, 'After I have become old, shall I have pleasure, my lord being old also?' And the

LORD said to Abraham, 'Why did Sarah laugh, saying, "Shall I indeed bear a child, when I am so old?" Is anything too difficult for the LORD? At the appointed time I will return to you, at this time next year, and Sarah will have a son.' Sarah denied it however, saying, 'I did not laugh'; for she was afraid. And He said, 'No, but you did laugh.'" Genesis 18:10–15*

This story of the angels' visit to Abraham on the way to Sodom, and giving the glad tidings about Isaac, is also told in the Quran in various places: verses 11:69–74, 15:51–58, and 51:24–37.

Abraham Sacrifices His Son, Isaac; Abraham Is Blessed

The story, told in many places in the Quran about Abraham sacrificing (actually attempting to sacrifice) his son, is also told in the Bible, except Genesis mentions Isaac by name as the son being sacrificed. The biblical account is noted in the following set of verses:

"Now it came about after these things, that God tested Abraham, and said to him, 'Abraham!' And he said, 'Here I am.' He said, 'Take now your son, your only son, whom you love, Isaac, and go to the land of Moriah, and offer him there as a burnt offering on one of the mountains of which I will tell you.'" Genesis 22:1–2

One may see a contradiction in this passage, in that though the name of the son mentioned is Isaac, he is also referred to as "your only son." The Bible already had told the story of Ishmael, as Abraham's first son, and so one would wonder why Isaac was referred to as the only son. The "only son" reference is repeated again in the following verse, after God told Abraham to stop:

"He said, 'Do not stretch out your hand against the lad, and do nothing to him; for now I know that you fear God, since you have not withheld your son, your only son, from Me.'" Genesis 22:12

The Quranic and biblical accounts are similar in that Abraham was prepared to sacrifice his son, before God called on to him to stop, informing him it was a test of his submissiveness and that Abraham had passed it with flying colors. The Quran follows that narration by saluting him, *"Peace and salutation to Abraham."* (37:109) Abraham was thus exalted and also was promised multiple nations as his followers, and that they too would be blessed:

"Then the angel of the LORD called to Abraham a second time from heaven, and said, 'By Myself I have sworn, declares the LORD, because you have done this thing and have not withheld your son, your only son, indeed I will greatly bless you, and I will greatly multiply your seed as the stars of the heavens and as the sand which is on the seashore; and your seed shall possess the gate of their enemies. In your seed all the nations of the earth shall be blessed, because you have obeyed My voice.'" Genesis 22:15–18

Ishmael (Ismail): Abraham's First Son

Prophet Ishmael is one of the highly revered prophets in the Quran. He is often mentioned in association with his father, Prophet Abraham. In addition to some of the verses already quoted, he is frequently mentioned elsewhere in high esteem:

"Also mention in the Book (the story of) Ismail: He was (strictly) true to what he promised, and he was a messenger (and) a prophet. He used to enjoin on his people Prayer and Charity, and he was most acceptable in the sight of his Lord." 19:54–55

"And Ishmael and Elisha, and Jonas, and Lot: and to all We gave favor above the nations:" 6:86. This is a culmination of a set of verses in reference to the exalted prophets that include Abraham, Isaac, Moses, and Jesus.

Ishmael in the Bible

Ishmael is mentioned in the Bible several times. In his first covenant, God promises Abraham a great number of descendants (Genesis 17:5) and then gave the news of a son. Before Ishmael was born, God promised Abraham that He would make a great nation out of Abraham. The following narration is at the time of news of the birth of Ishmael, long before the angels gave the news of Isaac's birth to Abraham:

"After these things the word of the LORD came to Abram in a vision, saying, 'Do not fear, Abram, I am a shield to you; Your reward shall be very great.' Abram said, 'O Lord GOD, what will You give me, since I am childless, and the heir of my house is Eliezer of Damascus?' And Abram said, 'Since You have given no offspring to me, one born in my house is my heir.' Then behold, the word of the LORD came to

him, saying, 'This man will not be your heir; but one who will come forth from your own body, he shall be your heir.'" Genesis 15:1–5

The New Living Translation version translates the last verse as *"No, your servant will not be your heir, for you will have a son of your own who will be your heir."* The following chapter of Genesis then goes on to describe the birth of Ishmael.

Muhammad, a Descendant of Ishmael: God's Promise to Make a Great Nation from Ishmael

The Bible also mentions that God promised Hagar that He would make a great nation from Ishmael's descendants. However, according to the Bible, God's covenant was to be confirmed with Isaac and his descendants, and not with Ishmael:

"And Abraham said to God, 'Oh that Ishmael might live before You!' But God said, 'No, but Sarah your wife will bear you a son, and you shall call his name Isaac; and I will establish My covenant with him for an everlasting covenant for his descendants after him. As for Ishmael, I have heard you; behold, I will bless him, and will make him fruitful and will multiply him exceedingly. He shall become the father of twelve princes, and I will make him a great nation.'" Genesis 17:18–20

Later as Ishmael grows, Sarah gets upset when Ishmael is said to have made fun of Isaac during his weaning celebration, so Sarah asked Abraham to take them away:

"Therefore she [Sarah] said to Abraham, 'Drive out this maid and her son, for the son of this maid shall not be an heir with my son Isaac.' The matter distressed Abraham greatly because of his son. But God said to Abraham, 'Do not be distressed because of the lad and your maid; whatever Sarah tells you, listen to her, for through Isaac your descendants shall be named. And of the son of the maid I will make a nation also, because he is your descendant.'" Genesis 21:10–13

Zamzam Well in the Bible

Though not mentioned by name, the Zamzam well is described in the Old Testament, when Abraham takes young Ishmael and Hagar away to eventually arrive in Mecca:

"So Abraham rose early in the morning and took bread and a skin of water and gave them to Hagar, putting them on her shoulder, and gave her the boy, and sent her away. And she departed and wandered about in the wilderness of Beersheba. When the water in the skin was used up, she left the boy under one of the bushes. Then she went and sat down opposite him, about a bowshot away, for she said, 'Do not let me see the boy die.' And she sat opposite him, and lifted up her voice and wept. God heard the lad crying; and the angel of God called to Hagar from heaven and said to her, 'What is the matter with you, Hagar? Do not fear, for God has heard the voice of the lad where he is. Arise, lift up the lad, and hold him by the hand, for I will make a great nation of him.' Then God opened her eyes and she saw a well of water; and she went and filled the skin with water and gave the lad a drink. God was with the lad, and he grew; and he lived in the wilderness and became an archer." Genesis 21:14–20

Ishmael's Descendants and His Death

Genesis 25:12–18 mentions the twelve sons of Ishmael by name and his age (137 years), something the Quran does not narrate.

Isaac: Abraham's Second Son and the Father of Jacob

Prophet Isaac (or *Ishaq,* as he is known in the Quran) is one of the highly revered prophets in Judaism, as well as in Christianity and Islam. The second son of Abraham and father of Jacob, God chose him, and his half brother, Ishmael, to carry the legacy of Abraham, though most of the prophets were from Isaac's progeny. His name is mentioned fifteen times in the Quran and eighty times in Genesis. Isaac is buried in the cave of the patriarchs, also known by Muslims as the mosque of Abraham (*Masjid-e-Ibrahimi*), in the city of Hebron in the West Bank. The graves of the other patriarchs and matriarchs are also located there (Abraham, Sarah, Rebecca—Isaac's wife, Jacob, and Leah—Jacob's wife). Thus the city of Hebron is considered the Second-holiest city in Judaism after Jerusalem. It is also considered the fourth-holiest city in Islam (after Mecca, Medina, and Jerusalem). The news of his birth was given to Abraham and Sarah by the angels, as it appears in the Bible

(Genesis chapter 18), and was reviewed earlier. The following is the narration in the Quran:

"And his wife was standing (there), and she laughed: But we gave her glad tidings of Isaac, and after him, of Jacob. She said: 'Alas for me! shall I bear a child, seeing I am an old woman, and my husband here is an old man? That would indeed be a wonderful thing!' They said [the angels visiting Abraham]: Do you wonder at Allah's bidding? The mercy of Allah and His blessings are on you, O people of the house, surely He is Praised, Glorious." 11:71–74

Isaac's righteousness and the prophethood in his progeny have been narrated elsewhere in the Quran.

"And We gave (Abraham) Isaac and Jacob, and ordained among his progeny prophethood and Revelation, and We granted him his reward in this life; and he was in the Hereafter (of the company) of the Righteous." 29:27

"And I [meaning Joseph] follow the ways of my fathers, Abraham, Isaac, and Jacob; and never could we attribute any partners whatever to Allah: that (comes) of the grace of Allah to us and to mankind: yet most men are not grateful." 12:38

Isaac in the Bible

Yishaq in Hebrew mean "he laughs," or "will laugh." The Testament of Isaac is part of the Old Testament Apocrypha. In it, the Archangel Michael is said to have visited Isaac before his impending death, and he visited heaven and hell. Compared to some of the other prophets, especially other patriarchs, Isaac's story and incidents are rather unremarkable, the family feud notwithstanding.

Isaac's wife was Rebekah, mother of Jacob and Esau. According to the calculation of Rabbi Solomon Izhaqi (a.k.a. *Rashi*, a well-respected eleventh-century Jewish scholar), Rebekah was three years old when she married Isaac. They were married for twenty years when they had Jacob and Esau. (Genesis 25:20) Another less well-known source puts Rebekah's age at marriage at fourteen years. This may seem strange, and a parallel can be drawn to the controversy surrounding the age of *Aisha* (one of Prophet Muhammad's wives), which at the time of her marriage is said to be anywhere from seven to about sixteen years.

The feud between their mothers apart, there is no suggestion of animosity between Isaac and Ishmael. Chapter 25 of Genesis describes Abraham's death and says that Ishmael returned to Hebron to bury his father along with his half-brother Isaac.

"Then his sons Isaac and Ishmael buried him in the cave of Machpelah, in the field of Ephron." Genesis 25:9

Jacob (Ya'qub)

Prophet Jacob (or *Ya'qub,* as he is known in the Quran) carried the progeny of Abraham and Isaac. His nickname in Arabic was *"Israeel"* (Is-ra-eel), which is derived from two words: "Isra" and "eel," translating to *"Abdullah,"* meaning "servant of God." Israel (Iz-ra-eel), or *Ysra'el* as he is known in the Hebrew Bible, also means something very close: "man of God." Israel is variously translated as "prince of God" (from the King James Version), "he who strives with God" (New American Standard Bible), and "God fights" (from the New Living Translation). According to Genesis 32:28, his name was changed from Jacob to Israel. His progeny and descendants are known in the Quran as *"Bani Israeel,"* meaning "children of Israel," and are frequently mentioned in references to the stories of the Israelites and Moses. The Quran describes Jacob as faithful, a possessor of power and vision, and a man in submission of God. Jacob taught the message of God to his twelve sons, who eventually made up the twelve tribes of Israel. The three patriarchs of Judaism (Abraham, Isaac, and Jacob) are a frequent subject of the Quran. In the following verses, they are mentioned simultaneously:

*"And commemorate Our Servants Abraham, Isaac, and Jacob, possessors of Power and Vision. Verily We did choose them for a special (purpose)—proclaiming the Message of the Hereafter. They were, in Our sight, truly, of the company of the **Elect** and the **Good**."* 38:45–47

The words bolded above are *"Mustafain,"* meaning "elite" (as translated by Yuksel) or "the elect" (as translated by Shakir, Pickthall, and Yousuf Ali), and *"Akhyar,"* meaning "the best," "the chosen," or "the good" (as translated by Shakir, Pickthall, and Yousuf Ali, respectively). Sarwar translates *Mustafain* as "the chosen" and *Akhyar* as "the virtuous." These verses are followed by references to

Ishmael, Elisha, and Ezekiel as the best and the virtuous also, but they do not use the word, *Mustafain*.

Jacob's story in the Quran is mentioned usually in association with other prophets but mostly with his twelve sons, specially his most beloved son, Joseph:

"When God commanded him [Abraham] to submit, he replied, 'I have submitted myself to the Will of the Lord of the universe.' Abraham left this legacy to his sons and, in turn, so did Jacob saying, 'God has chosen this religion for you. You must not leave this world unless you are a Muslim (submitted to the will of the Lord of the Universe).' Were you (believers) there when death approached Jacob? When he asked his sons, 'Whom will you worship after my death?' They replied, 'We will worship your Lord, the Lord of your fathers, Abraham, Ishmael, and Isaac. He is the only Lord, and to Him we have submitted ourselves.'" 2:131–133 (Sarwar)

Jacob in the Bible

Jacob's birth is described in Genesis chapter 25. He was the twin brother of Esau. Esau was the first one to be born, and he was red and hairy ("Esau" means "rough" or "hairy"). It is narrated that Jacob was born with his hand on the heel of Esau (*Ya'aqob* or *Ya'aqov* in Hebrew means "heel-catcher"). The Bible describes in much more detail many of his life struggles including hatred of his twin brother Esau; his deception of Isaac to receive his blessings (rather than Esau receiving it); him being more loved by his mother; the death of his favorite wife, Rachel; the rape of his daughter, Dinah; and his battle with an angel, who eventually gave the news of his name change from Jacob to Israel:

"Then God appeared to Jacob again when he came from Paddan-aram, and He blessed him. God said to him, 'Your name is Jacob; You shall no longer be called Jacob, But Israel shall be your name.' Thus He called him Israel." Genesis 35:9–10

Most of these stories (except for Joseph's) are not mentioned in the Quran. Jacob's stories and struggles are covered over many chapters in the book of Genesis, culminating in his death, when he gathered his twelve sons and gave them his will and wishes to be buried in the cave where Abraham and Isaac were buried:

"When Jacob finished charging his sons, he drew his feet into the bed and breathed his last, and was gathered to his people." Genesis 49:33

The book of Genesis takes sort of a detour between the narration of the birth of Jacob (chapter 25) and his death (chapter 49) to describe briefly the story of Esau and then Joseph (chapters 37 through 47).

Joseph, Son of Jacob (Yousuf)

Prophet Joseph (or *Yousuf,* as he is known in the Quran) was the eleventh son of Jacob and the only prophet among his twelve sons, according to the Islamic traditions. He is one of the most highly regarded prophets in Islam, Christianity, and Judaism. The Quran talks about Joseph along with other revered prophets in the following verse:

"We gave him (meaning Abraham) Isaac and Jacob: all (three) guided: and before him, We guided Noah, and among his [Abraham's] progeny, David, Solomon, Job, Joseph, Moses, and Aaron: thus do We reward those who do good." 6:84

Though he is mentioned in many chapters in the Quran, the story of Joseph is told in a chapter named after him (*Surah Yousuf*), in a rare continuous stream that is stunningly beautiful, formed, and heartfelt. Unlike many other chapters in the Quran named after other prophets, the chapter "Joseph" is almost entirely dedicated to his story, which in large part is similar to the story as told in Genesis. According to the Quran and the Bible, Joseph is a righteous person, in the footsteps of his forefathers Abraham, Isaac, and Jacob, and believes in One God and submits to His will. Jacob had twelve sons. Two of them, Joseph and Benjamin, were from Jacob's favorite wife, Rachel (Rachel and Benjamin are not mentioned by name in the Quran). Because of this, both the Quran and the Bible narrate how his other brothers grew jealous of him.

Surah Yousuf of the Quran almost immediately starts by a proclamation about a story to be told by the Almighty.

"We relate to you the <u>best</u> of stories through this Quran by Our revelation to you (O Muhammad), though before this you were one of those who did not know." 12:3 (Malik)

Yousuf Ali has translated the underlined word as "most beautiful" for the Arabic word *"Ahsan,"* used in the verse. This beautiful story starts with a young Joseph telling his father Jacob about a dream he had, and ends with the reunion of Joseph with his father, to complete the interpretation of the dream. The story that starts in verse 4 ends with a prayer by Joseph in verse 101.

"My Lord! You have given me of the kingdom and taught me of the interpretation of sayings: Originator of the heavens and the earth! You are my guardian in this world and the hereafter; make me die a Muslim [submitter] and join me with the good." 12:101 (Malik)

The last part of the verse is in line with many such verses in the Quran, where many prophets, from Abraham to Isaac and Jacob and others, have prayed and identified themselves as "Muslims," or submitters. As noted thought this book, various scholars have translated the Arabic word *"Muslimoon"* as either "Muslims" or as "submitters."

Chapter 12 ("Joseph") has one hundred and eleven verses. The actual story is told in verses from 12:4 to 12:101. There is an intro in verse 12:3: *"We narrate to you the best of the stories,"* with a short epilogue after the story in verse 12:102: *"This is of the announcements relating to the unseen (which) We reveal to you, and you were not with them when they resolved upon their affair, and they were devising plans."* (Shakir) A reading of the entire chapter is highly recommended.

Joseph's Dream

"When Joseph said to his father: O my father! Surely I saw eleven stars and the sun and the moon—I saw them prostrating to me." 12:4

When young Joseph tells his dream to Jacob, he is delighted, realizing this is a sign from God that the promise of the prophecy in Abraham's lineage will be fulfilled. Knowing that his ten half brothers are jealous of him, Jacob tells him not to tell this dream to his brothers.

Brothers Plot Against Him

Tired of Jacob's relentless love for Joseph, the half brothers plot against Joseph. They ask Jacob if they could take Joseph with them on a hunting trip, and during the trip, they consider killing him but instead decide to throw him in a well. They return to Jacob and tell him that a wolf ate Joseph, showing him his shirt that they had stained with wolf's blood as proof. Jacob does not believe them but is deeply saddened nonetheless to lose his dear son. Joseph ends up being picked up by a caravan on the way to Egypt and is sold to the king of Egypt; he ends up in the household of his chief, who bought him.

"The man in Egypt who bought him, said to his wife: 'Make his stay (among us) honorable: maybe he will bring us much good, or we shall adopt him as a son.' Thus did We establish Joseph in the land, that We might teach him the interpretation of stories (and events). And Allah has full power and control over His affairs; but most among mankind know it not." 12:21

Joseph Being Seduced

Joseph grows into a handsome, attractive young man of immense masculine beauty. The chief's wife, who is not named in the Quran but is said to be Zulaikha by Jewish and Islamic traditions, wants to have intimate relations with Joseph but he keeps resisting. One day when they were alone in the house, she makes advances toward him but he refuses again, citing fear of disobedience to God's rules as the reason for his resistance:

"And she in whose house he was, sought to make himself yield (to her), and she made fast the doors and said: Come forward. He said: I seek Allah's refuge, surely my Lord made good my abode: Surely the unjust do not prosper." 12:23 (Shakir)

Joseph starts to run for the door but is grabbed from behind by the chief's wife, ripping his shirt in the process. They find her husband at the door, and he naturally becomes furious. Joseph tells him it was his wife who was making the advances, and upon the advice of her family member, the torn shirt is shown as the proof of his innocence. The husband believes his version:

"So when he [meaning the husband] saw his shirt rent from behind, he said: Surely it is a guile of you women; surely your guile is great: O Joseph! turn aside from this; and (O my wife)! ask forgiveness for your fault, surely you are one of the wrong-doers." 12:28–29 (Shakir)

A while later, when the wife's lady friends mock her obsession with Joseph, she arranges for the ladies to cut oranges with a knife and calls on Joseph. The women get so spellbound by Joseph's beauty that they cut their fingers rather than the oranges. The wife then reminds her friends why she is so obsessed, as she has to deal with Joseph's beauty every day, since Joseph lives in the same household:

"She said: This is he with respect to whom you blamed me, and certainly I sought his yielding himself (to me), but he abstained, and if he does not do what I bid him, he shall certainly be imprisoned, and he shall certainly be of those who are in a state of ignominy. He said: My Lord! The prison house is dearer to me than that to which they invite me; and if You turn not away their device from me, I will yearn toward them and become (one) of the ignorant." 12:32 (Shakir)

And despite proving his innocence, Joseph ends up in the jail after all.

Joseph Interprets Dreams in the Prison

While in prison with two other inmates, Joseph correctly interprets their dreams, and he reaffirms his faith in the One God to the inmates:

"And I follow the ways of my fathers, Abraham, Isaac, and Jacob; and never could we attribute any partners whatever to God: that (comes) of the Grace of God to us and to mankind: yet most men are not grateful. O my two companions of the prison! (I ask you): are many lords differing among themselves better, or the One God, Supreme and Irresistible?" 12:38–39

When one of them is released, he tells the king (*Malik*, as he is noted in verses 43, 50, and 54) of Joseph's unique ability to correctly interpret dreams. The king himself had a dream of seven fat cows being eaten by seven skinny ones and seven ears of corn being replaced with shriveled ones, but none of his advisors could interpret it, and he decides to call on Joseph, who correctly informs the king of an impending drought that will last seven years, followed by a year of abundant rain. This impresses the king.

The Wife and Her Lady Friends Finally Confess

The chief's wife and her friends eventually retract their story and Joseph is exonerated:

"And the king said: Bring him to me. So when the messenger (meaning Joseph) came to him, he said: Go back to your Lord and ask him, what is the case of the women who cut their hands; surely my Lord knows their guile. He said: How was your [addressing the lady friends] affair when you sought Joseph to yield himself (to you)? They said: Remote is Allah (from imperfection), we knew of no evil on his part. The chief's [Aziz's] wife said: Now has the truth become established: I sought him to yield himself (to me), and he is most surely of the truthful ones." 12:50–51 (Shakir)

The king forgives Joseph and appoints him as one of his top aides, giving him a lot of authority:

"And the king said: Bring him to me, I will choose him for myself. So when he had spoken with him, he said: Surely you are in our presence today an honorable, a faithful one." 12:54 (Shakir)

Joseph's Brothers Visit Egypt

Joseph's brothers travel to Egypt for grain. Joseph instantly recognizes them but they don't know it is him. He asks them to bring him their half brother (Benjamin). The brothers go back to their home and tell Jacob they have to take Benjamin to Egypt:

"He [meaning Jacob] said: 'Shall I trust you with him with any result other than when I trusted you with his brother aforetime? But God is the best to take care (of him), and He is the Most Merciful of those who show mercy!'" 12:64

Jacob fears another plot like the one that took Joseph away from him, but eventually he relents. The half brothers then take Benjamin back to Egypt. Joseph reveals himself to his only real brother. He places his measuring cup in Benjamin's bag as his people distribute the grain. His people then call out that the chief's measuring cup has been stolen and the thief will be held back. The brothers' bags are searched and lo and behold, the measuring cup is found in Benjamin's bag. His brothers plead to Joseph's men that their brother is not a thief. They eventually return to their homes and Jacob, and once again break his heart by telling him that Benjamin had to be left behind. Jacob is deeply grief stricken:

"And he turned away from them, and said: 'How great is my grief for Joseph!' And his eyes became white with sorrow, and he fell into silent melancholy." 12:84

Joseph Finally Reveals Himself to His Brothers

Jacob asks the brothers to go back and find both Joseph and Benjamin. The brothers once again return to Egypt and plead with Joseph for the return of the two brothers:

"Then, when they came (back) into (Joseph's) presence they said: 'O exalted one! [Also translated as 'O chief or Aziz!'] Distress has seized us and our family: we have (now) brought but scanty capital: so pay us full measure (we pray you), and treat it as charity to us: for Allah does reward the charitable.' He (Joseph) said: (Do you) know how you dealt with Joseph and his brother, not knowing (what you were doing)?" 12:88–89

Then Joseph finally reveals his identity to his brothers:

"They said: Are you indeed Joseph? He said: I am Joseph and this is my brother; Allah has indeed been Gracious to us; surely he who guards (against evil) and is patient (is rewarded), for surely Allah does not waste the reward of those who do good." 12:90

The brothers then admit their wrongdoing and feel guilty and ask for forgiveness. Joseph forgives them and gives them his shirt to take back to Jacob. He asks them to rub it on Jacob's eyes as a healing, as he had gone blind weeping incessantly in Joseph's absence.

Joseph and Jacob Finally Reunite

The brothers take the shirt back to Jacob, who is not able to see much; he nonetheless feels the scent of Joseph's shirt as they near his house and announces that Joseph may be near. People think he is growing senile. Jacob indeed gets his eyesight back when Joseph's shirt is rubbed on his eyes:

"When the caravan left (Egypt), their father said: 'I do indeed scent the presence of Joseph: No, think me not a dotard' (or weak in judgment). They said: 'By Allah! truly you are in your old wandering mind.' So when the bearer of good news came he cast it on his face, so forthwith he regained his sight. He said: Did I not say to you that I know from Allah what you do not know? They said: O our father! ask forgiveness of our faults for us, surely we were sinners." 12:94–97

Jacob too forgives the sons and informs them that God also forgave them, since *"He is the Forgiving, compassionate."* Jacob then enters Egypt, and finally there is this long-awaited reunion with his most beloved son, Joseph.

The Dream Is Fulfilled

"Then when they entered the presence of Joseph, he provided a home for his parents with himself, and said: 'Enter Egypt (all) in safety if Allah wills.' And he raised his parents upon the throne and they fell down in prostration before him, and he [meaning Joseph] said: O my father! this is the significance of my vision of old; my Lord has indeed made it to be true; and He was indeed kind to me when He brought me forth from the prison and brought you from the desert after the Satan had sown dissensions between me and my brothers, surely my Lord is benign (Kind) to whom He pleases; surely He is the Knowing, the Wise." 12:99–100

The story ends with a prayer from Joseph in verse 12:101, as noted in the beginning of this section.

The short epilogue to the story of Joseph then follows:

"This is of the announcements relating to the unseen (which) We reveal to you [Muhammad] and you were not with them when they resolved upon their affair, and they were devising plans." 12:102 (Shakir)

Muslim scholars believe the chapter was revealed in its entirety in Mecca when the pagans of Mecca challenged the Quran's divinity and asked Muhammad about the story of Joseph in order to humiliate him. Though Genesis already had a description of

Joseph's story, they were stunned when Muhammad narrated the story that was fairly unknown within the pagan Arabs in Mecca.

Biblical Accounts of the Story of Joseph

Joseph's life story is told in great detail starting in chapter 37 of Genesis, with his father Jacob settling in the land of Canaan. It ends with Joseph's death at age of 110 years, in chapter 50, which is also the end of Genesis. By and large, the story of Joseph is very similar as told in the Bible and the Quran. They both hold Joseph in high esteem, mention his unique power to correctly interpret dreams, and portray him as the most beloved son of Jacob. The brothers are jealous and sell him to a caravan, Joseph ends up in Egypt where the chief's wife tries to seduce him, and he resists. He is put in jail, where he uses his ability as dream interpreter to the inmates, and this skill gets him out of prison when he correctly interprets the king's dreams. The accounts of the two dreams the king had are the same in the Quran and the Bible (the seven fat cows eating seven thin ones, and the seven green ears of corn with seven dry ones). He eventually is pardoned and rises up in the ranks quickly and holds a high post in the Egyptian kingdom. His brothers visit Egypt and don't recognize him. He holds his real brother ransom, sends his shirt back to his father, Jacob, who had been missing him dearly, and this eventually leads to a happy family reunion. Joseph forgives his brothers. Both the Quran and the Bible tell a continuous stream of events, a unique feature for the Quran, and a long narration in the Bible, even from biblical standards.

Some variations do exist in the story as told by the Quran and the Bible:

- The Quran uses the specific term *"Malik"* (with a short "a"), meaning "the king" or "the ruler," to describe the ruler in Egypt. The Quran uses the word *"Pharaoh"* (*Firon* in Arabic) for the king of Egypt during the times of Moses and never used this term to describe the Egyptian ruler in the story of Joseph (or Abraham). Genesis frequently refers to the Egyptian ruler as Pharaoh in Joseph's story. Though modern writers have used the term "Pharaoh" to describe all rulers of ancient Egypt, according to historical sources, the title Pharaoh for the rulers of Egypt was not used until the New Kingdom period of ancient Egypt (comprised of the eighteenth through the twentieth Egyptian dynasties), which started in the sixteenth century BCE.[36] By the time of the rule of Thutmose III in 1479 BCE, it became a common way of addressing the king. Until this time, the term "Pharaoh" was used to describe the royal palace. According to timelines by biblical scholars, Joseph died in the year 1805 BCE, well before the title was in use to indicate the Egyptian ruler. In fact, Genesis uses the title Pharaoh as early as the Abrahamic period, when Abraham took Sarah to Egypt.

"Pharaoh's officials saw her and praised her to Pharaoh; and the woman was taken into Pharaoh's house." Genesis 12:15

And in the story of Joseph, Genesis once again calls the king of Egypt a Pharaoh:

"Meanwhile, the Midianites sold him in Egypt to Potiphar, Pharaoh's officer, the captain of the bodyguard." Genesis 37:36

- The Quran refers to the man who took Joseph to his house by the generic word, "chief" (*Aziz*). True to its tradition of being specific, the Bible mentions his name as *Potiphar*, the captain of the guards of the Pharaoh, as noted in the verse above.
- In the Bible, when the advancing wife tears Joseph's shirt, Potiphar believes the wife's version and imprisons Joseph. The wife tells the story and blames Joseph instead for the advances when Potiphar came home *later that day*. In the Quran, the chief is described as being *at the door*, when Joseph is trying to flee, and he initially believes Joseph's defense for his innocence.

---

36 Aidan Dodson and Dyan Hilton, *The Complete Royal Families of Ancient Egypt*, Thames and Hudson, 2004.

- The story about the lady friends cutting their fingers is not described in the Bible.
- The Bible names Benjamin as Joseph's only real brother. The Quran does not name any of his brothers.

Points to Remember

- Abraham is considered the father of the monotheistic faiths of Islam, Christianity, and Judaism and is highly revered by all three. Abraham, Isaac, and Jacob are considered the patriarchs by all three religions. The Quran calls them among the elite prophets. The Quran proclaims Abraham "friend of Allah" *(Khaleel Allah)*—a very high rank.
- God promised Abraham great progeny through Isaac, as well as a great nation through Ishmael, according to Genesis and the Quran. The Hebrew prophets' lineage is through Isaac and Jacob. Muhammad's lineage is traced back to Ishmael.
- Abraham and Ishmael built Kaaba, the holiest shrine in Islam, located in the city of Mecca. The Bible also refers to Hagar and Ishmael in reverence and mentions the appearance of Zamzam well (without naming it) to quench young Ishmael's thirst, a well that is functional to this date; its water is considered holy by Muslims.
- According to the Quran, Islam is the faith of Abraham, and in addition to the progeny from Isaac, Abraham and Ishmael prayed for a prophet from *their* progeny while building Kaaba. Abraham, Jacob, and Joseph all asked their sons to be "Muslims," or submitters.
- Though the relationship between the two wives of Abraham, Sarah and Hagar, was not the most cordial, the Quran holds both of them in high esteem. The Bible also reassures Hagar in the wilderness and sends angels to help her and her young son, Ishmael.
- The story of Joseph is remarkably similar in the Quran and the Bible. Both scriptures describe his story in unusually long passages.

Time to Ponder

- All three monotheistic faiths hold the patriarchs in high esteem, along with their progeny and other prophets. Why has this (along with the belief in the same, One God) not translated into a better relationship between the followers of these faiths?
- Islam is categorized as the "religion of Abraham" *("Deen-e-Ibrahimi")* in the Quran, which then was completed by Prophet Muhammad. What makes many Muslims (as well as people of other faiths) view Islam as a religion mainly limited to the days of Prophet Muhammad and afterwards?

CHAPTER 16
MOSES (MUSA, MOSHE)

This chapter mainly reviews the life of Moses, but in the end it briefly goes over the story of David, a highly regarded king of Israel and a prophet of Islam.

Prophet Moses (known as Moshe in Hebrew or *Musa*) is the prophet most often mentioned by name in the Quran (136 times). The Torah (*Tawrat*) is the holy book revealed to him by God. "*Musa*" means "drawn out of water." His Hebrew name, *Moshe*, also means something similar: "to draw out." They both refer to him being drawn out of the Nile River, where his mother had left him as an infant in a basket. Moses is considered the prophet with the highest status in Judaism. Christianity also recognizes him as a highly revered prophet. He is known in the Quran as a messenger (*Rasool*), an exalted prophet, and a lawgiver.

"Also mention in the Book (the story of) Moses: for he was specially chosen, and he was a messenger (and) a prophet, and we called him from the right (blessed) side of Mount Sinai, and made him draw near to Us, for mystic (converse)." 19:51–52

His story, especially in reference to the pharaoh of Egypt and the children of Israel, is the most frequently told story in the Quran. Similarly, in the New Testament, Moses is mentioned more often than any of the other Old Testament prophets.

In a departure from the norm in this book, the life of Moses as told in the Bible will be reviewed first, before the Quranic narrations on the same subject. The life struggles and teachings of Moses are described in detail in the Torah, starting with the book of Exodus, and continuing on in Leviticus and Numbers, and ending with Moses's death in the book of Deuteronomy.

Birth: Moses was from the genealogy of Levi, one of the twelve sons of Jacob (Israel), and was born in Egypt, described anywhere from one hundred to four hundred years after the death of Joseph. When Joseph passed away, the children of Israel, or Israelites, were living rather well. However, that changed before Moses was born. By now, the king of Egypt, a cruel person, had enslaved the Israelites. Thutmose I, of the eighteenth Egyptian dynasty, is said to be the pharaoh at the time of Moses's birth, though other candidates have been put forth. The Israelites were oppressed and subjected to harsh labor. The children of Israel had multiplied, and there was a population explosion. According to some accounts, they numbered over half a million to about one million at the time. Pharaoh got concerned that the Israelites might take over the Egyptians, and he passed an executive order to kill all the Israeli baby boys. Moses's mother, fearing that he too would be killed, puts him in a basket and drops it in the Nile River, so he could float to safety. While his sister Miriam watches from the riverbank, he gets picked up by Pharaoh's daughter. Feeling pity for the crying baby, she takes him to Pharaoh's palace. (According to Islamic historians, it was Pharaoh's wife, *Asiya*, who picked him up and later adopted him.) She knew the baby was a Jewish boy and looks for an Israeli woman to breastfeed him. Miriam approaches Pharaoh's daughter and offers to find someone suitable to breastfeed him, and lo and behold finds Moses's real mother to do that. Moses then grows up in Pharaoh's palace.

Moses flees Egypt for Midian: Very little is mentioned about his youth in the book of Exodus. As he reached young adulthood, he starts to go outside the palace and realizes his people are mistreated. One day he sees an Egyptian beating up an Israelite slave. Moses gets angry and hits the Egyptian, who falls and dies. Moses eventually fears for his own life and flees Egypt and ends up in Midian, which is considered to be north of the Red Sea. There he meets his future wife and lives for many years, tending to the livestock of his father-in-law until around the age of eighty years. This is when his life changed, and that of a whole nation that followed.

The burning bush talks to Moses: One day when tending to his normal business, Moses sees a burning bush near Mount Sinai. He becomes curious as he sees the bush burn without being consumed. As he approaches the bush, God calls his name out and asks him to take his shoes off, since he is approaching holy ground (Exodus 3:4). This is the beginning of his prophecy and a long ordeal. God reminds Moses that while he is living comfortably with his family in Midian, the rest of the Israelites are still suffering in slavery in Egypt under the cruel rule of Pharaoh. The Torah does not name the pharaoh at the time of the Exodus; the many candidates include Thutmose III and Rameses I and II. God tells Moses to go to Pharaoh and ask for the release of the Israelites. According to the accounts in Exodus, after initial reluctance, Moses agrees but asks for his brother Aaron, also a prophet, to go with him to help. This is when God gave Moses the staff that can turn into a snake as well as the miracle in his hand that turns very bright (or very white). God endowed Moses with these miracles to convince the children of Israel, as well as Pharaoh, that he is a prophet sent by God to deliver the divine message. Armed by his belief in God, these two powerful tools, and Aaron, Moses returns to Egypt.

Upon his return, Moses relates to the Israelites what God had instructed him: that there is no god but God and to worship no one but Him and that he (Moses) has returned to liberate them. He then asks Pharaoh to release the Jews. He also gives Pharaoh the same message about the One God. Pharaoh does not take him seriously, even when he shows his miracles using his hand and the staff. Indeed, Pharaoh gets even more cruel to the Jewish slaves, and their affliction only gets worse. The children of Israel start to blame Moses for their sufferings, saying they wished he had never returned. Moses goes back for guidance to God, who then promises ten plagues upon the Egyptians to convince them to release the Israelites. These are the ten plagues mentioned in the book of Exodus:

1. The Nile turns to blood. (7:14–24)
2. Frogs came out of the Nile. (8:1–15)

3. Gnats, or lice, erupt from the ground. (8:16–19)
4. Flies swarm Egypt. (8:20–32)
5. A mysterious disease affects Egyptian livestock and kills them. (9:1–7)
6. Boils breaks out on Egyptians and their livestock. (9:8–12)
7. Hailstorm hits Egypt. (9:13–35)
8. Locusts kill the remaining crops of the Egyptians. (10:1–20)
9. Darkness covers Egypt for three days, except Goshen, where Israelites lived. (10:21–29)
10. The firstborns (humans and animals) die. (11:1)

First ever Passover, leading to Exodus: God goes on to instruct Moses to tell the children of Israel to sacrifice a lamb or a goat and smear their blood on their doors for identification. Detailed instructions are given regarding how the animals are to be slaughtered and eaten. The promise was that God would strike the firstborn of the Egyptians but pass over the Israelites' homes, sparing them.

The same night of the Passover, Pharaoh loses his firstborn son and relents to let the Israelites leave Egypt. Led by Moses and Aaron, the Israelites leave quickly. The book of Exodus describes how God guides Moses, in the form of a dark cloud during the day, and a large pillar of fire during the night, to show him the way. This path initially leads to the Red Sea (and eventually leads to the Promised Land—but not until after the death of Moses under the leadership of Moses's successor, Joshua).

The parting of the Red Sea: After letting the Israelites go, Pharaoh changes his mind and decides to chase them down with a huge army. He meets them near the Red Sea. Israelites are caught between Pharaoh's army on one side and the Red Sea on the other.[37]

"As Pharaoh drew near, the sons of Israel looked, and behold, the Egyptians were marching after them, and they became very frightened; so the sons of Israel cried out to the LORD. Then they

---

37 All biblical translations in this chapter are from the New American Standard Bible by the Lockman Foundation.

said to Moses, 'Is it because there were no graves in Egypt that you have taken us away to die in the wilderness? Why have you dealt with us in this way, bringing us out of Egypt? Is this not the word that we spoke to you in Egypt, saying, "Leave us alone that we may serve the Egyptians"? For it would have been better for us to serve the Egyptians than to die in the wilderness.' Exodus 14:10–12

Moses raises his miraculous staff and the sea parts, allowing Moses and the Israelites to pass on dry land and reach the other side of the sea.

"Then Moses stretched out his hand over the sea; and the LORD swept the sea back by a strong east wind all night and turned the sea into dry land, so the waters were divided. The sons of Israel went through the midst of the sea on the dry land, and the waters were like a wall to them on their right hand and on their left." Exodus 14:21–22

Pharaoh and his army follow, but by this time the water recedes and they drown in the Red Sea.

"Then the Egyptians took up the pursuit, and all Pharaoh's horses, his chariots, and his horsemen went in after them into the midst of the sea." Exodus 14:23

"Then the LORD said to Moses, 'Stretch out your hand over the sea so that the waters may come back over the Egyptians, over their chariots and their horsemen.' So Moses stretched out his hand over the sea, and the sea returned to its normal state at daybreak, while the Egyptians were fleeing right into it; then the LORD overthrew the Egyptians in the midst of the sea. The waters returned and covered the chariots and the horsemen, even Pharaoh's entire army that had gone into the sea after them; not even one of them remained. But the sons of Israel walked on dry land through the midst of the sea, and the waters were like a wall to them on their right hand and on their left." Exodus 14:26–29

Israelites complain: After successfully evading Pharaoh and his army, Moses and the Israelites wander in the desert for forty years in search of the Promised Land (Canaan). While wandering in the desert, people grumble more and more and openly complain that they are getting a raw deal. Exodus chapters 16 and 17 describe their frequent complaining. They complained frequently about the rough life in the desert and about not having the food they were used to eating:

"Then they [meaning Israelites] set out from Elim, and all the congregation of the sons of Israel came to the wilderness of Sin, which is between Elim and Sinai, on the fifteenth day of the second month after their departure from the land of Egypt. The whole congregation of the sons of Israel grumbled against Moses and Aaron in the wilderness. The sons of Israel said to them, 'Would that we had died by the LORD'S hand in the land of Egypt, when we sat by the pots of meat, when we ate bread to the full; for you have brought us out into this wilderness to kill this whole assembly with hunger.'"
Exodus 16:1–3

The Bible describes how *Manna* (a sticky breadlike substance) and *Salwa* (quails) descended from the sky to feed the Israelites.

They also complain of not having enough water. God told Moses to strike a rock with his staff and water gushes forth.

"Then all the congregation of the sons of Israel journeyed by stages from the wilderness of Sin, according to the command of the LORD, and camped at Rephidim, and there was no water for the people to drink. Therefore the people quarreled with Moses and said, 'Give us water that we may drink.' And Moses said to them, 'Why do you quarrel with me? Why do you test the LORD?' But the people thirsted there for water; and they grumbled against Moses and said, 'Why, now, have you brought us up from Egypt, to kill us and our children and our livestock with thirst?' So Moses cried out to the LORD, saying, 'What shall I do to this people? A little more and they will stone me.' Then the LORD said to Moses, 'Pass before the people and take with you some of the elders of Israel; and take in your hand your staff with which you struck the Nile, and go. Behold, I will stand before you there on the rock at Horeb; and you shall strike the rock, and water will come out of it, that the people may drink.' And Moses did so in the sight of the elders of Israel."
Exodus 17:1–6

Arriving at Mount Sinai: Two months into the journey from Egypt, Moses leads the Israelites to the wilderness of Sinai. He then ascends Mount Sinai and receives God's message, to make a covenant with God.

"Moses went up to God, and the LORD called to him from the mountain, saying, 'Thus you shall say to the house of Jacob and tell the sons of Israel: 'You yourselves have seen what I did to the Egyptians, and how I bore you on eagles' wings, and brought you to Myself. Now then, if you will indeed obey My voice and keep My covenant, then you shall be My own possession among all the peoples, for all the earth is Mine.'" Exodus 19:3–5

The Israelites respond as follows, promising they will follow God's commands:

"All the people answered together and said, 'All that the LORD has spoken we will do!'" Exodus 19:8

Moses receives the Ten Commandments at Mount Sinai: Moses leaves Aaron to look over the children of Israel in Sinai and ascends the mountain as God had instructed him to do. At first he receives the Ten Commandments. He later receives a number of other instructions that became law for the Jewish nation. All in all the five Books of Moses (the Torah) contain six hundred and thirteen laws. The Ten Commandments were inscribed on a tablet. Later on, God asks Moses to make two copies of the tablets (Exodus chapter 34). The Ten Commandments are:

1. I am the Lord, your God.
2. You shall have no gods before me. You shall not make yourself an idol.
3. Do not take Lord's name in vain (misuse His name).
4. Remember the Sabbath and keep it holy.
5. Honor your mother and father.
6. You shall not kill or murder.
7. You shall not commit adultery.
8. You shall not steal.
9. You shall not bear false witness.
10. You shall not covet your neighbor, his house, wife, male or female servants, ox or donkey, or anything else.

It should be noted that the imperatives known as the Ten Commandments appear twice in the Bible, initially in Exodus 20:1–17 and then repeated in Deuteronomy 5:6–21. The imperatives are the same but various religions have parsed them slightly differently. The Ten Commandments quoted above are from the Jewish (Talmudic) version. For example, Roman Catholics lump together the first two commandments mentioned above, whereas the last commandment is broken into two: 9 (*"Do not covet your neighbor's wife"*) and 10 (*"Or any other belonging of the neighbors"*).

Israelites make the golden calf: Moses was up on Mount Sinai for forty days, receiving the law; meanwhile, the Israelites grew impatient and asked Aaron to make an idol to worship. According to the biblical accounts, Aaron gathered gold jewelry from them, melted it, and carved it into a calf. The children of Israel, or at least some groups, started to worship the calf. God then asks Moses to go down quickly, as he was getting very angry with the people.

"Aaron said to them, 'Tear off the gold rings which are in the ears of your wives, your sons, and your daughters, and bring them to me.' Then all the people tore off the gold rings which were in their ears and brought them to Aaron. He took this from their hand, and fashioned it with a graving tool and made it into a molten calf; and they said, 'This is your god, O Israel, who brought you up from the land of Egypt.' Now when Aaron saw this, he built an altar before it; and Aaron made a proclamation and said, 'Tomorrow shall be a feast to the LORD.'

"So the next day they rose early and offered burnt offerings, and brought peace offerings; and the people sat down to eat and to drink, and rose up to play. Then the LORD spoke to Moses, 'Go down at once, for your people, whom you brought up from the land of Egypt, have corrupted themselves.'" Exodus 32:2–7

When Moses descends after receiving the Ten Commandments and the Torah, he gets furious when he sees many of his people worshipping the idol. He throws the tablets to the ground in disgust and burns the idol, grinds it into a powder, and throws it in the water and forces the people to drink it. He asks Aaron what happened under his command. Aaron essentially deflects the blame on to the Israelites. Moses then gets the people on Lord's side—all Levites—to separate from rest of the Israelites and asks the tribe of Levites to kill the rest of them. According to Exodus 32:28–29, "about 3,000 people died that day," in order to restore the truth and prevent the corruption of the rest of the Israelites by those who transgressed.

The Tabernacle and the Ark: Exodus goes on to talk about Moses building a place—a movable tent—to worship God. It describes in elaborate detail what it looked like—its dimensions and various compartments. In it were stored the tablets that were inscribed with the Ten Commandments; they were stored in a container called the Ark of the Covenant. The Ark contained many other relics from Moses and Aaron. The place that housed the Ark is called "the Holy of the Holies" (or *Mishkan,* in Hebrew).

Israelites fight many battles: Between this time and Moses's death, there were many wars between the Israelites and other groups on their way to the Promised Land. These included battles with communities like Canaanites and King Sihon of the Ammonites. These were battles for the establishment of truth and justice, rather than land. It is ironic that Moses himself never set foot in the Promised Land.

Moses passes away: Though Moses could not deliver the Israelites to the Promised Land, he accomplished a lot, according to biblical commentators. He liberated the children of Israel from slavery, gave them a code of ethics and law from God, and brought them to the edge of the Promised Land, to the plains of Moab. Only the Jordan River separated them from the Promised Land: Canaan (in current Israel). There in Moab, after God promised that he would lead the Israelites to the Promised Land, Moses passes away at the age of 120. The book of Deuteronomy (the last book of the Torah) ends by praising Moses:

"Since that time no prophet has risen in Israel like Moses, whom the LORD knew face to face, for all the signs and wonders which the LORD sent him to perform in the land of Egypt against Pharaoh, all his servants, and all his land." Deuteronomy 34:10–11

Moses in the Quran

Moses is known by the nickname of *"Kaleemullah,"* meaning, "One who spoke with God," obviously considered a great honor.

"Of some messengers We have already told thee the story; of others We have not; and to Moses Allah spoke direct." 4:164

A long sequence in the Quran tells the story of Moses: Chapter 20 tells the story of Moses. Verses 9 through 98 cover many aspects of his life, starting from the time when God first spoke with him from the burning bush, asking him to go back to Egypt to liberate the Israelites and reminding Moses of his birth and upbringing in Pharaoh's palace. It narrates his interaction with Pharaoh, Pharaoh's tyranny, rescuing the children of Israel from slavery, then their frequent complaints, and ends with their worshipping the golden calf. This is probably the second-longest sequence in the Quran (the longest being the one on Joseph in chapter 12). This sequence ends before the delivery of the Ten Commandments. That part of Moses's prophecy is mentioned elsewhere on various occasions. Most of the story told here is in chronological order (except the flashback to Moses's birth and the killing of the Egyptian, resulting in his escape to Midian). The verses are quoted here without much commentary. The following translation is compiled by Shakir, who uses the Arabic *"Musa"* for Moses and "Allah" for God:

Talking to the burning bush: *"And has the story of Musa come to you? When he saw fire, he said to his family: Stop, for surely I see a fire, haply I may bring to you there from a live coal or find guidance at the fire. So when he came to it, a voice was uttered: O Musa: Surely I am your Lord, therefore put (take) off your shoes; surely you are in the sacred valley, Tuwa, And I have chosen you, so listen to what is revealed: Surely I am Allah, there is no god but I, therefore serve Me and keep up prayer for My remembrance: Surely the hour is coming—I am about to make it manifest—so that every soul may be rewarded as it strives: Therefore let not him who believes not in it and follows his low desires turn you away from it so that you should perish."* 20:9–16

God then gives Moses two miracles: *"And what is this in your right hand, O Musa! He said: This is my staff: I recline on it and I beat the leaves with it to make them fall upon my sheep, and I have other uses for it. He said: Cast it down, O Musa! So he cast it down; and lo! it was a serpent running. He said: Take hold of it and fear not; We will restore it to its former state: And press your hand to your side, it shall come out white without*

evil: another sign: That We may show you of Our greater signs."
20:17–23

God instructs him to go to Pharaoh: *"Go to Firon [Pharaoh], surely he has exceeded all limits. He said: O my Lord! Expand my breast for me, And make my affair easy to me, And loose the knot from my tongue, (That) they may understand my word; And give to me an aider (helper) from my family: Haroun, [Aaron] my brother, Strengthen my back by him, And associate him (with me) in my affair, So that we should glorify You much, And remember You often. Surely, You are seeing us. He [Allah] said: You are indeed granted your petition, O Musa."* 20:24–36

God then reminds Moses of his mother: *"And certainly We bestowed on you a favor at another time; When We revealed to your mother what was revealed; Saying: Put him into a chest, then cast it down into the river, then the river shall throw him on the shore; there shall take him up one who is an enemy to Me and enemy to him, and I cast down upon you love from Me, and that you might be brought up before My eyes; When your sister went and said: Shall I direct you to one who will take charge of him? So We brought you back to your mother, that her eye might be cooled and she should not grieve ..."* 20:37–40

Moses kills the Egyptian (though not mentioned as an "Egyptian" in the Quran): *"... And you killed a man, then We delivered you from the grief, and We tried you with (a severe) trying. Then you stayed for years among the people of Madyan [Midian]; then you came hither as ordained, O Musa."* 20:40

Moses asks for Aaron and pleads to Pharaoh: *"And I have chosen you for Myself: Go you and your brother with My communications and be not remiss in remembering Me; Go both to Firon, surely he has become inordinate; Then speak to him a gentle word haply he may mind or fear. Both said: O our Lord! Surely we fear that he may hasten to do evil to us or that he may become inordinate. He [Allah] said: Fear not, surely I am with you both: I do hear and see. So go you both to him and say: Surely we are two messengers of your Lord; therefore send the children of Israel with us and do not torment them! Indeed we have brought to you a communication from your Lord, and peace is on him who follows* the guidance; surely it has been revealed to us that the chastisement will surely come upon him who rejects and turns back." 20:41–48

Moses delivers God's message to the Pharaoh: *"[When Moses and Aaron went to Pharaoh and delivered this message], (Firon) said: And who is your Lord, O Musa? He [Moses] said: Our Lord is He Who gave to everything its creation, then guided it (to its goal). He [Pharaoh] said: Then what is the state of the former generations? He [Moses] said: The knowledge thereof is with my Lord in a book, my Lord errs not, nor does He forget; Who made the earth for you an expanse and made for you therein paths and sent down water from the cloud; then thereby We have brought forth many species of various herbs. Eat and pasture your cattle; most surely there are signs in this for those endowed with understanding. From it We created you and into it We shall send you back and from it will We raise you a second time."* 20:49–55

Pharaoh disbelieves, challenges Moses: Verses 20:56–64 then go on to describe Pharaoh's contempt and disbelief; he calls Moses and Aaron "two magicians" and invites them to a duel with his own magicians. Moses accepts the challenge, and the duel takes place on the "day of the festival."

Duel with Pharaoh's magicians: *"They [magicians] said: O Musa! Will you cast, or shall we be the first who cast down? He said: No! Cast down. then lo! their cords and their rods—it was imaged to him on account of their magic as if they were running. So Musa conceived in his mind a fear. We [God] said: Fear not, surely you shall be the uppermost, And cast down what is in your right hand; it shall devour what they have wrought; they have wrought only the plan of a magician, and the magician shall not be successful wheresoever he may come from. And the magicians [seeing the miracle of Moses] were cast down making obeisance (in prostration); they said: We believe in the Lord of Haroun and Musa. (Firon) said: You believe in him before I give you leave [permission]; most surely he is the chief of you who taught you enchantment, therefore I will certainly cut off your hands and your feet on opposite sides, and I will certainly crucify you on the trunks of the palm trees, and certainly you will come to know which of us is the more severe and the more abiding in chastising. They said: We do not prefer you to what has come to us* *of clear arguments and to He Who made us, therefore decide what you are going to decide; you can only decide about this world's life. Surely we believe in our Lord that He may forgive us our sins and the magic to which you compelled us; and Allah is better and more abiding."* 20:65–73

Parting of the sea, Pharaoh drowns: *"And certainly We revealed to Musa, saying: Travel by night with My servants, then make for them a dry path in the sea, not fearing to be overtaken, nor being afraid. And Firon followed them with his armies, so there came upon them of the sea that, which came upon them. And Firon led astray his people and he did not guide (them) aright."* 20:77–79

Children of Israel are liberated, receive Manna and Salwa: *"O children of Israel! Indeed We delivered you from your enemy, and We made a covenant with you on the blessed side of the mountain, and We sent to you the manna and the quails. Eat of the good things We have given you for sustenance, and be not inordinate with respect to them, lest My wrath should be due to you, and to whomsoever My wrath is due he shall perish indeed. And most surely I am most Forgiving to him who repents and believes and does good, then continues to follow the right direction."* 20:80–82

Israelites start worshipping the golden calf: Verses 20:83–89 describe God telling Moses to go down from Mount Sinai, as the Israelites had made a golden calf and started worshipping it; these verses also describe Moses's anger over them.

Moses is upset with Aaron over the golden calf issue: *"And certainly Haroun had said to them before: O my people! you are only tried by it, and surely your Lord is the Beneficent (Gracious) Allah, therefore follow me and obey my order. They said: We will by no means cease to keep to its worship until Musa returns to us. (Moses) said: O Haroun! what prevented you, when you saw them going astray, So that you did not follow me? Did you then disobey my order? He said: O son of my mother! Seize me not by my beard nor by my head; surely I was afraid lest you should say: You have caused a division among the children of Israel and not waited for my word. He [Moses] said: What was then your object, O Samiri [the person who asked the Israelites to make the cal]? He said: I saw (Jibreel)[Gabriel] what they did not see, so I took a handful (of* *the dust) from the footsteps of the messenger, then I threw it in the casting; thus did my soul commend to me."* 20:90–96

The sequence ends with Moses's proclamation:

"Your Allah is only Allah [Your god is only God], there is no god but He; He comprehends all things in (His) knowledge." 20:98

Other Passages on Moses

There is yet another long passage about Moses in chapter 7 (*"Al-A'raaf"* or *"The Heights"*) that extends from verse 103 to 171. This set of verses mentions Moses's conversation with God on Mount Sinai and the deliverance of the Ten Commandments on the tablets and the Torah; it also covers some parts mentioned in chapter 20, verses 9–98. After mentioning the Torah's deliverance to Moses, the Quran interrupts the story of Moses to claim that Prophet Muhammad was mentioned in both the Torah and the Gospel and that he was sent as the messenger for all mankind. The long narration starts with the following verse:

"Then after them We sent Moses with Our signs to Pharaoh and his chiefs, but they wrongfully rejected them: So see what was the end of those who made mischief." 7:103

According to the Quran, Moses goes to Pharaoh and not only asks the release of the children of Israel, but starts with the proclamation that he is the messenger of Lord of the worlds:

"Moses said: O Pharaoh! I am a messenger from the Lord of the worlds, One for whom it is right to say nothing but truth about Allah. Now have I come unto you (people), from your Lord, with a clear (Sign): So let the children of Israel depart along with me." 7:104–105

Verses 7:117–122 then describe the duel with the magicians.

The plagues on the Egyptians: The chapter then goes on to narrate the plagues that were cast on Pharaoh's people. However, the Quran does not mention every single plague mentioned in the book of Exodus.

"We punished the people of Pharaoh with years (of droughts) and shortness of crops; that they might receive admonition. But when good (times) came, they said, 'This is due to us'; When gripped by calamity, they ascribed it to evil omens connected with Moses

and those with him! Behold! in truth the omens of evil are theirs in Allah's sight, but most of them do not understand! They said [to Mose]: 'Whatever be the Signs you bring, to work therewith your sorcery [magic] on us, we shall never believe in you.' So We sent (plagues) on them: Wholesale death, Locusts, Lice, Frogs, And Blood: Signs openly self-explained: but they were steeped in arrogance, a people given to sin. Every time the penalty fell on them, they said: 'O Moses! on your behalf call on your Lord in virtue of his promise to you: If thou wilt remove the penalty from us, we shall truly believe in you, and we shall send away the children of Israel with you.' But every time We removed the penalty from them according to a fixed term which they had to fulfill, Behold! they broke their word!" 7:130–135

Moses asks to see God on Mount Sinai: *"And remember We rescued you [addressing the Israelites] from Pharaoh's people, who afflicted you with the worst of penalties, who slew your male children and saved alive your females: in that was a momentous trial from your Lord. We appointed for Moses thirty nights, and completed (the period) with ten (more): thus was completed the term (of communion) with his Lord, forty nights. And Moses had charged his brother Aaron (before he went up): Act for me amongst my people: Do right, and follow not the way of those who do mischief. When Moses came to the place appointed by Us, and his Lord addressed him, He said: O my Lord! show (Yourself) to me, that I may look upon You. Allah said: By no means can you see Me (direct); But look upon the mount; if it abide in its place, then shall you see Me. When his Lord manifested His Glory on the Mount, He made it (turned) as dust. And Moses fell down in a swoon. When he recovered his senses he said: Glory be to You! to You I turn in repentance, and I am the first to believe. (Allah) said: O Moses! I have chosen you above (other) men, by the mission I (have given you) and the words I (have spoken to you): take then the (revelation) which I give you, and be of those who give thanks."* 7:141–144

Moses receives Torah on tablets: *"And We ordained laws for him in the tablets in all matters, both commanding and explaining all things, (and said): 'Take and hold these with firmness, and enjoin your people to hold fast by the best in the precepts: soon shall I show you the homes of the wicked.'"* 7:145

Verses 7:152–155 go on to describe the golden calf worshipping and Moses's disgust.

The Quran interrupts the story here to claim that Muhammad was mentioned in the Torah in verses 157–158, which will be addressed later in chapter 18 ("Muhammad"). After this, the Quran returns to the story of Moses by claiming:

"Of the people of Moses, there is a section who guide and do justice in the light of truth." 7:159

Quranic versus Biblical Accounts of the Story of Moses

As one can gather from the two accounts presented, the basic story as told in the Bible and the Quran is very similar, though there are some differences that are outlined below.

The similarities are summarized first:

- Prebirth: The ruthlessness of the pharaoh of Egypt, and his mistreatment of the Israelites. Male newborn babies of the Israelites were ordered to be killed. The Israelites were enslaved. Pharaoh was a transgressor, a nonbeliever, and a tyrant.
- Moses's mother puts him in a basket in the Nile, his sister offers a Jewish woman to breastfeed him, and that woman turns out to be his real mother. And he ends up in Pharaoh's palace.
- Moses kills the Egyptian, when he saw him mistreat a Jewish slave, eventually fleeing to Midian, and there he meets his future wife and raises his family.
- At Mount Sinai (called *"Mount of Tur"* in Arabic and the Quran), God from the burning bush talks to Moses for the first time, telling him to go back to Egypt and liberate the Israelites.
- The miracles given to Moses: the staff and the bright white hand. Moses talks about his speech impediment and a request to be "strengthened" by Aaron, his brother and another prophet. His request is granted.

- Pharaoh refuses to let go of the Israelites at first. The plagues hit Egyptians. (The Bible mentions ten of them, the Quran only few of them by name.) Pharaoh eventually lets the Israelites leave Egypt.
- Pharaoh then decides to chase them down; the sea parts, letting Moses and the Israelites cross the sea but Pharaoh and his army drown.
- The Israelites wander in the desert (for forty days, according to the Bible; however, the Quran, true to its style, does not mention the exact duration). The Israelites constantly grumble and complain. Manna and Salwa descend from the sky. The Israelites (or at least many of them) remain ungrateful. They make a golden calf and start worshipping it, when Moses is up on the mountain for forty days receiving the tablets on which the Torah is written. Moses gets furious at the Israelites for the idolatry and gets upset with Aaron, as he had left him in charge of the Israelites when he was away.
- The Torah is a source of mercy to the children of Israel (the Quran adds the word "*Furqa'n*," or "the criterion"). Both the Quran and the Bible use the words "guidance" and "law" frequently in reference to the Torah.

And following are some of the differences:

The entire story of Moses, the twelve tribes and their genealogy, and the laws of the Torah are described in much more detail in the Old Testament than in the Quran. For example, the Torah describes the Tabernacle, the holy place for worship, in great detail, along with the religious laws or commandments. In total, 613 commandments are described; 248 are considered "positive" (i.e., "Dos") and 365 are considered negative ("Don'ts"). The Quran makes a general references to the laws many times without specifics (*"And We ordained laws for him in the tablets in all matters, both commanding and explaining all things."* 7:145)

- The Bible talks about baby Moses being picked up by Pharaoh's sister. The Quran does not mention who picked him up, but many Muslim commentators and historians believe it was Pharaoh's wife, Asiya. The Quran specifically refers to her as a pious lady. *"And Allah sets forth, as an example to those who believe the wife of Pharaoh: Behold she said: 'O my Lord! Build for me, in nearness to You, a mansion in the Garden, and save me from Pharaoh and his doings, and save me from those that do wrong.'"* 66:11

- The Bible mentions Moses's father-in-law in Midian by two names: *Jethro* and *Ruel*. The Quran does not call him by name, but he is believed to be *Shoaib*, considered a prophet in Islam.

- In the Bible, Aaron helps the Israelites build the golden calf, which is then used for idol worship. In the Quran, Aaron is described as a prophet; he didn't help the Israelites with the idol, though Moses was upset with him for not preventing it. Aaron responds by basically stating he tried but feared for his life and thus didn't intervene with fuller force, as he was following Moses's command to maintain peace while he was gone.

- In the Quran, Pharaoh when drowning tried in vain to declare his belief in God just as he saw death approach him, but he was told it was too late for that kind of trickery: *"And We made the children of Israel to pass through the sea, then Pharaoh and his hosts followed them for oppression and tyranny; until when drowning overtook him, he said: 'I believe that there is no god but He in Whom the children of Israel believe and I am of those who submit.' (and it was said to him), 'What? Now!' and indeed you disobeyed before and you were of the mischief-makers. This day shall We save you in the body, that you may be a sign to those who come after you! But verily, many among mankind are heedless of Our Signs!"* 10:90–92 (Shakir). Many Muslim scholars feel that the Quran is referring to the mummification and preservation of Pharaoh's body. The Bible does not have such mention of his last-minute attempted reversal, or

God's promise to save his body as a sign for generations to come.

- In the Quran, Moses, while on Mount Sinai, wished to see God, and He warns Moses that he will not be able to sustain the sight (7:142–144). The Bible makes no mention of this event.
- In the Bible, Moses passes away before ever entering the Promised Land. The Quran makes no mention of this. Indeed the Quran does not address the passing away of Moses at all.

David (Dawud)

David (*Dawud* or *Daveed* in Hebrew and *Dawud*, as he is known in the Quran) is yet another important and highly regarded prophet in the Quran and the Bible. He is a messenger (*Rasool*) and a righteous king: the second king of the nation of Israel. He is among the select group of messengers, who received a named scripture, known as *"Zabur,"* in the Quran (biblical psalms). He was a soldier in the army of Saul (the first king of Israel) and eventually takes over the reign. He is given special powers by God as a judge and is famous for singing the praises of the Lord along with the birds and the mountains. He is perhaps most famous for killing a much bigger opponent, Goliath (*Jalut*), a famous warrior in the pagan Philistine army.

"Bear patiently what they say, and remember Our servant David, the possessor of power; surely he was frequent in returning (to Allah). Surely We made the mountains to sing the glory (of Allah) in unison with him at the evening and the sunrise, And the birds gathered together; all joined in singing with him. And We strengthened his kingdom and We gave him wisdom and a clear judgment." 38:17–20 (Shakir)

David's Melodious Singing of God's Praises

As mentioned above, David sings the praises of God, and the birds and the mountains join in. In addition to verse 38:18, David's singing of His praises along with mountains and birds is narrated in chapter 34 as well. It is not entirely clear in what physical form the birds and the mountains joined David in singing, except that it was indeed one of the miracles bestowed on David.

"We bestowed Grace aforetime on David from ourselves: O you Mountains! Sing back the Praises of Allah with him! and you birds (also)! And We made the iron soft [supple] for him." 34:10

Pooya Yazdi, in his commentary of verse 34:10 writes, "Dawud had been gifted with an enchanting melodious voice, and whenever he sang the glory of Allah the mountains around him would echo his praise, and the birds would join him in chorus. Allah made iron, one of the hardest metals, soft and pliant in his hands, so that without heating the metal he was able to manufacture coats of mail. It is said that Dawud was the first to manufacture coats of mail. As a prophet of Allah he only manufactured armor which is the means of defense, and not swords, which are the implements of aggression."

"And remember David and Solomon, when they gave judgment in the matter of the field into which the sheep of certain people had strayed by night: We did witness their judgment. To Solomon We inspired the (right) understanding of the matter: to each (of them) We gave Judgment and Knowledge; it was Our power that made the hills and the birds celebrate Our praises, with David: it was We Who did (all these things)." 21:78–79

"It was We Who taught him the making of coats of mail for your benefit, to guard you from each other's violence: will you then be grateful?" 21:80

David versus Goliath

The commentary by Pooya Yazdi is quoted first for verses 2:246–251 noted below, in references to the story of David and Samuel, the Israelite prophet who appointed Saul as the king of Israel.

"After Musa (Moses) several prophets were sent to maintain his law (Tawrat, the Torah), but as time passed, people started neglecting the law and took to idolatry. Ultimately a time came when the Jews had no prophet to guide them. In those days their enemies from the tribe of Jalut (Goliath) had captured all the land on the Mediterranean including Egypt and Palestine. They killed four hundred and forty princes and noblemen of *Bani*

Israil (children of Israel) and enslaved them. The *Bani Israil* prayed to Allah for a prophet. Allah appointed Samuel as their prophet. They asked Samuel to choose a king for them. Samuel warned them about what the kings would do, but they refused to listen to him. They said: 'No, we will have a king over us; then we shall be like other nations, with a king to govern us, to lead us out to war and fight our battles' (1 Samuel 8:19 and 20). Samuel again warned them that they might not fight even if fighting was ordained for them. And when fighting was ordained for them, they turned back, except for a few of them. In this verse fighting for the emancipation of the people from the tyranny of the oppressors has been described as fighting in the way of Allah."

"Have you not considered the chiefs of the children of Israel after Moses, when they said to a prophet of theirs: Raise up for us a king, (that) we may fight in the way of Allah. He said: May it not be that you would not fight if fighting is ordained for you? They said: And what reasons have we that we should not fight in the way of Allah, and we have indeed been compelled to abandon our homes and our children? But when fighting was ordained for them, they turned back, except a few of them, and Allah knows the unjust."
2:246 (Shakir)

The Ark of Moses, a source of tranquility: Though not named, the "prophet" being referred to in these verses is Samuel:
"And the prophet said to them: Surely the sign of His kingdom is, that there shall come to you the chest [ark] in which there is tranquility from your Lord and residue of the relics of what the children of Moses and the children of Aaron have left, the angels bearing it; most surely there is a sign in this for those who believe."
2:248 (Shakir)

God tests Saul's army: *So when Talut [Saul] departed with the forces, he said: Surely Allah will try you with a river; whoever then drinks from it, he is not of me, and whoever does not taste of it, he is surely of me, except he who takes with his hand as much of it as fills the hand; But with the exception of a few of them they drank from it. So when he had crossed it, he and those who believed with him, they* said: *We have today no power against Goliath and his forces. Those who were sure that they would meet their Lord said: How often has a small party vanquished a numerous host by Allah's permission, and Allah is with the patient."* 2:249 (Shakir)

David slays Goliath (*Jalut*): The Quran dubs David and Goliath's fight as a struggle between good and evil; verses 2:250–251 will be quoted in chapter 24, "Jihad (To Strive)".

David in the Bible

The Bible holds David in high esteem and, as is customary, describes his life in more detail than the Quran does. However, the Bible also talks about his sins and adultery with Bathsheba, wife of Uriah, who David had sent to the battlefield. According to the Old Testament, Bathsheba conceives a child, and David later marries her, but God was furious with David and sends Nathan, another prophet, to tell David about his sins. David later repents (Psalm 51:1–12 and 2 Samuel 12:1–15). David receives three rather graphic punishments that are referenced in 2 Samuel 12:11–12. The Quran clearly rejects all notions of any sins attributed to prophets, especially major sins like adultery, and holds David, one of the more revered prophets, above such sins.

Points to Remember

- Moses is believed to be one of the most exalted prophets in Islam. He is the prophet mentioned the most often by name in the Quran. His mother and sister, as well as Pharaoh's wife (named Asiya in Islamic traditions), are also mentioned with reverence in the Quran. Muslims often add, "Peace be upon him" after Moses's name to show respect (as they do with other prophets' names).
- According to both the Quran and the Bible, Pharaoh was an evil tyrant. The children of Israel were enslaved and the victims of his tyranny. After their release, the Israelites frequently grumbled and complained about the hardship as they wandered in the desert, in search of the Promised Land. Some of the children of Israel

reverted to idol worshipping and received the wrath of Moses and God.

- The Quran refers to David as one of the holiest prophets. He is highly regarded in the Bible and the Quran. The Quran labels Goliath and his army, who came to fight David, as *"Kafirs"* or nonbelievers (infidels). The Bible holds David in high esteem but also mentions David's transgressions (adultery). The Quran does not, as it typically holds the prophets above such fallible acts.

Time to Ponder

- The Quran is at times frowned upon by non-Muslims for its criticism of the Israelites' grumbling with Moses. Are the accounts of the similar stories in the Torah any less harsh? Does that criticism extend to all Jews of all generations?
- In the Quran, David's (a "Jewish" prophet) battle with Goliath is dubbed as Jihad, and Goliath's army is labeled *"Kafir"* or infidels. Is that consistent with the *prevailing perception* of Jihad and infidels?

CHAPTER 17
JESUS (ISA) AND
MARY (MARYAM)

This chapter will cover the life and teachings of Jesus Christ and his mother Mary, known in the Quran as "Isa" and "Maryam," respectively. The mother and the son are inseparable, like no other in history. In both the Quran and the Gospel, the two hold a very high and exalted status. Mary, though not described as a prophet in the Quran, is mentioned with reverence that is reserved for only the most exalted prophets.

Jesus Christ (Isa)

Prophet Jesus Christ is also known as Messiah in the Quran and known as *Yasu* among Arabic-speaking Christians. He is a messenger (*Rasool*), a lawgiver, and an exalted prophet. Muslims add "Peace be upon him" after his name as a sign of utmost respect. He was sent to the children of Israel and was given the Holy Book, *Injil*, or Gospel. The Quran mentions Jesus twenty-five times by name but he is referred to numerous other times without naming him. The specific details of his childhood and other teachings are not mentioned in details like the Gospel does. However, his miraculous birth is the focus of many sections of the Quran. Most of the references to Jesus revolve around his birth, his mother Mary, his prophecy, and his miracles. In the Quran, like all other prophets, he is considered to be a Muslim, or a submitter (to the will of God), and believed to have taught his followers the same message: that there is One God without any partners.

The miracles of Jesus

The Quran refers to him as *Roohallah*, or the spirit of God, in that God endowed him with many unique miracles, reflecting some of God's attributes. God bestowed these miracles upon him as a sign to prove his prophecy. Some of the miracles are mentioned below:

- Jesus speaks as a newborn from his cradle to defend the honor of his mother, Mary, and to proclaim his prophethood.
- He breathes life into clay and makes it into a bird.
- He cures the lepers.
- He cures the blind.
- He brings the dead back to life.

The Key Beliefs Taught by the Quran Regarding Jesus

1. He was born of a miraculous birth, without a father. The Quran gives a parallel with Adam's birth.
2. He was a prophet and a messenger of God. He was the word of God, the spirit of God, and the Messiah. All people in this world will honor him, and he will be honored in the hereafter.
3. However, he was neither divine nor Son of God.
4. He did not die on the cross, but rather God made him ascend to the heavens to protect his honor. He will return to earth before the Day of Judgment, bringing peace and justice to earth.
5. Jesus preached the unity of God.
6. He performed many miracles, as noted above, all of them *by the will of God*, and thus the ultimate power and supremacy lies with God.

The following segment quotes verses from the Quran to elaborate on these points:

Holy Spirit

The Quran repeatedly refers to Jesus as "son of Maryam" and says that God strengthened Jesus with *"Ruhul Quds,"* or "Holy Spirit."

"We gave Moses the Book and followed him up with a succession of messengers; We gave Jesus the son of Mary Clear (Signs) and strengthened him with the holy spirit." 2:87

"Those messengers We endowed with gifts, some above others: To one of them Allah spoke [referring to Moses]; others He raised to degrees (of honor); To Jesus the son of Mary We gave clear (Signs), and strengthened him with the Holy Spirit." 2:253

The following verse refers to the Holy Spirit as well as the miracles that Jesus performed (moreover, the Quran insists he performed the miracles with God's permission):

"Then God will ask: 'O Isa son of Maryam! Recall my favor upon you and to your mother, how I strengthened you with the Holy Spirit, so you could speak to the people in cradle and in old age, how I taught you the Book, Wisdom, the Tawrat [Torah], and the Injeel [Gospel]. How you were able to make the figure of a bird out of clay, by My permission, how you breathed into it and changed it into a real bird, by My permission. How you could heal the born-blind and the lepers by My permission. How you could bring the dead body back to life by My permission. How I protected you from the violence of the children of Israel when you came to them with clear signs and the unbelievers among them said: 'This is nothing but a clear sorcery.'" 5:110 (Shakir)

What or who is this Holy Spirit? On the surface, it resembles the Holy Spirit (Holy Ghost) component of the Trinity doctrine. In verse 16:102, the words *Ruhul Quds* (or Holy Spirit) is once again used, but this time it is not in relation with Jesus Christ:

"Say [addressing Muhammad]: The Holy Spirit has revealed it [meaning the Quran] from your Lord with the truth, that it may establish those who believe and as a guidance and good news for those who submit." 16:102 (Shakir)

Quran commentators take the Holy Spirit to mean Archangel Gabriel. Verse 16:102 confirms that belief. The previous verses mentioning the "strengthening" of Jesus "with the Holy Spirit" would then indicate that God empowered Jesus to perform his miraculous acts, or more specifically empowered him with words, through Archangel Gabriel.

The Annunciation and the Birth of Jesus

Much like the angels visiting Abraham and giving him the glad tidings about Isaac's birth, Jesus's birth was also announced in advance. In this case, it was Archangel Gabriel who made the announcement. In both cases, the mothers were surprised: Sarah because of old age, and Mary because she was a virgin. The following is the narration from chapter 19, named after Mary (*Surah Maryam*):

"O Muhammad, relate to them the story of Maryam in the Book (the Quran) when she withdrew from her family to a place in the East. She chose to be secluded from them. We sent to her Our angel and he appeared before her as a grown man. She said: 'I seek Rahman's (The Gracious-God's) protection against you, leave me alone if you are God fearing.' He said: 'Don't be afraid, I am merely a messenger from your Rabb [Lord] to tell you about the gift of a holy son.' She said: 'How shall I bear a son, no man has ever touched me nor am I unchaste?' The angel replied: 'So shall it be—Your Lord says: "It is easy for Me. We wish to make him a Sign for mankind and a blessing [mercy] from Us"—and this matter has already been decreed.' So she conceived the child and she retired with him to a remote place. The pains of childbirth drove her to the trunk of a palm-tree. She cried in her anguish: 'Ah! Would that I had died before this, and been long forgotten!' Then (the child) called out to her from beneath her: Grieve not, surely your Lord has made a stream to flow beneath you; If you shake the trunk of this palm-tree, it will drop fresh ripe dates in your lap. So eat, drink, and refresh yourself. If you see anyone, tell him: 'I have vowed a fast to Rahman (The Gracious-God), so I will not speak to anyone today.'" 19:16–26 (Malik)

Jesus talks in the cradle: The newborn baby Jesus then surprises everyone by speaking in the cradle and announcing his prophethood: a unique miracle that had never been seen before (or since). Though to the outside world, this was the first time a newborn spoke, but this seemingly is not the first time Jesus spoke.

The verses 19:23–24 quoted above mention something that the Bible does not: the matter of Mary's giving birth to Jesus Christ and the labor pains, indicating the "normalcy" of a human birth. Moreover, *"Then (the child) called out to her from beneath her"* (or *"the voice beneath her called out"* as some other Muslim scholars have translated the verse) indicates that Jesus spoke to his mother even *before* his birth.

"At length she [meaning Mary] brought the (baby) to her people, carrying him (in her arms). They said: O Mary! Truly an amazing thing hast thou brought! O sister of Aaron! [As a reminder of Mary's ancestry]: your father was not a man of evil, nor your mother a woman unchaste! But she pointed to the baby. They said: How can we talk to one who is a child in the cradle? He (Jesus) said: I am indeed a servant of Allah: He has given me revelation and made me a prophet; And He has made me blessed wheresoever I be, and has enjoined on me Prayer and Charity as long as I live; (He) has made me kind to my mother, and not overbearing (or hard to deal with); So peace [salaam] is on me the day I was born, the day that I die, and the day that I shall be raised up to life (again)! Such (was) Jesus the son of Mary: (it is) a statement of truth, about which they (vainly) dispute." 19:27–34

When questioned, she points to her baby to respond to the critics and doubters. How would she have known that the newborn could talk? Once again, the point made about Jesus talking before his birth would make more sense now. (The other possibility would be a prior divine revelation to her about Jesus's ability to speak as a newborn, as noted below in verse 3:45–46.) Also note that Mary is referred to as a sister of Aaron in these verses. This refers to her ancestry, rather than being a biological sister of Aaron. Zechariah was an uncle of Mary and her guardian. Zechariah's wife (known as Elizabeth in the Bible) and Mary were related and were descendants of Aaron, according to Muslim scholars.

The Quran then goes on to announce and make very clear that God does not have a son:

"It is not befitting to (the majesty of) God that He Himself should beget a son! He is far above this; for when He decrees a matter He need only say: 'Be' and it is. (Jesus declared), Verily God is my Lord

and your Lord: therefore serve Him. This is the Right Way. In spite of this, the sects from among them are divided concerning Jesus." 19:35–37

Jesus the Messiah: Jesus's birth is once again narrated in another set of verses in chapter 3, showing that not only did Mary know about Jesus's ability to talk from the cradle, she also knew what her son will mean to the world and that her son would be the long-awaited Messiah:

"Behold! The angels said: O Mary! Allah gives you glad tidings of a Word from Him: his name will be Christ [Messiah] Jesus, the son of Mary, held in honor in this world and the Hereafter and of (the company of) those nearest to Allah; He shall speak to the people in childhood and in maturity. And he shall be (of the company) of the righteous." 3:45–46

According to the Quran, Jesus was sent to confirm what's in the Torah and to make some of the things lawful that were previously forbidden:

"She said: O my Lord! How shall I have a son when no man has touched me? He said: Even so: Allah creates what He wills: When He has decreed a plan, He but says to it, 'Be,' and it is! And Allah will teach him the Book and Wisdom, the Law [Torah] and the Gospel, And (appoint him) a messenger to the children of Israel, (with this message): 'I have come to you, with a Sign from your Lord, in that I make for you out of clay, as it were, the figure of a bird, and breathe into it, and it becomes a bird by Allah's leave: And I heal those born blind, and the lepers, and I quicken the dead, by Allah's leave; and I declare to you what you eat, and what you store in your houses. Surely therein is a Sign for you if you did believe; (I have come to you), to attest the Law which was before me. And to make lawful to you part of what was (Before) forbidden to you; I have come to you with a Sign from your Lord. So fear Allah, and obey me. It is Allah Who is my Lord and your Lord; then worship Him. This is a Way that is straight." 3:47–51

"Fear Allah" is according to the translation by Yousuf Ali. However, other translators have interpreted this differently, generally to mean to serve and worship him: "Worship Him" (Malik,

Mir Ali, and Unal), "keep your duties to Allah" (Pickthall), "be aware of God" (Yuksel), and "serve Him" (Emerick and Shakir)

As noted in many of the verses quoted in this section, Jesus repeatedly declares that God (Allah) is his Lord and commands his followers to worship Him.

While the Quran mentions the miracles of Jesus and his high status, the emphasis is clearly on God's ultimate authority. As with other prophets, the Quran's underlying teachings are about God's supremacy, whether the matter in question is his miraculous birth or miracles shown by Jesus Christ.

Jesus's Teachings to the Children of Israel and the Disciples

Many of Jesus Christ's teachings are not directly quoted but are mentioned in the form of God's foretelling Mary of his birth, what he will teach, and his miracles. This was outlined in the set quoted above (3:47–51).

The Quran does not name the disciples or indicate their number but mentions them as true believers. The disciples when asked by Jesus go on to pledge their allegiance to Jesus and that they believe him and his message to submit to One God.

"When Jesus found unbelief on their part He said: 'Who will be my helpers to (the work of) Allah?' Said the disciples: 'We are Allah's helpers: We believe in Allah, and you bear witness that we are Muslims [Submitters].'" 3:52

Once again, the Quran uses the word "Muslims" in a more broad sense here than what is typically perceived. It affirms the Quran's teachings that Islam is the same, universal religion taught by all prophets and thus their followers are submitters, or Muslims.

After the attestation of their faith in God, the disciples then went on to plead to God:

"Our Lord! we believe in what You have revealed, and we follow the Messenger; then write us down among those who bear witness." 3:53

Ascension

Muslims believe that Jesus did not die on the cross but rather ascended to heaven in bodily form, only to return in his second coming before the Day of Judgment, when he will bring peace, rule the world with justice, and kill the antichrist. They believe that he was made to appear to die on the cross. Who actually died on the cross is not mentioned in the Quran, and commentators widely vary in their opinion, from Judas Iscariot to Simon of Cyrene.

"Behold! Allah said: O Jesus! I will take you and raise you to Myself and clear (purify) you (of the falsehoods) of those who blaspheme; I will make those who follow you superior to those who reject faith, to the Day of Resurrection: Then shall you all return unto me, and I will judge between you of the matters wherein you dispute." 3:55

According to the commentary by Pooya Yazdi, the followers of Jesus believed his message and accepted him as a prophet of God, believed in his teachings and his prophecy about the coming of Muhammad.

"That they said (in boast), We killed Christ Jesus the son of Mary, the Messenger of Allah; but they killed him not, nor crucified him, but so it was made to appear to them, and those who differ therein are full of doubts, with no (certain) knowledge, but only conjecture to follow, for of a surety they killed him not. Nay! God took him up to Himself; and God is Mighty, Wise." 4:157–158

"And they contrived and Allah contrived and Allah is best of the contrivers." 3:54 (Fakhry). Most translators use the word "planned" for "contrived."

The majority of Muslim scholars and interpreters of the Quran believe the message in the Quran is that God will not allow His faithful servant to suffer and succumb to the enemies' plots and allow the enemies of Jesus, and in turn of God, a final victory. Thus his whole life was a miracle—from his conception, to his life, to the miracles he performed, and to his (apparent) death, or ascension.

Jesus in the Bible

The story of Jesus's life and teachings are captured in much more detail in the four Gospels. Even the Synoptic Gospels are said to have different perspectives on the life of Jesus. Like the Quran, Jesus is also known as the Messiah in the Gospels. "Messiah" comes from a Hebrew word *Mashiach*, meaning "anointed one." In Greek, this word is *Christos*, which became "Christ" in English.

The annunciation and birth of Jesus in the Gospel: Like the Quran, the Gospel speaks about the announcement of the birth of Jesus. However, the announcement from Archangel Gabriel to Mary is mentioned in the Gospel of Luke only. Matthew talks about an unnamed angel approaching Joseph, who was engaged to be married to Mary. The verses 26 to 36 from Luke, chapters 1, are quoted below:

"In the sixth month of Elizabeth's pregnancy, God sent the Angel Gabriel to Nazareth, a village in Galilee, to a virgin named Mary. She was engaged to be married to a man named Joseph, a descendant of King David. Gabriel appeared to her and said, 'Greetings, favored woman! The Lord is with you!'

"Confused and disturbed, Mary tried to think what the angel could mean. 'Don't be afraid, Mary,' the angel told her, 'for you have found favor with God! You will conceive and give birth to a son, and you will name him Jesus. He will be very great and will be called the son of the Most High. The Lord God will give him the throne of his ancestor David. And he will reign over Israel forever; his Kingdom will never end!' Mary asked the angel, 'But how can this happen? I am a virgin.'

"The angel replied, 'The Holy Spirit will come upon you, and the power of the Most High will overshadow you. So the baby to be born will be holy, and he will be called the son of God. What's more, your relative Elizabeth has become pregnant in her old age! People used to say she was barren, but she's now in her sixth month. For nothing is impossible with God.'" Luke 1:26–36

Though not using the exact words, there are striking similarities in this account and the Quranic verses quoted earlier. Both refer to the angel appearing to Mary, her being afraid, the angel talking about a holy son, and Mary's questioning as to how that is possible since she is a virgin.

According to the Gospel, Mary at the time of the annunciation was living in Nazareth; later she moved to Bethlehem, where Jesus was born. The Gospel, unlike the Quranic account, does not mention Jesus talking in the cradle. The Gospels go on to mention his circumcision when he was eight days old—a common practice among the Jews. After this, the Gospels are relatively quiet about his childhood till he was about twelve years old, when his family traveled to Jerusalem for Passover festivities.

Jesus, the king of Israel and the savior: The Gospel refers to Jesus as the king of Israel from David's progeny, who will liberate the Israelites once again—this time from the evil Roman Empire— and that he was the fulfillment of the prediction for the Davidic Messiah.

Baptism and temptation by Satan: Jesus was baptized by John the Baptist. Though John was surprised that Jesus asked him to be baptized, since Jesus was sinless, he proceeded with it anyway. Jesus then goes into a desert, where he fasts for forty days. There Satan appears to him and tempts him three times—by asking him to turn stones into bread, by asking him to jump off the top of Jerusalem's temple, and lastly by asking Jesus to worship him. Every time, Jesus quotes verses from scripture, and in the end, he tells Satan to leave:

"'Get out of here, Satan,' Jesus told him. 'For the scriptures say, "you must worship the LORD your God and serve only Him."'" Matthew 4:10

His teachings and the disciples: The rest of the Gospels then go on to describe the teachings of Jesus and the establishment of his ministries: how he starts to gather large crowds, and his showing of miracles, including curing lepers, giving eyesight to the blind, and giving life to the dead. The Roman Empire, as well as the religious leadership at the time, become alarmed by his teachings and popularity and begin plotting against him, eventually leading to his crucifixion.

The twelve disciples are named in the Gospel. Judas and Peter were among the twelve. Judas is said to have betrayed him when he informed the authorities of his whereabouts for thirty pieces of silver. He later commits suicide, but the vision of his torments in hell for betraying Jesus has been reported by many. Peter also backs off, when he was approached by the authorities when interrogated about Jesus's whereabouts, and he responds by saying he does not know Jesus (as was foretold by Jesus), but provides no information about Jesus's whereabouts. Peter later cries and repents and becomes a cornerstone for the early church. Another disciple was John the Baptist. John is known in the Quran as *Yahya*, son of Zechariah, and a prophet. The Gospel describes the last week of Jesus Chris in significant detail, including his seclusion, Judas's betrayal, his last supper with the disciples, his trial by the religious authorities and Roman Empire, and his sentencing.

The crucifixion: The cross was set up on a mountaintop. Jesus was put on the cross with nails through his hands and feet. On the way to the cross, he was beaten repeatedly; he was bloodied and made to carry his own cross. While on the cross, many people mocked him, including the chief priests. On the cross, Jesus then shouts out his final words: *"At about three o'clock, Jesus called out with a loud voice, 'Eli, Eli [Eloi, Eloi, according to Mark], lema sabachthani?' which means 'My God, my God, why have you abandoned me?'"* Matthew 27:46, Mark 15:34

True to his character and tradition, even at this tumultuous time, he asks God for forgiveness for the people, for "they don't know what they are doing."

Jesus appears to his disciples and other people: It's reported that after the crucifixion, Jesus appears to many people, including Mary Magdalene (John 20:10–18) and Peter and other disciples (John 21:1–23). Many of them note that the tomb that was supposed to contain his body was empty. Jesus also suddenly appears to two men walking in a village near Jerusalem:

"And just as they were telling about it, Jesus himself was suddenly standing there among them. 'Peace be with you,' he said. But the whole group was startled and frightened, thinking they were seeing a ghost." Luke 24:36–37

It is interesting to note that Jesus greets these two people by "Peace be with you," which is strikingly similar to what Muslims typically say to greet each other (*"**Assalamu Alaikum**"*). The Arabic translations of the New Testament for this verse also bear striking resemblance to Islamic greetings.

Muslims argue that the sighting of Jesus, as noted above, is consistent with the Quranic accounts of Jesus not really dying on the cross, but that he ascended to heaven and will return to earth before the Day of Judgment.

Ascension: Jesus is said to have appeared to some five hundred people after his resurrection. He then ascends to heaven as his disciples look on.

Trinity

A review of Jesus Christ's life cannot be complete without mentioning the Trinity. The following discussion is undertaken objectively, but with the utmost care and sensitivity, realizing its central importance among many Christian denominations.

The word "Trinity" is derived from Latin *trinitas*, meaning, "number three" or "a triad." A widely debated doctrine, it is near and dear to most Christians, while opposed by Judaism and Islam as well as some Christian churches. It is accepted and vigorously defended by most Christians, including Roman Catholics and most Protestants. The gist of this doctrine is that God exists in three persons: God the father, God the Son, and God the Holy Spirit, but He is really One divine being who merely exists in three forms. All three aspects represent the nature of God. Jesus Christ, according to the dogma, represents all three. God the Father is God the Creator. He is All-Powerful and All-Knowing. God the Son is in the form and flesh of Jesus Christ, who was both man and God at the same time (or God appearing in flesh). God the Holy Spirit (or Holy Ghost) is the Spirit of God as an inner presence and describes how God touches human affairs. It holds that the Holy Spirit descends on people. Whatever attributes God the Father has, God the Son and God the Holy Spirit have as well.

The history: Though the concept of Trinity probably started in the Pauline era, in the early Church there were various competing views of Jesus Christ: from being a prophet only to being God in the flesh. The doctrine of Trinity did not have its roots firmly established until a Christian church council in 325 CE in Nicaea (a village in the current Turkey) fixed the Christian belief of Jesus being the same substance as the Father and the son; several decades later, in 381, a council in Constantinople added the Holy Spirit in the Trinity as having the same substance as God. Triune scholars take the position that even though the doctrine was not established till the late fourth century, it existed in various forms starting with the Pauline era. Modern nontrinitarian groups still exist; perhaps the most well known are Reformist Protestant groups such as Jehovah's Witness and Unitarians, as well as Christian Scientists and the United Church of God (though these groups clearly represent a minority Christian viewpoint). Christian scholars acknowledge that Trinity is a complex and difficult concept to comprehend, especially for non-Christians. Michael Lodahl, a Christian scholar and professor of theology, defends Trinity, but in his book *Claiming Abraham*, he acknowledges, "Orthodox Christian teaching in fact does not encourage the idea that God is Jesus, the Messiah, period."[38] He goes on to further state, "It is not difficult to comprehend the logic of divine power as presented in the Qur'an. This is the God of sheer Omnipotence; the God worshiped not only by Muslims but also by many Jews and Christians—and a great many others, for that matter. It is, however, more difficult to comprehend the logic of divine power in John's Gospel. This God is indeed the Creator of all things, and in an important sense does indeed exercise 'power over everything' and yet this God has 'given all things into [Jesus'] hands.'" He returns to the subject of Trinity later in the book and points out, "The doctrine (Trinity) itself, of course, did not come ready-made from the Bible but required centuries of reading, reflection, and dispute within the Christian community."[39]

Though the word "Trinity" does not appear in the New Testament, Triune scholars cite numerous passages from the Gospel to support the doctrine:

"Then the eleven disciples left for Galilee, going to the mountain where Jesus had told them to go. When they saw him, they worshiped him but some of them doubted! Jesus came and told his disciples, 'I have been given all authority in heaven and on earth. Therefore, go and make disciples of all the nations, baptizing them in the name of the Father and the Son and the Holy Spirit.'" Matthew 28:16–19

---

38 Michael Lodahl, *Claiming Abraham*, Brazos Press, 2010, pp. 154-155.
39 Lodahl, *Claiming Abraham*, p. 184.

"After his baptism, as Jesus came up out of the water, the heavens were opened and he saw the Spirit of God descending like a dove and settling on him. And a voice from heaven said, 'This is my dearly loved Son, who brings me great joy.'" Matthew 3:16–17

The above passage is also mentioned in John 1:32 and Luke 3:22. There are numerous other mentions of God, the son, and the Holy Spirit that are interpreted by many Christian scholars and theologians as references to the Triune God. The Gospel of John is viewed as the one that most emphasizes the divinity of Jesus Christ:

"Jesus replied, 'I have already told you, and you don't believe me. The proof is the work I do in my Father's name. But you don't believe me because you are not my sheep. My sheep listen to my voice; I know them, and they follow me. I give them eternal life, and they will never perish. No one can snatch them away from me, for my Father has given them to me, and he is more powerful than anyone else. No one can snatch them from the Father's hand. The Father and I are one.' Once again the people picked up stones to kill him. Jesus said, 'At my Father's direction I have done many good works. For which one are you going to stone me?' They replied, 'We're stoning you not for any good work, but for blasphemy! You, a mere man, claim to be God.'" John 10:25–33

The Christian scholars are quick to point out that Trinity is *not* tritheistic idolatry and that the doctrine calls for One God, who appeared in three forms.

Arguments Against Trinity

Those arguing against the concept of Trinity point out that the concept only took firm root centuries after Jesus Christ and was introduced to please the Greco-Roman culture of paganism, when gods had many worldly attributes. They argue that the Old Testament, the Quran, and even the New Testament do not support it. The following are among the verses quoted in support of their argument:

Old Testament

"Hear O Israel, the Lord is our Lord, One Lord." Deuteronomy 6:4

"This is what the LORD says, Israel's King and Redeemer, the LORD of Heaven's Armies: 'I am the First and the Last; there is no other God.'" Isaiah 44:6

"I am the LORD; there is no other God." Isaiah 45:5

New Testament

"'Get out of here, Satan,' Jesus told him. 'For the scriptures say, "you must worship the LORD your God and serve only Him."'" Matthew 4:10

"Once a religious leader asked Jesus this question: 'Good Teacher, what should I do to inherit eternal life?' 'Why do you call me good?' Jesus asked him. 'Only God is truly good. But to answer your question, you know the commandments: "You must not commit adultery. You must not murder. You must not steal. You must not testify falsely. Honor your father and mother."'" Luke 18:18–19

Just before his death, on the cross, Jesus cries out: *"At about three o'clock, Jesus called out with a loud voice, 'Eli, Eli ('Eloi, Eloi,' according to Mark), lema sabachthani?' which means 'My God, my God, why have you abandoned me?'"* Matthew 27:46, Mark 15:34

"The people were surprised when they heard him. 'How does he know so much when he hasn't been trained?' they asked. So Jesus told them, 'My message is not my own; it comes from God who sent me.'" John 7:15–16

Son of God as a metaphor?

They further argue that the Jews before Jesus Christ often referred to people as "sons of God" to mean the servants of God. The sons of God served God and worked in His cause to please Him and to seek His nearness. Therefore "son of God" should not be taken in its literal sense to mean a biological son. "Son of God" and "Sons of God" are metaphorically mentioned numerous times in the Old and New Testaments:

"Then the people began to multiply on the earth, and daughters were born to them. The sons of God saw the beautiful women and took any they wanted as their wives." Genesis 6:1–2

"And the LORD told Moses, "When you arrive back in Egypt, go to Pharaoh and perform all the miracles I have empowered you

to do. But I will harden his heart so he will refuse to let the people go. Then you will tell him, 'This is what the LORD says: Israel is my firstborn son. I commanded you, "Let my son go, so he can worship me." But since you have refused, I will now kill your firstborn son!'" Exodus 4:21–23

"God blesses those who work for peace, for they will be called the children of God." Matthew 5:9

Before the last supper, when Jesus washed the feet of his disciples, he gave some last minute advice. Among other instructions, he told his disciples:

"I tell you the truth, slaves are not greater than their master. Nor is the messenger more important than the one who sends the message." John 13:16

Jesus's Lineage and Trinity

After describing his baptism, the Gospel of Luke, in keeping with the Bible's tradition of outlining the lineage of the prophets in detail, describes Jesus's lineage all the way to Adam:

"Jesus was about thirty years old when he began his public ministry. Jesus was known as the son of Joseph. Joseph was the son of Heli. Heli was the son of Matthat. Matthat was the son of Levi. Levi was the son of Melki. Melki was the son of Jannai." Luke 3:23–24

The rest of the verses (23–38) continue in the same fashion and end like this:

"Enosh was the son of Seth. Seth was the son of Adam. Adam was the son of God." Luke 3:38

Opponents of the Trinity doctrine point out again the reference to Adam as the son of God as a metaphor. They further ask why there is such a long lineage if one is to accept the "Jesus, the son of God" dogma. In that case, the description should have started and ended without anyone in between.

Jesus Acted with God's Will

"I can do nothing on my own. I judge as God tells me. Therefore, my judgment is just, because I carry out the will of the one who sent me, not my own will." John 5:30

"So Jesus told them, 'My message is not my own; it comes from God who sent me.'" John 7:16

These verses seem to concur with the ones quoted earlier from the Quran indicating the miracles were shown by God's permission.

Jesus the Messiah

"Then he (meaning Jesus) asked them (meaning his disciples), 'But who do you say I am?' Peter replied, 'You are the Messiah sent from God!'" Luke 9:20

The above verse essentially states that Jesus was the "anointed" (Messiah) and God was the "anointer."

The Quran and Trinity

Like Judaism and many other religions, Islam does not believe in the doctrine of Trinity. The Quran specifically rejects, in no uncertain terms, the notion that Jesus is God, or the Son of God. It states that the birth of Jesus was similar to the birth of Adam, different only in that Adam was born without a father *and* a mother.

"The similitude of Jesus before God is as that of Adam; He created him from dust, then said to him: 'Be'. And he was." 3:59

The Quran mentions that Jesus was a prophet who taught the Oneness of God (*Tawheed*), a fundamental belief taught by the scriptures.

"They take their priests and their anchorites to be their lords in derogation of Allah, and (they take as their Lord) Christ the son of Mary; yet they were commanded to worship but One God: there is no god but He. Praise and glory to Him: (Far is He) from having the partners they associate (with Him)." 9:31

"The Messiah, son of Mary is but a messenger; messengers before him have indeed passed away; and his mother was a truthful woman." 5:75

"O People of the Book! do not exceed the limits in your religion, and do not speak (lies) against God, but (speak) the truth; the Messiah, Jesus son of Mary is only a messenger of God and His Word which He communicated to Mary and a spirit from Him; believe therefore in God and His messengers, and say not, Three. Desist, it is better for you; God is only one God; far be It from His glory that He

should have a son, whatever is in the heavens and whatever is in the earth is His, and God is sufficient for a Protector." 4:171 (Shakir)

"Say: He is God, the One and Only; God, the Eternal, Absolute; [or Self-sufficient]. He begets not, nor is He begotten. And there is none like unto Him." 112:1–4

Another parallel between the Quran and the Gospel can be drawn in the following passages about Jesus and his disciples (God speaks in the first person in the Quranic passage quoted below):

"And when I revealed to the disciples, saying, Believe in Me and My messenger, they said: We believe and bear witness that we submit." 5:111 (Shakir)

Once again, the Quranic focus is on Jesus's teachings on belief in God *and* his messenger (Jesus), indicating they are two separate entities. Compare that to the Gospel of John, when Jesus instructs his disciples:

"Let not your heart be troubled: you believe in God, believe also in me." John 14:1

Final thoughts on Jesus Christ

The opposing views of Trinity aside, the Quran holds Jesus in extremely high esteem. He is a lawgiver, a messenger, nicknamed *"Roohallah,"* or "Spirit of God": a very high honor indeed. However, this Spirit of God is interpreted as an indication of God's power to create by the simple command, "be," and that Jesus represented God's word and some attributes that only he was bestowed with.

Mary (Maryam) in the Quran

Like her son Jesus Christ, Mary (or *Maryam*, as she is known in the Quran) is held in very high esteem, and though not considered a prophetess, or divine, she is mentioned with utmost respect. Many of the Quranic verses quoted in the prior section also refer to Mary. She is known to have spoken with angels, a great honor in itself, usually reserved for messengers and prophets. The Quran defends her vigorously and testifies to her chastity. Jesus himself is repeatedly mentioned in the Quran as "Jesus, son of Mary." She is one of only eight people in the Quran to have a chapter named after them (and the only woman). She is mentioned by name more often in the Quran than in the New Testament. In fact, she is the *only* woman mentioned by name in the Quran. She is among the four holiest ladies mentioned in Hadith (sayings of Prophet Muhammad). The other three are Fatima (his daughter), Khadijah (his first wife), and Asiya (pious wife of Pharaoh of Exodus, who picked Moses out of the Nile).

Mary's father was Amram (known as *Imran* in Arabic and *Joachim* in Christian literature). It is said that Mary's mother prayed to God to give what's "in her womb" to the service of God. She was raised by her uncle, Zechariah, and she often secluded herself to temple in remembrance of God, where it was said she received food from the angels.

"Behold! a woman of Imran said: O my Lord! I do dedicate unto You what is in my womb for Your special service: So accept this of me: For You hear and know all things. When she was delivered, she said: O my Lord! Behold! I am delivered of a female child! and Allah knew best what she brought forth. And no wise is the male Like the female. I have named her Mary, and I commend her and her offspring to Your protection from the Evil One, the Rejected.

"Graciously did her Lord accept her: He made her grow in purity and beauty: To the care of Zechariah was she assigned. Every time that he entered (her) chamber to see her, He found her supplied with sustenance. He said: O Mary! Where (comes) this to you? She said: From Allah: for Allah Provides sustenance to whom He pleases without measure." 3:35–37

Chosen above all women and purified by God: The Quran declares that Mary was chosen above all women of the world—a declaration not found in the New Testament. While announcing the birth of Jesus to Mary, the proclamation is made:

"Behold! the angels said: O Mary! God has chosen you and purified you, chosen you above the women of all nations." 3:42

Shia Muslim scholars and commentators like Pooya Yazdi go on to state that Fatima, daughter of Muhammad, was given the status and the title of the "leader of the ladies of the worlds" *(Syedatun Nisa)*, for chastity and purity, citing many authentic Hadith to support that belief. The last part of Quranic verse 33:33 is often quoted in support of that belief as well. Nonetheless, Mary retains a very high stature and is highly regarded among all Muslims.

Mary Was a Devout Worshiper and Guarded Her Chastity: The Quran testifies to Mary's pious character and her chastity, leaving no doubts in the mind of followers and readers of the Quran. The Quran refers to this perhaps more strongly and more often than the New Testament itself.

"O Mary! Worship Your Lord devoutly: Prostrate yourself, and bow down (in prayer) with those who bow down." 3:43

"And Mary the daughter of Imran, who guarded her chastity; and We breathed into (her body) of Our spirit; and she testified to the truth of the words of her Lord and of His Revelations, and was one of the devout (servant)." 66:12

"And (remember) her who guarded her chastity: We breathed into her of Our spirit, and We made her and her son a sign for all peoples." 21:91

God made Mary (and her son) a sign for all people: In addition to the verse quoted above, here is another one with the same declaration:

"And We made the son of Mary and his mother a symbol [of Our grace], and provided for both an abode in a lofty place of lasting restfulness and unsullied springs." 23:50

It is interesting to note that in the verse above, Jesus is referred to as the "son of Mary," without naming him; and Mary herself is referred to as "his mother," without naming her.

The Quran does not mention much about Mary's whereabouts at the time of the Crucifixion, or about her death. The Quran also does not mention her betrothal to Joseph. (Betrothal, also called espousal, is a formal state of engagement to be married, a Jewish tradition that has been practiced since the times of Abraham). In fact, the Quran is entirely quiet about any mention of Joseph, who the New Testament says married Mary after the miraculous conception of Jesus.

Mary in the New Testament

Highly revered by all Christian groups, some more than others, Mary is mentioned by name fewer than fifteen times in the New

Testament, most often in the Gospel of Luke (twelve times by name). The Gospel of Matthew mentions her by name five times, Mark's Gospel once, whereas John's Gospel does not mention her by name at all, though "the mother of Jesus" is mentioned on a couple of occasions. There are two nativity accounts in the Gospels. Matthew tells the story from Joseph's perspective, whereas Luke narrates it with the focus on Mary—something that it shares with the Quran. Please see section above under "Jesus in the Bible" and Luke 1:26–36. John's Gospel says that Mary witnessed the crucifixion of her son, Jesus Christ:

"But standing by the cross of Jesus were his mother and his mother's sister, Mary the wife of Clopas, and Mary Magdalene. When Jesus saw his mother and the disciple whom he loved standing nearby, he said to his mother, 'Woman, behold, your son!'" John 19:25–26

Mary is mentioned as a caring, loving, and concerned mother. Her motherly side is evident from the passage in Luke when Jesus accompanies her to Jerusalem at the age of twelve and went to a temple during the Passover festival, apparently without her knowledge, and she gets very anxious when she does not find him around.

"When they couldn't find him, they went back to Jerusalem to search for him there. Three days later they finally discovered him in the Temple, sitting among the religious teachers, listening to them and asking questions. All who heard him were amazed at his understanding and his answers. His parents didn't know what to think. 'Son,' his mother said to him, 'why have you done this to us? Your father and I have been frantic, searching for you everywhere.'" Luke 2:45–48

Mary's high position varies somewhat among Christians. The Roman Catholics highly revere her (but do not consider her divine); they ask her for intercession, believe in her assumption (taken up in to heavens), and believe in her perpetual virginity. These views are also shared by Eastern Orthodox Christians. Protestants, on the other hand, believe in the virgin birth of Jesus and that she was an ordinary, but a highly pious woman devoted to God. They believe that Jesus had brothers and sisters, thereby opposing the view of her perpetual virginity. All groups agree on her being a very pious lady, one who is highly regarded in God's view. Mary is believed to have lived for a varying period after the ascension of Jesus, from three days to twenty-four years.

Points to Remember

- Jesus Christ (or Isa, as he is known in the Quran, which also considers him one of the elite prophets) is highly revered both in the New Testament and the Quran. The Quran calls Jesus the Messiah. Muslims add "Peace be upon him" whenever saying Jesus's name (as they do with other prophets' names in a show of respect).
- The New Testament and Quranic accounts of the angelic announcement of the nativity are strikingly similar, though some differences exist. Jesus Christ was bestowed with many miracles; his conception itself is considered miraculous. The Quran portrays that as a sign of God's supremacy, rather than Jesus's divinity.
- The doctrine of Trinity didn't take firm root until a few centuries after Jesus, though it existed starting from the Pauline era. According to the doctrine, God presented Himself in three forms: the Father, the Son, and the Holy Spirit. Christian theologians point out that Trinity does not mean tritheistic idolatry. The Quran, like many non-Christian faiths, opposes the doctrine of Trinity.
- Mary, the only woman mentioned by name in the Quran, is highly revered and "chosen among the women of all nations." In fact, there is an entire Surah, or chapter, named after her (*Surah Maryam*).

Time to Ponder

- While the Quran gives elite status to Jesus, what is the purpose of its denial of the account of Jesus dying on the cross and the proclamation that he was raised to heaven?

CHAPTER 18
MUHAMMAD

Many non-Muslims, as well as many Muslims, often think of Muhammad as the "founder" of Islam. The Quranic view is that Islam (or submission to God) is the universal message revealed to humanity through a series of prophets and that Muhammad was the last prophet in that chain of prophethood. Prophet Muhammad was sent with a set of religious laws, or *Sharia*, making him a *Nabi*, or messenger (similar to other messengers like Prophets Moses and Jesus Christ). The Quranic view is that Prophet Muhammad did not bring a "new religion" per se, but rather *completed* the religion of other prophets before him—that religion being Islam, or submission. The singularity of the religion will be discussed in more detail in chapter 19.

Names of Muhammad

The name "Muhammad" means "the praised one" or "worthy of praise." He was also known as *"Ahmad,"* with similar meanings: "most worthy of praise" or "highly praised." He was also known as *Mustafa*, meaning the "chosen one." Other nicknames include *"Rehmatul Alaimeen"* ("blessing for all the worlds"), *"Habiballah,"* ("the beloved of Allah"), and *"Ad-Dahuk"* ("the one who smiles," "cheerful," or simply a pleasant, kind person).

PBUH: You might see the letters "PBUH" following his name, which stands for "Peace be upon him". This is derived from the Quranic verses whereby God instructs followers to send their peace and blessing unto him.

"God and His angels send blessings on the Prophet [Muhammad]: O you who believe! Send your blessings on him, and salute him with all respect." 33:56

"He it is Who sends blessings on you [Muhammad], (as do) His angels, that He may bring you [believers] out from the depths of darkness into light: and He is Full of Mercy to the Believers." 33:43

As noted before, in a show of respect, Muslims use the words "peace be upon him" after the names of all prophets. Though I have not always used these words in this book while mentioning the prophets, the respect for them is always intended and never ignored.

Brief Life History

In order to understand the Quran fully, it is critically important to study and understand the life of Muhammad. Without it, it would be like trying to understand the Torah without knowing the life history of Moses and the children of Israel, or understand the Gospel without knowing the history involving Mary and Jesus Christ. It is beyond the scope of this book to cover his life story in depth, but a brief synopsis is submitted here.

His life can be summarized in three parts: From birth to the first revelation at age forty, his prophetic life in Mecca, and lastly the postemigration (Hijra) years in Medina.

Birth to the Announcement of Prophecy (570 CE to 610 CE):

Prophet Muhammad was born in the city of Mecca in the year 570 CE. His lineage is from Abraham through his first son Ishmael through Kedar (Qedar), one of the twelve sons of Ishmael. In those days, Mecca was a trade center and a trade route from Yemen in the south to Syria in the north. He was born in a clan known as Quraish. Most Meccans were pagans and polytheists. Ka'aba, the holiest shrine in Islam, built by Abraham and Ishmael, was by now riddled with many idols. The chief god's name was *Hubal*. Allah was considered one of the gods and was called upon only in crisis; there was not the same monotheistic concept of Allah as the Muslims have now, or as taught by prior prophets. In addition, there were three goddesses in Ka'aba named *al-Lat, Manat,* and *al-Uzza*. The pagans considered them daughters of Allah. Despite being covered with gods by the pagans, in violation of the monotheistic intentions of its founders, Ka'aba retained its sacred status (though for entirely different deities) and was a vital center for pilgrimage.

Muhammad's father, Abdullah, died before his birth. His mother, A'mina, and grandfather, Abdul Muttalib, raised him. His mother passed away when he was six years old, and two years later, his grandfather also passed away, leaving him with one of his uncles, Abu Talib, as his guardian and, as we will see, his protector. Abu Talib was a trader and highly respected tribal leader in Mecca.

Muhammad's noble character and high ethical and moral standards were apparent well before his announcement of prophethood. He accompanied his uncle on many trade caravans. When he was still very young, the caravan stopped in Basra, Iraq, where a Christian monk named *Bahira* is believed to have seen a light above the caravan and took it as a sign that the awaited prophet was amongst them. He examined Muhammad for the signs of prophecy, reportedly a mark on his back between the shoulders (a birthmark?), and recognized him as the prophet promised by the scriptures. (Some authors state this happened on a journey to Syria, not Iraq.) Throughout this period of his life, people respected him for his honesty, kindness, and trustworthiness. It was a common practice for people to leave their earnings and other valuable belongings in his possession without any witnesses or agreements, trusting him that he would return it without any issues and thus received the nicknames *As-Sadiq* (the truthful) and *Al-Amin* (the trustworthy).

One of the wealthiest persons in all of Arabia, a tradeswoman named Khadijah, became aware of his attributes and employed him to lead her trade caravan. She sent a trusted employee to observe him. His report was nothing short of stellar for Muhammad's honest dealings, and he spoke highly of his ethical standards and mannerisms. Impressed by these attributes, it's reported that she eventually proposed to Muhammad, and he accepted. It was by all means a very happy marriage, built on mutual respect and love. Khadijah and Muhammad were very supportive of each other. Muhammad did a lot of his own household chores, like preparing food, sewing his clothes, and repairing his shoes.

First Revelations, 610 CE

The Meccans were mostly illiterate, though they excelled in poetry. The pre-Islamic culture of Mecca was not pretty; it is known as *"Jahilia,"* or the age of ignorance. In addition to idol worshipping, fights were common among the tribes for petty issues. A newborn daughter brought shame to a family's honor, and many were buried alive or abandoned. Women had practically no rights, and neither did slaves. Muhammad wanted no part of it and often went on reclusive trips for days to a cave near Mecca, called *Hira*. He meditated hard and worshipped God for long periods of time. Then one day, his whole life changed, which started a new chapter in the history of religions when the first five verses of the Quran were revealed to him through Archangel Gabriel.

"Read! [Or some translate as 'Recite']: In the name of your Lord Who created—created man from a clot [leechlike mass]. Read! Your Lord is the Most Honorable, Who taught by the pen. Taught man what he knew not." 96:1–5 (Shakir)

The question "when did he 'become' a prophet?" is somewhat controversial. Most Muslims believe he "became a prophet" at this time. Others believe that, like all other prophets, he was sinless and was born a prophet. Regardless, all Muslims agree that the message he received at the age of forty was the start of the revelations of the Quran and his ministry.

Early preaching: Muhammad initially kept his prophecy to his own circle of family and close friends. The first one to hear about the experience was Khadijah herself. Soon thereafter his cousin, Ali, and other family members heard about it. As one might guess, his first public announcement didn't go very well. He gathered the pagans of Mecca and asked them, "If I told you there is an army waiting behind these mountains to attack you, would you believe it?" They responded, "Of course, you are *As-Sadiq* (the truthful) and you never lie." Muhammad then followed up by saying something to the effect of, "Then let me tell you that there is no god but God (Allah) and I am his messenger." The animosity shown by the Meccan pagans was rather instantaneous. The "truthfulness" and "trustworthiness" he earned over decades of immaculate character dissolved within moments after this declaration. He continued to preach the unity of God and asked the pagans to stop worshipping the powerless gods. His uncle, Abu Talib, continued to protect and support him.

New converts are persecuted: Since Prophet Muhammad himself was relatively protected at this time due to the reputation and status of Abu Talib, the wrath of the pagans fell on the new converts. The pagans of Mecca reverted to torturing the few who converted. Among them was an African slave named *Bilal,* from Ethiopia. He was dragged on hot desert sand, heavy rocks were put on his chest, and he was asked to repeal his newfound belief. He, like all other converts, refused. Years later, Muhammad, along with his family and most of the converts, were expelled to a valley and were cut off from the mainstream. This was a social and economical boycott. Many died due to insufficient food and other hardships. Three years later, they eventually returned to Mecca. However, this difficult experience took a heavy toll on him and his family, and in the year 619, he lost both Khadijah and Abu Talib. This year is called "the year of sorrow," as he lost two of his most beloved and staunch supporters.

Christian ruler grants refuge in Abyssinia (Ethiopia): In the times preceding the deaths of Khadijah and Abu Talib, around 615, Prophet Muhammad allowed the immigration of about eighty new converts to Abyssinia (currently Ethiopia). A group of Meccan Quraish tribesmen followed them. Their pagan leader brought gifts to the ruler and met them in the palace of the Christian king named *Ashama Ibn Abjar* (commonly known in Islamic traditions as *Al-Najashy*); they asked him to extradite the immigrant Muslims to Mecca, so they could be persecuted. He described the immigrants as unruly people who disobeyed the gods of Mecca, explaining that they preached Oneness of God. The Christian ruler, known for his mercy and fairness, brought the Muslims back to the palace to respond. Jafar Ibne Abu Talib, Muhammad's cousin and one of the Muslim immigrants' leaders, went on to plead his case. He stated that they were ignorant people before Prophet Muhammad's message, worshipping idols and acting like wild animals. "We acted badly," he admitted, adding that they abandoned relatives and mistreated their neighbors. "Strong oppressed the weak," he stated.

After this background, Jafar goes on to describe how Prophet Muhammad changed them, in that he invited them to worship One God, to be honest and truthful, to visit their relatives, to be good neighbors, to give in charity, to avoid committing atrocities, and to prevent spreading evil against women or taking orphans' money. He went on to describe how this resulted in their persecution and torture by the pagan Meccans, resulting in their escape to Abyssinia as they preferred this king over many others, knowing he would treat them justly.

Al-Najashy then asked Jafar if this prophet had brought any revelations, to which Jafar quoted the following verses from the chapter 19 (*Surah Maryam*) of the Quran (these were also quoted in this book in the previous chapter):

"And mention Maryam [Mary] in the Book when she drew aside from her family to an eastern place. So, she took a veil (to screen herself) from them; then We sent to her Our Spirit, and there appeared to her a well-made man (an angel). She said: Surely I fly for refuge from you to the Beneficent God, if you are one guarding (against evil). He said: I am merely a messenger from your Lord to tell you about the gift of a holy son. She said: When shall I have a boy and no mortal has yet touched me, nor have I been unchaste? He said: Even so; your Lord says: It is easy to me: and that We may make him a sign to men and a mercy from us; and it is a matter which has been decreed. So, she conceived him; then withdrew herself with a remote place and the throes (of childbirth) compelled her to take herself to the trunk of a palm tree. She said: Oh, would that I had died before this, and had been a thing quite forgotten! Then (the child called out to her from beneath her): Grieve not, surely your Lord has made a stream to flow beneath you. And shake toward you the trunk of the palm tree, it will drop on you fresh ripe dates. So, eat and drink and refresh the eye. Then if you see any mortal, say: Surely I have vowed a fast to the Beneficent God."

It is said that by now, the Christian ruler Al-Najashy was in tears. Jafar went on to recite more verses; the last segment is quoted below (after people questioned Mary about the baby Jesus):

"But she pointed to him. They said: How should we speak to one who was a child in the cradle? He said: 'Surely I am Allah's servant;

he has given me the Book and made me a prophet, and has made me blessed wherever I may be, and he has enjoined on me prayer and poor-rate so long as I live and dutiful to my mother; and he has not made me insolent, unblessed and peace be on me on the day I was born, and on the day I die, and on the day I am raised to life.'"

It is reported that the priests and the monks wept humbly, too. At this time, Al-Najashy angrily told the Meccan pagans that he believed the Muslims' story and he returned their gifts. He then asked Jafar, "How do you greet each other?" Jafar responded, "By saying *Assalamu Alaikum* ("Peace be upon you")." At which time, Al-Najashy said, *"Assalamu Alaikum.* You are welcome to stay in my land."

The stories of most other Muslim converts were not nearly as cordial or heartwarming, where they were severely persecuted by Meccan pagans.

Miraj/Isra (Ascension to Heaven): 620 CE

The year after the "year of sorrow," Muhammad is said to have ascended to heaven one night, a journey called *Miraj.* To this date, this night, on the eve of the 27th of Rajab (the seventh month of Islamic calendar), is observed in many Muslim countries as "the night of Miraj." According to the Islamic traditions, in the first part of the trip, called *Isra,* Prophet Muhammad was taken by Gabriel on *Buraq,* the mythological steed, from Ka'aba to the "farthest mosque," or the Al-Aqsa mosque in Jerusalem. From there he was taken into heaven. At each station of heaven, he met various prophets from Adam to Abraham to Moses to Jesus, accompanied by Archangel Gabriel. He was then led directly in close proximity to God, so close that it's reported that even Archangel Gabriel had to excuse himself. There, Prophet Muhammad spoke directly to God at a distance of "two bows or less," according to the Quran as noted below. The matters of Islamic jurisprudence were handed to him. It is widely believed by Muslims that the Miraj was to honor and reward him for his hard work, to show him God's signs, and also to boost him when he was feeling down following the deaths of his two dearest supporters: Khadijah and Abu Talib. After his dialogue with God, Prophet Muhammad was brought back on the

Buraq to Mecca and his bed. It is said that the time it took on earth for his door chain to swing only once is the time it took for the entire night's journey. Ibne Ishaq, the author of the first biography on Muhammad, believed the journey was spiritual, whereas later authors like Ibne Kathir and Al Tabari believe the journey was physical. Most of the details are part of the Hadith or Islamic history, and the Quran does not give many specifics of the night journey. The Miraj is mentioned in the opening verse of chapter 17, named *Al-Isra* (or "The Night Journey"):

"Glory to (Allah) Who did take His servant [meaning Muhammad] for a Journey by night from the Sacred Mosque to the farthest Mosque, whose precincts We did bless, in order that We might show him some of Our Signs." 17:1

And in chapter 53, the night journey is referred to once again in a bit more detail. The verses assert that the journey was physical and the prophet was not dreaming:

"Endued with Wisdom: for he appeared (in stately form). While he was in the highest part of the horizon. Then he approached and came closer, So did (Allah) convey the inspiration to His Servant, (conveyed) what He (meant) to convey. The (Prophet's) (mind and) heart in no way falsified that which he saw. Will you then dispute with him concerning what he saw? For indeed he saw him at a second descent, Near the Lote-tree beyond which none may pass: [said to be at the farthest end of the seven heavens, beyond which none can pass]. Near it is the Garden of Abode. Behold, the Lote-tree was shrouded (in mystery unspeakable!) (His) sight never swerved, nor did it go wrong! For truly did he see, of the Signs of his Lord, the Greatest!" 53:6–18

Emigration to Medina or Hijra: 622 CE

Back in Mecca, life was getting harder for the new Muslims. After the death of his uncle, Abu Talib, the pressure mounted. There were more direct threats to Prophet Muhammad's life. He had given permission for many of his followers to immigrate to Medina, known as *Yathrib* at the time. The enemies were planning an attack on him during his sleep. They surrounded his house. It is reported that God informed him of their plans, and he made his cousin,

Ali, lie in his bed, to give the impression Muhammad was home and asleep. He then left his house in the dark, accompanied by his close friend, Abu Bakr. When the pagans entered the house, they were surprised and furious to see Ali instead of Muhammad and went on to chase him into the desert. Muhammad and Abu Bakr hid in a cave. Muslim narrations speak of a tree that grew overnight as well as a spider web that spread across the opening of the cave, making the enemies believe no one could be hiding inside the cave. They eventually gave up the chase, and Prophet Muhammad safely proceeded to Medina.

The emigration to Medina became a landmark event and is the beginning of the Islamic calendar. The event is known as *Hijra*. The year 2012 CE corresponds to 1433 AH (After Hijra)

Life in Medina: Muhammad was warmly greeted by people in Medina, which means "the city"—the full name being *Medina tul Nabi*, or "the City of the Prophet." He quickly became not only a spiritual leader but a statesman, a military leader, and a strategist as well. He paired each immigrant Muslim with one of the Medinites, called *Ansar* (helper), and declared them brothers. He made joint agreements with the two main Jewish clans in Medina, which stipulated the two groups would support each other if either party came under attack, and started a social system of fairness and justice, as the new religious laws were revealed. There the first Muslim community took roots, with its own set of laws, justice, and religious and social reforms.

The emigration only fueled the hatred and animosity of the pagans of Mecca toward him and his newfound ministry; this led to many wars between the two parties when the pagans attempted to overcome the new community. These were fought mostly near or around Medina. During his time in Medina, the nature of the revelations in the Quran changed from issues related to the unity of God and avoiding polytheism to setting religious and social laws, and verses on interfaith issues as the audience changed from pagan Meccans to a newly formed Muslim community and the Jews and the Christians of Medina.

Conquering of Mecca, 630 CE: By now, Islam had spread from a handful of followers to tens of thousands due to rapid conversion, without the use of force. Prophet Muhammad entered into an agreement with pagan Meccans, called the Treaty of Hudaibiyya. It called for a ten-year truce. However, the pagans broke the treaty repeatedly when they continued to attack small groups of Muslims from Medina, which eventually prompted Muhammad to respond with force, in accordance with the terms of the treaty. In January of 630, Prophet Muhammad, accompanied by an army of ten thousand, marched into Mecca after the pagans again broke the terms of the treaty. In a completely bloodless takeover, Prophet Muhammad announced general amnesty. However, he continued to live in Medina, his adopted city.

Last pilgrimage and death, 632 CE: Prophet Muhammad led Muslims on a Hajj, a pilgrimage to Mecca, where he gathered all the pilgrims in the plains of Arafat for his last sermon. This included part of a verse from chapter 5, verse 3:

"This day have I perfected your religion for you, completed My favor upon you, and have chosen for you Islam as your religion."

The Shia Muslims believe that as the crowd started to disperse after the sermon, he called them back at a place called "the pond of Khum," and the following verse was revealed, contending this was in reference to the announcement of Ali as his successor:

"O Messenger! Proclaim the (message) which has been sent to you from your Lord. If you did not, you would not have fulfilled and proclaimed His mission. And Allah will defend you from men (who mean mischief)." 5:67

By now Islam had spread beyond the confines of Arabia. People were highly impressed with Prophet Muhammad's humble, benevolent nature and the simple message of fairness, justice, and peace for all, while protecting the rights of the oppressed and neglected (women, blacks, slaves, and orphans, among others). Soon after the return from Mecca, Prophet Muhammad fell ill and, after a brief illness, passed away on June 8, 632, at the age of sixty-two. Even to his detractors, his amazing story of establishing a social and religious system within a very short span of twenty-two years, that exists till this age, is nothing short of astounding and one of the all-time success stories.

References in the Quran

Prophet Muhammad is referred to by name (Muhammad) only four times in the Quran and by his other name, Ahmad, one more time. However, there are numerous references to him in other passages that start with *"Qul,"* meaning, "say" (O Muhammad), and also by "O, messenger," "O, prophet," and other indirect references, including "you," *"Yaseen,"* and others.

Muhammad, the prophet for mankind: The Quran considers Muhammad a prophet sent for mankind, not just a specific group of people:

"(O Muhammad,) say: "O mankind! I am the Rasool [apostle] of Allah toward all of you from He to whom belongs the kingdom of the heavens and the earth. There is no deity but Him. He brings to life and causes to die. Therefore, believe in Allah and His Rasool, the unlettered Prophet (Muhammad) who believes in Allah and His Word. Follow him so that you may be rightly guided." 7:158 (Malik)

"We have sent you (O Prophet!), to mankind as a messenger; and God is sufficient as a witness." 4:79 (Malik)

"O Muhammad! This is a Book which We have revealed to you so that you may bring mankind out of utter darkness to the light, by the leave of their Lord, to the Way of the Mighty, the Praiseworthy." 14:1 (Malik)

Muhammad: The Answer to the Prayer of Abraham

Many Muslim scholars believe that Prophet Muhammad was the answer to the prayers of Abraham and Ishmael, while building Ka'aba in Mecca. The following prayers are the culmination of their prayers:

"Our Lord! And make us both submissive (Muslims) to You and (raise) from our offspring a nation submitting to You [Muslims], and show us our ways of devotion and turn to us (mercifully), surely You are the Oft-returning (to mercy), the Merciful. Our Lord! And raise up in them a Messenger from among them who shall recite to them Your communications and teach them the Book and the wisdom, and purify them; surely You are the Mighty, the Wise." 2:128–129 (Shakir)

Muhammad's character: Addressing and referring to Muhammad and dispelling the claim of his opponents, the Quran proclaims his noble character:

"Nay, verily for you [meaning Muhammad] is a reward unfailing: And you (stand) on an exalted standard of character." 68:3–4

When he was forced to immigrate to Medina, fearing for his life, he was still in possession of many of the valuables of the Meccans, as was their custom. Rather than keeping them to himself, he asked Ali, who stayed behind in Mecca for a little while, to return them to their rightful owners—the same pagans who were after his life.

Mercy for the believers: The Quran calls him mercy to the believers.

"Now has come unto you a Messenger from amongst yourselves: it grieves him that you should perish: ardently anxious is he over you: to the believers is he most kind and merciful." 9:128

Muhammad, mercy for mankind: He showed mercy to everyone regardless of their creed. This is based on his life stories, full of examples when he showed a tender heart and mercy to people, including those who tortured him, his family, and companions. An often-told story about him goes as follows:

Muhammad went to Taif, a town near Mecca, to preach to the locals. The trip was rather discouraging, in that no one took heed, and in fact they mocked and ridiculed him. He was physically tortured, and one old woman threw garbage over him every day when he passed near her house. One day, when he passed through the same street, no one threw garbage on him from that house. He inquired and found out the old woman had fallen ill. He then spent time consoling her, tended to her illness, and cleaned her house, as it had gotten dirty during her illness.

People also threw rocks at him and put thorny bushes in his path so much that his shoes would be filled with blood. Battered and disappointed, he returned to Mecca, and on his way back, it is narrated, Archangel Gabriel met him and offered to turn the whole town upside down as punishment. Prophet Muhammad instead showed his benevolent nature and forgave his tormentors and offered a prayer for them.

Upon his triumphant return to Mecca, the same Meccans who tortured him and his supporters now feared for their lives. But it was a bloodless coup. He asked the Meccan pagans who were awaiting his decision about them, "How do you expect me to treat you?" They responded unanimously: "You are a noble one, the son of a noble one." He then told them, "You may go free! No reproach this day shall be on you; may God forgive you."

Muhammad, a blessing and mercy for all the worlds: The Quran goes on to proclaim him as mercy, or blessing, not just for "Muslims," or mankind, but all of the worlds (the plural). This is the verse where Muhammad is called the *"Rehmatul Alaimeen,"* meaning "mercy to all the worlds."

"And We have not sent you [O Muhammad] but as a mercy to the worlds." 21:107 (Shakir). Yousuf Ali translates this verse as *"a mercy to all the creatures."*

The Hadith is full of narrations of his instructions to show mercy to others, including animals.

Not divine: Despite his noble character, Muhammad is not believed to be divine. The Quran warns those who might be tempted to think otherwise (or who might have lost their belief after Muhammad's death) in the following verse:

"And Muhammad is no more than a messenger; the messengers have already passed away before him; if then he dies or is killed, will you turn back upon your heels? And whoever turns back upon his heels, he will by no means do harm to Allah in the least and Allah will reward the grateful." 3:144 (Shakir)

Does not say anything on his own: Prophet Muhammad is believed by Muslims to have said nothing on his own, except what was revealed to him by God through revelations.

"By the star when it goes down. Your Companion is neither astray nor being misled. Nor does he say (aught) of (his own) desire. It is naught but revelation that is revealed, the Lord of Mighty Power has taught him." 53:1–5

This in many ways is not different from Jesus proclaiming that his words are not his own but essentially are inspired by God, as told in the Gospel of John:

"So Jesus told them, 'My message is not my own; it comes from God who sent me.'" John 7:16

"Jesus replied, 'All who love me will do what I say. My Father will love them, and we will come and make our home with each of them. Anyone who doesn't love me will not obey me. And remember, my words are not my own. What I am telling you is from the Father who sent me.'" John 14:23–24

Obey Muhammad: Since Prophet Muhammad's words are believed to be under divine control, obeying him and obeying God go hand in hand. The Quran has many verses with the phrase "Obey God and obey the messenger."

"O you who believe! Obey God and obey the Messenger and those in authority from among you; then if you quarrel about anything, refer it to God and the Messenger, if you believe in God and the last day; this is better and very good in the end." 4:59 (Shakir)

Muhammad, the judge: The following is another verse, in addition to the verse quoted above, asking believers to seek and accept his judgments:

"But no, by the Lord, they can have no (real) Faith, until they make you judge in all disputes between them, and find in their souls no resistance against your decisions, but accept them with the fullest conviction." 4:65

Muhammad a warner and bearer of good tidings: Like all other prophets before him, the Quran refers to Muhammad frequently as a warner and the bearer of glad tidings:

"Surely We have sent you with the truth as a bearer of good news and a warner; and there is not a people but a warner has gone among them." 35:24

"Say: I am not the first (new) of the messengers, and I do not know what will be done with me or with you: I do not follow anything but that which is revealed to me, and I am nothing but a plain warner." 46:9 (Shakir)

Muhammad the last prophet: A key Islamic belief is that Muhammad is the seal, or the last of the prophets:

"Muhammad is not the father of any of your men, but he is the Messenger of God and the last of the prophets; and God is cognizant of all things." 33:40 (Shakir)

Muhammad in the Bible?

Muslim scholars and commentators of the Quran contend that Muhammad *was* foretold in the Bible, and in fact many Jews and Christians of Arabia were awaiting the coming of the prophet to fulfill the prophecy in the Bible. (Similar to the Christian belief that Jesus was foretold in the Old Testament.) It must be pointed out here, however, that Prophet Muhammad is not considered the Messiah. According to most Muslim scholars, the two persons who foretold Muhammad's prophecy (to Muhammad) were Christian monks, first when he was a young boy, accompanying his uncle on a trade journey, and then after the first revelation of Quranic verses, when Khadijah is said to have taken him to her cousin, a Christian, for advice on his experience. (The Shia Muslim commentators disagree with the latter, believing that he did not need a confirmation of his prophecy from another human.) The Quran refers to the prophecy being foretold in the Bible in the following verses:

"And remember, Jesus, the son of Mary, said: 'O children of Israel! I am the messenger of God (sent) to you, confirming the Law [Torah] before me, and giving Glad Tidings of a Messenger to come after me, whose name shall be Ahmad.' But when he [meaning Muhammad] came to them with Clear Signs, they said, 'this is evident sorcery!'" 61:6

In a long sequence previously quoted in chapter 16, the Quran interrupts the story on Moses to proclaim the following:

"Those who follow the messenger, the unlettered Prophet, whom they find mentioned in their own (scriptures), in the law [Torah] and the Gospel, for he commands them what is just and forbids them what is evil; he allows them as lawful what is good (and pure) and prohibits them from what is bad (and impure); He releases them from their heavy burdens and from the yokes that are upon them. So it is those who believe in him, honor him, help him, and follow the light, which is sent down with him, it is they who will prosper. Say [O Muhammad]: O men! [Mankind] I am sent unto you all, as the Messenger of Allah, to Whom belongs the dominion of the heavens and the earth: there is no god but He: it is He That gives both life and death. So believe in Allah and His Messenger, the Unlettered

Prophet, who believes in Allah and His words: follow him that (so) you may be guided." 7:157–158

These verses naturally sent the Muslim scholars to search for verses in the Bible to find these statements, even though they believe the Bible is in altered form since its original divine revelations.

Deuteronomy 18:15 and 18:17–18 and Acts 3:22

The following are the verses often quoted by Muslim scholars to point out that Moses in the Torah spoke about the coming of Muhammad:

"The Lord, your God will raise up for you a Prophet like me from your midst, from your brethren. Him you shall hear." Deuteronomy 18:15

"And the Lord said to me (meaning Moses): 'What they have spoken is good. I will raise up for them a Prophet like you from among their brethren, and will put My words in His mouth, and He shall speak to them all that I command Him." Deuteronomy 18:17–18

"Moses said, 'The Lord your God will raise up for you a Prophet like me from among your own people. Listen carefully to everything he tells you." Acts 3:22

However, these verses are a subject of controversy and contradictory claims, as outlined in the following sections.

The Likeness of Moses and Muhammad

Muslim scholars go on to point out the similarities between Moses and Muhammad to highlight the verse in Deuteronomy 18:15 ("a prophet like me"). Jesus shared some, but not all, of the following:

- Lawgiver
- Spiritual leader
- Judge and arbitrator for their communities
- Political leader of their communities
- Military leader
- Raised by someone other than their parents (at least most of their early lives)

The above translation of the verses from Deuteronomy is from the King James Version. A similar translation is found in the New International Version of 1984 (*"I will raise up for them a prophet like you from among their brothers"*). The newer translations of the Old Testament have translated the highlighted words differently:

"I will raise up for them a prophet like you from among their fellow Israelites." (New International Version)

"I will raise up a prophet like you from among their fellow Israelites." (New Living Translation)

Many Christian scholars argue that the Deuteronomy verses were actually in reference to the coming of Jesus, since he was an Israelite and Muhammad was from the progeny of Ishmael in Arabia. They point out that God indeed put His words in Jesus's mouth and that Jesus *was* the word of God. Matthew Henry in his commentary of Deuteronomy 18:15–18 goes on to quote the following verses in support of the belief that God spoke through Jesus:

"Long ago God spoke many times and in many ways to our ancestors through the prophets. And now in these final days, he has spoken to us through his Son." Hebrews 1:1–2

Muslim scholars counter by referring to the older translations, using the word "brethrens," rather than "fellow Israelites." Moreover, Jesus's birth was miraculous, without a father, and thus he couldn't have been a "prophet like Moses." The debate goes on. Regardless of who these particular verses refer to, there is a general consensus among Christian and Muslim scholars that the coming of Jesus *was* also foretold in the Torah and that the Jews were indeed awaiting for the Messiah.

Paraclete: The Comforter

In the Gospel of John, Jesus spoke of a comforter, or Paraclete, who will come after him:

*"But I will send you the **Advocate** (comforter, from the Greek 'Paraclete"), the "spirit of truth". He will come to you from the Father and will testify all about me."* John 15:26

*"But the **Comforter**, which is the Holy Ghost, whom the Father will send in my name, he shall teach you all things, and bring all things to your remembrance, whatsoever I have said unto you."* John 14:26

The bolded words are the English translation of the original Greek word, *"Peraclytos."* In Christianity, "Paraclete" has been used to mean a helper, an advocate, and an intercessor (Jesus Christ). Later on, the early church around the fourth century used the word "Paraclete" to mean the Holy Spirit. Some Muslim scholars have pointed out that the original Greek word used was *"Periklytos,"* which has almost the same meaning as the Arabic word "Muhammad" or "Ahmad": "the praised one" or "praiseworthy" (Ibn Kathir, David Benjamin Keldani), and this word in some *older* Arabic translations of the New Testament has been translated as *"Ahmad."* (The current Arabic versions of the New Testament mostly translate the word as *"Ruhul Quds"* or Holy Spirit.) They contend that "Periklytos" got replaced with *"parakletos"* (or *Paraclete* in English).

Moreover, Muslim scholars claim that the Paraclete is spoken of in the future tense and as such couldn't have meant Jesus himself, as Jesus was foretelling a future prophet. (*"He will come to you from the Father and will testify all about me."*) Therefore, they conclude that these biblical verses are what the Quranic verse 61:6 perhaps refers to (*"And remember, Jesus, the son of Mary, said: 'O children of Israel! I am the messenger of God (sent) to you, confirming the Law (Torah) before me, and giving Glad Tidings of a Messenger to come after me, whose name shall be Ahmad.'"*). Moreover the *spirit of truth*, in John 15:26, Muslims contend, once again refers to Muhammad, whose nickname as mentioned before was *As-Sadiq* (the truthful). The matter largely remains unresolved without a consensus between Christian and Muslim scholars.

The great nation from Ishmael: According to the Torah, God's first covenant to Abraham about having great numbers of descendants and having an heir occurred before the birth of Ishmael, the ancestor of Muhammad.

"Then the Lord took Abram outside and said to him, 'Look up into the sky and count the stars if you can. That's how many descendants you will have!'" Genesis: 15:5

The covenant described in Genesis is then followed by the birth of Ishmael in chapter 16.

And in narrating the story of Hagar and young Ishmael in the desert crying for water, Genesis refers to creating a great nation from Ishmael:

"But God heard the boy crying, and the angel of God called to Hagar from heaven, 'Hagar, what's wrong? Do not be afraid! God has heard the boy crying as he lies there. Go to him and comfort him, for I will make a great nation from his descendants.'" Genesis 21:17–18

"As for Ishmael, I will bless him also, just as you have asked. I will make him extremely fruitful and multiply his descendants. He will become the father of twelve princes, and I will make him a great nation." Genesis 17:20

The great nation reference, one may contend, tells nothing about Muhammad's prophecy. However, one may wonder, in terms of biblical lineage and legacy of prophecy, how else can a "great nation" from Ishmael be defined *without* a prophet? And if that prophet wasn't Muhammad, then who else was a prophet from Ishmael's lineage with a great nation? Please refer to Quran verses 2:127–129, noted earlier in this section, when they prayed for a great nation from their progeny and a messenger.

Points to Remember

- The name "Muhammad" means "the praised one." His other name, "Ahmad," means "most worthy of praise" or "highly praised." Even his pagan enemies in Mecca recognized Muhammad's highly ethical and moral practices and gave the nicknames of "the truthful" (*Al-Sadiq*) and "the trustworthy" (*Al-Amin*).
- Prophet Muhammad's lineage to Abraham is through his first son, Ishmael. The story of Ishmael and Abraham in the book of Genesis refers to a "great nation" from the descendants of Ishmael. The Quran insists that the coming of Muhammad was foretold in the Bible, and that his name will be Ahmad (the name given to him by his mother). The Greek word *"Paraclete,"* in the New

Testament, has been interpreted by Christians and Muslims to indicate Jesus and Ahmad, respectively.

- The first set of revelations of the Quran occurred when Muhammad was forty years old in the year 610 CE. Among the first to confirm his prophethood were two Christian monks.
- Prophet Muhammad is referred to in the Quran as a mercy (blessing) to believers, mankind, and all the worlds.

Time to Ponder

- Jesus in the Gospel of John (14:26 and 15:26) speaks of a comforter/advocate to come after him and that he *"will testify all about me"* and *"he shall teach you all things."* If one believes it was not a reference to Prophet Muhammad, then who else fits the description?

CHAPTER 19
SCRIPTURES AND PEOPLE OF THE BOOK

This chapter will cover the Quranic references to the prior scriptures, specifically the Torah (*Tawrat*), the Psalms (*Zabur*), and the Gospel (*Injil*), as well as the references to the "People of the Book" *(Ahlul Kitab)*. While presenting here the Quranic and biblical viewpoints in an accurate and objective manner, the sensitive nature of this subject is never overlooked.

In their basic forms, the three faiths have their roots in Abraham. They all believe in the same God—the Creator of Adam and the heavens and earth; in the Day of Judgment; and in the hereafter. They believe in the prophets, though Jesus and Muhammad are not shared by all (Jesus by Jews, Muhammad by Jews and Christians). The moral and ethical values and laws are also very similar in their essence, as discussed later in this book. Where they diverge significantly seem to be in the details of how they interpret religious practices, laws, and rituals as well as on historical perspectives on prophetic stories, and they are often colored by geopolitical complexities.

Quranic View of the scriptures

The Quran has a clear view of the prior scriptures: The scriptures, as set down by Moses and Jesus and other prophets, are sacred and to be respected but exist today (and as they did in the days of Prophet Muhammad) in an altered state from their original divine revelations. Muslims are commanded to "believe" in all scriptures. In the very beginning of the Quran, it asks believers to respect the Quran and the prior scriptures.

The Quran is a continuation of the revelations from the same God.

"This Book, there is no doubt in it, is a guide to those who guard (against evil) Those who believe in the unseen and keep up prayer and spend out of what We have given them. And who believe in that which has been revealed to you [meaning Muhammad] and that which was revealed before you and they are sure of the hereafter." 2:2–4 (Shakir)

"Say: Whoever is an enemy to Gabriel, for he brings down the (revelation) to your heart by Allah's will, a confirmation of what was (revealed) before, and guidance and glad tidings for those who believe." 2:97

"This Quran is not such as can be produced by other than God; on the contrary it is a confirmation of (revelations) that went before it, and a fuller explanation of the Book—wherein there is no doubt—from the Lord of the worlds." 10:37

The Quran, in addition to generic references to "what was sent before," also mentions the Torah and the Gospel by name. In the following set of verses, the Quran confirms the divine source of the Torah, the Gospel, and "the Book" (meaning the Quran). The Quran declares that the Torah and the Gospel were "guidance and light." The following is a small sample:

The Quran on the Torah

"It was We who revealed the law [Torah] (to Moses): therein was guidance and light. By its standard have been judged the Jews, by the prophets who bowed (as in Islam) to Allah's will, by the rabbis and the doctors of law: for to them was entrusted the protection of Allah's book, and they were witnesses thereto: therefore fear not men, but fear me, and sell not my signs for a miserable price. If any do fail to judge by (the light of) what Allah has revealed, they are (no better than) Unbelievers. We ordained therein for them: 'Life for life, eye for eye, nose for nose, ear for ear, tooth for tooth, and wounds equal for equal.' But if anyone remits the retaliation by way of charity, it is an act of atonement for himself." 5:44–45

"We gave Moses the Book and followed him up with a succession of messengers." 2:87

Other Passages on the Torah: A Criterion, Light, and Mercy

"And remember We gave Moses the scriptures and the [Furqa'n] Criterion (Between right and wrong): There was a chance for you to be guided aright." 2:53

"In the past We granted to Moses and Aaron the Furqa'n and a Light and a Message **for those who would do right [or guard against evil]***."* 21:48

It is of note that the Quran uses the word *"Furqa'n"* for the Torah also, as it has for itself. *Furqa'n* means the criterion, between good and evil or right and wrong.

Moreover, the Torah is described as a guide for the *"Muttaqeen"* (bolded above), another word often used for believing, pious Muslims, meaning those who guard against evil.

"And certainly We gave the Book to Musa, so be not in doubt concerning the receiving of it, and We made it a guide for the children of Israel." 32:23 (Shakir)

"And We gave Musa the Book and made it a guidance to the children of Israel, saying: Do not take a protector besides Me." 17:2 (Shakir)

"And before this, was the Book of Moses as a guide and a mercy: And this Book [meaning the Quran] confirms (it) in the Arabic tongue; to admonish the unjust, and as Glad Tidings to those who do right." 46:12

The following verses do indeed refer to the Torah being a more detailed description of the laws:

"Moreover, We gave Moses the Book, completing (Our favor) to those who would do right, and explaining all things in detail, and a guide and a mercy, that they might believe in the meeting with their Lord." 6:154

"And We ordained for him [referring to Moses] in the tablets admonition of every kind and clear explanation of all things; so take hold of them with firmness and enjoin your people to take hold of what is best thereof; I will show you the abode of the transgressors." 7:145 (Shakir)

Quran on the Gospel (Injil): Guidance and Light

In the verses preceding the one quoted below, the Quran makes references to the Torah and the prophets that followed Moses and the rabbis who protected the Torah, followed by Jesus being given the *Injil* and that it was a guidance for the *Muttaqeen.*

"And We sent after them in their footsteps Jesus, son of Mary, verifying what was before him of the Torah and We gave him the Gospel in which was guidance and light, and verifying what was before it of the Torah and a guidance and an admonition for those who guard (against evil). And the followers of the Gospel should have judged by what God revealed in it; and whoever did not judge by what God revealed, those are they that are the transgressors." 5:46–47 (Shakir)

Other Passages on the Gospel

In the first verse quoted below, the Quran addresses Mary in reference to Jesus Christ and says that he was born with the knowledge of the prior scriptures, including the Torah:

"And He [meaning God] will teach him [Jesus] the scriptures and wisdom, and the Torah and the Gospel." 3:48 (Shakir)

"Then We made Our messengers to follow in their footsteps, and We sent Jesus son of Mary afterwards, and We gave him the Gospel and We put in the hearts of those who followed him kindness and mercy." 57:27 (Shakir)

"When Allah will say: O Jesus son of Mary! Remember My favor on you and on your mother, when I strengthened you with the Holy Spirit, you spoke to the people in the cradle and when of old age, and when I taught you the Book and the wisdom and the Torah and the Gospel." 5:110 (Shakir)

"It is He Who sent down to you (step by step), in truth, the Book [meaning the Quran], confirming what went before it; and He sent down the Law (of Moses) [Torah] and the Gospel (of Jesus) before this, as a guide to mankind, and He sent down the criterion (of judgment between right and wrong)." 3:3

People of the Book

The Quran often refers to Jews and Christians as "the People of the Book." This subject is even more emotionally charged and often a source of criticism of the Quran, especially in the West—usually by those who are not scholars of, or well versed with, the Quran. Before delving into this topic, the concept of Islam as a religion, as described in the Quran, is examined.

Islam: *One* Religion from Adam to Muhammad

Many people around the world, including many Muslims, tend to think of Islam as being born in Arabia in the seventh century; they consider Muhammad as its "founder," and the Quran as its Holy Book. Was Islam a result of Jewish and Christian influence on Prophet Muhammad? Did it start as an independent religion and borrow some concepts from the other two monotheistic religions prevalent in Arabia at the time? Many Western Muslim scholars have argued in favor of the latter. A review of the Quran, however, would reveal a broader perspective on Islam and Muslims.

"And We gave Moses the Book, in order that they might receive guidance. And We made the son of Mary and his mother as a Sign: We gave them both shelter on high ground, affording rest and security and furnished with springs." 23:49–50

After these verses, the message is put in perspective in the next set of verses:

O messengers! [Note the plural used.] Eat of pure things and do good deeds, certainly I have knowledge of all your actions. In fact, your religion is one religion, and I am your Lord: so fear Me Alone. Yet people have divided themselves into factions and each faction rejoices in its own doctrines—well! Leave them in their heedlessness for an appointed time." 23:51–53 (Shakir)

The universality of Islam is addressed in other places in the Quran as well:

"The same religion has He established for you [meaning Muhammad] as that which He enjoined on Noah—that which We have sent by inspiration to you—and that which We enjoined on Abraham, Moses, and Jesus: Namely, that you should remain

steadfast in religion, and make no divisions therein: to those who worship other things than God, hard to the unbelievers is that which you call them to. God chooses to Himself those whom He pleases, and guides to Himself those who turn (to Him)." 42:13

"*Verily! This, your religion, is one religion, and I am your Lord, so worship Me.*" 21:92

The word used above for religion, "*Umma,*" has been variously translated as "group," "brotherhood," and "nation."

"*And certainly We raised in every nation a messenger saying: Serve God and shun the false gods [or Satan].*" 16:36 (Shakir)

One might argue that the "one religion" is not named, or perhaps "*my* religion" is "*that* one religion." In the following verses of the Quran, that universal one religion is spelled out:

"*This day have I perfected for you your religion and completed My favor on you and chosen for you Islam as a religion.*" 5:3 (Shakir)

"*The Religion before God is Islam (submission to His Will).*" 3:19

The religions have typically been named by their followers after their prophet's departure from this world, but as noted above, Islam was named as a religion by God in the Quran. After the Quran proclaims that the prophets brought one religion, and names it Islam, the Quran spells out what *that* religion is:

"*Do they seek for other than the Religion of Allah? While all creatures in the heavens and on earth have, willing or unwilling, bowed to His Will (Accepted Islam), and to Him shall they all be brought back. Say (O Muhammad): We believe in God and what has been revealed to us, and what was revealed to Abraham, and Ishmael and Isaac and Jacob and the tribes, and what was given to Moses and Jesus and to the prophets from their Lord; we do not make any distinction between any of them, and to Him do we submit.*" 3:83–84

After this broad definition, the Quran urges people to accept no other religion:

"*And whoever desires a religion other than Islam, it shall not be accepted from him.*" 3:85 (Shakir)

Chain of Prophets and Islam

In one very long sequence in chapter 21 of the Quran, many prophets are mentioned, one after another, and at the end, the Quran declares that they all belong to the same nation (*Umma*). Each section talks about a particular prophet or a group of prophets:

"Certainly, We granted to Musa and Haroon the Criterion of right and wrong, a light and a reminder for those righteous people who fear their Lord though they have not seen Him, and dread the Day of Judgment. And now We have revealed this blessed Reminder (the Quran). Will you then deny it?" 21:48–50 (Shakir)

"Even before that We blessed Ibrahim with rectitude, for We knew him well. Remember that occasion when Ibrahim asked his father and his people, 'What are these images to which you are so devoted?' They replied, 'We found our forefathers worshipping them.' He said, 'Then certainly both you and your forefathers have been in manifest error.' They asked, 'Have you brought us the truth or are you one of the triflers?' He replied, 'No! Your Lord is the Lord of the heavens and the earth. It is He Who has created them; and I am of those who bear witness to this.'" 21:51–56 (Shakir)

The passage from verse 57 to 71 goes on to tell the story of Abraham breaking the idols and the idolaters putting him in fire and the cooling of fire under divine order. Then the focus shifts to other prophets:

"We gave him a son Ishãq [Isaac] and then a grandson Ya'qoob [Jacob]; and We made each of them a righteous man. We made them leaders (Imams) who guided other people by Our command and We sent them revelations to do good deeds, establish Salah [prayer] and pay Zakah [regular charity]. Us Alone did they serve. To Lüt [Lot] We gave wisdom and knowledge, and We delivered him from the town which practiced abominations—surely its inhabitants were very wicked transgressors—and We admitted him to Our mercy: for he was of the righteous people." 21:72–75 (Malik)

"Before them Nüh [Noah] prayed to Us, We accepted his prayer and delivered him and his family from the great calamity. We helped him against those people who had denied Our revelations; surely they were an evil people, so We drowned them all in the Great Flood." 21:76–77 (Malik)

"And remember David and Solomon, when they gave judgment in the matter of the field into which the sheep of certain people had strayed by night: We did witness their judgment. To Solomon We inspired the (right) understanding of the matter: to each (of them) We gave Judgment and Knowledge; it was Our power that made the hills and the birds celebrate Our praises, with David: it was We Who did (all these things). It was We Who taught him the making of coats of mail for your benefit, to guard you from each other's violence: will you then be grateful? (It was Our power that made) the violent (unruly) wind flow (tamely) for Solomon, to his order, to the land which We had blessed: for We do know all things. And of the evil ones, were some who dived for him, and did other work besides; and it was We Who guarded them." 21:78–82

"And (remember) Job, when He cried to his Lord, 'Truly distress has seized me, but You are the Most Merciful of those that are merciful.' So We listened to him: We removed the distress that was on him, and We restored his people to him, and doubled their number, as a Grace from Ourselves, and a thing for commemoration, for all who serve Us." 21:83–84

"And (remember) Ishmael, Idris, and Zul-kifl, all (men) of constancy and patience; We admitted them to Our mercy: for they were of the righteous ones. And remember Zun-nun [Jonah], when he departed in wrath: He imagined that We had no power over him! But he cried through the depths of darkness, 'There is no god but You: Glory to You: I was indeed wrong!' So We listened to him: and delivered him from distress: and thus do We deliver those who have faith. And (remember) Zechariah, when he cried to his Lord: 'O my Lord! leave me not without offspring, though you are the best of inheritors.' So We listened to him: and We granted him Yahya [John]: We cured his wife's (Barrenness) for him. These (three) were ever quick in emulation in good works; they used to call on Us with love and reverence, and humble themselves before Us. And (remember) her [meaning Mary] who guarded her chastity: We breathed into her of Our spirit, and We made her and her son a sign for all peoples." 21:85–91

After the long sets of passages on many prophets, the Quran puts it all in perspective:

"Verily this Islam is your religion, is one religion, and I am your Lord, so worship Me and I am your only Lord, therefore worship Me Alone. And they broke their religion (into sects) between them: to Us shall all come back. Therefore whoever shall do of good deeds and he is a believer, there shall be no denying of his exertion, and surely We will write (It) down for him." 21:92–94 (Shakir)

Islam: Religion of Abraham (*Deen-e-Ibrahim*)

The Quran describes Islam as a universal religion with broader meaning as well as the *"Deen-e-Ibrahim,"* or the religion of Abraham. There are numerous references to "this religion" as the "way of Abraham" and that he, as well as his descendants, were Muslims, as defined by the Quran.

"And who forsakes the religion of Abraham but he who makes himself a fool, and most certainly We chose him in this world, and in the hereafter he is most surely among the righteous. When his Lord said to him, Be a Muslim (submit), he said: I submit myself to the Lord of the worlds." 2:130–131 (Shakir)

And this message echoes the one in verse 42:13 quoted earlier, regarding making no distinction between the prophets:

"And they say: Be Jews or Christians, you will be on the right course. Say: No (we follow) the religion of Abraham, the upright (true), and he was not one of the polytheists. Say: We believe in God and (in) that which had been revealed to us, and (in) that which was revealed to Abraham and Ishmael and Isaac and Jacob and the tribes, and (in) that which was given to Moses and Jesus, and (in) that which was given to the prophets from their Lord, we do not make any distinction between any of them, and to Him do we submit." 2:135–136

Other verses in references to the religion of Abraham:

"Who can be better in religion than one who submits his whole self to God, does good, and follows the way [faith or religion] of Abraham the true in Faith? For God did take Abraham for a friend." 4:125

"Say (O Muhammad): Surely, (as for) me, my Lord has guided me to the right path; (to) a most right religion, the faith of Abraham, the upright one, and he was not of the polytheists." 6:161 (Shakir)

"In fact Ibrahim was a nation in himself, an upright man obedient to Allah, and he was not of the polytheists. He was always grateful for the favors of Allah, Who chose him and guided him to the Right Way. We gave him a good life in this world, and in the hereafter he will be among the righteous. And now We have revealed to you Our will, saying: "Follow the faith of Ibrahim the upright, he was not of the polytheists." 16:120–123 (Malik)

"He has chosen you and has not laid upon you a hardship in religion; the faith of your father Abraham; He named you Muslims before and in this (scripture)." 22:78 (Shakir)

One might find an apparent contradiction in calling Islam the one religion God sent down, as well as the "religion of Abraham." So how about the prophets before Abraham? What religion were they preaching? The Quran, as mentioned in preceding discussions, praises Abraham as a noble servant of God, and one may conclude that by referring to the universal religion Islam as the religion of Abraham, the Quran intended to highlight Abraham's key role in propagating that religion by linking it to him, who in turn was following the same universal religion.

It is interesting to note that the words "Islam" and "Muslim" (or their derivatives) appear frequently in the Quran, but the word "Judaism" does not appear in the Torah (though references to the Israelites are frequent in the Torah and to Jewish people in later revelations), and "Christianity" does not appear in the Gospel, even though the teachings of the two religions are derived from their respective scriptures. This may be an argument to support the view that God intended to send down one universal religion—that of submission to the will of God—but people differed in their opinion and interpretation, resulting in multiple religions, divisions, and subdivisions.

Who Is a *Kafir*/Nonbeliever ("Infidel")?

Some non-Muslims, as well as some Muslims, assume that Islam considers People of the Book and all other non-Muslims as *Kafirs*, or infidels. The Quranic commandments on this topic are examined here.

The word "Kafir" is variously translated as "nonbeliever," "unbeliever," or "disbeliever." A Kafir, according to the concepts laid out by the Quran, is a faithless soul, one who rejects the truth, an anti-submitter. Just like a Muslim is in a state of submission, a Kafir similarly is in a state of rejection of the truth. The first Kafir was Satan, when he refused to bow to Adam at God's command:

"And when We said to the angels: Make obeisance (bow down) to Adam they did obeisance, except Iblis (did it not). He refused and he was proud, and he was one of the unbelievers." 2:34 (Shakir)

A Kafir rejects the truth knowingly and disbelieves in God, the angels, the messengers, and the hereafter. This would include pagans, idolaters, polytheists (*Mushrikoon*), and atheists. The word "Kafir" comes from a root word that means "a farmer who covers the seed with soil." "Kafir" in this sense refers to someone who covers the truth. The term "infidel" was originally used by Christians to describe those who do not believe the inspirations of the scriptures. "Infidel" is not used here to describe Jews and Christians and is regardless considered an inaccurate translation of "Kafir."

Verse 98:1 (*"Those who disbelieved from among the People of the Book"*) supports the argument that People of the Book do *not* equate with Kafirs or disbelievers. Since they are said to have among them disbelievers, therefore they must have believers among them as well. To refer to People of the Book as infidels, or nonbelievers, as a group is thus *not* in accordance with Quranic teachings.

In fact, the Quran calls those who were opposing and fighting against David as unbelievers or Kafirs.

"And when they went out against Jalut [Goliath] and his forces they said: Our Lord, pour down upon us patience, and make our steps firm and assist us against the unbelieving people [Kafirs]." 2:250 (Shakir)

Those who fought *with* Moses were believers: Similarly, those who were fighting with Moses were called believers in the

Quran. When Moses led the children of Israel near the edge of the Promised Land, he spoke to his people:

"And when Musa said to his people: O my people! Remember the favor of Allah upon you when He raised prophets among you and made you kings and gave you what He had not given to any other among the nations." 5:20 (Shakir)

"Two men of those who feared [were God-fearing], upon both of whom Allah had bestowed a favor, said: Enter upon them by the gate, for when you have entered it you shall surely be victorious, and on Allah should you rely if you are believers." 5:23 (Shakir). The word used for believers is *Momineen*, a term often used for pious, believing Muslims.

Other verses in the Quran on nonbelievers among the Israelites:

"Those who disbelieved [i.e., who were Kafirs] from among the children of Israel were cursed by the tongue of David and Jesus, son of Mary; this was because they disobeyed and used to exceed the limit." 5:78 (Shakir)

It is clear from the verses noted above that the Quran refers to the various factions among People of the Book (and children of Israel)—some were believers, others were nonbelievers. This account is no different than the Tanakh, which frequently refers to the Israelites who reverted to polytheism; many of them were killed by Moses and the believing Israelites.

Pagan: Defined by *Webster's Dictionary* as "one who worships false gods, or idolater, one who is neither a Christian, a Mohammedan, or a Jew." In the Quran, the word used for this group is *Mushrikoon.* They typically associate other gods with God.

People of the Book

This term is used in the Quran for the followers of the Torah and the Gospel, implying Jews and Christians. At times the Quran addresses the "children of Israel"—referring to the Israelites, or more directly as "Jews and Christians," usually in references to the Jews and Christians of Medina. In the early days of the prophecy in Mecca, most of Muhammad's interactions, and thus the Quranic verses, were related to pagan beliefs and practices. After the *Hijra*, or emigration to Medina, as the Muslim community took shape, the Quran then spells out the new law for this community as well as the guidelines for interactions with the Jews and Christians who lived in and around Medina.

And according to the following verse, the fate of all nations will be in the hands of God only:

"As for those who have faith and do righteous deeds, We shall soon admit them to gardens beneath which rivers flow to live therein forever. This is the promise of Allah, true indeed, and who can be truer in his words than Allah? The final result will neither be in accordance with your desires nor in accordance with the desires of the People of the Book. He who does evil will be requited with evil: he will find no protector or helper besides Allah. But the one who does righteous deeds, whether a male or a female—and he or she is a believer—shall enter paradise and will not be harmed a speck." 4:122–124 (Malik)

Who Is Righteous?

This verse defines who is righteous without saying if one must be a "Muslim" or a "Jew" or a "Christian." It defines what one must do to be counted among the *Mutiqoon*, or God-fearing, righteous, pious people. The first part involves beliefs and the second part deals with actions—what one must do to be righteous:

*"It is not righteousness that you turn your faces toward the East and the West, (meaning facing Ka'aba for prayers) but righteousness is this that one should believe in God and the last day and the angels and the Book and the prophets, AND give away wealth out of love for Him to the near of kin and the orphans and the needy and the wayfarer and the beggars and for (the emancipation of) the captives, and keep up prayer (Salah) and pay the poor-rate (Zakah); and the performers of their promise when they make a promise (or keep their pledges when they make a pledge), and the patient in distress and affliction and in time of conflicts—these are they who are true (to themselves) and these are **they who guard (against evil)**."* 2:177 (Shakir).

The bolded phrase is also translated as "pious" (Mir Ali, Malik), "Allah-fearing" (Yousuf Ali, Pickthall), "God-fearing" (many modern translators), or "righteous" (Yuksel). The Arabic word used in the Quran is *"Mutaqoon."*

The following verse is not nearly as detailed but revolves around the same theme:

"And they [referring to People of the Book] say: None shall enter the garden [meaning paradise] except he who is a Jew or a Christian. These are their vain desires. Say: Bring your proof if you are truthful. Yes! Whoever submits himself entirely to God and he is the doer of good (to others) he has his reward from his Lord, and there is no fear for him nor shall he grieve [meaning on the Day of Judgment]." 2:111–112 (Shakir)

Muslims, Jews, and Christians and the Sabean Verses

"For, verily, those who have attained to faith (in this divine writ), as well as those who follow the Jewish faith, and the Sabeans, and the Christians—all who believe in God and the Last Day and do righteous deeds—no fear need they have, and neither shall they grieve (on the Day of Judgment)." 5:69 (Asad)

An almost identical message is sent by verse 2:62.

According to these verses, all the groups mentioned above shall have "their reward" if they follow the instructions as noted. Some commentators of the Quran, however, mention that only the "believing (who turned Muslim) Jews, Christians, and Sabeans" are implied in this verse. Other Muslim commentators alternatively claim the verse refers to the "good Jews, Christians, and Sabeans who lived before Muhammad." For example, in his commentary, Pooya Yazdi points out another verse that says, *"And whoever desires a religion other than Islam, it shall not be accepted from him, and in the hereafter he shall be one of the losers."* *3:85* He further comments, "And to remove misunderstanding, it should be noted that this verse refers to those Sabeans, Jews, and Christians who, as sincere faithful, followed the original teachings of their respective prophets, without ever corrupting the true message, and believed in the prophecy of the advent of Muhammad made known by Musa, Isa, and other prophets."

With due respect to him and others with similar interpretation of the verse, it can be argued here that if the condition in this verse includes "those Jews, Christians, and Sabeans who turned Muslim," then they *should be* counted among "those who attained faith," or "Muslims," and thus no longer are "Jews or Christians." (In fact, many of the early Muslim converts *were* either pagans, Christians, or Jews living in Mecca or Medina.) Moreover, Muslims are one of the four groups mentioned in this verse side by side in the *present* tense, and not in the past tense. Thus this verse includes the Muslims (believers in Muhammad and the Quran) AND the Jews, Christians, and Sabeans—as long as the other conditions are met, as spelled out in the second part of the verse. Secondly, verse 3:85, quoted by Pooya Yazdi in his commentary, should be put in context with the prior verses that preceded it. These were quoted in the previous chapter:

"Are they looking for a religion other than the religion of Allah [God] knowing well that everything in the heavens and in the earth, willingly or unwillingly, has submitted to Him? And to Him they shall all return. (O' Prophet) say: 'We believe in Allah and what is revealed to us and what was revealed to Abraham, Ishmael, Isaac, Jacob, and their descendants; and in that which was given to Moses, Jesus, and other Prophets from their Lord; we do not discriminate between any one of them, and to Allah do we submit. And whoever desires a religion other than Islam [submission to God], it shall not be accepted from him, and in the hereafter he shall be one of the losers.'" 3:83–85 (Shakir)

One cannot conclude the discussion on this verse without pointing out that in addition to all other beliefs spelled out above, the belief in Muhammad as the last prophet and the Quran is considered an integral part of the religion of Islam, without which the faith in this universal religion is incomplete.

Interfaith Dialogue as Taught by the Quran

The differences and the tensions that currently exist between Jews, Christians, and Muslims are nothing new; they have existed for centuries. The Quran acknowledges that and provides broad guidelines and instructs its followers on how to approach interfaith dialogue:

"Do not argue with the People of the Book except in the best manner—except for those wicked amongst them, and say: 'We acknowledge what was revealed to us and in what was revealed to you; Our God and your God is the same. To him we peacefully surrender.'" 29:46 (Yuksel)

The underlined word is *"Ahsan"* (with a short "a" sound) and is translated as "by what's best" (Shakir, Mir Ali), "with means better than mere disputation" (Yousuf Ali), "in good taste" (Malik), and "in the best way" (Unal).

"Call to the way of your Lord with wisdom and goodly exhortation, and have disputations with them in the best manner." 16:125 (Shakir)

"Say: O People of the Book! come to common terms as between us and you: That we worship none but Allah[God]; that we associate no partners with him; that we take not, from among ourselves, Lords and patrons other than Allah." 3:64

People of the Book: Some Were "Good," Some Were Not

The Quranic narrations involving the children of Israel with Moses are similar in many ways to the biblical accounts. The following is a review of some of these verses, along with some "controversial" verses, cited by some in the West to accuse the Quran of "promoting hatred." The Quran, like the Torah, is often critical of the Israelites who accompanied Moses in the wilderness in search of the Promised Land. The Quran also talks about their favored status:

"O' children of Israel! Remember My favors which I bestowed upon You; that I exalted you above all other nations." 2:47 and 2:122 (Malik)

"And there are, certainly, among the People of the Book, those who believe in God, in the revelation to you, and in the revelation to them, bowing in humility to God: They will not sell the Signs of God for a miserable gain! For them is a reward with their Lord, and God is swift in account." 3:199

Not all of them were alike:

"Not all of them are alike: Of the People of the Book are a portion that stand (For the right): They rehearse [recite] the Signs [revelations] of God all night long, and they prostrate themselves in adoration. They believe in God and the last day, and they enjoin what is right and forbid the wrong and they strive with one another in hastening to good deeds, and those are among the good. And whatever good they do, they shall not be denied it, and God knows those who guard (against evil). (As for) those who disbelieve, surely neither their wealth nor their children shall avail them in the least against God; and these are the inmates of the fire; therein they shall abide." 3:113–116

"Among the People of the Book are some who, if entrusted with a hoard of gold, will (readily) pay it back; others, who, if entrusted with a single silver coin, will not repay it unless you remain firm in demanding, because, they say, 'there is no call on us (to keep faith) with these Gentiles', and they tell a lie against God, and (well) they know it. Yea, whoever fulfills his promise and guards (against evil)—then surely God loves those who guard (against evil). (As for) those who take a small price for the covenant of God and their own oaths—surely they shall have no portion in the hereafter, and God will not speak to them, nor will He look upon them on the day of resurrection nor will He purify them, and they shall have a painful chastisement." 3:75–77

The Quran on Arabs: Some Were "Good," Some Were Not

The Quran's criticism is not limited to the pagans and the transgressors among the People of the Book. Similarly the due praise is given to the righteous:

"The Arabs of the desert are the worst in Unbelief and hypocrisy, and most fitted to be in ignorance of the command which Allah has sent down to His Messenger: But Allah is All-knowing, All-Wise." 9:97

"But some of the desert Arabs [Bedouins] believe in God and the Last Day, and look on their payments as pious gifts bringing them nearer to God and obtaining the prayers of the Messenger. Surely it

shall be means of nearness for them. Soon will God admit them to His Mercy: for God is Oft-forgiving, Most Merciful." 9:99

The Quran Allows Marrying People of the Book

The Quran allows believers of the Quran and Muhammad (commonly viewed as "Muslims") to marry Jews and Christians with certain conditions:

"Today all good clean things have been made lawful for you; and the food of the People of the Book is also made lawful for you and your food is made lawful for them. Likewise, marriage with chaste free believing women and also chaste women among the People who were given the Book before you is made lawful for you, provided that you give them their dowries and desire chastity, neither committing fornication nor taking them as mistresses." 5:5 (Malik)

Conversely, many Jewish sages have argued against interfaith marriages between Jewish and non-Jewish people, citing some Tanakh verses such as Deuteronomy 7:1–5, revealed in reference to how the Israelites should treat other tribes like the Ammonites and Canaanites. The verses for obvious reasons refer to the nonbelievers of the time, predating the followers of the Gospel and the Quran:

"Nor shall you make marriages with them. You shall not give your daughter to their son, nor take their daughter for your son. For they will turn your sons away from following Me, to serve other gods." Deuteronomy 7:3–4

Friendship with People of the Book Forbidden?

In a verse that has been flashed on TV screens and is equally misused by critics of the Quran, as well as by Muslims at times, the believers in Muhammad and the Quran (Muslims) are asked to forbid "friendship" with Jews and Christians. I will quote a common translation first:

"O you who believe! do not take the Jews and the Christians for friends; they are friends of each other; and whoever amongst you takes them for a friend, then surely he is one of them; surely Allah does not guide the unjust people." 5:51 (Shakir, and similarly by Pickthall).

There are two points that need to be reiterated here. First, the verses of the Quran (like the Bible) should be viewed within the proper context. Second, it must be pointed out that the word used for "friendship" used in the verse is *"Awliya,"* which means allies or a protector, or protecting friend, which has a very different connotation than just a "friend." Yuksel thus translates this verse as *"do not take the Jews and the Christians for allies"* and comments that the word is not to be taken in the context of social, personal, or financial interactions, but rather in the case of religious conflict. In addition, it does not refer to all People of the Book, as will be discussed below.

The context: The verse was revealed in Medina, where the local Jews started to show hostilities against the new converts and the budding Islamic community. According to Muslim historians, they were mocking and ridiculing the new Muslims. This verse was revealed in reference to *these* Jews, not all of them; and for that matter, not all of the Jews and Christians "who will ever live." The verses 5:57–58 that followed verse 5:51 quoted above address that:

"O you who believe! Take not for friends and protectors those who take your religion for a mockery or sport [or joke], whether among those who received the scriptures before you, or among those who reject Faith; but fear Allah, if you have faith (indeed)." 5:57

"When you proclaim your call to prayer [Adhan] they take it (but) as mockery and sport; that is because they are a people without understanding." 5:58

The Quran commands us to deal in kindness and respect those who have not done injustice to the believers.

"God does not forbid you respecting those who have not made war against you on account of (your) religion, and have not driven you forth from your homes, that you show them kindness and deal with them justly; surely God loves the doers of justice." 60:8 (Shakir)

And one should take the entire Quran for a proper context; verse 5:5 on interfaith marriages (quoted above) has significant relevance to the discussion here. The allowance of food in the same verse as marriage is a call for social interaction between people of faith and implies inviting each other for and sharing meals. The allowance of interfaith marriages and promoting social interaction is clearly a far cry from the call of "don't make friends with People of the Book."

Biblical Accounts of the Children of Israel

Many in the West criticize the Quran for being too harsh on the Israelites, saying that it promotes hatred toward them. However, the Torah seems equally as harsh, if not more so. The Quran and the Torah seem to take a similar view: God chose and favored the children of Israel, showing mercy to them. God cursed the enemies of the children of Israel, including the pharaoh and others who fought them on their way to the Promised Land. However, the journey in wilderness from Egypt to the Promised Land was not exactly an easy one.

The Quran and the Old Testament describe many stories about the transgressions of the children of Israel, their rebellious nature, and their constant grumbling. Some of the verses related to this topic were quoted in chapter 16. Other Israelites, however, remained pious and steadfast, and they trusted in God despite their adversities.

"The Lord told Moses, 'Quick! Go down the mountain! Your people whom you brought from the land of Egypt have corrupted themselves.'" Exodus 32:7

"Then the Lord said, 'I have seen how stubborn and rebellious these people are. Now leave me alone so my fierce anger can blaze against them, and I will destroy them.'" Exodus 32:9–10

Recurrent Rebellion by the Children of Israel

The following is a small sample from the Torah:

- Two noble spies (Caleb and Joshua): When nearing the Promised Land, Moses sent spies out to find out about it. They reported that the people there were giants, making them look like grasshoppers, and said the city had fortified walls. The spies further reported they had no chance against them, except Caleb and Joshua, who maintained that by having trust in God, they could overcome their apparent shortcomings. The Israelites then rebelled against them.

"Why is the Lord taking us to this country only to have us die in battle?" Numbers 14:3.

"But the whole community began to talk about stoning Joshua and Caleb. Then the glorious presence of the LORD *appeared to all the Israelites at the Tabernacle. And the* LORD *said to Moses, 'How long will these people treat me with contempt? Will they never believe me, even after all the miraculous signs I have done among them? I will disown them and destroy them with a plague. Then I will make you into a nation greater and mightier than they are!'"* Numbers 14:10–12

"Then the Lord said to Moses and Aaron, 'How long must I put up with this wicked community and its complaints about me? Yes, I have heard the complaints the Israelites are making against me. Now tell them this: "As surely as I live, declares the LORD*, I will do to you the very things I heard you say. You will all drop dead in this wilderness! Because you complained against me, every one of you who is twenty years old or older and was included in the registration will die. You will not enter and occupy the land I swore to give you. The only exceptions will be Caleb son of Jephunneh and Joshua son of Nun."'"* Numbers 14:26–30

- Israelites' idolatry and sexual relations with Moabite women: *"While the Israelites were camped at Acacia Grove, some of the men defiled themselves by having sexual relations with local Moabite women. These women invited them to attend sacrifices to their gods, so the Israelites feasted with them and worshiped the gods of Moab. In this way, Israel joined in the worship of Baal of Peor, causing the* LORD'S *anger to blaze against his people."* Numbers 25:1–3

Gospels' Criticism of the Religious Leaders

Not just the Quran and the Old Testament but the New Testament also spoke negatively of many of the religious leaders at the time. Jesus often called them hypocrites. Matthew chapter 23 opens up with Jesus calling on his disciples. These are strong words from anyone—especially from someone as kindhearted, merciful, and loving as Jesus:

"What sorrow awaits you teachers of religious law and you Pharisees. Hypocrites! For you build tombs for the prophets your ancestors killed, and you decorate the monuments of the godly people your ancestors destroyed. Then you say, 'If we had lived in the days of our ancestors, we would never have joined them in killing the prophets.' But in saying that, you testify against yourselves that you are indeed the descendants of those who murdered the prophets. Go ahead and finish what your ancestor started. Snakes! Sons of vipers! How will you escape the judgment of hell?" Matthew 23:29–33

"Then Jesus said to the crowds and to his disciples, 'The teachers of religious law and the Pharisees are the official interpreters of the law of Moses. So practice and obey whatever they tell you, but don't follow their example. For they don't practice what they teach.'" Matthew 23:1–3

The purpose of these references from the Quran, the Old Testament, and the New Testament is not to be critical of any group but to show the consistency of the scriptures in reference to historical events. It is noteworthy that the scriptures also praise the pious and the righteous among these groups, putting their criticism in perspective.

Points to Remember

- The Quran repeatedly refers to the original Torah and the Gospel (*Injil*) as "guidance," "light," and "mercy." It also states the original scriptures have been altered. The Muslims are commanded to believe in the divine nature of their scriptures.

- The Quran views Islam as one universal religion and that all prophets, from Adam to Muhammad, preached the same basic religion.
- Contrary to the common belief, the Quran does not forbid Muslims from being friends with Jews and Christians in terms of daily social and personal interactions. It refers to specific instances of religious conflicts that existed in Medina or those who waged war against Muslims. In fact the Quran allows interfaith marriages with People of the Book.
- Even in case of differences, the Quran asks Muslims to interact with the People of the Book in "good taste" or "best manner" and gives guidelines on interfaith dialogue.
- In the Quran's description of righteousness, Jews, Christians, and Muslims are mentioned side by side, as long as they all meet the prescribed criteria (see verses 2:62, 2:177 and 5:69).
- The Quran commands believers to leave the judgment involving the differences between various faiths to God (i.e., they should not be the ones judging each other).

Time to Ponder

- The distrust and, at times, frank animosity between various interfaith groups has existed for centuries. In such situations, is the behavior of the followers when approaching interfaith relationship consistent with the teachings and the guidelines established by the scriptures they follow?

SECTION 5
THE QURAN AND
ESCHATOLOGY

Chapter 20
Life and Death

"Eschatology" is derived from Greek work *"eskhatos,"* meaning "last". *Oxford English Dictionary* defines "eschatology" as "the part of theology concerned with death, judgment, and the final destiny of the soul and mankind." This section reviews life and death and the hereafter.

This chapter will cover life and death. The Day of Judgment and the concept of the hereafter will be reviewed in the next two chapters, though these concepts are closely intertwined and rather inseparable.

Life and Death

According to the scriptures, life in this world is a transient journey, compared to the hereafter. Death is simply a transition from the life on earth to the hereafter, with an intermediary period. No matter how transient earthly life is, the Quran emphasizes it is the only life people will be judged by, emphasizing an individual's accountability. The hereafter is eternal. Some will indeed live "happily ever after"; others will not. The Quran, the Old Testament, and the New Testament describe the hereafter in varying details.

Where Did We Come from and Where Are We Going?

"Verily, it is We who have created man out of a drop of sperm intermingled, so that We might try him (in his later life): and therefore We made him a being endowed with hearing and sight. Verily, We have shown him the way: (and it rests with him to prove himself) either grateful or ungrateful." 76:2–3 (Malik)

Life is part of a round trip: Muslims often recite this verse when they hear the news of someone passing away:

"To Allah We belong, and to Him is our return." 2:156 *(or "We are from God and to Him is our return.")*

A similar message is found in the following verse:

"To Allah is your return, and He has power over all things." 11:4

Life is a journey, and according to the Quran and the Bible, it is a round trip: we came from God, and to Him we shall return. The word "return" in itself implies man's origin from God.

Purpose of Life

This topic was discussed in chapter 4 ("God, the Creator") in more detail but some of the verses are quoted here again.

"He Who created Death and Life, that He may try which of you is best in deed: and He is the Exalted in Might, Oft-Forgiving." 67:2

If life is a test, how has God prepared humans to take this test? The Quran repeatedly talks about the mission of the prophets: to convey the message from the divine and serve as warners and bearers of glad tidings.

"(We sent) messengers as the givers of good news and as warners, so that people should not have a plea against Allah after the (coming of) messengers; and Allah is Mighty, Wise." 4:165

The Quran explains that prophets' messages alone wouldn't have been enough to prepare humans for the test, and thus man is endowed with the power to comprehend and a free will to make choices.

"It is He Who has created for you (the faculties of) hearing, sight, feeling, and understanding: little thanks it is you give!" 23:78

Though overly simplistic, the underlying theme can be summarized as follows: We came from God, and to Him we shall return. Man has no choice with either situation. The Quran and the Bible teach that between the coming and going, this life serves as a test. We have been given the capacity and the free will to choose the paths shown by God's messengers, thus making us accountable for our actions.

Reward Ratio 10:1 for Good and Bad Deeds

"Whoever brings a good deed, he shall have ten like it, and whoever brings an evil deed, he shall be recompensed only with the like of it, and they shall not be dealt with unjustly." 6:160 (Shakir)

Repentance: The concept of repentance is not unique to the Quran. The Bible frequently refers to people who repented, starting right from the beginning when Adam and Eve sinned and God accepted their repentance. There are numerous verses on His mercy, and accepting repentance is considered a sign of His mercy in the Quran. One of the ninety-nine names of God is *Al-Ghaffar*, or "The Forgiving." *Al-Ghafur* and *Al-Afu* carry similar meanings. The following is a small sample of verses on repentance and His forgiveness:

"The revelation of this Book is from Allah, Exalted in Power, Full of Knowledge, Who forgives sin, accepts repentance." 40:2–3

"But verily your Lord, to those who do wrong in ignorance, but who thereafter repent and make amends, your Lord, after all this, is Oft-Forgiving, Most Merciful." 16:119

"He is the One that accepts repentance from His Servants and forgives sins: and He knows all that you do." 42:25

The Quran narrates the story when Pharaoh was about to drown in the Red Sea, he saw death and in his desperation stated his belief in God. God essentially told him it was too late. Therefore the acceptance of repentance comes with an expiry date—no pun intended.

"Of no effect is the repentance of those who continue to do evil, until death faces one of them, and he says, 'Now have I repented indeed'; nor of those who die rejecting Faith." 4:18

Death

The Quran (and the Bible) views death as a mere transition. Death is not viewed as an end of life, but rather a beginning of another phase. Man started in the presence of God, then moved on to this life on earth, and will eventually move on to the life of hereafter, which will be eternal.

"Every soul shall have a taste of death: and We test you by evil and by good by way of trial. To Us must you return." 21:35

"Every soul must taste of death, then to Us you shall be brought back." 29:57

Note that the word used is "soul" (*"Nafs"* in Arabic). It does not say "man" or "humans," indicating that everything will perish—except the person of the Lord.

"Everyone on it must pass away (perish). And there will endure for ever the person of your Lord, the Lord of Glory and Honor." 55:26–27 (Shakir)

"Every soul shall taste of death, and you shall only be paid fully your reward on the resurrection day; then whoever is removed far away from the fire and is made to enter the garden he indeed has attained the object; and the life of this world is nothing but a provision of vanities [chattels of deception]." 3:185 (Shakir)

It must be pointed out that though the Quran reminds us of the transient nature of life on earth, it does not trivialize it and does not recommend we simply cut ourselves off from worldly affairs or just worship God all the time. In fact, the Quran asks for moderation in worship and recommends we make efforts to be successful in this world as long as God's guidelines and laws are adhered to. For instance, the Quran does not forbid making a lot of money. However, it provides guidelines for how one should earn it (and spend it). The following is a famous verse often recited as a prayer by Muslims:

"Our Lord! Give us good in this world and good in the Hereafter, and defend [save] us from the torment of the Fire!" 2:201

The Bible and Life and Death

The Bible does not describe life and death or the hereafter in as much detail, but it conveys a similar message nonetheless: that life is short, with the eventual return to God.

However, in his book *The Torah for Dummies*, Rabbi Kurzweil explains, "A common misconception about Judaism is that Jewish teachings don't say much about death and afterlife. This is a gross distortion of Judaism based in part on the fact that the written Torah has little to say about death. The oral Torah, including the

Talmud and the teachings of Kabbalah, is where you find extensive treatment of death and the afterlife."[40]

He further explains very eloquently on page 65 of his book that "the body comes from the earth and ultimately returns to the earth after death. The soul comes from God and it lives after the death of the body. People aren't bodies with souls but rather souls with bodies. The soul existed before the body, it uses the body as an instrument, and then the soul drops the body and continues on."

This indeed is strikingly similar to the Islamic views on the body and soul.

The following is a small sample that paints the same picture as the Quran about the brevity of life as well as the eventual return to God, though the references are not as direct and pointed:

"My days fly faster than a weaver's shuttle. They end without hope. O God, remember that my life is but a breath, and I will never again feel happiness." Job 7:6–7

"Remember that you made me from dust; will you turn me back to dust so soon." Job 10:9

"Remember how short my life is, how empty and futile this human existence! No one can live forever; all will die. No one can escape the power of the grave." Psalm 89:47–48

"I am here on earth for just a little while; do not hide your commands from me." Psalm 119:19 (Good News Translation)

"Lord, what are mortals, that you notice mere mortals, that you pay attention to us? We are like a puff of wind; our days are like a passing shadow." Psalm 144:3–4

The Bible and Repentance

The Bible invites followers to repent for their sins and narrates many occasions when people repented. The repentance should be sincere. The Old Testament refers to the many times the children of Israel rebelled, but many repented, and God accepted their repentance. The confession of sins is a key concept in Christianity and Judaism. Confession and repentance go hand in hand. Repentance is considered opening the gates to the mercy of God.

---

40 Kurzweil, *The Torah for Dummies*, p. 198.

"The Lord isn't really being slow about His promise, as some people think. No, He is being patient for your sake. He does not want anyone to be destroyed, but wants everyone to repent." 2 Peter 3:9

"Peter replied, 'Each of you must repent of your sins and turn to God, and be baptized in the name of Jesus Christ for the forgiveness of your sins. Then you will receive the gift of the Holy Spirit.'" Acts 2:38

"Seek the LORD while you can find Him. Call on Him now while He is near. Let the wicked change their ways and banish the very thought of doing wrong. Let them turn to the LORD that He may have mercy on them. Yes, turn to our God, for He will forgive generously.'" Isaiah 55:6–7

Repentance in Judaism

Known as *teshuva* in Judaism, repentance is a way for atonement for sins. The Jewish traditions spell out the conditions for repentance that include confession (*viduy*), acting with humility, refraining from committing the same sins, and in fact doing the opposite of the sins committed. *Yamim Noraim*, or Days of Awe (Days of Repentance), are ten days starting from *Rosh Hashanah* and ending with *Yom Kippur* in which Jewish people are directed to ask for forgiveness and repent. During this ten-day period, it is believed that God writes down what is to happen in the next year: who will live, who will die, who will have good and bad things happen. Thus it is a period for repentance (*teshuva*), prayers (*tefilah*), and good deeds or charity (*tzedakah*). This concept is strikingly similar to the Muslim beliefs regarding the night of the power (*Shab-e-Qadr*), which occurs on one of the last ten days of Ramadan. According to the Talmud, Yom Kippur only atones for men's sins against God; to atone for sins committed against another person, one should ask for forgiveness from, and reconciliation with, that person, yet another concept entirely consistent with Islamic traditions.

Repentance in Christianity

Repentance has central significance in Christianity, as is evident from the start of the ministry of Jesus and John the Baptist.

"From then on Jesus began to preach, 'Repent of your sins and turn to God, for the Kingdom of Heaven is near.'" Matthew 4:17

"In those days John the Baptist came to the Judean wilderness and began preaching. His message was, 'Repent of your sins and turn to God, for the Kingdom of Heaven is near.'" Matthew 3:1–2

Many of the conditions for repentance remain the same in the three faiths: sincerity, confession, avoiding the same sins in the future as well as other sins, and asking for God's mercy.

Points to Remember

- The Quran and the Bible consider life a journey, on the way to the hereafter, and instruct followers to spend this life wisely.
- Life is a test, and because of the guidance God has sent, as well as the intellect He endowed us with, we are accountable for our actions and beliefs.
- Repentance is a major tool, reflecting God's mercy and forgiveness. The Quran and the Bible frequently invite followers to confess their wrongdoings and repent to clean their slates. The Quran asks for repentance before it is too late (when one "sees death").
- Death is inevitable. Every soul will have the taste of death, which is considered not an end to life but a beginning to eternal life. Death occurs to the body, while the soul lives on.

Time to Ponder

- If one is to believe God will pardon everyone in the hereafter, does that imply there is no accountability for the actions in *this* life? If everyone is destined to pass the test, what then is the purpose of administering the test? Can we act justly and fairly without having a sense of accountability?

CHAPTER 21
THE DAY OF JUDGMENT

The Quran and the Bible have numerous references to the Day of Judgment and leave no doubt whatsoever about its occurrence. The Quran refers to it as *Yaum-e-Qiyamah* (Day of Resurrection), *Yaum-e-Hisab* (Day of Accounting), or simply "the Day." Chapter 75 of the Quran is named *Al-Qiyamah*. There are many other shorter chapters that describe various aspects of the Day of Judgment. Though the Bible is typically more descriptive, this is one subject that is described in significantly more detail in the Quran, indicating its emphasis on accountability of individuals.

"Does man think that We shall not be able to put his bones together? Why not? We are able to put together, in perfect order, the very tips of his fingers. But man wishes to keep on doing evil in the future as well. He questions: 'When will this Day of Resurrection be?' Well, it will come when the sight shall be dazed, the moon will be eclipsed, and the sun and the moon will be brought together." 75:3–9 (Malik)

The key elements on the Day, as outlined in the Quran, can be put together as follows:

- To start off, a mighty disaster of astronomical proportion will occur, no pun intended, when the universe will fold upon itself. A trumpet will sound. There are rather graphic descriptions of what it will be like on the Day. Every soul will perish, except the person of God.
- Resurrection of the souls, followed by:
- Accounting (*Hisab*) and Judgment.

The Quran is often said to be harsh, painting a picture of doom and gloom. But contrary to this common perception, the Quran describes in an equitable manner paradise and hell and the fate of good people and evil people. In fact, the depiction of heaven as an eternally peaceful and joyful abode is presented in more vivid details.

The Quran describes the final Day as terrifying and chaotic. It will be the end of life as we know it. Upon resurrection, everyone will be given their report card, and every deed will be counted and judged upon justly and mixed with divine mercy along with the intercession by those whom God has given permission to intercede. However, the Quran makes it clear that there will be only one Judge that Day: God Himself, and He will have complete authority over everyone and everything. Some will be sentenced to paradise, others to hell, and still others to an intermediary place.

What It Will Be Like

Earth will crumble, the moon and sun will be together, and the earth will shake like never before and will "spit" everything it has. In chapter 101, called *Al-Qariyah* (or "The Calamity"), the entire, short chapter is reserved for describing the picture of the Day:

"The Qariyah! [The Calamity] What is the Qariyah? And what will explain to you what the Qariyah is? It is that Day when men shall be like scattered moths and the mountains like colorful carded wool. On that Day, he whose scale of good deeds is heavy shall live a pleasant luxurious life. But he whose scale of good deeds is light shall abode in Hāviah [bottomless pit/abyss]; and what will explain to you, what it (Hāviah) is? It is a blazing fire." 101:1–11 (Malik)

Other passages describing the rather sobering events on the final Day:

"And when the trumpet is blown with a single blast, And the earth is moved, and its mountains, and they are crushed to powder at one stroke, On that day shall the great event come to pass, And heaven shall cleave asunder, so that on that day it shall be frail." 69:13–16 (Shakir)

"On the day when heaven shall be as molten copper. And the mountains shall be as tufts of wool. And friend shall not ask of friend. Though they will be given sight of them. The guilty man will long to be able to ransom himself from the punishment of that day at the price of his children, And his wife and his brother. And the nearest of his kinsfolk who gave him shelter. And all those that are in the earth, (wishing) then (that) this might deliver him. By no means! Surely it is a flaming fire." 70:8–15 (Shakir)

The following verses indicate the destruction will not be only in the solar system but elsewhere in the universe as well:

"On the Day of Resurrection the whole earth shall be in His grasp and all the heavens shall be rolled up in His right hand. Glory be to Him! Exalted be He above what they associate with Him." 39:67 (Shakir)

Pooya Yazdi comments that this is symbolic to indicate the heavens are and will be under His power, the right hand being a symbol of power.

"On the day when We will roll up heaven like the rolling up of the scroll for writings, as We originated the first creation, (so) We shall reproduce it; a promise (binding on Us); surely We will bring it about." 21:104 (Shakir)

"When the sun (with its spacious light) is folded up; When the stars fall, losing their luster; When the mountains vanish (like a mirage); When the she-camels, ten months with young, are left untended; When the wild beasts are herded together (in human habitations); When the oceans boil over with a swell; When the souls are sorted out, (being joined, like with like); When the female (infant) buried alive, is questioned, For what crime she was killed?; When the Scrolls are laid open; When the World on High (heavens) is unveiled: When the Blazing Fire is kindled to fierce heat; And when the Garden [Paradise] is brought near (Then) shall each soul know what it has put forward." 81:1–13

A Trumpet Will Sound

The Quran frequently mentions the sounding of a loud trumpet starting the sequence of events leading up to the destruction of earth and the heavens, and another one will blow before the resurrection.

"In fact what they are waiting for is a single blast, which will seize them while they are yet disputing among themselves in their worldly affairs. Then, neither they will be able to make a will, nor be able to return to their families. Then a trumpet shall be blown and, behold, they will rise up from their graves and hasten to their Lord. They will say: 'Oh, Woe to us! Who has raised us up from our graves?' (They will be told:) 'This is what the Compassionate (Allah) had promised and true was the word of the messengers.' It will be no more than a single blast, and then they will all be gathered before Us. On that Day no soul will suffer the least injustice and you shall be rewarded according to your deeds." 36:49–54 (Malik)

"The Trumpet shall be blown, and all that is in the heavens and the earth shall swoon except those whom Allah will please to exempt. Then the Trumpet will be blown for the second time and behold! They shall all stand up, looking around. The earth will be shining with the light of her Lord, the Book of record will be laid open, the Prophets and other witnesses will be brought in, and justice shall be done between people with all fairness: none shall be wronged. Every soul will be paid in full according to its deeds, for He knows fully well as to what they did." 39:68–70

Resurrection

All the dead will be brought back to life for the accounting and judgment. Some of the verses quoted above already have references to resurrection.

"They say: 'What! When we are reduced to bones and dust, shall we really be raised up again into a new creation?' Tell them: 'even if you be stones or iron or even something harder than this that you may think of.' Then they will ask: 'Who will restore us?' Say: 'The One Who created you the first time.' Then they will shake their heads at you and ask: 'Well, when will this be?' Say, 'It may be quite soon! It will be on the Day when He will call you and you will rise up in response to it, with His praise, and you will think that you remained in the state of death but a little while." 17:49–52 (Malik)

"And verily the Hour will come: there can be no doubt about it, or about (the fact) that Allah will raise up all who are in the graves." 22:7

Accounting and Judgment: Everyone Will Be Given a Record (Report Card)

"Every man's fate We have fastened on his own neck: On the Day of Judgment We shall bring out for him a scroll, which he will see spread open, (It will be said to him:) 'Read your (own) record: Sufficient is your soul this day to make out an account against you.' Whoever goes aright (does well), for his own soul does he go aright (does well); and whoever goes astray, to its detriment only does he go astray: nor can the bearer of a burden bear the burden of another, nor do We chastise until We have sent a messenger." 1713–15 (verse 15 is from Shakir's compilation)

Though the concept of intercession is widely accepted in Islam (as it is in Christianity), the preceding set of verses essentially declares that no one will bear anyone else's sins and everyone is responsible for their own deeds—good and bad.

"And everything they have done is in the writings. And everything small and great is written down." 54:52–53 (Shakir)

"And We will set up a just balance on the day of resurrection, so no soul shall be dealt with unjustly in the least; and though there be the weight of a grain of mustard seed, (yet) will We bring it, and sufficient are We to take account." 21:47 (Shakir)

"And the Book shall be placed, then you will see the guilty fearing from what is in it, and they will say: 'Ah! woe to us! what a book is this! it does not omit a small one nor a great one, but numbers them (all);' And what they had done they shall find present (there); and your Lord does not deal unjustly with anyone." 18:49 (Shakir)

"One day We shall call together all human beings with their (respective) Imams: those who are given their record in their right hand will read it (with pleasure), and they will not be dealt with unjustly in the least." 17:71

The Fate of the Righteous and the Evil

In addition to verse 17:71 noted above, the Quran gives good news to the ones receiving their report card in their right hands:

"When heaven bursts asunder, and obeys its Lord and it must. And when the earth is stretched [flattened out]. And casts forth what is in it and becomes empty, and obeys its Lord and it must. O

man! Surely you must strive (to attain) to your Lord, a hard striving until you meet Him. Then as to him who is given his book in his right hand, He shall be reckoned with by an easy reckoning, and he shall go back to his people joyful. And as to him who is given his book behind his back, He surely will invoke destruction and enter into burning fire." 84:1–12 (Shakir)

Chapter 56 (*Al-Waqiyah*, or "The Inevitable"): This chapter, like many others near the end of the Quran, is mostly dedicated to describe the Day of Judgment, but perhaps in more detail than others. The people will be divided into three categories: those who are foremost and exalted, those who are righteous (people of the right hand), and those who disbelieved (people of the left hand).

The "foremost" group: *"When the inevitable event will come to pass—no one will be able to deny it's coming to pass—then some shall be abased and some exalted. The earth shall be shaken with severe shaking and the mountains shall be made to crumble with awful crumbling and become like scattered dust. Then you shall be divided into three groups: the companions of the right hand—who will be the companion of the right hand; And the companions of the left hand—who will be the companions of the left hand; and foremost shall be the foremost. They will be nearest to God, in the gardens of bliss. Most of them will be from the former and a few from the later generations. They shall have the jeweled couches, reclining on them facing each other, and there shall wait on them the eternal youths with goblets, shining beakers and cups of pure drink—which will neither pain their heads nor take away their senses. They shall have fruits of their own choice and flesh of fowls that they may desire, and dark eyed Hurs (damsels) as lovely as well guarded pearls as a reward for their good deeds that they had done. There they shall not hear any vain talk nor sinful words, but only the greetings of 'Peace be upon you! Peace be upon you.'"* 56:1–26 (Malik)

People of the right hand and their reward: The verses 17:71 and 84:1–12, noted above, mention people whose records will be given on their right hand. *Surah Al-Waqiyah* goes on to describe these people again:

"Those of the right hand—happy shall be those of the right hand! They shall be among the thornless lote trees [lush orchards]

clusters of bananas, extended thick shades, constantly flowing water, abundant fruits of unforbidden never ending supply, and will be reclining on high raised couches. We have created their wives [Companions] of special creation, And made them virgin [virgin_ pure and undefiled], beloved by nature, equal in age, for those of the right hand. Many of them will be from the former and many from the later generations." 56:27–40 (Malik)

People of the left hand and their punishment: Those receiving the record on their left hand will not be a happy bunch. The Quran does not mince words when warning the consequences of evil deeds:

"*As for those of the left hand—how unfortunate will be the people of the left hand! They will be in the midst of scorching winds and in boiling water: in the shade of a pitch-black smoke, neither cool nor refreshing. For they lived in comfort before meeting this fate. They persisted in heinous sins and used to say: 'When we are dead and turned to dust and bones, shall we then be raised to life again? And our forefathers, too?' Tell them: 'Surely those of old and those of present age shall certainly be brought together on an appointed time of a known Day. Then, O the mistaken rejecters, you shall eat of the Zaqqum tree [tree of bitterness], and fill your bellies with it; and drink on top of it scalding water; yet you shall drink it like a thirsty camel.' Such will be their entertainment on the Day of Reckoning.*" 56:41–56 (Malik)

Another chapter, called *Al-Intifaar,* or "The Cleaving," is entirely dedicated to a description of the Day of Judgment. It describes the two scribes, or guardian angels, assigned to each person. One writes the good deeds, the other the bad deeds. Moreover, it states God will be the only authority on the Day of Judgment. Here is the chapter in its entirety:

"*When heaven will cleft asunder, when the stars will scatter, when the oceans will be torn apart; and when the graves will be laid open: then each soul shall know what it has sent forth and what it left behind. O man! What has lured you away from your Gracious Lord, Who created you, fashioned you, proportioned you, and molded you in whatever form He pleased? Nay! In fact you deny the Day of Judgment. You should know that guardian angels have indeed been appointed over you, who are noble writers, they know all that you do. On that Day the righteous will surely be in bliss; while the wicked will indeed go to hell, they shall enter it on the Day of Judgment, and they shall not be able to escape from it. What will explain to you what the Day of Judgment is? Again, what will explain to you what the Day of Judgment is? It will be the Day when no one shall have the power to do anything for another: for, on that Day, Allah shall keep the entire command to Himself."* 82:1–19 (Malik)

God's Mercy on the Day of Judgment

Every deed, good or bad, "worth an atom," will be accounted for and rewarded, using a 1:10 scale in favor of good deeds, as noted earlier. Though the events of the Day of Judgment can be horrifying, it is also noted frequently that the righteous will have nothing to grieve. The people of Abrahamic faiths uniformly believe that God will indeed judge mankind on the Day of Judgment for their deeds, but His Mercy will be in full force on the Day. They further believe that ultimately those who enter paradise will do so mostly on the basis of God's mercy and His forgiveness, with varying connotations—involving intercession from Prophet Muhammad and his progeny, Prophet Jesus Christ, Prophet Moses, and others. *Surah Al-Fatiha* is referenced here again to point out the Quran's emphasis on His kindness and mercy right before the mention of the Day of Judgment:

"In the name of God, the Most Kind, the Most Merciful. Praise be to God, the Lord of the worlds. The Most Kind, the Most Merciful. Master of the Day of Judgment." (1:1–4)

Biblical Accounts of the Day of Judgment

The Bible's references to the Day of Judgment are not as detailed and not nearly as graphic. Nonetheless, the Bible clearly sends the message about the Day when everyone will be resurrected, followed by accounting and judgment. Though not as specific as the Quran's promise that every deed worth an atom will be accounted for, the following verse reminds believers to be mindful of their words:

"I tell you, on the Day of Judgment people will give account for every careless word they speak." Matthew 12:36

About resurrection and His Judgment:

"And just as it is appointed for man to die once, and after that comes judgment." Hebrew 9:27

"The one who rejects Me and does not receive My words has a judge; the word that I have spoken will judge him on the last day." John 12:48

And about a matter that is consistent with the message in the Quran, the Bible declares:

"But concerning that day and hour no one knows, not even the angels of heaven, nor the Son, but the Father only." Matthew 24:36

In a passage that does bear resemblance to the graphic details of the Quran, the Bible paints a picture of doomsday:

"But the day of the Lord will come like a thief, and then the heavens will pass away with a roar, and the heavenly bodies will be burned up and dissolved, and the earth and the works that are done on it will be exposed. Since all these things are thus to be dissolved, what sort of people ought you to be in lives of holiness and godliness, waiting for and hastening the coming of the day of God, because of which the heavens will be set on fire and dissolved, and the heavenly bodies will melt as they burn! But according to his promise we are waiting for new heavens and a new earth in which righteousness dwells." 2 Peter 3:10–13

Points to Remember

- The Quran gives vivid details of the Day of Judgment. The Day will come quickly and without much warning. The description of the Day is unique in its details.
- The destruction will be complete—not just the earth or the sun but the "heavens will be folded" and the stars will lose their lights.
- The main criteria for judgment will be the beliefs and deeds of the people. Every single deed recorded will be displayed to the person. No one will be treated unjustly. In the end, people of the three monotheistic faiths believe, God's mercy will be in full force.

Time to Ponder

- It is a widely held belief among the scientific community that our solar system will eventually collapse, ending all life on earth. The Quran and the Bible insist the destruction will be complete—all on the same Day. The sun and earth's fatality was not well known until recent times within the scientific community. Is science still "behind" on its calculations for the life span of the rest of the universe?

CHAPTER 22
THE HEREAFTER:
PARADISE AND HELL

Along with the unity of God, the angels, the scriptures, and the prophets, belief in the *Qiyamah* (Day of Resurrection) and hereafter is an essential part of the faith, according to the teachings of the Quran and the Bible. Paradise is often mentioned as "the garden," and hell as "the blazing fire." The vivid descriptions are in stark contrast with the Old Testament, which is relatively quiet when it comes to the Day of Judgment and the hereafter, though the Jewish traditions point out that the oral Torah is much more descriptive on this subject. The New Testament descriptions of the hereafter and the last Day are somewhere in between those of the Quran and the Old Testament in their depth and detail.

Hell (*Jahannum* in Arabic)

Like the serenity, happiness, and calm of paradise, the torments of hellfire are equally hard to imagine by human minds, but a very sobering picture is painted in the Quran nonetheless:

"To those who reject Our signs and treat them with arrogance, no opening will there be of the gates of heaven, nor will they enter the garden, until the camel can pass through the eye of the needle: Such is Our reward for those in sin. For them there is Hell, as a couch (below) and folds and folds of covering above: such is Our requital of those who do wrong." 7:40–41

The Torments of Hell

The following description may warrant a PG-13 or higher rating, for its graphic nature. In addition to the mention of hellfire, other torments are mentioned. The following is a small sample:

"In front of such a one is Hell, and he is given, for drink, boiling fetid water. In gulps will he sip it, but never will he be near swallowing it down his throat: death will come to him from every quarter, yet will he not die: and in front of him will be a chastisement unrelenting." 14:16–17

"On the day when the earth shall be changed into a different earth, and the heavens (as well), and they shall come forth before God, the One, the Supreme. And you will see the guilty on that day linked together in chains. Their shirts made of pitch and the fire covering their faces." 14:48–50 (Shakir)

"(As for) those who disbelieve in Our communications, We shall make them enter fire; so oft as their skins are thoroughly burned, We will change them for other skins, that they may taste the chastisement; surely God is Mighty, Wise." 4:56 (Shakir)

Scary reality: Many, including some Muslims, feel the Quran is very "harsh" and scares readers when it comes to the description of hell. The Quran maintains that the purpose is not to scare people into believing but to give a fair warning and inform mankind of the consequences of their deeds and belief (or unbelief). Hell is described as a terrible abode. As the saying goes, you can put lipstick on a pig, but it is still a pig. The Old Testament, though not very descriptive of hell, nonetheless narrates many instances of severe punishment and wrath of the Lord for sinners and wrongdoers—in *this* world alone.

A few years ago, I attended a program showing the consequences of teen drunk-driving in our small town. It was sponsored by the local high school, the city police, and the fire department. The purpose was to educate high school students about drunk-driving and its consequences. It was rather graphic. There was a "real" car wreckage; teenage (actors) laid bloodied and injured—some were "dead" at the crash scene; police and fire trucks were on hand, and sirens were blowing. There was even "blood" on the street and bodies scattered on the roadside. The event was well advertised and there were hundreds of people watching, with their children. There was an eerie silence and a somber mood in the crowd despite a nice sunny weekend day. Why the graphic presentation, one might ask? Because the graphic nature of the reenactment sent a much stronger message than just telling teenagers "drunk driving is unsafe." My teenage daughter, a high school student at the time, confirmed these sentiments to me and mentioned it many times after the event. It indeed had a deep impact on everyone who watched the whole scene.

The Quran gives graphic descriptions of hell to ensure that we get the message loud and clear. Having said that, it is important to remember that the underlying message of the Quran is not to scare us or to make us "greedy" for heaven but rather to nurture a state of submission and deep love as the foundation of a relationship between God and His creation. The fear (of hell) or greed (for heaven), though implied, should not be the driving factor for the worship. To worship and submit to One God is to seek His nearness and His pleasure, which is the ultimate goal for the believer, with heaven a natural consequence of this relationship. According to Jewish traditions, not being near Him in the hereafter in and of itself will be torment for believers.

Heaven: Paradise (*Jennah*)

Paradise is variously described as a place of immense peace, joy, comfort, and holiness, without any worries. Believers and their families will live in luxury, in the presence of God. As is the case on practically all occasions, a passage or reference to hell is followed by a description of paradise (or vice versa)—often in more detail. For example, in the verses that follow verse 76:4 (describing the fate of disbelievers), the fate of believers is described in much greater detail. It paints a picture of comfort, luxury, and eternal peace:

"Surely the righteous shall drink of a cup the admixture of which is camphor. A fountain from which the servants of God shall drink; they make it to flow a (goodly) flowing forth. They fulfill vows and fear a day the evil of which shall be spreading far and wide. And they give food out of love for Him to the poor and the orphan and the captive: We only feed you for God's sake; we desire from you neither

reward nor thanks: Surely we fear from our Lord a stern, distressful day. Therefore God will guard them from the evil of that day and cause them to meet with ease and happiness; And reward them, because they were patient, with garden and silk, Reclining therein on raised couches, they shall find therein neither (the severe heat of) the sun nor intense cold. And close down upon them (shall be) its shadows, and its fruits shall be made near (to them), being easy to reach. And there shall be made to go round about them vessels of silver and goblets, which are of glass, (transparent as) glass, made of silver; they have measured them according to a measure. And they shall be made to drink therein a cup the admixture of which shall be ginger, (of) a fountain therein, which is named Salsabil. And round about them shall go youths never altering in age; when you see them you will think them to be scattered pearls. And when you see there, you shall see blessings and a great kingdom. Upon them shall be garments of fine green silk and thick silk interwoven with gold, and they shall be adorned with bracelets of silver, and their Lord shall make them drink a pure (holy) drink. Surely this is a reward for you, and your striving shall be recompensed." 76:5–22 (Shakir)*

Another example of the passages on a description of the torments of hell followed by a description of paradise is the set of verses 44:43–57, initially describing hell (43–50) and immediately followed by a description of paradise.

"As to the Righteous (they will be) in a position of Security, among Gardens and Springs; Dressed in fine silk and in rich brocade, they will face each other; So; and We shall join [wed] them to fair women with beautiful, big, and lustrous eyes. There can they call for every kind of fruit in peace and security; Nor will they there taste Death, except the first death; and He will preserve them from the Penalty of the Blazing Fire, As a Bounty from your Lord! that will be the supreme achievement!" 44:51–57

What type of people will enter paradise, one may ask? The belief in One God is mandatory. The following is one of the many verses in the Quran addressing this question:

"Be quick in the race for forgiveness from your Lord, and for a Garden whose width is that (of the whole) of the heavens and of the earth, prepared for the righteous, Those who spend (benevolently)

in prosperity as well as in adversity, and those who restrain (their) anger and pardon men; and Allah loves the doers of good (to others). And those who, having done something to be ashamed of, or wronged their own souls, earnestly bring Allah to mind, and ask for forgiveness for their sins, and who can forgive sins except Allah? and are never obstinate in persisting knowingly in (the wrong) they have done. For such the reward is forgiveness from their Lord, and Gardens with rivers flowing underneath, an eternal dwelling: How excellent a recompense for those who work (and strive)!" 3:133–136

Parents United with Offspring (If the Offspring Followed in Faith)

"Surely those who guard (against evil) shall be in gardens and bliss Rejoicing because of what their Lord gave them, and their Lord saved them from the punishment of the burning fire. Eat and drink pleasantly for what you did, Reclining on thrones set in lines, and We will unite (wed) them to large-eyed beautiful ones. And (as for) those who believe and their offspring follow them in faith, We will unite with them their offspring and We will not diminish to them aught (any) of their work; every man is responsible for what he shall have wrought [earned]." 52:17–21 (Shakir)

The Inhabitants of Paradise Will Live with Their Families

The Quran emphasizes the importance of a family system—one that loves and cares for each other. This will be extended to the life in paradise for the righteous. Not only will they live with their offspring but they will also be united with their (righteous) families.

"Those who patiently persevere, seeking the countenance of their Lord; Establish regular prayers; spend, out of (the gifts) We have bestowed for their sustenance, secretly and openly; and turn off Evil with good: for such there is the final attainment of the (eternal) home—Gardens of perpetual bliss: they shall enter there, as well as the righteous among their fathers, their spouses, and their offspring: and angels shall enter unto them from every gate (with the salutation)." 13:22–23

"And grant, our Lord! That they enter the Gardens of Eternity, which You have promised to them, and to the righteous among their

fathers, their wives, and their offspring. For You are the Exalted in Might, Full of Wisdom." 40:8 (Shakir)

The Inhabitants of Paradise Will Have Their Pure (Holy) Mates (*Azwaj-e-Mutahhara*)

The Quran variously describes the inhabitants living comfortably with their *Azwaj-e-Mutahhara,* or "pure (and holy) mates." This phrase has also been translated as "pure companions" or "pure spouses." This is in contrast to the word *"Azwajohum,"* simply meaning spouses. The following are some of the verses describing these pure mates. Does it mean people whose spouses were not righteous will get new, "pure companions," in paradise?

"And convey good news to those who believe and do good deeds, that they shall have gardens in which rivers flow; whenever they shall be given a portion of the fruit thereof, they shall say: This is what was given to us before; and they shall be given the like of it, and there for them are pure mates; there for ever they shall abide." 2:25 (Shakir)

"Say: Shall I give you glad tidings of things far better than those? For the righteous are Gardens in nearness to their Lord, with rivers flowing beneath; therein is their eternal home; with companion pure (and holy); and the good pleasure of Allah. For in Allah's sight are (all) His servants." 3:15

"Pure, Chaste-Eyed Mates" (*Qasiratut tarfi*), Also Called "Mates of Modest Gaze"

The Quran frequently mentions the righteous in paradise living comfortably with "pure mates of modest gaze." This phrase is variously translated as "mates of restrained gaze" or "whose gaze will be fixed at their mates only." The phrase *"Qasiratut tarfi"* is often followed by another word like *"eyn"* (of lovely big eyes) or *"atrab"* (of equal age). Many have translated the words as gender neutral (Unal: "pure chaste-eyed spouses"; Muhammad Ali and Pickthall: "those modest in gaze"; and Shakir and Asad: "mates with modest gaze"). However, some translators use the words "chaste women with modest gaze." These include Yousuf Ali and Mir Ahmad Ali/Pooya.

"And with them shall be mates with modest [restrained] gaze, equals in age." 38:52 (Shakir)

"In them shall be mates with modest [restrained] gaze; before them neither man nor Jinn shall have touched them." 55:56 (Pickthall)

A quick reading may lead one to conclude that this means female mates for man since "neither man nor Jinn" has touched them before. However, the word for "man" used in Arabic here is *"Ins,"* derived from *"Naas,"* meaning mankind, and not a male. Thus the references to the holy companions are for both righteous males and females.

Hoor, or Pure Maidens

Another word used to describe the pure mates in paradise is *Hoor,* which is translated as "pure maidens," "companions pure," or "pure spouses," and usually means female companions of righteous male inhabitants.

"And (there will be) Companions with beautiful, big, and lustrous eyes." 56:22

"(As against this) verily, the God-conscious will find themselves in a state secure, amid gardens and springs, wearing (garments) of silk and brocade, facing one another (in love). Thus shall it be. And We shall pair [wed] them with companions pure, most beautiful of eye." 44:51–54 (Asad)

Other verses mentioning the Hoors or pure maidens can be found in 55:72 and 52:20.

Regardless, all commentators agree this is going to be a holy union without lust, as some might think at a cursory review of the verses, or when the verses are read out of context. After all, these are the mates assigned and wedded by God. The Quran states that these couples will enjoy each other's company in a pure, holy, and nonsensual way in a manner unlike the bodily experiences on earth. The overall experiences in paradise, and hell, will be unlike any other. For instances, in hell, there will be blazing fire, hot enough to char the earthly body instantly, yet the inhabitants will experience that without succumbing to it. Similarly, the joyful existence in paradise, even with the "pure maidens," will be unlike any other. The Quran clearly asserts that there will be no lewd or lusty acts in paradise.

This perhaps applies to the references to the "drinks" in paradise as well, sometimes translated as wine, but one that's pure and holy. This is not the same earthly alcohol we know about (which is forbidden by the Quran). To make the point, the Quran mentions that these drinks will not cause intoxication, lewdness, headaches, or other undesirable effects like earthly wine can. Thus the picture painted by some, of men in paradise having sensual sexual relations with maidens while drinking and having a "good time," is far from the picture painted by the Quran.

A Place between Hell and Heaven

The Quran refers to a veil between hell and paradise known as *Al-Araf*, a plural of *Arf*, meaning the elevated places or heights. Though varying opinions on this concept and the interpretation of these verses exist, many Muslim commentators believe this to be a temporary place for believers who sinned and will eventually enter heaven. This is similar to the concept of purgatory in Christianity. According to the doctrine, some people who did not earn entrance into heaven, but were not bad enough to go to hell, will be purified in purgatory, before being allowed into heaven. Similar concepts are found in Judaism, where such people will spend up to forty-nine days (according to Nuri) or twelve months (according to Akiba) in this transitional place.

In chapter 7, *Al-Araf*, there is a long passage that talks about the conversations between the people of heaven and hell; and people in *Al-Araf* with those in heaven and hell.

"Between the two, there shall be a veil, and on the Arāf (heights/ elevated places) there will be people who will recognize them by their features. They will call out to the residents of Paradise: 'Peace be upon you!' They will not have yet entered it, though they hope. When their eyes shall turn toward the inmates of the hell-fire they will say: 'Our Lord, Do not cast us among these wrongdoers.' And the dwellers of the most elevated places shall call out to men whom they will recognize by their features saying: 'Of no avail were to you your amassing and your arrogance'. Behold! Are these not the men

whom you swore that God with His Mercy would never bless? Enter the Garden: no fear shall be on you, nor shall you grieve." 7:46–49 (Malik)

Should One Fear Hell or Be Greedy for Heaven?

Ali, the fourth caliph of Islam and Prophet Muhammad's son-in-law, eloquently addressed this question:

"Islam in fear of hell is the Islam of a slave, and Islam in the hope of Heaven is that of a merchant. The best Islam is the Islam for the sake of God's Glory alone."

This was further highlighted by yet another sermon:

"O' God, I worship you, not because of fear of hell or because of the greed of Heaven. I worship you because I have found you to be the only one worthy of worship."

Biblical References[41]

Day of Judgment, Heavens, and Hell

As noted previously, all three Abrahamic faiths do believe in a final day when every person's sins and good deeds will be weighed and a divine decision will be made whether to redeem that person. After that, the concept of hell and heaven varies somewhat in Islam, Judaism, and Christianity.

The New Testament

The Day of Judgment will occur after the second coming of Jesus and the resurrection of the dead. Various churches have varying doctrine. Roman Catholics, for example, believe in two judgments: the "particular judgment" and the "last judgment". The *particular judgment* occurs right after death and the soul goes to heaven, hell, or purgatory: heaven for believers and those who did good; hell for unbelievers and evildoers; and purgatory for those whose fate hangs in the balance. According to the Eastern Orthodox Church doctrine, the particular judgment occurs on the fortieth day after

---

41 All biblical translations in this chapter are from the New American Standard Bible by the Lockman Foundation.

death. Then after the second coming of Jesus, there will be end of times and the *last judgment* will take place. At that time, a final judgment will be passed; the good will stay in heaven, evildoers in hell, and those in purgatory will go to heaven.

Hell has been described as a fiery, extremely undesirable place for the souls of the sinners who were not saved on the Day of Judgment. The New Testament speaks about the after-death fate of the wicked by using the Greek words *"gehenna"* (derived from the Hebrew word *"ge-hinnom"*) and *tartaro*, words with striking phonetic closeness to the Arabic word *"Jahannum."* It is generally defined as the fate of unrepentant sinners, those who reject Jesus, and those who did not believe in God.

"But I say to you that everyone who is angry with his brother shall be guilty before the court; and whoever says to his brother, 'You good-for-nothing,' shall be guilty before the Supreme Court; and whoever says, 'You fool,' shall be guilty enough to go into the fiery hell." Matthew 5:22

"Woe to the world because of its stumbling blocks! For it is inevitable that stumbling blocks come; but woe to that man through whom the stumbling block comes! 'If your hand or your foot causes you to stumble, cut it off and throw it from you; it is better for you to enter life crippled or lame, than to have two hands or two feet and be cast into the eternal fire. If your eye causes you to stumble, pluck it out and throw it from you. It is better for you to enter life with one eye, than to have two eyes and be cast into the fiery hell.'" Matthew 18:7–9

Mark refers to the same passages but adds the presence of maggots (translated by NASB as "worms") and says that the fire will never go out:

"If your eye causes you to stumble, throw it out; it is better for you to enter the kingdom of God with one eye, than, having two eyes, to be cast into hell, where their worm does not die, and the fire is not quenched." Mark 9:47–48

The references to cutting off limbs or gouging out eyes are of course metaphoric and should not be taken literally. Jesus says this to his disciples:

"I say to you, My friends, do not be afraid of those who kill the body and after that have no more that they can do. But I will warn

you whom to fear: fear the One who, after He has killed, has authority to cast into hell; yes, I tell you, fear Him!" Luke 12:4–5

Hell: Raging Fire/Lake of Fire

"But a terrifying expectation of judgment and the fury of a fire which will consume the adversaries." Hebrews 10:27

"Just as Sodom and Gomorrah and the cities around them, since they in the same way as these indulged in gross immorality and went after strange flesh, are exhibited as an example in undergoing the punishment of eternal fire." Jude 1:7

"Then I saw a great white throne and Him who sat upon it, from whose presence earth and heaven fled away, and no place was found for them. And I saw the dead, the great and the small, standing before the throne, and books were opened; and another book was opened, which is the book of life; and the dead were judged from the things which were written in the books according to their deeds. And the sea gave up the dead, which were in it, and death and Hades gave up the dead which were in them; and they were judged, every one of them according to their deeds. Then death and Hades were thrown into the lake of fire. This is the second death, the lake of fire. And if anyone's name was not found written in the book of life, he was thrown into the lake of fire." Revelation 20:11–15

Heaven

According to Christian teachings, heaven is an eternally peaceful and joyful place, with no pain, worries, or any type of suffering. The believers will live with their families near God. There will be no death in heaven, only righteous people will enter it, and one must be a follower of Jesus to be an inhabitant. In the following verse, Jesus, while addressing his disciples, talks about his second coming and explains that his followers will live with him:

"Do not let your heart be troubled; believe in God, believe also in Me. In My Father's house are many dwelling places; if it were not so, I would have told you; for I go to prepare a place for you. If I go and prepare a place for you, I will come again and receive you to Myself, that where I am, there you may be also." John 14:1–3

The book of Revelation, consisting of the visions of John, describes the hereafter and heaven in great detail:

"And He will wipe away every tear from their eyes; and there will no longer be any death; there will no longer be any mourning, or crying, or pain; the first things have passed away." Revelation 21:4

"Then he showed me a river of the water of life, clear as crystal, coming from the throne of God and of the Lamb, in the middle of its street. On either side of the river was the tree of life, bearing twelve kinds of fruit, yielding its fruit every month; and the leaves of the tree were for the healing of the nations. There will no longer be any curse; and the throne of God and of the Lamb will be in it, and His bond-servants will serve Him; they will see His face, and His name will be on their foreheads. And there will no longer be any night; and they will not have need of the light of a lamp nor the light of the sun, because the Lord God will illumine them; and they will reign forever and ever." Revelation 22:1–5

The Gospel of Matthew declares there will be no marriages in heaven:

"But Jesus answered and said to them, 'You are mistaken, not understanding the scriptures nor the power of God. For in the resurrection they neither marry nor are given in marriage, but are like angels in heaven.'" Matthew 22:29–30

The Old Testament

The Torah, though very detailed when it comes to historical events and the law, is relatively quiet on the subject of the last day and the afterlife. However, as mentioned before, the oral Torah, including the Talmud, is said to be where one will find more details on the Day of Judgment and the hereafter. Like Islam and Christianity, Judaism believes in a Day of Judgment. The Old Testament books of Daniel and Malachi make a relatively cursory reference to such day:

"Many of those who sleep in the dust of the ground will awake, these to everlasting life, but the others to disgrace and everlasting contempt." Daniel 12:2

"'For behold, the Day is coming, burning like a furnace; and all the arrogant and every evildoer will be chaff; and the day that is coming will set them ablaze,' says the Lord of hosts, 'so that it

will leave them neither root nor branch. But for you who fear My name, the sun of righteousness will rise with healing in its wings; and you will go forth and skip about like calves from the stall. You will tread down the wicked, for they will be ashes under the soles of your feet on the day which I am preparing,' says the Lord of hosts."
Malachi 4:1–3

The Jewish eschatology refers to *Mashiach*, the Jewish equivalent of Messiah, which also means the same: anointed one. Considered to be from the lineage of David, he will unite the people of Israel and rule with peace and justice. Unlike Christian belief, *Mashiach* is not considered divine, or Jesus.

The Tanakh refers briefly to the rising of the dead:

"Your dead will live; Their corpses will rise. You who lie in the dust, awake and shout for joy, For your dew is as the dew of the dawn, And the earth will give birth to the departed spirits."
Isaiah 26:19

Hell

Hell, or at least the eternal hell with blazing fire, does not get much mention in the Torah. *Gehinnom* is believed to be a place where sinners will stay for varying periods lasting up to twelve months, according to various Jewish traditions. The main consequence of sin is a separation from God in the hereafter, which is a terrible punishment in itself. In many ways, *Gehinnom* resembles purgatory in Christianity, rather than a place for eternal punishment for the sinners with blazing fires.

Paradise

Similarly, paradise is not part of the Tanakh descriptive. Though the righteous will spend time in the hereafter in the presence of God, the physical description of heaven is lacking in the Hebrew Bible, save for references as the house of the Lord or before the creation of man (the garden of Eden, where Adam and Eve lived). The Hebrew word *"shamayim"* is derived from *"shameh"* (which means lofty) and is used for heaven. This includes atmosphere, the inter-celestial matter, as well as heaven, where God and angels "live." Living in the presence of God is considered the ultimate reward.

"For thus says the high and exalted One Who lives forever, whose name is Holy, 'I dwell on a high and holy place, and also with the contrite and lowly of spirit In order to revive the spirit of the lowly and to revive the heart of the contrite.'" Isaiah 57:15

Points to Remember

- The Quran, the New Testament, and the Hebrew Bible refer to the Day of Judgment and the life hereafter. However, they differ greatly in the details.
- The description of the Day of Judgment and life in the hereafter is presented in vivid details in the Quran, but the Hebrew Bible offers scant descriptions of them. The New Testament's accounts are somewhere in between the two.
- Hell is an eternal abode according to the Quran and the New Testament (or at least according to the majority view). The Jewish concept of hell is rather unique. It is not described in terms of an eternal fiery place but rather a temporary residence lasting up to twelve months according to various traditions. The residents eventually will move on to get near God after paying for their sins.
- Heaven, according to the Quran, is a place for eternal joy and peace without any grief and worries, with families of faithful enjoying the bounties of God together. The New Testament has somewhat similar views, without the details presented in the Quran. The Old Testament is fairly quiet on the physical descriptions of paradise, though oral traditions are more descriptive.

Time to Ponder

- Is heaven an exclusive place for the followers of Prophets Moses, Jesus, or Muhammad? Does any group have an "automatic right" to enter heaven based on their faith alone? Is it even under our purview to debate it in the first place?

Section 6
The Quran
and Daily Life

CHAPTER 23
PILLARS OF ISLAM

This section will cover the teachings of the Quran and the Bible on social aspects of life in accordance with the divine law. A detailed description of Islamic law and jurisprudence (*Fiqh*) is beyond the scope of this book. Most of the topics outlined in this section are mostly relevant to individuals rather than society in general.

Before getting into the specific topics, it is worth emphasizing that the Quran's view of religion is much broader than just a set of religious instructions and laws. Islam is viewed as a way of life and covers every aspect of daily life: from "purely religious" instruction like prayers and other mandatory forms of worship, to the laws that govern daily lives like marriage, divorce, inheritance, personal finances, personal behavior, and ethics, as well as the societal issues.

Pillars of Islam

There are five basic, mandatory commandments, or pillars, of Islam, as interpreted by most Muslim jurists, and they are listed as follows:

1. *Shahada*, or Testimony
2. *Salah (Salat)*, or Daily Prayers
3. *Zakah (Zakat)*, or Helping the Poor (Charity)
4. *Sawm*, or Fasting
5. *Hajj*, or Pilgrimage

According to the interpretation by Shia Muslims, there are five roots of faith ("Usul-e-Deen"). These are the basic, mandatory beliefs: *Tawheed* (Oneness of God), *Adl* (Justice of God), *Nabuwwat*

(Prophethood), *Imamat* (Leadership, or Succession to Imams after Prophet Muhammad by Divine Instructions), and *Qiyamah* (the Day of Resurrection). Moreover, there are eight branches of the faith (*Furu-e-Deen*). These are the same as the last four pillars of Islam noted above plus *Khums*, *Jihad*, *Amr-bil-Ma'ruf* (Enjoin What's Good), and *Nahi-Anil-Munkar* (Forbid What's Evil). It is of note that Jihad is also considered obligatory by Sunni Muslims but not considered part of the five pillars of faith. Similarly, the enjoining of the good and forbidding of the evil is highly recommended, but without defining them as pillars of Islam. The following should be viewed only as a brief introduction to the pillars of Islam:

Shahada (Testimony)

This is the basic statement, or testimony to faith. It simply states:
"I testify that there is no god but God, and Muhammad is the messenger of God."

The Quran has numerous passages that form the basis for the *Shahada*. The first part (there is no god but God) also forms one of the Ten Commandments and is the basic tenet of the three Abrahamic faiths. The main difference in the creed is the second part: "Muhammad is the messenger of God."

"There is no god but He: That is the witness of God, His angels, and those endued with knowledge, standing firm on justice. There is no god but He, the Exalted in Power, the Wise." 3:18

"Say: He is Allah the One and Only." 112:1

"That is Allah, your Lord, there is no god but He; the Creator of all things, therefore serve Him, and He has charge of all things." 6:102 (Shakir)

"God! There is no god but He—the Living, the Self-subsisting, Eternal. No slumber can seize Him nor sleep." 2:255

As for the second part of *Shahada*, there are numerous passages addressing Muhammad, or referring to Muhammad as the warner or the bearer of glad tidings, or calling him, "O' Prophet." Some examples are noted here:

"We have sent you (O Prophet!), to mankind as a messenger; and God is sufficient as a witness." 4:79 (Shakir)

The following addresses Muhammad by name and as the messenger in the same verse:

"Muhammad is the messenger of God." 48:29

Though typically "no god but God" and Muhammad's prophecy are mentioned separately, the following verse combines the two commandments:

"Say (O Muhammad): 'O mankind! Verily, I am an apostle (messenger) of God to all of you (sent by Him) unto Whom the dominion over the heavens and the earth belongs! There is no deity save Him; He (alone) grants life and deals death!' Believe, then, in God and His Apostle—the unlettered Prophet who believes in God and His words—and follow him, so that you might find guidance!" 7:158 (Asad)

Salah (Daily Prayers)

Salah, also spelled *Salat*, is the ritual prayers that are obligatory for all Muslims. It is more than "the prayers" as might be perceived by the English translation. It follows a prescribed pattern and recitation of specific verses and supplications in a particular sequence. There are five mandatory prayers each day from dawn to late evening. In each Salah, there are a prescribed number of *Rakah,* or cycles. In addition, Muslims also offer the prayers on Friday in congregation and on the occasion of two festivals: *Eid al Fitr* (after Ramadan) and *Eid al Ad'ha* (after Hajj). The congregational prayers on Friday are emphasized in the following verse:

"O you who believe! when the call is made for prayer on Friday, then hasten to the remembrance of Allah and leave off trading; that is better for you, if you know." 62:9 (Shakir)

The prayers can be done in private (individually) at home and work but are more highly recommended to be offered in a congregation in a mosque (*masjid*). Before one starts the prayers, one must cleanse with water by performing ablution (*Wadhu*). Many consider this a spiritual rather than physical cleansing. Each prayer is announced with a call to prayer, known as *Adhan*.

More than just a set of ritualistic verses or postures, it is considered a way to purify one's soul and attain spiritual health by seeking nearness to God by worshipping Him and remembering

Him often. The daily prayers are constant reminders of one's duty to God and are intended to prevent one from getting perverted or deviate from the right path. One must be entirely devoted and maintain the entire focus on remembrance of God during Salah, and not merely fulfill the mechanical requirements. Salah can be viewed as a means for a person communicating with God, whereas the recitation of the Quran can be considered God talking to the person, completing a two-way communication.

"Recite that which has been revealed to you of the Book and keep up prayer (Salah); surely prayer keeps (one) away from indecency and evil, and certainly the remembrance of Allah is the greatest, and Allah knows what you do." 29:45 (Shakir)

Salah is often mentioned in combination with *Zakah* (charity).

"And be steadfast in prayer; practice regular charity; and bow down your heads with those who bow down (in worship)." 2:43

"And be steadfast in prayer and pay the regular charity and whatever good you send before for yourselves, you shall find it with Allah; surely Allah sees what you do." 2:110 (Shakir)

Salah Was Also Ordained on Abraham, Moses, Jesus, and Other Prophets

Non-Muslims and many Muslims erroneously believe the Salah was ordained on Prophet Muhammad and subsequently on his followers. But the Quran indicates it was ordained on other prophets as well:

"And We bestowed on him [meaning Abraham], Isaac, and, as an additional gift, (a grandson), Jacob, and We made righteous men of every one (of them). And We made them leaders, [or Imams] guiding (men) by Our Command, and We sent them inspiration to do good deeds, to establish regular prayers [Salah], and to practice regular charity [Zakah]; and they constantly served Us (and Us only)." 21:72–73

"And mention Ishmael in the Book; surely he was truthful in (his) promise, and he was a messenger, a prophet. And he enjoined

on his family prayer and almsgiving [Zakah], and was one in whom his Lord was well pleased." 19:54–55 (Shakir)

Salah and *Zakah* were ordained on the children of Israel: *"And remember We took a covenant from the children of Israel (to this effect): Worship none but Allah; treat with kindness your parents and kindred, and orphans and those in need; speak fair to the people; be steadfast in prayer [Salah]; and practice regular charity [Zakah]."* 2:83

Similar passages are repeated when recalling prophets prior to Muhammad and their communities: on the children of Israel (2:43, 2:83); on Shoaib, a prophet in Midian, often said to be described by Muslims as Jethro of the Hebrew Bible (11:87); on Moses (*"And I have chosen you [referring to Moses], so listen to what is revealed. Verily, I am Allah: There is no god but I: So serve you Me (only), and establish regular prayer for celebrating My praise."* 20:13–14); and on Jesus (*"He said [referring to Jesus' testimony from the crib]: Surely I am a servant of Allah; He has given me the Book and made me a prophet. And He has made me blessed wherever I may be, and He has enjoined on me prayer [Salah] and poor-rate [Zakah] so long as I live."* 19:30–31).

Zakah (Almsgiving, Charity)

There are three forms of charitable giving in Islam. *Zakah* is obligatory. *Sadaqah* is above and beyond the mandatory giving and is highly recommended. *Khums*, according to the Shia Muslim theology only, is also mandatory.

Every religion has some form of charitable giving for religious, social, and educational services. Islam has institutionalized the charitable giving in the name of God. *"Zakah"* means "to purify" and refers to purifying one's wealth and soul. Purification of the soul implies freedom from selfishness and greed, and to unattach one's self from worldly wealth and to seek nearness of God. It helps fulfill the societal obligations of the individual. It is intended to prevent wealth hoarding and meets the needs of the poor in the community through altruistic acts.

Zakah is due as a fixed proportion of one's surplus wealth and earnings after meeting one's financial obligations and liabilities.

It is mentioned by name (Zakah) thirty times alongside *Salah*, in addition to numerous other references to spend in the way of God.

"And be steadfast in prayer; practice regular charity; and bow down your heads with those who bow down (in worship)." 2:43

"And be steadfast in prayer and regular in charity: And whatever good you send forth for your souls before you, you shall find it with Allah: for Allah sees well all that you do." 2:110

"Only God is your Guardian [protecting friend or Wali] and His Messenger and those who believe, those who keep up prayers and pay the poor-rate while they bow." 5:5 (Mir Ali). Shia Muslim commentators believe the last part of the verse revealed refers to Ali, Muhammad's son-in-law, who reportedly dropped his ring to a beggar while bowing down during a prayer.

In the following verse, Zakah and other giving are termed *"Qarz-e-Hasna"* or "a loan to God," which will be paid back on the Day of Judgment in the form of mercy and forgiveness to the donor:

"Read, therefore, as much of the Quran as may be easy (for you); and establish regular Prayer and give regular Charity; and loan to Allah a Beautiful Loan [Qarz-e-Hasna]. And whatever good you send forth for your souls you shall find it in Allah's Presence—yes, better and greater, in reward and seek the Grace of Allah: for Allah is Oft-Forgiving, Most Merciful." 73:20

And in the "who is righteous" verse that has been quoted a few times in this book, Zakah is mentioned as one of the many deeds one must do to be counted as righteous:

"It is righteousness to believe in God and the Last Day, and the Angels, and the Book, and the Messengers; to spend of your wealth, out of love for Him, for your kin, for orphans, for the needy, for the wayfarer, for those who ask, and for the ransom of slaves; to be steadfast in prayer, and practice regular charity." 2:177

Giving Openly Is Fine; Giving in Secret Is Even Better

"Those who (in charity) spend of their goods by night and by day, in secret and in public, have their reward with their Lord: on them shall be no fear, nor shall they grieve." 2:274

Thus the Quran encourages giving openly or secretly, but giving secretly, without showing off, is even better. Giving, for the purpose of showing off, is highly undesirable:

"If you do deeds of charity openly, it is well; but if you bestow it upon the needy in secret, it will be even better for you, and it will atone for some of your bad deeds. And God is aware of all that you do." 2:271 (Asad)

In fact, one cannot be righteous until he gives in the way of God to the needy:

"By no means shall you attain to righteousness until you spend (benevolently) out of what you love; and whatever thing you spend, Allah surely knows it." 3:92 (Shakir)

God is the recipient of charitable giving:

"Do they not know that Allah accepts repentance from His servants and takes the alms [gifts of charity], and that Allah is the Oft-returning (to mercy), the Merciful?" 9:104 (Shakir)

And the reward for charity is manifold:

"God deprives usurious gains of all blessing, whereas He blesses charitable deeds with manifold increase." 2:274

"For those who give in Charity, men and women, and loan to Allah a Beautiful Loan, it shall be increased manifold (to their credit), and they shall have (besides) a liberal reward." 57:18

Warning to the Stingy

The Quran, true to its tradition of highlighting the consequences, praises those who give but also sends out warnings to those who cling to their wealth and do not give to the needy:

"And let not those who covetously withhold of the gifts which Allah has given them of His Grace, think that it is good for them: Nay, it will be the worse for them: soon shall the things which they covetously withheld be tied to their necks Like a twisted collar, on the Day of Judgment." 3:180

Sadaqah (Voluntary Charity)

Sadaqah means voluntary charity, though it is highly recommended in the Quran as well as Hadith (the sayings of Muhammad):

"Alms [Sadaqaat—plural] are for the poor and the needy, and those employed to administer the (funds); for those whose hearts have been (recently) reconciled (to truth); for (the ransom of) those in bondage and in debt; in the cause of God; and for the wayfarer: (thus is it) ordained by God, and God is full of knowledge and wisdom." 9:60

The purpose of charitable giving is to seek nearness to God, and not for a "thank-you" note from the recipient.

"And they feed, for the love of Allah, the indigent, the orphan, and the captive. (Saying) 'We feed you for the sake of Allah alone: no reward do we desire from you, nor thanks.'" 76:8–9

Khums is the Arabic word for one-fifth. According to Shia Muslim theology, *Khums* is mandatory on the profit or surplus of the past year's income. Income is defined as anything one earns from business, wage or salary, dividend income, or other means of possession. Shia scholars cite the following verse to support their view:

"And know that whatever thing you gain, a fifth of it is for Allah and for the Messenger and for the near of kin and the orphans and the needy and the wayfarer." 8:41 (Shakir)

The view of Sunni Muslim scholars is that this verse was revealed in reference to the spoils of the war and not meant for general wealth or income.

Sawm (Fasting)

Sawm, or fasting, is mandatory during the month of Ramadan, the ninth month of the Islamic calendar. The fasting starts at dawn with a meal (called *Sehri*) and lasts till sunset with another meal (called *Iftar*). During this time, one is not to eat or drink anything. Contrary to a common perception, fasting is considered much more than simply avoiding food and drinks, and in fact is an example where English translation loses the essence of the original concept. It's a time for spiritual healing, strengthening faith, and reflection. The time is spent in remembrance of God, getting near to Him, repenting, avoiding all major and minor sins, and spending for the needy in the way of God. Though at a glance, fasting may seem "unnatural" and harsh, those who fast regularly insist that fasting actually is an uplifting experience. This is the time to renew one's vows and relationship with God. According to Muslim view, fasting teaches the virtues of self-discipline and self-control over bodily desires (hunger, sexual feelings, anger, etc.).

"O you who believe! Fasting is prescribed for you, as it was prescribed for those before you, so that you may guard (against evil)." 2:183 (Shakir)

The word used in the above verse is "prescribed." Indeed, many Muslim scholars and Muslim physicians point out many health benefits of fasting, including cleansing of the gastrointestinal tract, and better control of blood glucose, weight, and cholesterol. In addition, fasting seems to stimulate endorphins, considered an important neurochemical that controls pain and emotional well-being. Religious scholars point out that the physical benefits are just one small though important element of fasting, and the real benefit is spiritual growth and healing. The verse also points out that fasting was prescribed before the time of Prophet Muhammad. Indeed many other religions and cultures such as Judaism, Christianity, Hinduism, and Buddhism observe fasting in one form or another.

What's Forbidden During Fasting?

- Physical needs: Avoiding food, drink, smoking, and sexual intercourse
- Morals: Avoiding sins, major and minor
- Spiritual: Avoiding distractions that move one away from God

A festival called *"Eid al Fitr"* follows at the end of the month. It is not to celebrate the *end* of Ramadan, but Muslims view it as a day to give thanks to God for all the blessings and bounties received during the month of Ramadan.

"The month of Ramadan is that in which the Quran was revealed, a guidance to men and clear proofs of the guidance and the distinction; therefore whoever of you is present in the month, he shall fast therein, and whoever is sick or upon a journey, then (he shall fast) a (like) number of other days; Allah desires ease for you, and He does not desire for you difficulty, and (He desires) that you should complete

the number and that you should exalt the greatness of Allah for His having guided you and that you may give thanks." 2:185 (Shakir)

According to many Muslim traditions, all good deeds during the month of Ramadan, as an added incentive, are multiplied many times. One particular night, known as the night of the power (*Lailatul Qadr*), is of great importance to Muslims. Chapter 97 is named after that night (*Qadr*). This is the night when the Quran is said to have been revealed in its entirety from God to the lower heaven, and the angels are said to descend upon earth all night till the dawn, to bring peace, mercy, and forgiveness, and all matters for the next year are decreed. The Muslims spend the night in prayers, repentance, and seeking His nearness. As mentioned before, in its basic concept, the night has many parallels to the Jewish *Yamim Noraim,* or Days of Awe (Days of Repentance). The translation of the entire chapter is quoted below:

"Surely We have revealed this (Quran) in the night of the power. And what will make you understand, what the night of the power is! The night of the power is better than one thousand months. The angels and the Spirit (Gabriel) come down with every decree, by the leave of their Lord, that night is the night of Peace, till the break of dawn." 97:1–5 (Malik)

Hajj (Pilgrimage to Mecca)

Unlike daily prayers, charity, and fasting, Hajj is mandatory only once in a lifetime, for those who are able and can afford to travel to Mecca during the month of *Dhul-Hijja*, the twelfth month of the Islamic calendar. Each year, millions of Muslims from all around the world from various ethnicities, colors, and socio-economic backgrounds meet in the city of Mecca and perform various rituals in a show of unity, simplicity, harmony, and submission to God.

A life changing experience for many: During this whole time, pilgrims spend time in remembrance of God, supplications, and deeds of charity; they avoid major and minor sins. The experience is considered a purification of mind and soul, and pilgrims after performing the Hajj are said to be as pure as a newborn. Most people upon their return from the Hajj report that it was a life-changing experience, and that they had never felt so much peace in their hearts before. Malcolm X, in one of the letters he wrote from Mecca during Hajj, noted, "Never have I witnessed such sincere hospitality and overwhelming spirit of true brotherhood as is practiced by people of all color and races here in this ancient Holy land, the home of Abraham, Muhammad, and all the other prophets of the Holy scriptures. For the past week, I have been utterly speechless and spellbound by the graciousness I see displayed by all around me by people of all colors. There were tens of thousands of pilgrims, from all over the world. They were of all colors, from blue-eyed blondes to black-skinned Africans. But we were all participating in the same ritual, displaying a spirit of unity and brotherhood that my experiences in America had led me to believe never could exist."[42]

A 2008 study conducted in conjunction with Harvard University's JFK School of Government, entitled "Estimating the Impact of the Hajj: Religion and Tolerance in Islam's Global Gathering," found that Muslim communities become more open after the Hajj experience. The authors of the study (Clingingsmith, Khwaja, and Kremer) concluded that the Hajj "increases belief in equality and harmony among ethnic groups and Islamic community and that Hajjis (those who have performed the Hajj) show increased belief in peace, and in equality and harmony among adherents of different religions. The evidence suggests that these changes are more a result of exposure to and interaction with Hajjis from around the world, rather than religious instruction or a changed social role of pilgrims upon return."[43]

The rituals: Most of the rituals are to commemorate and honor the acts of Abraham, Ishmael, and Hagar. For example, the *Sayee* (walking between the mountains of *Safa* and *Marwa*) after Hagar's running back and forth in the desert, looking for water for Ishmael, her very young son; drinking from the well of Zamzam; animal sacrifice after Abraham's attempted sacrifice when he received vision from God; and stoning the devil where he is said to have appeared to Abraham to deceive him.

---

42 http://www.malcolm-x.org/docs/let_mecca.htm.
43 http://papers.ssrn.com/sol3/papers.cfm?abstract_id=1124213##.

Quranic References to Hajj

Verses 196–203 of chapter 2 address Hajj and its rituals in depth:

"Hajj is in the well known months. One who undertakes to perform it must abstain from husband-wife relationship, obscene language, and wrangling during Hajj. Whatever good you do, Allah knows it. Take necessary provisions with you for the journey, and piety is the best provision of all. Fear Me, O People endowed with understanding." 2:197 (Malik)

Amr-bil-Ma'ruf (Enjoin What's Good) and *Nahi-Anil Munkar* (Forbid What's Evil)

Often mentioned together and emphasized frequently in the Quran, this commandment is self-explanatory. This will be described in more detail in chapter 26.

The Bible and the Pillars of Islamic Faith

As mentioned earlier, the Quran claims that in their basic forms, the pillars and other acts (or branches) of Islamic faith mentioned above were commanded to other prophets and their communities before Muhammad. A review of the Bible would seem to collaborate this claim. Though not as specific as the Quranic references or in conformity with current traditional practices of Muslims, there are numerous references in both the Old and the New Testament to prayers, fasting, charity, doing good, and forbidding evil.

Biblical References on Daily Prayers, Fasting, and Charitable Giving

Salah is not mentioned by name in the Bible but there are references on regular prayers and ablutions (washing before prayers, known as *Wadhu* in Islam).

- **Ablution/washing before prayers:** The Torah describes Moses, Aaron, and the priests washing their hands and feet before entering the altar:

"Next Moses placed the washbasin between the Tabernacle and the altar. He filled it with water so the priests could wash themselves. Moses and Aaron and Aaron's sons used water from it to wash their hands and feet. Whenever they approached the altar and entered the Tabernacle, they washed themselves, just as the LORD *had commanded Moses."* Exodus 40:30–32

Not only were they supposed to wash, it was made a permanent law for their descendants:

"Then the LORD *said to Moses, "Make a bronze washbasin with a bronze stand. Place it between the Tabernacle and the altar, and fill it with water. Aaron and his sons will wash their hands and feet there. They must wash with water whenever they go into the Tabernacle to appear before the* LORD *and when they approach the altar to burn up their special gifts to the* LORD*—or they will die! They must always wash their hands and feet, or they will die. This is a permanent law for Aaron and his descendants, to be observed from generation to generation."* Exodus 30:17–22

- **Kneeling (*Ruku*) and prostration (*Sajdah*)** are considered signs of humility before God and part of the rituals of the Muslim prayers. These have been mentioned many times in the Bible, without using the specific terms:

"Moses and Aaron turned away from the people and went to the entrance of the Tabernacle, where they fell face down on the ground. Then the glorious presence of the LORD *appeared to them."* Numbers 20:6

"'Neither one,' he replied. 'I am the commander of the LORD's *army.' At this, Joshua fell with his face to the ground in reverence. 'I am at your command,' Joshua said. 'What do you want your servant to do?'"* Joshua 5:14

"Then Jesus went with them to the olive grove called Gethsemane, and he said, 'Sit here while I go over there to pray.' He took Peter and Zebedee's two sons, James and John, and he became anguished and distressed. He told them, 'My soul is crushed with grief to the point of death. Stay here and keep watch with me.' He went on a little

farther and bowed with his face to the ground, praying, 'My Father! If it is possible, let this cup of suffering be taken away from me. Yet I want your will to be done, not mine.'" Matthew 26:36–39\

- **Praying regularly/prayer times:** Though the regular prayers five times a day are not practiced by Christians and Jews today, there are some references to daily prayers performed at particular hours of the day:

"In Caesarea there lived a Roman army officer named Cornelius, who was a captain of the Italian Regiment. He was a devout, God-fearing man, as was everyone in his household. He gave generously to the poor and prayed regularly to God. One afternoon about three o'clock ..." Acts 10:1–3. It further goes on to describe Cornelius's experience: *"Cornelius replied, 'Four days ago I was praying in my house about this same time, three o'clock in the afternoon.'"* Acts 10:30 (This would roughly correspond to the midafternoon Muslim prayer time.)

"Now Peter and John went up together into the temple at the hour of prayer, being the ninth hour." Acts 3:1 (King James Version) The New Living Translation's version is as follows: *"Peter and John went to the Temple one afternoon to take part in the three o'clock prayer service."*

The *Qiblah,* or direction of prayers: In the early days of Prophet Muhammad, the first *Qiblah* was Jerusalem (Al Quds Mosque/Dome of the Rock, believed by Muslims to have been built by Solomon). The *Qiblah* was changed to Kaaba according to the Quranic verses 2:142–144. The Bible points out that when Solomon prayed to the Lord, he used to face toward the temple in Jerusalem.

"May you watch over this Temple night and day, this place where you have said, 'My name will be there.' May you always hear the prayers I make toward this place. May you hear the humble and earnest requests from me and your people Israel when we pray toward this place. Yes, hear us from heaven where you live, and when you hear, forgive." 1 Kings 8:29–30

Daniel, another Jewish prophet, used to pray regularly (though three times a day, according to the Bible) and faced Jerusalem during the prayers:

"But when Daniel learned that the law had been signed, he went home and knelt down as usual in his upstairs room, with its windows open toward Jerusalem. He prayed three times a day, just as he had always done, giving thanks to his God." Daniel 6:10

It appears then that some form of daily prayers were regularly performed by these biblical figures, with many rituals similar to the Muslim prayers as ordained by the Quran, like ablution, kneeling, prostration, and facing the Qiblah.

- **Fasting:** Moses fasted for forty days and forty nights. He did it twice, once before receiving the tablets, and the other time when he found out about the idolatry of the children of Israel upon coming down from Mount Sinai:

"This happened when I was on the mountain receiving the tablets of stone inscribed with the words of the covenant that the LORD had made with you. I was there for forty days and forty nights, and all that time I ate no food and drank no water." Deuteronomy 9:9

"So I took the stone tablets and threw them to the ground, smashing them before your eyes. Then, as before, I threw myself down before the LORD for forty days and nights. I ate no bread and drank no water." Deuteronomy 9:17–18

King David fasted to humble himself:

"Yet when they were ill, I grieved for them. I denied myself by fasting for them, but my prayers returned unanswered." Psalm 35:13

Prophet Joel fasted to avert the Judgment of God:

"Announce a time of fasting; call the people together for a solemn meeting. Bring the leaders and all the people of the land into the Temple of the LORD your God, and cry out to him there." Joel 1:14

Jesus fasted for forty days and night, like Moses did, while he was in the desert and the devil tried to tempt him:

"Then Jesus was led by the Spirit into the wilderness to be tempted there by the devil. For forty days and forty nights he fasted and became very hungry." Matthew 4:1–2

Jesus not only fasted but also taught how to fast properly:

"'We have fasted before you!' they say. 'Why aren't you impressed?'" Isaiah 58:3

This indicates the people in the days of Jesus observed regular fasting. Jesus then goes on to teach what fasting entails and the true spirit of fasting (something that Muslims can readily relate to):

"'I will tell you why!' I respond. 'It's because you are fasting to please yourselves. Even while you fast, you keep oppressing your workers. What good is fasting when you keep on fighting and quarreling? This kind of fasting will never get you anywhere with me. You humble yourselves by going through the motions of penance, bowing your heads like reeds bending in the wind. You dress in burlap and cover yourselves with ashes. Is this what you call fasting? Do you really think this will please the Lord? No, this is the kind of fasting I want: Free those who are wrongly imprisoned; lighten the burden of those who work for you. Let the oppressed go free, and remove the chains that bind people. Share your food with the hungry, and give shelter to the homeless. Give clothes to those who need them, and do not hide from relatives who need your help.'" Isaiah 58:3–17

- **Charity:** *"Teach those who are rich in this world not to be proud and not to trust in their money, which is so unreliable. Their trust should be in God, who richly gives us all we need for our enjoyment. Tell them to use their money to do good. They should be rich in good works and generous to those in need, always being ready to share with others. By doing this they will be storing up their treasure as a good foundation for the future so that they may experience true life."* 1 Timothy 6:17–19

Jesus Taught to Give in Secret, Not for Show

"Watch out! Don't do your good deeds publicly, to be admired by others, for you will lose the reward from your Father in heaven.

When you give to someone in need, don't do as the hypocrites do—blowing trumpets in the synagogues and streets to call attention to their acts of charity! I tell you the truth; they have received all the reward they will ever get. But when you give to someone in need, **don't let your left hand know what your right hand is doing.** *Give your gifts in private, and your Father, who sees everything, will reward you."* Matthew 6:1–5

The teachings of Jesus in bold fonts above are practically identical to a famous Hadith (saying of Muhammad). In reference to certain deeds that will earn God's special mercy and protection on the Day of Judgment, Prophet Muhammad declared:

"A person who practices charity so secretly that his left hand does not know what his right hand has given."

"And (God does not love) those who spend their possessions on others (only) to be seen and praised by men, the while they believe neither in God nor in the Last Day." 4:38 (Asad)

In the following sermon, Jesus Christ emphasized the private, not-for-show acts of worship—not just charitable giving but also prayers and fasting:

"When you pray, don't be like the hypocrites who love to pray publicly on street corners and in the synagogues where everyone can see them. I tell you the truth, that is all the reward they will ever get. But when you pray, go away by yourself, shut the door behind you, and pray to your Father in private." Matthew 6:5–6

"And when you fast, don't make it obvious, as the hypocrites do, for they try to look miserable and disheveled so people will admire them for their fasting. I tell you the truth that is the only reward they will ever get. But when you fast, comb your hair and wash your face. Then no one will notice that you are fasting, except your Father, who knows what you do in private. And your Father, who sees everything, will reward you." Matthew 6:16–17

Jewish Prayers and Positions

In a book titled *To Pray as a Jew: A Guide to the Prayer Book and the Synagogue Service,* Rabbi Hayim H. Donin discusses the prayers of the ancient Jews and shows illustrations of various positions during the regular prayers that included bowing and prostration.

The images of the various positions during the prayers have striking resemblance to those of the Muslim daily prayers.

He goes on to comment, "In most contemporary congregations very few people keep to the tradition of falling prostrate. Sometimes it is only the prayer leader and the rabbi who does so. In more traditional congregations, however, some worshipers, men and women, will join the prayer leader and rabbi in the act of prostrating themselves. In Israeli synagogues, the practice is more widespread than in synagogues elsewhere."[44]

Do Good and Forbid Evil

The Bible has numerous instructions on doing good and staying away from evil. This will be discussed in more detail in chapter 26. The following is a small sample.

"Keep your tongue from evil and your lips from telling lies. Turn from evil and do good; seek peace and pursue it. The eyes of the LORD are on the righteous, and his ears are attentive to their cry; but the face of the LORD is against those who do evil, to blot out their name from the earth. The righteous cry out, and the LORD hears them; he delivers them from all their troubles." Psalm 34:13–17

"Do not be overcome by evil, but overcome evil with good." Romans 12:21

Points to Remember

- The five pillars of Islamic faith are Testimony to One God and Muhammad as His Prophet (Shahada), Prayers (Salah), Charity (Zakah), Fasting (Sawm), and Pilgrimage to Mecca (Hajj).
- The Bible makes many references to fasting, regular prayers (and some of its rituals) and charity, and the Oneness of God, though not in the exact manner as the Quran does. The Quran insists that Salah (regular prayers), fasting, and Zakah (charity) were also ordained on prior prophets and communities.

---

44 Hayim H. Donin, *To Pray as a Jew: A Guide to the Prayer Book and the Synagogue Service.* BasicBooks, USA, 1980.

- Some of the ancient Jewish traditions of prayer resemble Muslim prayers, though they are not often practiced currently.

Time to Ponder

- Is there one universal way to worship God? Are rituals more important than the spiritual connection one needs to make with God during prayers and various other forms of worship? Does God accept or prefer one form of worship over others? If so, is that belief supported by the scriptures?

Chapter 24
Jihad (To Strive)

Jihad is the most misunderstood and misused article of Islamic faith—both by Muslims and non-Muslims. Used at times for political purposes by Muslims and non-Muslims alike, it has become a subject of great intrigue recently, though many still don't seem to have a clear understanding of it.

"Jihad" means "to strive" or "to struggle." The struggle must be in the path of God. (Struggling to get onto a college football team, for example, would not be considered Jihad.) There are two basic forms of Jihad: the nonmilitary form and the military form (described as *Qital* in the Quran). The military struggle is in self-defense and not an act of aggression. The "Greater Jihad" refers to personal struggles with one's self. The "Lesser Jihad" refers to group struggle and includes armed conflicts. The word "Jihad" and its derivatives are mentioned by name six times in the Quran. The word *Qital*, the military form of Jihad, appears eight times. Jihad is often, wrongly, translated loosely as "holy war."

The Nonmilitary Form of Jihad

This is the more common form of Jihad referenced in the Quran. Ironically, it is the less emphasized form of Jihad by both Muslims and non-Muslims. This form includes personal struggles to find the right path (an internal struggle within one's self and against desires), as well as a group struggle. This may be in the form of standing up for justice and against tyranny, oppression, and evil. Jihad can be accomplished by the tongue and by pen (speaking up and writing against injustice, for example). As mentioned above, the struggles must be in the path of God, not just for political or personal reasons. In this regard, striving against intoxicants and indecent acts like pornography and prostitution would be considered Jihad. Striving to "enjoin what is good and forbidding evil" is a form of Jihad.

*"The believers are those who believe in God and His Messenger, who do not change their belief into doubt and who **strive hard** for the cause of God with their property and persons. They are the truthful ones."* 49:15 (Sarwar)

"Have faith in God and His messenger and strive hard for His cause with your wealth and in persons. This is better for you if only you knew it." 61:11 (Sarwar)

(The bolded words are the Arabic word for "Jihad" or its derivative—translated as "striving" even by older translations like Pickthall and Asad, as well as modern translators like Yuksel.)

Greater Jihad *(Jihad e Akbar)*

Greater Jihad is the personal struggle against evil. This is warfare, but within the individual and not on the battlefield. The struggling, once again, is in the path of God. The personal struggles against desires and temptations are forms of Greater Jihad.

Verse 25:52 instructs believers to make Jihad with the Quran. The words used for the phrase bolded below are *"Jihadan Kabeera."* This "mighty striving with it" instructs believers to use the Quran, its wisdom, blessings, and teachings when doing Jihad; this refers to the nonmilitary form.

*"So do not follow the unbelievers, And strive against them a **mighty striving** with it [meaning the Quran]"*, as translated by Shakir. Asad translates the same verse as follows:

*"Hence, do not defer to those who deny the truth, but strive hard against them, by means of this (divine writ), with **utmost striving**."*

Military Form of Jihad/Lesser Jihad (*Qital*)

The Quran permits, and in fact encourages, armed resistance in self-defense, when believers are under attack and when the way of God is in jeopardy. These verses spell out various situations and reasons for such struggle:

"And fight in God's cause against those who wage war against you, but do not commit aggression—for, verily, God does not love aggressors." 2:190 (Asad)

"Permission (to fight) is given to those upon whom war is made because they are oppressed, and most surely God is well able to assist them." 22:39 (Shakir)

"Therefore let those fight in the way of God, who sell this world's life for the hereafter; and whoever fights in the way of God, then be he slain or be he victorious, We shall grant him a mighty reward. And what reason do you have not to fight in the cause of God, to rescue the helpless oppressed old men, women, and children who are crying: 'Our Lord! Deliver us from this town whose people are oppressors; send us a protector by Your grace and send us a helper from Your presence?' Those who are believers fight in the cause of God, and those who are unbelievers fight in the cause of Taghut [evil]: so fight against the helpers of Taghut; surely, Satan's crafty schemes are very weak." 4:74–76 (Shakir)

When resisting, the Quran instructs believers to defend with utmost resistance. Some who criticize the Quran for "preaching violence" often cite this verse, but an examination of the context will shed light on its perspective:

"And kill them wherever you find them, and drive them out from where they drove you out, and persecution is severer than slaughter, and do not fight with them at the Sacred Mosque until they fight with you in it, but if they do fight you, then slay them; such is the recompense of the unbelievers." 2:191 (Shakir)

The verse is put in context by the previous verse (2:190 quoted above): "And fight in God's cause against those who wage war against you." This refers to the pagans of Mecca, who persecuted early Muslim converts, tortured them, drove them out of Mecca, and continued to wage war when they settled in Medina. Their purpose was to wipe out this early, small community of believers. It was critical to use force to defend that small, budding community.

And even so, the Quran commanded not to start the aggression (verse 2:190), and if the enemy initiated the hostilities, the instructions were to stop fighting when they do and to deal with them with fairness and kindness.

"But if they cease (their hostilities), Allah is Oft-forgiving, Most Merciful. And fight them on until there is no more tumult or oppression, and there prevail justice and faith in Allah; but if they cease, let there be no hostility except to those who practice oppression." 2:192–193

Moreover, war *cannot* be used to propagate the name of God. The following verse is true for the armed struggle, as well as in the matters of everyday observance of the faith. Coming close to God must be at one's own free will:

"There is no compulsion in religion." 2:256 (Shakir)

When You Do Fight, Do So Justly: Code of Conduct

Military Jihad is allowed in self-defense and to help the oppressed in the cause of God, but even then, the code of conduct as ordained by God must be followed. It must not be done out of simple hatred for people or personal reasons.

"O you who believe! Be upright for Allah, bearers of witness with justice, and let not hatred of a people (toward you) incite you not to act equitably; Act equitably, that is nearer to piety, and be careful of (your duty to) Allah; surely Allah is Aware of what you do." 5:8 (Shakir)

Ali, son-in-law of Prophet Muhammad and his trusted commander, was once involved in a one-on-one combat during a battle between the Muslims of Medina and the pagans of Mecca. The enemy fell and lay helplessly, and as Ali was about to kill him, he spat on Ali's face out of desperation and hatred. Ali instantly stood up and started to walk away. Startled, the enemy asked Ali why he spared his life, Ali responded by saying that the battle was in the cause of God, and the spitting had made him angry; he didn't want to kill him for a personal insult.

Verse 4:90 indicates military Jihad is not allowed against noncombatants. This is in conformity with verse 2:190, prohibiting aggression. Islam forbids annihilation of trees, crops, and livestock during military struggles.

Fight to Protect Mosques, Churches, and Synagogues

In the following verses, the Quran explains why fighting in the cause of God is allowed. If it weren't for the armed struggle, the unbelieving forces would have demolished places of worship and the name of God and His message. In fact, places of worship like mosques, churches, and synagogues must be protected, as they are places of remembrance of God. Military jihad is allowed to *protect* mosques, churches, and synagogues against those who were bent on destroying them.

"Permission to fight back is hereby granted to the believers against whom war is waged and because they are oppressed. Certainly Allah has power to grant them victory—those who have been unjustly expelled from their homes only because they said, 'Our Lord is Allah.' Had Allah not repelled some people by the might of others, the monasteries, churches, synagogues, and mosques in which Allah's praise is daily celebrated, would have been utterly demolished. Allah will certainly help those who help His cause; most surely Allah is Mighty, Powerful. These are the people who, if We establish them in the land, will establish Salah and pay Zakah, enjoin justice and forbid evil; the final decision of all affairs is in the hands of Allah." 22:39–41 (Malik)

Here is a compendium of armed struggle (*Qital*/Lesser Jihad):

- Purpose. Defend life and the way of God (2:190–193) and defend human rights for the oppressed and to protect the freedom to worship (22:39–41).
- One cannot be the aggressor. It is in self-defense (2:190, 22:39), when war is waged upon you.
- One must follow a code of conduct. If the enemy stops fighting you, you should cease hostilities (2:192–193). One must not harm noncombatants (4:90).

What About Verse 9:5?

Another verse that has been flashed on TV screens by some in the past to point out the Quran's "preaching violence" is quoted here:

"So when the sacred months have passed away, then slay the idolaters wherever you find them, and take them captives and

besiege them and lie in wait for them in every ambush, then if they repent and keep up prayer and pay the poor-rate, leave their way free to them; surely Allah is Forgiving, Merciful." 9:5 (Shakir)

This is another example where reading one verse out of context can be very misleading. The context of the verse is examined here by a review of the start of chapter 9 of the Quran.

Verse 9:1 announces the treaty between the pagans of Mecca and the Muslims of Medina under Prophet Muhammad, known as the Treaty of Hudaibiyya. It guaranteed peace for ten years between the two parties, unless one group broke the treaty by violating its clauses. The pagans of Mecca continued to harass and ambush some Muslim groups, eventually leading to the Muslims marching back into Mecca in a bloodless takeover of the city, where a general amnesty was given by Muhammad.

"(This is a declaration of) immunity by Allah and His Messenger toward those of the idolaters with whom you made an agreement." 9:1 (Shakir)

Verse 9:4 then goes on to instruct that the pagans who still followed the treaty should be left alone:

"Except those of the pagans with whom you made an agreement, then they have not failed you in anything and have not backed up anyone against you, so fulfill their agreement to the end of their term; surely Allah loves those who are careful (of their duty)." 9:4 (Shakir)

This was then followed by verse 9:5, which instructs believers to kill that particular brand of pagans who kept breaking the treaty and continued their hostilities and attacking ordinary Muslims. However, believers were not to fight the pagans who kept the treaty; the next verse instructs the believers to show mercy and give asylum to the pagan enemies seeking refuge:

"If one amongst the Pagans ask you for asylum, grant it to him, so that he may hear the word of Allah; and then escort him to where he can be secure. That is because they are men without knowledge." 9:6

This whole sequence would now seem to be a far cry from a picture painted whereby Muslims were "bent on just killing all infidels," if verse 9:5 was to be discussed in isolation.

Jihad Ordained for the Pre-Muhammad Prophets

The military form of Jihad (*Qital*), according to the Quran, was not limited to Prophet Muhammad's time. The Quran refers to the battles of other biblical prophets as Jihad against the unbelievers and calls them (who fought against the prophets' armies) "Kafir," the same term used for the nonbelievers fighting Muhammad.

"How many of the prophets fought (in Allah's way), and with them (fought) large bands of devoted men? But they never lost heart if they met with disaster in Allah's way, nor did they weaken (in will) nor give in. And Allah Loves those who are firm and steadfast." 3:146

The following verse refers to Moses returning from Mount Sinai and finding his people worshipping the golden calf:

"And when Moses said to his people: O my people! you have surely been unjust to yourselves by taking the calf (for a god), therefore turn to your Creator (in repentance), so kill your people, that is best for you with your Creator: so He turned to you (mercifully), for surely He is the Oft-returning (to mercy), the Merciful." 2:54 (Shakir)

(Compare with quote from Exodus 32:27–28 below.)

Moreover, in reference to when Saul and David fought against the unbelievers in Goliath's army, the Quran states:

*"When they advanced to meet Goliath and his forces, they [the army of Saul and David] prayed: 'Our Lord! Pour out constancy on us and make our steps firm: Help us against the **unbelieving people**.'"* 2:250 (Shakir). The bolded words are the plural of *Kafir*.

*"So they put them to flight by Allah's permission. And David **slew** Goliath, and Allah gave him kingdom and wisdom, and taught him of what He pleased."* 2:251

The word bolded above is a derivative of *Qital*, the word for the military form of Jihad used in the Quran.

The purpose of such struggles between good and evil: *"And were it not for Allah's repelling some men with others, the earth* *would certainly be in a state of disorder; but Allah is Gracious to the creatures."* 2:251 (Shakir)

Jihad (*Qital*) Armed Struggle for the Sake of God in the Bible

The word "Jihad" does not appear in the Bible. However, fighting in the cause of God is justified and mentioned frequently, especially when chronicling the Israelites' battles in search of the Promised Land. The Israelites were engaged in many battles with various armies and communities—including some within themselves. The following is in reference to Moses's return from receiving the Torah on Mount Sinai, when he found the people worshipping idols and creating mischief:

"Moses told them, 'This is what the LORD, the God of Israel, says: Each of you, take your swords and go back and forth from one end of the camp to the other. Kill everyone—even your brothers, friends, and neighbors.' The Levites obeyed Moses' command, and about 3,000 people died that day." Exodus 32:27–28

Deuteronomy chapter 9 covers some of the reasons why God wanted the Israelites to destroy various Canaanite cities:

"After the LORD your God has done this for you, don't say in your hearts, 'The LORD has given us this land because we are such good people!' No, it is because of the wickedness of the other nations that he is pushing them out of your way. It is not because you are so good or have such integrity that you are about to occupy their land. The LORD your God will drive these nations out ahead of you only because of their wickedness, and to fulfill the oath he swore to your ancestors Abraham, Isaac, and Jacob. You must recognize that the LORD your God is not giving you this good land because you are good, for you are not—you are a stubborn people." Deuteronomy 9:4–6

Rules of Wars for Moses and the Children of Israel

Deuteronomy chapter 20 goes on to describe the regulations concerning war for the Israelites:

"When you go out to fight your enemies and you face horses and chariots and an army greater than your own, do not be afraid. The

LORD *your God, who brought you out of the land of Egypt, is with you!"* Deuteronomy 20:1

Offer peace first: According to chapter 20 in Deuteronomy, the Israelites were instructed to offer peace first:

"As you approach a town to attack it, you must first offer its people terms for peace. If they accept your terms and open the gates to you, then all the people inside will serve you in forced labor. But if they refuse to make peace and prepare to fight, you must attack the town. When the LORD *your God hands the town over to you, use your swords to kill every man in the town. But you may keep for yourselves all the women, children, livestock, and other plunder. You may enjoy the plunder from your enemies that the* LORD *your God has given you."* Deuteronomy 20:10–14

For the rest of the towns, the destruction was to be total, not sparing anyone, even livestock: The purpose of such destruction, it goes on to explain, was to prevent future generations from imitating (replicating) the perversions of the destroyed nations.

"But these instructions apply only to distant towns, not to the towns of the nations in the land you will enter. In those towns that the LORD *your God is giving you as a special possession, destroy every living thing. You must completely destroy the Hittites, Amorites, Canaanites, Perizzites, Hivites, and Jebusites; just as the* LORD *your God has commanded you. This will prevent the people of the land from teaching you to imitate their detestable customs in the worship of their gods, which would cause you to sin deeply against the* LORD *your God."* Deuteronomy 20:15–18

After Moses passed away, the children of Israel were led by Joshua and eventually entered the Promised Land (Canaan) and took Jericho. The battle and its regulations, similar to the ones mentioned above, are described in detail in Joshua chapter 6.

Points to Remember

- "Jihad" means "to strive" or "to struggle." The struggle must be in the path of God.
- Though often translated as such, Jihad is not equal to "holy war."

- Two forms of Jihad: There is the nonmilitary as well as the military form of Jihad (known as *Qital* in the Quran). The military struggle is in self-defense and not an act of aggression. Thus, using the word "Jihad" to only mean the military form is erroneous. In fact, the "Greater Jihad" refers to personal struggles with desires and temptations. The "Lesser Jihad" refers to group struggle against oppression and tyranny and military form.
- The Quran enforces a strict code of conduct and behavior during armed struggles.
- The military form of Jihad is not unique to Muslims or Prophet Muhammad. The Quran used a derivative of *Qital* (military Jihad) to describe David's war against Goliath. The Bible describes many battles between the Israelites and nonbelievers.

Time to Ponder

- The Quran and the Bible consider killing a grave sin. However, the scriptures do allow it during military struggles and, in fact, make it mandatory as long as certain conditions are met. What are the defining criteria separating a grave sin from an obligation? Is there only a fine line between the two, subject to an *individual's* interpretation?

CHAPTER 25
WOMEN AND THE FAMILY

The Quran puts great emphasis on forming a society that is based on sound moral values and justice, and it provides guidelines for doing so. It views individuals as building blocks, the family as a small unit of individuals, and the society as a multitude of many such units. Individuals are given their own set of *rights*, as well as *responsibilities* within the family and the society. The Quran delineates laws related to financial undertakings, property, inheritance, and a system of justice. In short, the Quran describes a way of life set forth by God. It is worth pointing out that though some of these laws or guidelines are described in detail, the Quran is not meant to be an instruction manual. It provides broad guidelines, and the *Sunnah* (Prophet Muhammad's actions) describes them in more detail. However, that can be complex and is a source of diverging opinions. There are many schools of thought or jurisprudence that interpret the same rules somewhat differently, at least on certain issues. Shia Muslim theologians add Prophet Muhammad's noble family and imams for interpretation of the guidelines set forth in the Quran. Other Muslim scholars, though not representing the majority view, believe that the Quran itself is detailed enough and good enough that no additional help (neither the *Sunnah* of Prophet Muhammad nor his noble family) are needed for interpretation or further guidance, though they are to be respected. These varying opinions notwithstanding, there is clear unanimity among all Muslims that man has no right to change the divine laws; that the Quran is the basic source of all such rules and guidance; and that the verdict of the Quran being the literal word of God is final.

In much the same way, the Torah ordains its own set of laws. The word "Torah" itself is variously translated as "instructions," "teach," or, simply, "law."

This chapter will focus on the rights and responsibilities of individuals within a family—husband, wife, parents, and children— with special emphasis on women, since this issue is often a source of intense debate.

The Quran and Women

Women are considered a crucial part of the family. Their role as daughter, wife, and mother forms the building blocks, and their role as mother is considered one of great significance and respect. Chapter 4 of the Quran is named *Al-Nisa*, meaning "The Women." However, the subject is not limited to this chapter only.

Spiritual equality: It is worth reviewing the status of women, as it existed in pre-Islamic days, in Arabia as well as in India, China, Rome, and Greece, the other prominent civilizations at the time the Quran was revealed. Women had few if any legal rights and were considered spiritually inferior. In Arabia, newborn girls brought shame to a family; they were often buried or abandoned. It is also reported that women were forced to strip naked and dance in public for the pleasure of viewing men. It was considered a coup when the Quran protected the honor of women and gave equal rights to men and women. Men are not superior to women, and women are not superior to men. What separates them in the eyes of God from each other is the level of their piety, not their gender.

"Whoever works righteousness, man or woman, and has Faith, verily, to him will We give a new Life, a life that is good and pure and We will bestow on such their reward according to the best of their actions." 16:97

"For Muslim men and women [or men and women who submit]—for believing men and women; for devout men and women; for truthful men and women; for men and women who are patient and constant; for men and women who humble themselves; for men and women who give in Charity; for men and women who fast; for men and women who guard their chastity; and for men and women

who engage much in Allah's praise, for them has Allah prepared forgiveness and great reward." 33:35

This spiritual equality was an alien concept in the seventh century, until the Quran declared men and women equal in God's sight. The above verse clearly indicates that men are not necessarily superior to women in their spirituality. The Quran goes on to state that God will not waste the work of anyone regardless of his or her gender, for He is an equal opportunity Lord.

"So their Lord accepted their prayer: That I will not waste the work of a worker among you, whether male or female." 3:195 (Shakir)

The Quran and Marriage

The relationship between a husband and wife is established on a foundation of mutual respect, kindness, and love:

"And one of His signs is that He created mates for you from yourselves that you may find rest [tranquility] in them, and He put between you love and compassion; most surely there are signs in this for a people who reflect." 30:21 (Shakir)

Moreover, the husband and wife are "cloth" or garments for each other. This is not interpreted in terms of its physical aspects but rather implies they cover and support each other during hard times and protect each other's faith.

"Permitted to you, on the night of the fasts, is the approach to your wives. They are your garments and you are their garments." 2:187

No Marriage Against Women's Will: Equal Status for Husband and Wife

In pagan, pre-Islamic Arabia, widows were often divided amongst the heirs of a deceased as goods. The heir either married the widow himself against her will or gave her to marry someone else and kept her dowry or demanded a payment as settlement to give her away. In addition, the wives were at times imprisoned in their homes in order that they may ask for separation and thus relinquish their dowry or inheritance. The following verse abolished these practices:

"O you who believe! You are forbidden to inherit women against their will. Nor should you treat them with harshness, that you may take away part of the dowry you have given them, except where they have been guilty of open lewdness. On the contrary live with them on a footing of kindness and equity." 4:19

Polygamy

The Quran allows multiple marriages for men (up to four) *with* certain conditions. However, it clearly made polygamy much less desirable than monogamy:

"And if you fear that you cannot act equitably toward orphans, then marry such women as seem good to you, two and three and four; but if you fear that you will not do justice (between them), then (marry) only one or what your right hands possess; this is more proper, that you may not deviate from the right course." 4:3 (Shakir)

It must be pointed out that polygamy was practiced before the revelation of the Quran but was uncontrolled and without regulations. The Quran does not encourage or promote polygamy and, on the contrary, attempts to limit polygamy (to having four wives) and attaches conditions to it. This verse and the idea of having multiple wives has been misunderstood and misused by non-Muslims and, perhaps more so, by Muslims. In some parts of the Muslim world, men are reported to have married women with the clear intention of divorcing them after a very short period (at times, after a day or two). This is done for obvious reasons of satisfying physical needs and in clear violation of the concept and purpose of marriage: achieving a harmonious relationship built on love and companionship to fulfill both physical and spiritual needs.

The Quran acknowledges later in chapter 4 that it is very difficult for men to be fair and do justice with multiple wives, thus again implying it is much preferred to marry one woman:

"It is not possible for you to do justice between your wives even if you wish to do so; therefore, in order to comply with Divine Law, do not lean toward one wife to the extent that you leave the other hanging in air. If you work out a friendly understanding and fear Allah, Allah is Forgiving, Merciful." 4:129 (Malik)

Many Muslim scholars believe that polygamy was allowed for a specific time and for a specific reason. They point out that the allowance in verse 4:3 was related to the mothers of orphans *only*, to provide them psychological, social, and economical support (see Yuksel's commentary on the verse). The other intended purpose was to prevent indecent, illicit sexual activities. In any event, marrying other women without the free will and consent of the first wife is not allowed; and one can draw the conclusion that this in itself should put a stop to polygamy in most cases.

Polygamy According to Islamic Principles in the United States

It must be noted that polygamy is illegal in the Unites States as well as many other countries. Many Muslim scholars point out that putting US law and the Quranic commandments together makes it illegal *and* against the teachings of the Quran to have multiple wives. They argue that such practice, in addition to being a violation of the law of the land, would mean that the second wife will not have the same rights (for example, inheritance, property ownership, and health insurance) as the first wife under local laws, and thus one would be dealing with her unjustly, thereby *also* violating the teachings of the Quran.

Women's Right for Divorce or Separation: Compromise Is Better

Divorce, considered distasteful, is nonetheless allowed by the Quran but only after all attempts at reconciliation fail. Even in this setting, God orders men to not take advantage of women.

"If a wife fears cruelty or desertion on her husband's part, there is no blame on them if they arrange an amicable settlement [reconciliation] between themselves; and such settlement [reconciliation] is best; And peoples' souls are swayed by greed." 4:128

"O Prophet! When you divorce women, divorce them for their prescribed time, and calculate the number of the days prescribed, and be careful of (your duty to) Allah, your Lord. Do not drive them out of their houses, nor should they themselves go forth, unless they commit an open indecency." 65:1 (Shakir)

This is the opening of the chapter called *At-Talaq,* or "Divorce." This verse addresses Muhammad in the beginning, as is the norm on many occasions, but the message is clearly intended for the community. It refers to a period of time called *Iddat,* which is a waiting period before a woman should remarry. In case of a divorce, it is three months. This allows for a cooling-off period among other reasons. It also protects women from being evicted from their house, as was often the custom at the time. It then goes on to instruct men to treat their wives (or ex-wives) kindly. The following verse gives two options at the end of this period. In either scenario, men are ordered to treat women with kindness:

"Then, when they have reached their term, take them back in kindness or part from them in kindness." 65:2 (Shakir)

And the Quran sends a warning to those men who keep women as their wives as an excuse so they can abuse them:

"When you divorce women, and they fulfill their prescribed term, either take them back on equitable terms or part ways on equitable terms; but do not take them back to injure them, (or) to take undue advantage; if anyone does that; He wrongs his own soul. Do not treat Allah's signs [meaning verses] as a jest [mockery]." 2:231

No Legal Parity?

The subject matter in verse 2:282 seems to be another area of criticism or misunderstanding, again, by both Muslims and non-Muslims. The verse is in relation to the number of witnesses needed:

"And call in to witness from among your men two witnesses; but if there are not two men, then one man and two women from among those whom you choose to be witnesses, so that if one of the two errs, the second of the two may remind the other." 2:282 (Shakir)

Critics claim that by requiring the testimony of either two men, OR one man and two women, the Quran implies that women are inferior to men in intellect.

The defendants of the verse claim that first of all, this verse refers to a very specific issue: that of a business transaction involving contracts. Here is a fuller portion of the verse (which goes on to describe other aspects of the contract and the responsibilities of the witnesses):

"O you who believe! When you deal with each other in contracting a debt for a fixed time, then write it down; and let a scribe write it down between you with fairness; and the scribe should not refuse to write as Allah has taught him, so he should write; and let him who owes the debt dictate, and he should be careful of (his duty to) Allah, his Lord, and not diminish anything from it; but if he who owes the debt is unsound in understanding, or weak, or (if) he is not able to dictate himself, let his guardian dictate with fairness; and call in to witness from among your men two witnesses; but if there are not two men, then one man and two women from among those whom you choose to be witnesses, so that if one of the two errs, the second of the two may remind the other." 2:282 (Shakir)*

Muslim commentators point out that the witness requirement of one man and two women does not imply that women are inferior; rather, it points to the fact that women were not as involved and familiar with business transactions and contract negotiations. Moreover, one may not extend this very specific scenario to other situations where testimony is required, let alone deducing the women's intellectual status. In other verses related to the requirement of witnesses, for example in case of false accusation of adultery, this equation does not exist:

"And those who launch a charge against chaste women, and produce not four witnesses (to support their allegations), flog them with eighty stripes; and reject their evidence ever after: for such men are wicked transgressors." 24:4

Not only are four witnesses required (with no mention of the gender mix in this scenario), but this ordinance calls for severe punishment of men falsely accusing women of adultery, a charge the Quran does not take lightly.

Wife Beating Allowed by the Quran?

By examining the verses at the beginning of this chapter, it would seem hard to imagine that the Quran would sanction wife beating, though that's what some critics accuse. And many Muslim scholars have translated the following verse as such:

"Men shall take full care of women with the bounties which God has bestowed more abundantly on the former than on the latter, and

*with what they may spend out of their possessions. And the righteous women are the truly devout ones, who guard the intimacy, which God has (ordained to be) guarded. And as for those women whose ill-will you have reason to fear, admonish them (first); then leave them alone in bed; then **beat them**; and if thereupon they pay you heed, do not seek to harm them. Behold, God is indeed most high, great!" 4:34 (Asad)*

The first part about "Men shall take full care of women" has been variously translated as "Men are the maintainers of women" (Shakir), "Men are the protectors and maintainers of women" (Yousuf Ali), and "Men are to support women" (Yuksel). All translators agree it does not make men "superior" to women but actually refers to men's *responsibility* to earn and bring sustenance on account of his physical attributes. It does not necessarily mean that a woman cannot work. The bolded words in the verse are the source of controversy. Because of the mistranslation, the commentators have gone on the defensive and scrambled to find an explanation. Some have translated the word as "beat lightly" and commented that men should "beat lightly as with a toothbrush" or with a handkerchief. The defensive posture seems to be for naught, as the Quran never allowed a man to beat his wife, under any circumstances.

The most appropriate translation and commentary seem to be from Yuksel and Emerick. In his commentary, especially for the bolded words "beat them," Yuksel states: *"The second key word that is commonly misunderstood is IDRIBuhunna. In almost all translations, you will see it translated as 'scourge,' or 'beat.' The verb DaRaBa is a multiple-meaning word akin to English 'strike' or 'get.' The Quran uses the same verb with various meaning such as to travel, to get out (3:156, 4:101, 38:44, 73:20, 2:273), to strike (2:60,73, 7:160, 8:12*[and many others]), *to beat (8:50), to beat or regret (47:27), to set up (43:58,57:13), to give (examples) (14:24, 16:75*[and many others]), *to take away, to ignore (43:5)."* He goes on to say, *"It is again interesting that the scholars pick the meaning BEAT, among the many other alternatives, when the relationship between men and women is involved, a relationship that is defined by the Quran with mutual love and care (30:21)."*

Some of the verses with the same verb and its derivatives used elsewhere are reviewed.

"What! Shall We then take away [Na'drib] the reminder [Message] from you, because you are an extravagant people?" 43:5 (Shakir)

"As for the poor who face hardship in the cause of God, and they cannot leave [Durban] the land." 2:273 (Yuksel)

Therefore, in the most logical translation, and the one most consistent with the Quran's overall message, the last part of verse 4:34 is translated as follows (Yuksel and Emerick):

"As for those women from whom you fear disloyalty, then you shall advise them, abandon them in bedchamber, and separate (from) them."

In summary, the appropriate translation for this homonymous Arabic word seems to indicate that men should "separate" or ignore their spouse, or get out of the relationship if other advice doesn't work out, but not beat them. This is not dissimilar to the English use of the word "beat," which has been used in multiple situations, for example, "beat around the bush," or "beat an egg," or "we can beat their baseball team" (meaning winning a game, not physically beating the team). Nonetheless, this verse remains poorly understood and continues to generate debate with varying point of view, even among Muslims.

The following verses, already quoted earlier, clearly contradicts the "beat them" translation:

"When you divorce women, and they fulfill their prescribed term, either take them back on equitable terms or part ways on equitable terms; but do not take them back to injure them, (or) to take undue advantage." 2:231

"Then, when they have reached their term, take them back in kindness or part from them in kindness." 65:2 (Shakir)

Modesty (*Hijab*)

Yet another topic that has generated tremendous interest in recent time is the issue of Muslims wearing *Hijab*, or head coverings. It must be emphasized at the outset that the essence of *Hijab* in the Quran is more than a dress code; it revolves around modesty and piety, without public showing of one's physical beauty. It is interesting to note that the word *"Hijab"* does *not* appear in the Quran. The interpretation of the extent of the covering varies between various Muslim scholars and countries.

The Quran considers sexuality sacred and sets rules for its expression. Sexuality is limited to a marital relationship and has no place in public, nor is there ever a reason for a public display, which may lead to sensual feelings and eventually immorality, which the Quran (and the Bible) detests. In this sense, Hijab seems to be a preemptive effort to guard against eventual immorality. Chapter 24 verses 30 and 31 of the Quran address this issue:

"Tell the believing men to lower their gaze and to be mindful of their chastity: this will be most conducive to their purity—(and) verily, God is aware of all that they do." 24:30 (Asad)

Note that men are addressed first—a fact often lost upon many Muslim men, eager to enforce Hijab on the women. The verse is then followed by instructions for women:

"And tell the believing women to lower their gaze and to be mindful of their chastity, and not to display their charms (in public) beyond what may (decently) be apparent thereof; hence, let them draw their head-coverings over their bosoms [chest]. And let them not display (more of) their charms to any but their husbands, or their fathers, or their husbands' fathers, or their sons, or their husbands' sons, or their brothers, or their brothers' sons, or their sisters' sons, or their womenfolk, or those whom they rightfully possess, or such male attendants as are beyond all sexual desire, or children that are as yet unaware of private aspects of women; And let them not swing their legs [in walking] (or strike their feet) so as to draw attention to their hidden charms [or ornaments]. And O you believers—all of you—turn unto God in repentance, so that you might attain to a happy state!" 24:31 (Asad)

According to these verses, men and women have equal responsibility for maintaining modesty.

Women and the Bible[45]

Women and their place in the family are mentioned frequently in the Bible. Many are mentioned by name, including prophets' wives: Eve, Hagar, Sarah, and Rebekah among others. Mary is highly revered. So are Sarah, Rebekah, and the wives of Jacob and Joseph.

Husband-and-Wife Relationship and Their Roles

The following is an attempt to summarize the teachings of the Bible, realizing it is an extensive subject:

The husband-and-wife relationship is built on love and respect. Wives are to submit to the authority of the husband, and husbands are considered head of the household and the breadwinners. Modesty for wives is emphasized. One of the greatest sins is adultery. Women should make themselves presentable to their husbands. The holy union and nearness to God is invoked in this relationship.

The concept of marriage in the Torah is one of companionship. Women and men are considered two halves of one whole. After creating Adam, God created Eve and made them husband and wife:

"Then the LORD God said, 'It is not good for the man to be alone; I will make him a helper suitable for him.'" Genesis 2:18

Responsibilities of Wives

Wives are to remain modest, chaste, and obedient to their husbands. Their outward beauty is minimized, and their inner beauty and spirituality is what makes them dearer to God.

"In the same way, you wives, be submissive to your own husbands so that even if any of them are disobedient to the word, they may be won without a word by the behavior of their wives, as they observe your chaste and respectful behavior. Your adornment must not be merely external—braiding the hair, and wearing gold jewelry, or putting on dresses; but let it be the hidden person of the heart, with the imperishable quality of a gentle and quiet spirit, which

---

45 All biblical translations in this chapter are from the New American Standard Bible by the Lockman Foundation, unless specified otherwise.

is precious in the sight of God. For in this way in former times the holy women also, who hoped in God, used to adorn themselves, being submissive to their own husbands; just as Sarah obeyed Abraham, calling him lord, and you have become her children if you do what is right without being frightened by any fear." 1 Peter 3:1–6

"Wives, be subject to your own husbands, as to the Lord. For the husband is the head of the wife, as Christ also is the head of the church, He Himself being the Savior of the body. But as the church is subject to Christ, so also the wives ought to be to their husbands in everything." Ephesians 5:22–24

Responsibilities of Husbands

The husband is responsible for the provision of food, clothing, and sexual intimacy:

"If a man who has married a slave wife takes another wife for himself, he must not neglect the rights of the first wife to food, clothing, and sexual intimacy. If he fails in any of these three obligations, she may leave as a free woman without making any payment." Exodus 21:10–11 (NLT)

Compare these verses to the Quranic verses relating to multiple wives and how men should approach the idea of multiple wives (verses 4:3, 4:19, 4:129).

According to the Torah, the husband should also take time off for a year to spend time with his wife, highlighting the importance of time needed to develop a healthy relationship between husband and wife. In fast-paced world of today, this seems like a luxury, but the Torah is clear on the requirement:

"A newly married man must not be drafted into the army or be given any other official responsibilities. He must be free to spend one year at home, bringing happiness to the wife he has married." Deuteronomy 24:5 (NLT)

And defaming the wife by false accusations of unchastity (before marriage when she was a virgin) is taken very seriously:

"The elders must then take the man and punish him. They must also fine him 100 pieces of silver, which he must pay to the woman's father because he publicly accused a virgin of Israel of shameful

conduct. *The woman will then remain the man's wife, and he may never divorce her.*" Deuteronomy 22:18–19 (NLT)

Compare that with Quranic verse quoted earlier (verse 24:4) for punishment of men for false accusation.

The wife, though submitting to the "authority of the husband," is an equal partner in this relationship. Compare these verses to the Quranic verses 30:21 and 65:2 (calling for kindness even if separating):

"In the same way, your husbands must give honor to your wives. Treat your wife with understanding as you live together. She may be weaker than you are, but she is your equal partner in God's gift of new life. Treat her as you should, so your prayers will not be hindered." 1 Peter 3:7 (NLT)

Polygamy

Most churches and Jewish traditions disallow polygamy. However, polygamy is mentioned throughout the Old Testament, and many prophets are known to have had multiple wives, including the patriarchs: Abraham, Isaac, and Jacob. The first mention of polygamy in the Old Testament starts with Lamech, seven generations removed from Cain:

"Lamech took to himself two wives: the name of the one was Adah, and the name of the other, Zillah." Genesis 4:19

The first prohibition is found in Deuteronomy, even though this was meant for kings, and not a general commandment:

"He [referring to the king to be chosen] shall not multiply wives for himself, or else his heart will turn away; nor shall he greatly increase silver and gold for himself." Deuteronomy 17:17

However, there are other verses that seem to make polygamy legal but with certain conditions:

"If he takes to himself another woman, he may not reduce her food, her clothing, or her conjugal rights." Exodus 21:10

Many scholars acknowledge that the New Testament did not specifically prohibit polygamy. However, when asked about it, Jesus responds in Matthew 19:5 and Mark 10:8, making references to God's creation of Adam and Eve as man and wife and uniting them as one. This and other passages are generally taken as indications that Jesus promoted monogamy. Perhaps the strongest argument quoted by many is Matthew 19:8–9:

"He [meaning Jesus] said to them, 'Because of your hardness of heart Moses permitted you to divorce your wives; but from the beginning it has not been this way. And I say to you, whoever divorces his wife, except for immorality, and marries another woman commits adultery.'"

Divorce

Like the Quran, divorce is allowed but considered distasteful in the Bible:

"'For I hate divorce,' says the LORD, the God of Israel, 'and him who covers his garment with wrong,' says the LORD of hosts. 'So take heed to your spirit, that you do not deal treacherously.'" Malachi 2:16

However, divorcing a wife seems relatively easier than the procedures outlined in the Quran.

"When a man takes a wife and marries her, and it happens that she finds no favor in his eyes because he has found some indecency in her, and he writes her a certificate of divorce and puts it in her hand and sends her out from his house." Deuteronomy 24:1

And in one of his sermons, Jesus gives instructions regarding divorce, clearly disliking it and making one think twice before divorcing:

"You have heard the law that says, 'A man can divorce his wife by merely giving her a written notice of divorce.' But I say that a man who divorces his wife, unless she has been unfaithful, causes her to commit adultery. And anyone who marries a divorced woman also commits adultery." Matthew 5:31–32 (NLT)

Veil (*Hijab*) in the Bible

Hijab is typically viewed as an Islamic dress code for women. Both accounts seem erroneous. *Hijab* is *not* merely a dress code, and it is not just for women; it also may not be an Islamic-only dress code. Some biblical passages on the teachings of Paul and practices of highly acclaimed biblical women are quoted below:

"Isaac went out to meditate in the field toward evening; and he lifted up his eyes and looked, and behold, camels were coming. Rebekah lifted up her eyes, and when she saw Isaac she dismounted from the camel. She said to the servant, 'Who is that man walking in the field to meet us?' And the servant said, 'He is my master.' Then she took her veil and covered herself." Genesis 24:63–65

In the following set of verses, Paul addresses Timothy in one of his letters, giving him many instructions:

"And I want women to be modest in their appearance. They should wear decent and appropriate clothing and not draw attention to themselves by the way they fix their hair or by wearing gold or pearls or expensive clothes. For women who claim to be devoted to God should make themselves attractive by the good things they do." 1 Timothy 2:9–10 (NLT)

In 1 Corinthians, chapter 11, Paul gives instructions for women to cover their head, at least when worshipping. The head covering is specifically meant for women only.

"For this reason, and because the angels are watching, a woman should wear a covering on her head to show she is under authority." 1 Corinthians 11:10

"Judge for yourselves: is it proper for a woman to pray to God with her head uncovered?" 1 Corinthians 11:13

Quran and Parents

Serving one's parents and respecting them is considered paramount and is frequently emphasized in the Quran. The verses are self-explanatory:

"And serve God and do not associate any thing with Him and be good to the parents." 4:36 (Shakir)

"Say: 'Come, I will rehearse what Lord has (really) prohibited you from': Join not anything as equal with Him; be good to your parents." 6:151

"Your Lord has decreed that you worship none but Him, and that you be kind to parents. Whether one or both of them attain old *age in your life, say not to them a word of contempt (even 'ugh'), nor repel them, but address them in terms of honor."* 17:23

Polytheism (associating other gods with God) is the greatest sin according to the Quran. It is of note that in many of the verses, avoiding polytheism and showing kindness to parents are ordained side by side, highlighting their emphasis:

"And make yourself submissively gentle to them with compassion, and say: O my Lord! Have compassion on them, just as they brought me up (when I was) little." 17:24 (Shakir). Yousuf Ali's translation of the same verse: *"And, out of kindness, lower to them the wing of humility, and say: 'My Lord! Bestow on them your Mercy even as they cherished me in childhood.'"*

"And We have enjoined on man (to be good) to his parents: in travail [hardship] upon travail [hardship] did his mother bear him, and in year two was his weaning: (hear the command), Show gratitude to Me and to your parents: to Me is (your final) goal." 31:14

Bible and Parents/Children

The responsibilities of children and parents are topics frequently addressed in the Bible as well.

Respecting Parents

"Every one of you shall reverence his mother and his father, and you shall keep My Sabbaths; I am the LORD your God." Leviticus 19:3

"Children, obey your parents because you belong to the Lord, for this is the right thing to do. Honor your father and mother. This is the first commandment with a promise." Ephesians 6:1–2 (NLT)

It is interesting to note that parents' respect and obedience is mentioned next to the name of the Lord, like in the Quran.

The following verses from Colossians chapter 3 provide a summary of roles and responsibilities of various members of a family:

"Wives, be subject to your husbands, as is fitting in the Lord." (3:18)

"Husbands, love your wives and do not be embittered against them." (3:19)

"Children, be obedient to your parents in all things, for this is well-pleasing to the Lord. Fathers, do not exasperate your children, so that they will not lose heart." (3:20–21)

"Slaves, in all things obey those who are your masters on earth, not with external service, as those who merely please men, but with sincerity of heart, fearing the Lord." (3:22)

Points to Remember

- Women were subjected to abuse in pre-Islamic Arabia. The Quran gave women many rights they didn't have before and protected them from abusive practices. Women and men have their own set of rights and responsibilities and equal status in the Quran. What separates them in God's sight is their level of piety. The husband-and-wife relationship is built on mutual love and respect, though the Bible gives the husband authority over the wife and the Quran puts the husband "a degree above" the wife, in an apparent reference to their physical stature and role as breadwinner.

- The Quran allows polygamy but only under certain conditions; it clearly favors monogamy. The Old Testament makes references to many prophets with multiple wives without objection. The reference against polygamy relates to the kings. Most churches and scholars interpret many verses as an indication of the New Testament's prohibition of polygamy. As mentioned in the main body of the chapter, compliance with the prohibition of polygamy by local laws is in line with the teachings of the Quran.

- Divorce is allowed in the Quran and the Bible but is considered distasteful; every effort should be made to reconcile. When divorcing, one must do so with fairness and kindness.

- Hijab is more than just a dress code and is considered a sign of chastity and modesty; it equally applies to men and women. The Bible narrates passages of noble women covering their heads or faces when in front of strangers. Paul has instructions for women to cover their heads, at least during worship.

Time to Ponder

- Is the notion of men's superiority (spiritual or otherwise) over women in accordance with the teachings of the scriptures? If so, is that more akin to a higher level of responsibility rather than absolute authority?

CHAPTER 26
PERSONAL BEHAVIOR AND
CODE OF CONDUCT

The Quran gives instructions on how an individual can attain a high level of spiritual and moral standards. The spiritual health and moral values of individuals and families would thus determine the health of a society. Muslims insist that though the concept seems idealistic, the structure provides a sound basis for a functional and just society. The Quran commands individuals to maintain purity of body and mind, calls for honesty in thoughts and actions, and with an objective to form an altruistic society, commands individuals to fulfill social obligations in the form of assisting other people (the sick, poor, needy, widows, orphans, etc.).

This chapter will review some of the teachings of the Quran and the Bible concerning ethical and moral values for individuals. This is laid out in the form of the "Dos" and the "Do Nots" here; it is not meant to be an exhaustive list.

The "Dos"

Enjoin What's Good (*Amr-bil-Ma'ruf*)

As mentioned under "Pillars of Islam," followers are strongly encouraged to enjoin and promote what's good. The Quran has repeatedly defined what is considered "good":

"And from among you there should be a party who invites to good and enjoin what is right and forbid the wrong, and these it is that shall be successful." 3:104 (Shakir)

"Those who follow the Messenger, the unlettered prophet, whom they find written down with them in the Torah and the Gospel (who) enjoins them good and forbids them evil." 7:157 (Shakir)

Honesty and Truthfulness

Muslims believe that Prophet Muhammad was a "walking and talking Quran," since he is considered to have exemplified the teachings of the Quran with his words and actions. One of the nicknames the pagan Arabs gave Muhammad, before the revelation, was *"Al-Sadiq,"* or "the Truthful," on account of his unblemished record of never telling a lie and always keeping his word.

"Truly Allah guides not one who transgresses and lies!" 40:28

The truthfulness implies more than being true with one's words or tongue. It means consistency between the inside and outside; actions and intentions; and conformity of speech with belief:

"O you who believe! Be careful of (your duty to) Allah and be among the truthful." 9:119 (Shakir)

The Quran praises prophets and other noble persons for their truthfulness:

"And mention Abraham in the Book; surely he was a truthful man, a prophet." 19:41 (Shakir)

"The Messiah, son of Mary was but a messenger; messengers before him have indeed passed away; and his mother was a truthful woman." 5:75 (Shakir)

Similar passages are found testifying to the truthfulness of Ishmael (19:54) and Joseph (12:46).

The Quran warns those who are not honest in their businesses by not measuring items correctly (verses 83:1–3). They are referred to as "defrauders." One Hadith states that truthfulness leads to righteousness and falsehood leads to wickedness and evil-doing.

Forgiveness/Anger Management

The Quran instructs individuals on many life skills, and prominent among them is taking charge of one's temperament. Managing anger goes hand in hand with self-control, kindness, and forgiveness. The Quran gives numerous examples of prophets who, despite their nation's rebellion and hatred toward them, always asked for their forgiveness. The Quran mentions forgiveness and controlling anger together in the same verses on many occasions:

"Those who avoid the greater crimes and shameful deeds, and, when they are angry even then forgive." 42:37

"Those who spend (freely), whether in prosperity, or in adversity; who restrain anger, and pardon (all) men—for Allah loves those who do good." 3:134

Those who forgive can also expect God's forgiveness for their shortcomings. The verse 3:134 quoted above is immediately followed by such a promise. One of the many attributes of God in the Quran is *"Al Ghafoor,"* or "the Most forgiving."

"If you do good openly or do it in secret or pardon an evil then surely Allah is Pardoning, Powerful." 4:149 (Shakir)

"The recompense for an injury is an injury equal thereto (in degree): but if a person forgives and makes reconciliation, his reward is due from Allah: for (Allah) loves not those who do unjust [the tyrants]." 42:40

"But indeed if any show patience and forgive, that would truly be an exercise of courageous will and resolution in the conduct of affairs." 42:43

Kindness and Mercy

Forgiveness is an important ingredient for controlling anger, but kindness is essential for forgiveness, and as in the case of forgiveness, the Quran declares that God will show mercy to those who show mercy to others. In its fundamental form, all humans possess some portion of divine attributes, kindness and mercy being two of the most important. The Quran asks believers to show kindness in many ways: in speech, in their treatment of others, and in actions. These include "random acts" of kindness, as well as more organized forms like charitable giving:

"And serve Allah and do not associate any thing with Him and be kind to the parents and to the near of kin and the orphans and the needy and the neighbor of (your) kin and the neighbor who are strangers, and the companion in a journey and the wayfarer and those whom your right hands possess; surely Allah does not love him who is proud, boastful." 4:36 (Shakir)

Prophet Muhammad was a symbol of mercy and kindness to everyone around him, friends and foes alike. The Quran refers to that as a gift from God:

"Thus it is due to mercy from Allah that you (O Muhammad) deal with them gently, and had you been rough, hard hearted, they would certainly have dispersed from around you; forgive them therefore and ask pardon for them." 3:159 (Shakir)

Many Hadiths (sayings of Muhammad) instruct the importance of kindness and mercy to all—humans and nonhumans.

"Those who are kind and considerate to Allah's creatures, Allah bestows His kindness and affection on them. Show kindness to the creatures on the earth so that Allah may be kind to you." (Hadith)

The Quran ordains kindness to parents (verse 6:151); to spouses, even during the course of a divorce (2:229); and toward people of other religion and captives, who are not waging wars against you (60:8). There are numerous other narrations for other groups, including orphans and the needy.

Repel Evil with What's Good

"Nor can goodness and Evil be equal. Repel (Evil) with what is better." 41:34

Verse 25:63, noted in the next section, also specifically instructs believers to respond in kindness, even to the taunts of the enemy.

Humility, Simplicity, and Modesty

The very essence of Islam, or submission, is to humbly submit to God. The prostration, performed many times during each daily prayer, is the ultimate symbol of humility shown to God.

The Quran also instructs followers to be humble toward each other; of course, in ways other than the way to submit to God. The Quran makes it very clear that God does not like arrogance. Satan, in fact, was labeled a disbeliever when he showed arrogance and refused to prostrate to Adam when ordered by God to do so. He reasoned that Adam was made up from the clay (verses 2:34, mentioned elsewhere in this book, and 15:30–35).

"And do not turn your face away from people in contempt, nor go about in the land exulting overmuch; surely Allah does not love any self-conceited boaster." 31:18 (Shakir)

"And the servants of Most Gracious (Allah) are those who walk on the earth in humility, and when the ignorant [in reference to pagans of Mecca] address them, they say, 'Peace!' [Salaam]." 25:63

"And be moderate [humble] in your pace, and lower your voice." 31:19

Modesty also extends to one's life style. Extravagant, wasteful spending and materialism are discouraged, and followers are instructed to treat life as a short journey, without losing sight of the ultimate goal of seeking nearness to God.

"Fair in the eyes of men is the love of things they covet: Women and sons; Heaped-up hoards of gold and silver; horses branded (for blood and excellence); and (wealth of) cattle and well-tilled land. Such are the possessions of this world's life; but in nearness to God is the best of the goals." 3:14

The verses on wasteful spending will be reviewed later in this chapter under "Don't Be Stingy or Wasteful (Be Moderate)."

Protect Life

Preserving and honoring life is a basic human imperative, according to the Quran. The Quran instructs that killing one person is akin to killing all of humanity. The description of the murder of Abel by his older brother Cain (sons of Adam) is followed by this verse:

"Whoever kills a person, except as a punishment for murder or mischief in the land, it will be written in his book of deeds as if he had killed all the human beings, and whoever will save a life shall be regarded as if he gave life to all the human beings." 5:32 (Malik)

The following verse probably should be listed under the "Do Nots," but it is relevant to note here that slaying a soul is mentioned in the Quran along with two other major prohibitions:

"And they, who do not call upon another god with God and do not slay the soul, which Allah has forbidden except in the requirements of justice, and (who) do not commit fornication; And he who does

this [meaning the three prohibitions] shall find a requital of sin."
25:68 (Shakir)

The "Do Nots"

Forbid What's Evil (*Nahi-Anil-Munkar*)

The opposite of "enjoin what's good" is forbidding what's "evil." In the following section, the focus is primarily on avoiding bad deeds in the context of personal behavior, rather in reference to "major" or "minor" sins.

Slander

The Quran sends clear warning to those who engage in backbiting and slandering. It is distasteful in the eyes of God:

"O you who believe! Avoid suspicion as much (as possible): for suspicion in some cases is a sin: And spy not, neither backbite one another. Would any of you like to eat the flesh of his dead brother? No you would hate it. But fear Allah: For Allah is Oft-Returning [Accepter of repentance], Most Merciful." 49:12

And falsely accusing chaste women is a grave sin:

"Those who slander chaste women, indiscreet but believing, are cursed in this life and in the Hereafter: for them is a grievous Penalty." 24:23

Don't Be Stingy or Wasteful (Be Moderate)

The Quran repeatedly gives instructions for charity. Whereas there is plenty of praise for charitable work, being stingy, on the other hand, is considered distasteful:

"And let not those who hoard up that which God has bestowed upon them of His bounty, think that it is better for them. No, it is worse for them." 3:180

However, extravagant spending is also discouraged:

"And He it is Who produces gardens (of vine), trellised and untrellised, and palms and seed-produce of which the fruits are of various sorts, and olives and pomegranates, like and unlike; eat of its fruit when it bears fruit, and pay the due of it on the day of its

reaping, and do not act extravagantly; surely He does not love the extravagant [wasteful]." 6:141

The Quran asks for moderation where one does not go from being stingy to being wasteful. Elsewhere, in a series of verses describing the characteristics of the good servants of God, moderation in spending is emphasized:

"*Who, when they spend, are neither extravagant nor stingy, but keep the balance between those two extremes.*" 25:67

Forgiving Debts

"*If the debtor is in a difficulty, grant him time till it is easy for him to repay. But if you remit it by way of charity [that is forgive the loan], that is best for you if you only knew.*" 2:280

Transgression

According to *Merriam-Webster's Dictionary*, "transgression" means "infringement or violation of law, command, or duty." From the scriptures's perspective, it means disobeying God and exceeding the limits and the laws set forth by Him. This can take many forms. Denying God is the worst form of transgression. Mistreating prisoners of war is a transgression in the battlefield, and tyranny is a violation of basic human rights, as ordained by God and one of the worst types of transgressions (Pharaoh being a prime example in the Quran).

"*Successful indeed are the believers, who are humble in their prayers, And who keep aloof from what is vain, And who are givers of poor-rate [Zakah], And who guard their private parts, except before their mates or those whom their right hands possess, for they surely are not blamable, But whoever seeks to go beyond that, these are they that exceed the limits [transgressors].*" 23:1–7 (Shakir)

"*And do not eat up your property among yourselves for vanities, nor use it as bait for the judges, with intent that you may eat up wrongfully and knowingly a little of (other) people's property.*" 2:188

Tyranny and Oppression

Tyranny is considered a form of severe transgression when a person (often a ruler), or a group, oppresses another group of people. The

Quran is very harsh on oppressors and tyrants and warns them of a painful fate. Justice is the opposite of oppression. The story of the plight of the children of Israel at the hands of Pharaoh is given as an example of tyranny:

"And We made the children of Israel to pass through the sea, then Pharaoh and his hosts followed them for oppression and tyranny." 10:90 (Shakir)

Adultery

Adultery in its basic form is a sexual transgression. It is considered among the major sins in the Quran and is repeatedly condemned:

"Nor come near to adultery: for it is a shameful (deed) and an evil, opening the road (to other evils)." 17:32

In the verse above, the Arabic word for adultery is *"Zina,"* which essentially means sexual relations outside the marital and legal boundaries as set forth by the divine. In this context, commentators agree it refers to adultery. Note that the instructions are to not just avoid adultery but to not even "come near" it. Adultery is considered an unethical act—one that breaks the basic fabric of a loving relationship, thus destroying the family unit.

Verse 25:68, quoted already in this chapter, puts adultery in the same category as associating others with God and murder.

Alcohol

The Quran forbids alcohol, even for social purposes. One does not have to get drunk to disobey the divine ordinance. Drinking alcohol is considered a major offense in Islam:

"They ask you about intoxicants and games of chance [gambling]. Say: In both of them there is a great sin [harm] and means of profit [benefit] for people, and their sin [harm] is greater than their profit [benefit]. And they ask you as to what they should spend. Say: What you can spare. Thus does Allah make clear to you the communications, that you may ponder." 2:219 (Shakir)

In the verse above, "intoxicants" refers to alcoholic beverages, though the word used is generic for all intoxicants. Note the "harm" is not in the intoxication, but the intoxicants, thus the commandment to avoid the use of intoxicants, and not merely the state of intoxication. The verse acknowledges some benefits of alcohol but states that its benefits are far outweighed by the harmful effects (for example, gastric ulcers, cirrhosis of the liver, dementia, pancreatitis, neuropathy, and cardiomyopathy, to name a few, as well as its negative effects on social life). Moreover, it is also well known now that a glass of grape juice can provide the same amount of protective antioxidant effects without any of the harmful effects of alcohol. This is referenced in the following verse.

*"And of the fruits of the palms and the grapes—you obtain from them intoxication ["**Sakar**"], and goodly provision; most surely there is a sign in this for a people who ponder."* 16:67 (Shakir)

Personal Behavior and Conduct in the Bible

The equivalent of *Amr-bil-Ma'ruf* (enjoin what's good) in Hebrew might be *Ma'asim tovim,* meaning "good works and actions." The Torah and the Gospel frequently give instructions to do good deeds. Similarly, there are commands to avoid certain acts and deeds. The Jewish Talmud describes 613 commandments, derived from the Torah, of which 248 are "positive commandments" (the Dos) and 365 are "negative commandments" (the Don'ts). These commandments are not limited to personal conduct but cover a full spectrum of personal and social life including worship, charity, marital laws, treatment of servants, judicial system, and war.

Righteousness

Righteousness is defined broadly as fearing God and obeying the decrees and the commands of the Lord. This verse does not spell out the deeds like verse 2:177 in the Quran does, but it makes a reference to obeying "all the commands" to be counted as righteous:

"And the Lord our God commanded us to obey all these decrees and to fear Him so He can continue to bless us and preserve our lives, as He has done to this day. For we will be counted as righteous when we obey all the commands the Lord our God has given us." Deuteronomy 6:24–25

And in Job chapter 29, Prophet Job talks about his righteous deeds as being a father figure to the poor, assisting strangers, helping the blind, and rescuing victims from the godless.

Honesty and Truthfulness

Both the Old and the New Testaments frequently underscore the importance of truthfulness and honesty:

"Who may climb the mountain of the Lord? Who may stand in His holy place? Only those whose hands and hearts are pure, who do not worship idols and never tell lies." Psalm 24:3–4

"Better to be poor and honest than to be dishonest and a fool." Proverbs 19:1

"Whoever can be trusted with very little can also be trusted with much, and whoever is dishonest with very little will also be dishonest with much." Luke 16:10

And in the book of Proverbs, Solomon's advice to his son is described over many chapters. The set of instructions include avoiding lying:

"There are six things the Lord hates—no, seven things he detests: haughty eyes, a lying tongue, hands that kill the innocent, a heart that plots evil, feet that race to do wrong, a false witness who pours out lies, a person who sows discord in a family. My son, obeys your father's commands, and don't neglect your mother's instruction." Proverbs 6:16–20

Kindness/Mercy/Forgiveness

These attributes are at the center of the teachings of Jesus Christ as well as frequent subject of the teachings of the Torah. Many of the verses quoted are fairly self-explanatory even without a reference to their context:

"Do not seek revenge or bear a grudge against a fellow Israelite, but love your neighbor as yourself. I am the Lord." Leviticus 19:18

"Get rid of all bitterness, rage, anger, harsh words, and slander, as well as all types of evil behavior. Instead, be kind to each other, tenderhearted, forgiving one another, just as God through Christ has forgiven you." Ephesians 4:31–32

In the above verse, the Christians were asked to be kind to fellow Christians.

"Make allowance for each other's faults, and forgive anyone who offends you. Remember, the Lord forgave you, so you must forgive others." Colossians 3:13

Just like the Quranic commandments, the Gospel also instructs people to be merciful to and forgiving of others, so God can show mercy and forgiveness.

"For if you forgive men their trespasses, your heavenly Father also will forgive you." Matthew 6:14

"Judge not, and you will not be judged; condemn not, and you will not be condemned; forgive, and you will be forgiven." Luke 6:37

Anger

The book of Genesis indicates that Cain killed Abel out of anger (as well as jealousy):

"'Why are you so angry?' the Lord asked Cain. 'Why do you look so dejected? You will be accepted if you do what is right. But if you refuse to do what is right, then watch out! Sin is crouching at the door, eager to control you. But you must subdue it and be its master.'" Genesis 4:6–7

And in the following verses, Jesus teaches his followers to guard against anger as well as a host of other negative behaviors, including immorality, slander, lust, and dirty language:

"You have heard that our ancestors were told, 'You must not murder. If you commit murder, you are subject to judgment.' But I say, if you are even angry with someone, you are subject to judgment! If you call someone an idiot, you are in danger of being brought before the court. And if you curse someone, you are in danger of the fires of hell." Matthew 5:21–22

"So put to death the sinful, earthly things lurking within you. Have nothing to do with sexual immorality, impurity, lust, and evil desires. Don't be greedy, for a greedy person is an idolater, worshipping the things of this world. Because of these sins, the anger of God is coming. You used to do these things when your life was still part of this world. But now is the time to get rid of anger, rage, malicious behavior, slander, and dirty language. Don't lie to each

other, for you have stripped off your old sinful nature and all its wicked deeds." Colossians 3:5–9

"Understand this, my dear brothers and sisters: You must all be quick to listen, slow to speak, and slow to get angry. Human anger does not produce the righteousness God desires." James 1:19–20

Humility versus Arrogance

Jesus Christ preached humility and is widely believed to have led by personal example. Throughout his life, Jesus spoke against arrogance and false pride.

"But he gives us even more grace to stand against such evil desires. As the scriptures say, 'God opposes the proud but favors the humble.' So humble yourselves before God. Resist the devil, and he will flee from you." James 4:6–7

It further goes on to say, "Humble yourselves before the Lord, and he will lift you up in honor." James 4:10

The following verse refers to the fate on the Day of Judgment:

"But those who exalt themselves will be humbled, and those who humble themselves will be exalted." Matthew 23:12 (and Luke 14:11)

Charity

"Teach those who are rich in this world not to be proud and not to trust in their money, which is so unreliable. Their trust should be in God, who richly gives us all we need for our enjoyment. Tell them to use their money to do good. They should be rich in good works and generous to those in need, always being ready to share with others. By doing this they will be storing up their treasure as a good foundation for the future so that they may experience true life." 1 Timothy 6:17–19

"And don't forget to do good and to share with those in need. These are the sacrifices that please God." Hebrews 13:16

"If anyone gives you even a cup of water because you belong to the Messiah, I tell you the truth, that person will surely be rewarded." Mark 9:41

"There will always be some in the land who are poor. That is why I am commanding you to share freely with the poor and with other Israelites in need." Deuteronomy 15:11

Similar to the disdain shown by the Quran for those who like to show off, the Bible is equally harsh against such actions. Giving in secret is much preferred.

"Watch out! Don't do your good deeds publicly, to be admired by others, for you will lose the reward from your Father in heaven. When you give to someone in need, don't do as the hypocrites do—blowing trumpets in the synagogues and streets to call attention to their acts of charity! I tell you the truth, they have received all the reward they will ever get. But when you give to someone in need, don't let your left hand know what your right hand is doing. Give your gifts in private, and your Father, who sees everything, will reward you." Matthew 6:1–4

Adultery

Adultery is repeatedly condemned in the Bible. Prohibited by one of the Ten Commandments, adultery is considered a great sin. Exodus 20:14 commands:

"You must not commit adultery." (Period)

And in a verse that comes very close to the spirit of verse 17:32 of the Quran (that instructs "not to come near to adultery"), Jesus instructs his followers in the Gospel of Matthew:

"You have heard the commandment that says, 'You must not commit adultery.' But I say, anyone who even looks at a woman with lust has already committed adultery with her in his heart." Matthew 5:27–28

And the punishment for adultery in the Torah was stoning of the guilty.

"Jesus returned to the Mount of Olives, but early the next morning he was back again at the Temple. A crowd soon gathered, and he sat down and taught them. As he was speaking, the teachers of religious law and the Pharisees brought a woman who had been caught in the act of adultery. They put her in front of the crowd. 'Teacher,' they said to Jesus, 'this woman was caught in the act of adultery. The Law of Moses says to stone her. What do you say?'" John 8:1–4

The passage then goes on to describe Jesus's response that only those who have not sinned can stone the guilty, and since everyone else had sinned, the crowd filed out without stoning the woman.

Alcohol

Alcohol is often mentioned in the Old Testament as *"shekar"*, an intoxicating drink distilled from corn, honey, or dates. Compare that to *Sakar,* the word used by the Quran in verse 16:67, quoted earlier in the chapter.

Wine and other alcoholic beverages are commonly consumed in Christianity and Judaism and are generally not considered sinful; only drunkenness is considered a sin, though some have divergent views. One can still find prohibition for alcohol for various people under certain situations.

"You and your descendants must never drink wine or any other alcoholic drink before going into the Tabernacle. If you do, you will die. This is a permanent law for you, and it must be observed from generation to generation." Leviticus 10:9

The above-mentioned verse does not outlaw alcohol outright but prohibits its consumption before entering the Holy of the Holies. The following verse is a set of instructions for Nazirites. The word "Nazirite" comes from a Hebrew verb which means "to dedicate or separate oneself." The Torah set strict guidelines for a person who volunteered for such an office:

"Then the Lord said to Moses, 'Give the following instructions to the people of Israel. If any of the people, either men or women, take the special vow of a Nazirite, setting themselves apart to the Lord in a special way, they must give up wine and other alcoholic drinks. They must not use vinegar made from wine or from other alcoholic drinks, they must not drink fresh grape juice, and they must not eat grapes or raisins." Numbers 6:1–3

While foretelling the birth of John the Baptist, the angel from the Lord described the pious character of John the Baptist, including his abstaining from drinking alcohol:

"While Zechariah was in the sanctuary, an angel of the Lord appeared to him, standing to the right of the incense altar. Zechariah was shaken and overwhelmed with fear when he saw him. But the angel said, 'Don't be afraid, Zechariah! God has heard your prayer. Your wife, Elizabeth, will give you a son, and you are to name him John. You will have great joy and gladness, and many will rejoice at his birth, for he will be great in the eyes of the Lord. He must never

touch wine or other alcoholic drinks. He will be filled with the Holy Spirit, even before his birth. And he will turn many Israelites to the Lord their God.'" Luke 1:11–16

The following verses represent more generic prohibition rather than being directed at a specific person or a priest or for a specific place:

"What sorrow for those who get up early in the morning looking for a drink of alcohol and spend long evenings drinking wine to make themselves flaming drunk. They furnish wine and lovely music at their grand parties—lyre and harp, tambourine and flute—but they never think about the Lord or notice what He is doing." Isaiah 5:11–13

"Wine produces mockers; alcohol leads to brawls. Those led astray by drink cannot be wise." Proverb 20:1

Organizers at soccer matches and other sporting events probably would testify to the accuracy of the above verse.

No Booze Parties

"Because we belong to the day, we must live decent lives for all to see. Don't participate in the darkness of wild parties and drunkenness, or in sexual promiscuity and immoral living, or in quarreling and jealousy. Instead, clothe yourself with the presence of the Lord Jesus Christ. And don't let yourself think about ways to indulge your evil desires." Romans 13:13–14

"When you follow the desires of your sinful nature, the results are very clear: sexual immorality, impurity, lustful pleasures, idolatry, sorcery, hostility, quarreling, jealousy, outbursts of anger, selfish ambition, dissension, division, envy, drunkenness, wild parties, and other sins like these. Let me tell you again, as I have before, that anyone living that sort of life will not inherit the Kingdom of God." Galatians 5:19–21

Many Christian scholars argue that the Bible does not forbid alcohol, though it prohibits drunkenness; they point to passages that refer to wine in positive terms. The Gospel of John in chapter 2, verses 2–11 describes one of the miracles of Jesus, when he was at a wedding in Cana; he changed the water in the waterpots to wine, turning his disciples into believers. Wine is considered a gift from God for enjoyment.

"So go ahead. Eat your food with joy, and drink your wine with a happy heart, for God approves of this! Wear fine clothes, with a splash of cologne!" Ecclesiastes 9:7–8

"You cause grass to grow for the livestock and plants for people to use. You allow them to produce food from the earth—wine to make them glad, olive oil to soothe their skin, and bread to give them strength." Psalm 104:114–115

"Is anyone thirsty? Come and drink—even if you have no money! Come, take your choice of wine or milk—it's all free! Why spend your money on food that does not give you strength?" Isaiah 55:1–2

Points to Remember

- The Quran, the Old Testament, and the New Testament have striking similarities on personal codes of conduct. All of them repeatedly instruct followers on matters such as honesty, humility, kindness, charity, and truthfulness. All of them prohibit the opposite acts like rudeness, cruelty, lying, anger, stealing, and oppression.
- The Quran and the Bible forbid lewdness, adultery, and alcohol (or at least drunkenness). Most Christian scholars have interpreted the verses to mean that only drunkenness is prohibited and refer to passages where alcohol consumption is used in positive terms and consumed during feasts. Adultery and drinking alcohol are considered major offenses in Islam.

Time to Ponder

- The similarity of the code of personal conduct and behavior as commanded in the Quran and the Bible is striking. When differences do exist, are they a reflection of different interpretations of the same laws, or different sets of laws for different communities, to address their unique needs?

In Closing …

I have made a humble attempt to group various themes presented by the Quran and compared them with passages on similar themes in the Bible to highlight the often unrealized commonality of these scriptures. This book only scratches the surface of the themes covered in the Quran and the Bible, but hopefully it will serve to stimulate an interest in studying the Quran and the Bible further. I have made a conscious effort to provide candid answers to many of the questions people may have always wanted to ask but couldn't find in one concise format.

Though Muslims around the world often recite the Quran in Arabic, I have emphasized that for non-Arabic-speaking people, the Quran needs to be read in the native language also, in order to understand the intended message. It must be added that for a truer appreciation of the message and beauty of the Quran, one must *study* the Quran in its original Arabic language. In much the same way, the Old Testament loses its luster when translated from Hebrew to English (or any other language). Unfortunately, there are no copies of the original Aramaic Gospel available anywhere currently. Reading the Arabic text of the Quran without understanding it at all would seem to defeat the purpose of the revelations. Thus reading the scriptures in one's native language is a practical (but inferior) alternative to the study in the original language of the revelations.

The Quran and the Bible do not believe in being politically correct, hence we will find many passages in the scriptures that modern societies may not find to their liking. If one believes in the divine source of the scriptures and that the ultimate authority belongs to God, then it becomes easy to accept that the divine laws don't always correspond to man-made laws or opinions: they don't have to. It is not to imply, however, that one should ignore the law of the land. The scriptures do not encourage people to "take the law into their hands" if there is a discrepancy between the divine laws and the law of the land. A case in point might be the issue of polygamy. In most Western countries, it is illegal to have multiple wives. Even when allowed by the scriptures, the law of the land must be followed. Conversely, at an individual level, even when the local laws allow certain actions, for example gambling and prostitution, the scriptures continue to prohibit their followers from engaging in such activities.

This book was written for the "common person" with an open and investigative mind, with the objective of addressing the need to gain a basic understanding of the scriptures, and thus I have tried to use plain English to discuss passages from the Quran and the Bible. At times, I might have tried to oversimplify matters. In order to maintain the brevity of the book, yet address the major themes, I have addressed some topics relatively superficially without going into deep theological debates. This book should not be treated as an exegesis, because it is not one. As I mentioned in the beginning of the book, I have stayed focused on the similarities of the message in the scriptures, rather than the differences. It is up to the individual whether one wants to promote the similarities to find common ground or latch onto the differences that continue to widen the gulf between the followers of the world's most read scriptures. Even when we have reasons for disagreements, can we agree to disagree *respectfully*? In doing so the followers of the Abrahamic faiths, I believe, will only be acting in accordance with the scriptures they trust and respect.

Sincerely
Ejaz Naqvi, MD

Bibliography

Ali, Abdullah Yusuf. *The Holy Qur'an,* Elmhurst, New York: Tahrike Tarsile Qur'an, 2001.

Ali, Maulana Muhammad. *The Holy Qur'an with English Translation*, Lahore, Pakistan: Ahamadya Press, 1951.

Asad, Muhammad. *The Message of the Qur'an*, Gibraltar: Dar al-Andalus Limited, 1980.

Aslan, Reza. *No god but God. The Origins, Evolution, and Future of Islam*, New York, NY: Random House Trade, 2011.

Bucaille, Maurice. *The Bible, the Qur'an, and Science*, Qum, Iran: Ansariyan Publications, 2007.

Clark, Malcolm. *Islam for Dummies*, Hoboken, NJ: Wiley Publishing, 2003.

Emerick, Yahya. *The Meaning Of The Holy Qur'an in Today's English*, Charleston, SC: Extended Study Edition, 2000.

Fakhri, Majid. *The Qur'an: A Modern English Version*, Ithaca, New York: Garnet Publishing, 1997.

Fazley, Rabbi A. K. M. *Topics from the Holy Quran,* Tallahassee, FL: Father and Son Publishing, 2005.

Geoghegan, Jeffrey and Michael Homan. *The Bible for Dummies*, Hoboken, NJ: Wiley Publishing, 2003.

Ghattas, Rauf and Carol B. Ghattas. *A Christian Guide to the Qur'an*, Grand Rapids, MI: Kregel Publications, 2009.

Hadith of Bukhari. www.sahih-bukhari.com.

Haleem, M. A. S. Abdel. *The Qur'an: A New Translation*, New York, NY: Oxford University Press, 2005.

Holy Bible, New American Standard Bible, LaHabra, CA, Lockman Foundation, 2008.

Holy Bible, New Living Translation, Carol Stream, IL: Tyndale House Publishers, 2007.

Khan, Aftab Ahmad. *The Creator,* http://aftabkhan.blog.com, 2009.

Kurzweil, Arthur. *The Torah for Dummies,* Hoboken, NJ: Wiley Publishing, 2008.

Liepert, David. *Muslim, Christian, and Jew,* Toronto, Canada: Faith and Life Publishing, 2010.

Lodahl, Michael. *Claiming Abraham,* Grand Rapids, MI: Brazos Press, 2010.

Malik, M. Farooq-i-Azam. *Al-Qur'an, Guidance for Mankind: The English Translation of the Meaning of Al Qur'an,* Houston, Texas: Institute of Islamic Knowledge, 1997.

Pickthall, Muhammad M. *The Glorious Qur'an,* Hyderabad, India: Government Central Press, 1938.

Sarwar, Shaykh Muhammad and Brandon Toropov. *The Complete Idiot's Guide to the Koran,* Indianapolis, IN: Beach Brook Productions, 2003.

Shakir, M. H. *The Quran: Arabic Text and English Translation,* Elmhurst, New York: Tahrike Tarsile Qur'an, 1999.

Sultan, Sohaib. *The Koran for Dummies,* Hoboken, NJ: Wiley Publishing, 2004.

Ünal, Ali. *The Quran with Annotated Interpretation in Modern English,* Clifton, NJ: Tughra Books, 2010.

Yazdi, Ayatullah Agha Pooya and S. V. Mir Ahmad Ali. *The Holy Qur'an—The Final Testament,* Elmhurst, New York: Tahrike Tarsile Qur'an, 2002.

Yuksel, Edip; L. S. Al-Shaiban and M. Schulte-Nafeh. *The Quran: A Reformist Translation,* Breinigsville, PA: Brainbow Press, 2007.

22814555R00229

Made in the USA
Lexington, KY
14 May 2013